NAFTA@10

John M. Curtis and Aaron Sydor

Editors

Foreword

The research assembled in this volume has been undertaken by academic and government researchers writing in a personal capacity. Foreign Affairs and International Trade Canada managed and assembled this volume with the objective of contributing to, and encouraging, debate on an issue of major importance to the Department, to the Government of Canada, and to Canadians. The views expressed in this volume, however, are those of authors and do not reflect the views of the departments represented in this volume or of the Government of Canada.

NAFTA@10

John M. Curtis and Aaron Sydor

Editors

© Minister of Public Works and Government Services Canada 2006

Cat: IT5-1/2006E
ISBN: 0-662-43036-0

(Publié également en Français)

Table of Contents

Part 2: The Way Forward?

Acknowledgements

We would like to thank a number of people who were instrumental to assembling this volume, including: Jean-Pierre Voyer, Executive Director of the Policy Research Initiative (PRI), for his support as well as that of the numerous PRI staff who contributed chapters to this volume. Richard Roy, who was then A/Director General of the Mico-Economic Policy Analysis (MEPA) Branch at Industry Canada, and the contributions from that group. Bill Jarvis and Troy Joseph, with the Strategic Analysis and Research Directorate at Environment Canada, also are to be thanked for their enthusiastic early support for this project. We appreciate the contribution of all those who reviewed and commented on the papers contained in this volume.

Editors' Overview

John M. Curtis & Aaron Sydor

Foreign Affairs and International Trade Canada

Introduction

It has been more than ten years since the implementation of the North American Free Trade Agreement (NAFTA) and fifteen years since its precursor, the Canada-U.S. Free Trade Agreement (Canada-U.S. FTA), came into force. For Canada, those two agreements were important, and hotly debated, turning points in its trade and in its economic policy more generally.

The Canada-U.S. FTA was the first major bilateral trade agreement for two countries that were founding members of the post-war multilateral system and regarded it as the cornerstone of their respective trade policies. The expansion of that agreement to include Mexico, five years later, was significant in that it was the first major free trade agreement between the "rich north" and "poor south", a highly innovative initiative at the time and still controversial in several sectors of society in each of the countries involved.

Part 1: A Look Back

A considerable amount of analysis has taken place evaluating the effects of the Canada-U.S. FTA and the NAFTA from a Canadian perspective. Harris, in the opening chapter, provides an overview of this work. In economic terms, Canada is a small open economy, therefore free trade agreements, he argues, must be primarily seen as economic agreements with the goal of improving the standard of living for Canadians. Although the popular press often engage in job counting exercises in order to evaluate the impact of a trade agreement, this is a fool's errand. As Harris points out, trade agreements, although potentially shifting the composition of production and employment and thus temporarily dislocating workers, have no impact on employment levels in the long run. Rather, trade agreements improve economic efficiency through a better allocation of resources; they contribute to increased competition; they provide access to a greater variety of goods and services; and they improve productivity through greater innovation and economies of scale.

Evaluating the Canada-U.S. FTA and NAFTA in this context, Harris provides a review of the literature. He finds that the two agreements did result in an adjustment in employment and output for the sectors most affected. While domestic macro-economic policies, including the Bank of Canada's move to a low inflation environment and the government's fiscal tightening, were primarily responsible for the protracted downturn of the early 1990s, the Canada-U.S. FTA did play a role in the downturn and provides a cautionary tale for policy coordination. The lasting impacts of the agreement, however, are of greater interest. Harris argues that the Canada-U.S. FTA and NAFTA did indeed have a significant and positive impact on the Canadian economy. The estimates of the direct impact on Canadian exports range from a low of 10 percent to a high of over 50 percent. Increasing trade, however, is not the goal of a trade agreement. Citing work by Trefler (1999) Harris shows that the Canada-U.S. FTA produced a

1

productivity gain of 0.6 percent per year within the manufacturing sector and 3.2 percent per year for those sectors most affected (Those that experienced a drop in average tariff rates of more the 8 percentage points) for the years examined. It is these gains that improve the standard of living of Canadians and allow for Canadian-based businesses to compete successfully in the global marketplace.

Through his analysis, Harris also identifies areas for further work. One such area is the impact of trade agreements on the access to increased variety of products. Trade theory predicts that, through the creation of a larger market and with greater competition, the number of varieties of goods and services available to consumers increases. This greater variety of products allows producers to meet individual tastes and thus improve the standard of living for those involved. Difficulties in measuring product varieties, however, have led to few quantitative estimates of the impact of free trade agreements on the variety of goods available. In chapter 2, using data on trademarks, Chen finds that not only did the Canada-U.S. FTA increase the variety of products available to Canadians by 60 percent per year, but also because of the size difference and a positive relation between the size of a market and the number of varieties available in that market, Canada benefited more in terms of number of new products available as a result of trade, gaining access to three times as many new varieties as did the U.S. This finding has important implications for smaller countries entering into trade agreements with larger partners.

In his analysis, Chen argues that scale effects from the Canada-U.S. FTA have been surprisingly small. As a result, much of the gains from trade, in his opinion, have come from the increase in the variety of products traded. In chapter 3, Acharya evaluates the various theoretical motivators for trade, including scale effects, in the context of the NAFTA. According to his findings, for most industries, a number of factors play a role in determining the composition of trade. He finds that economies of scale play the most important role in industries that require significant capital expenditures and also involve product differentiation, and are therefore limited to only a few industries such as the Aerospace and Automotive industries. Relative abundance of either capital or labour (as per the Heckscher-Ohlin theory) and technological advantage (as per Ricardian theory), on the other hand, were important for most industries to some degree. These results are useful for policy-makers evaluating the potential benefits and adjustment costs of trade liberalization

Gu and Rennison examine, in the subsequent chapter, the impact of trade on skills and wages within Canada. The authors find that, somewhat surprisingly, despite Canada having one of the highest rates of post-secondary educational attainment among the OECD, this does not appear to be a source of comparative advantage for Canada as one might expect. Canada's skill content of exports was not substantially different from that of imports and only somewhat higher than the business sector average. Further, they find that there has not been a significant change over time. The authors provide a number of possible explanations for this result including that our primary trading partner, the U.S., has an even higher skills profile, particularly in university education.

Capital intensity, on the other hand, does appear to be a source of comparative advantage for Canada, with the capital intensity of exports exceeding

2

imports by 53 percent. Linked to this, labour productivity in the export sector was found to be not only twice as high as the over-all business sector but also growing twice as fast. It is therefore not surprising that wages were also, on average, eight percent higher in the export sector.

Included in the NAFTA, were side agreements on labour and the environment. Kirton, in a chapter devoted to one of those side agreements evaluates the effectiveness of the environmental side agreement (the North American Agreement on Environmental Co-operation or NAAEC) in meeting its objectives from a Canadian perspective. He concludes that the agreement has, for the most part, lived up to its objectives, although meeting some more successfully than others.

Part 2: The Way Forward

Part 2 moves away from a historic evaluation of the impact of the Canada-U.S. FTA and the NAFTA for Canada to be more forward looking. While titled "The Way Forward", this analysis does not reflect the intentions or policy directions of the government of Canada as such; rather, the chapters in this part explore some possible scenarios that have been put forward for deeper integration with North America.

One such scenario has been that of a common currency being instituted within North America. While interest in this form of closer integration has subsided somewhat, the debate was based on the premise that operating different currencies within and integrated North American production system imposes unnecessary costs and frictions. It is within this context that Laidler examines the issue of increased cooperation in monetary policy between Canada and the U.S. providing an assessment of the entire spectrum of alternate monetary orders from increased exchange of information up to and including a common currency.

Professor Laidler acknowledges that there may be efficiency gains to be had from increased monetary integration resulting from reduced frictions to trade. Separate and floating currencies, however, also allow for a cushion in adjusting to shocks, and Canada and the U.S. still have significantly different industrial structures that face separate shocks. Probably the most convincing argument put forward by Laidler, though, is the simple fact that for any common currency arrangement, U.S. cooperation would be required and this does not seem likely at this point in time, especially as it relates to cooperation in setting policy or in sharing seignorage revenues. Without this cooperation, Canada would be required to give up a significant degree of policy control and revenue which would substantially reduce, if not eliminate, any potential efficiency gains.

It has been argued that, short of a common currency, better coordination of monetary policy could achieve similar gains. This could potentially include a greater sharing of information to a dual goal for monetary policy of price stability and exchange rate stability. Professor Laidler shows, however, that there is already a relatively high level of information sharing at both formal and informal levels and it is difficult to see what additional gains can be achieved on this front. As for dual goals for monetary policy, Laidler argues quite convincingly that attempts to influence the exchange rate have been largely ineffective in the past.

3

He also suggests that having two goals for monetary policy would only make its operation less transparent and thus less effective.

Rao and Sharma, in "International Competitiveness and Regulatory Framework: A Canadian Perspective" explore the role of regulations in contributing to Canada's much cited innovation and productivity gaps with the U.S. Using data from the OECD and the Institute for Management Development (IMD), they show that Canada has a more restrictive regulatory environment than the U.S. in a number of areas including product market regulations and labour market regulations. Using a very simple reduced form equation for their estimation, the authors find that two areas of regulation in particular; intellectual property rights and restrictions to foreign direct investment, explain about one-third of the gap in R&D intensity and 55 percent of the labour productivity gap between Canada and the U.S. Even if one questions the precise estimates of these regulations on innovation and productivity performance, the sheer size of these impacts deserves greater attention by researchers and policy makers.

Blair, Downs and Ndayisenga build on the theme established by Rao and Sharma and examine the potential gains from a specific regulatory reform: cooperation between Canada and the U.S. for human drug approvals. The authors suggest that increased cooperation with the U.S. would allow for economies of scale in drug approvals, resulting in shorter delays for drug approvals without requiring additional resources. According to their analysis, speeding up drug approval times by 6 months would contribute to increased output of 2.4 percent as well as employment of 4.1 percent and R&D of 2 percent for the human drug industry in Canada. Reducing delays by 12 months would essentially double these gains. Possibly more importantly, however, speeding up time to market would increase the availability of new drugs to Canadians; reducing health care costs and improving the quality of life of Canadians. The primary obstacle, as the authors note, would be that of accountability in the system.

Beaulieu and Emery, in the next chapter, examine whether there is any benefit to increasing the geographic diversification of Canada's trade, particularly exports. As has already been noted, even prior to the Canada-U.S. FTA, Canadian exporters were heavily dependant on the U.S. as a market. This, as would be expected, increased after the agreement, peaking with 87 percent of Canadian merchandise exports going to the U.S. in 2000. While the authors note that some risks increase with this concentration, especially those that stem from national economic power such as trade, national fiscal and monetary policy, the U.S. is not, in fact, one market. Rather, it is 300 million plus individual consumers, many different levels of government with many different interests and objectives. Possibly most importantly, the authors point out that Canada-U.S. trade is the summation of many individual argents making their own export, investment and consumption decisions.

Having noted this, Beaulieu and Emery ask whether, through some coordination of activities, would it be possible to make Canadians better off by diversifying trade? Specifically, they test whether incomes in Canada have become more volatile as a result of an increased concentration of exports on the U.S. and also, through a more diversified export pattern, would it be possible to reduce the volatility of incomes in Canada. On both accounts they conclude that

4

neither did the increased reliance on the U.S. as an export market increase income volatility nor would it be possible to reduce current levels of volatility through increased geographic diversification of export markets. Furthermore, they suggest that history has shown that policies designed to diversify trade simply do not work and by interfering with market system can result in lower incomes for Canadians without significantly impacting on income stability.

Kunimoto and Sawchuk examine the issue of rules of origin and the potential benefits of less restrictive rules of origin within NAFTA. They illustrate that NAFTA rules of origin are the most restrictive of any major free trade agreement and therefore there may be not insignificant gains to be had from reducing their restrictiveness. Rules of origin are necessary to the operation of any preferential trade agreement as they allow the benefits of the agreement to accrue to its members and allow signators the ability to maintain different tariffs to non-members (as opposed to a common external tariff and a defacto customs union). The cost of maintaining rules of origin can therefore be interpreted as an upper bounds to the gains from their elimination as they can not be eliminated completely. The authors place the costs of the status quo at about 1% of GDP. They also report a declining use of NAFTA which peaked in 1998, but have since fallen to 50% of Canada-US bilateral trade. This, the authors conclude, is largely as a result of the shrinking gap between MFN and NAFTA rates.

Papadaki et al examine the economic impact of two policy shocks using a CGE model. The first scenario involves the creation of a Canada-US customs union with a common external tariff for both countries set to either US MFN rates or the minimum rate of either Canada or the U.S. which the authors refer to as scenarios 1a and 1b respectively. In each of the two scenarios, the authors find a minimal impact for either country at an aggregate level. At a more detailed level, the impact for some sectors that had been protected by high tariffs is more significant, such as; the Agricultural and Forestry, Food Beverage and Tobacco, Textiles, and Clothing industries.

The second scenario explored involves the elimination of all "unobserved trade costs". The authors make no distinction between the possible sources for these costs and interpret their results as the upper bounds for the potential gains from complete Canada-US economic integration. As would be anticipated, the expected gains from this experiment are quite significant, producing a welfare improvement in the range of 6-7% of GDP as well as a substantial increase in two-way trade flows.

Papadaki et al, also provide a useful comparison of computable general equilibrium (CGE) ex ante predictions for the Canada-U.S. FTA and the NAFTA based on a variety of assumptions. Early models, based on the assumption of constant returns to scale and perfect competition, showed modest gains for Canada. Later models, however, relaxing these assumptions and expanding the models to include such things as capital mobility, showed much larger gains. Comparing these predictions to the ex post results summarized by Harris, one might conclude that the early CGE models provided the lower bound to the impacts while later models provided an upper bound. Furthermore, while all of the CGE models consistently underestimated the impacts of the two agreements on trade flows, the simplest assumptions may have come the closest to measuring impacts for GDP and welfare.

Conclusions

After ten and fifteen years respectively, we are now confidently able to say that the Canada-U.S. FTA and NAFTA did indeed have a significant and positive impact on the Canadian economy. They contributed to Canadian productivity growth which will allow Canadian-based companies to compete effectively in international markets and improved the standard of living for Canadians.

NAFTA@10

Part 1:

A Look Back

The Economic Impact of the Canada-U.S. FTA and NAFTA Agreements for Canada: A Review of the Evidence

Richard G. Harris
Simon Fraser University

Introduction

Canada entered into a free trade agreement with the United States on January 1, 1989 after a lengthy debate and considerable dispute as to its ultimate effects. That agreement, the Canada-US Free Trade Agreement, was extended in 1994 to include Mexico with the North American Free Trade Agreement (NAFTA). For Canada these trade agreements represented both a substantial opening of Canadian markets to foreign competition, together with a number of provisions on services and investment which generally increased the importance of markets and international competition within the Canadian economy. One of the principal reasons that countries enter into regional free trade agreements is to secure long-term economic benefits and to provide a business environment in which investment and commerce can effectively contribute to the well-being of its citizens. While there may be exceptions to this, such as when countries enter trade agreements for humanitarian or national security reasons, in the absence of significant expected economic benefits it would be unlikely that governments would willingly give up instruments of national economic control. The history of the free trade debate is that the benefits of trade far outweigh any presumed loss of control over the national economy by forgoing protectionism.

The world is an imperfect place, however, and regional trade agreements are not perfect arrangements. In a world of complex overlapping jurisdictions, different national histories, and the realistic political constraints on governments' ability to change domestic laws and institutions, all trade agreements are a complex set of rules reflecting compromise. The NAFTA and the Canada-U.S. FTA moved all three countries some way towards free trade but, as all are aware, protectionism and departures from the general principle of national treatment are still common. Not surprisingly, therefore, these agreements are routinely criticized on a range of criteria from economic to political to social. The purpose of this paper is not to review those complaints but to step back and ask what can be said after more than 15 years (more than 10 years for the NAFTA) about the impact of these agreements on the economy and economic outcomes in Canada. Did these agreements deliver substantial economic benefits to Canadians? The impact of international trade agreements does not take hold overnight. Generally their impact is only felt after a number of years. However, after 15 years we have a fairly good idea what the impact has been. There are a large number of studies covering a range of economic outcomes on the ex post impact of the FTA and then NAFTA. While there are gaps in the research, the overall picture is clear. These agreements had a major positive economic impact on Canada.

This chapter proceeds to make this case by first documenting the current state of trade in the economy, and provide some indication of its overall importance. Section two lays out the basic facts on the current state and structure of the Canadian economy. The basic point of this section is to highlight the extraordinary degree to which the Canadian economy is integrated into the global economy. In order to understand how Canada got to where it is now, and the role of the Canada-U.S. FTA and NAFTA agreements. Section three provides a historical overview of the economic development of Canada and the role of international trade agreements after World War II. The bulk of the study is contained in section four, which is a review of academic and government research of the impact of these trade agreements on a range of economic outcomes. These include trade volumes and patterns, foreign direct investment, employment, wage and income distribution effects, productivity gains, effects on competition and consumers, and the impact on the long-run growth prospects of the economy through increased international flows of knowledge and diffusion of technology. Most studies are Canadian or NAFTA focused, relying on data covering the first ten years after the agreement. In addition, when necessary, related international evidence is used. The bulk of the evidence is quantitative but some is qualitative. Section five of the study deals specifically with the issue of market access and dispute settlement. Use of unfair trade laws by the national governments within NAFTA was not eliminated by these agreements, despite the economic merits of doing so. An enhanced dispute settlement process was the resulting compromise. As such, it represented an improvement over the status quo at the time, but how effective it would be in increasing security of market access was only to be determined with experience. In section five we review that experience and look at evidence on what its impact has been. Section six concludes with an overall assessment.

Trade and Investment in the Canadian Economy: an Overview

Canada is a nation that is heavily dependent upon trade to sustain incomes and living standards. A few numbers put this in perspective. In 2004, Canada's exports and imports were $928.5 billion—this is an average trade volume of $2.5 billion per day, or about $29,000 for each and every Canadian. Canada's GDP was approximately 1.29 trillion dollars that year. Therefore trade, measured against GDP, is about 72.0 percent of GDP. This number has risen fairly steadily over the decades, but accelerated sharply between 1991 and 2000. In fact, the ratio of trade to GDP for Canada rose 34 percentage points over that nine year period, more than double the increase over the preceding three decades peaking at 85.2% in 2000.

Canada, by virtue of geography and history, trades a great deal with the United States. In 2004, the US was the market for 78.8 percent of Canada's exports. As a much smaller country, what is perhaps more extraordinary is the importance of Canada as the largest trading partner for the US. In 2004, Canada took 19.2 percent of US exports, and Canadian-produced goods and services accounted for 15.8 percent of total US imports. Canada's trade with other countries is important, although an order of magnitude smaller, with the E.U. accounting for 9.3 percent and Japan 2.7 percent of Canadian trade in 2004.

10

Canada has a substantial trade surplus with the United States, reaching $93.9 billion in 2004 - a very large number when judged against total trade volume for example. It is important to recognize, however, that whether a country has surplus or deficit on its trade account has little to do with the state of trade liberalization between countries, but is more accurately a reflection of relative macroeconomic conditions between countries.

International trade allows countries to specialize both at the industry level and at the detailed individual product level within specific firms. At the broader level, Canada's exports, in order of importance in 2004 were; Automotive products (21.2 percent), Machinery and Equipment (19.5 percent), Industrial products (17.5 percent), Energy (16.5 percent), Forestry (9.7 percent), Agriculture and Fishing (7.2 percent) and Consumer goods (3.7 percent). It is interesting, however, that two-way trade in similar goods (at least at the broad level) is an important feature of modern trade. Canada's three largest imports are also Machinery and Equipment (29.2 percent), Automotive products (21.7 percent) and Industrial products (20.4 percent).

Similar to goods trade, increased specialization together with globalization has brought about larger transactions in services such as travel services, transportation services, commercial services (which includes accounting, legal, insurance, architecture, engineering, and management consulting), and government services. Canadian exports of services in 2004 were $62.3 billion, or 12.7 percent of total Canadian exports of goods and services. Imports of services were $73.5 billion in 2004, or 16.8 percent of total Canadian imports of goods and services. Interestingly, the share of the United States in Canada's two-way trade is smaller for services (57.3 percent) than for merchandise (75.9 percent). Also, services trade, while rising as a share of Canadian GDP, as it is for all the advanced countries, has fallen somewhat as a share of total trade throughout the 1990s, further highlighting the boom in goods trade.

The openness of Canada to trade parallels closely the importance of Foreign Direct Investment (FDI) in the economy, both inward and outward. In 2004 the stock of inward FDI was $357.5 billion. Of that, $232.0 billion (64.9 percent) was accounted for by US firms. The stock of outward FDI by Canadian firms was $399.1 billion of which $224.4 billion (56.2 percent) was in the US economy. Globally, FDI has grown more rapidly than has trade, as in the case of Canada. Two-way FDI carries with it many benefits as will be discussed in due course.

These statistics only partially convey the importance of international trade to Canadians at the beginning of the 21st century. Economic models and theories can be used to ask questions such as "how will a fall in exports of 10 percent impact on Canadian employment?" or "how will Canadian living standards adjust if Canada were to withdraw from NAFTA?" The reality is, however, that these questions cannot be answered with any great quantitative precision. At one level, the export-import numbers suggest that, to a first approximation, one in five jobs is "export dependent" in Canada. This simply reflects an accounting of how much of current aggregate demand, or total spending in the economy, is accounted for by exports.[1] However, in another sense this vastly understates how dependent Canada is on trade. The structure and the entire organization of the Canadian economy is crucially dependent on trade and on its integration with the United States.

It is important to remember that the real purpose of exports is to import—i.e. to consume what you do not or cannot produce. The level of income in a country reflects both the efficiency with which your resources are used to produce the goods exported, and the relative value or price of goods exported versus those imported. As a small country, Canada produces a small share of the range of technologically advanced goods in the world. In a world of much reduced trade most of those goods would not be available, and it would be folly to think that a small country could undertake the investments necessary to produce even a fraction of those. Thus our access to computers, books, MRI machines, commercial jet aircraft and the Internet reflects the ability of Canadians to sell other goods in international markets.

Trade Liberalization and the role of Trade Agreements as Economic Instruments

While very large economies such as the United States have historically had good economic growth while trading relatively little, this is emphatically not the case for Canada and virtually all smaller industrial economies. In general, international trade has conferred enormous benefits on modern nations, and the history of economic progress has been coincident with the internationalization of the world's economy. While there have been periods in which, for a variety of reasons, nations and regions within have sought to become self-sufficient, trade, or more generally exchange between geographically distinct regions, is generally thought to be one of the principal driving factors behind the industrial revolution and economic advance over the last two centuries. Canada's fortunes are ample testimony to these forces. Canada began as a colony that exported raw materials to Europe, and imported finished goods. By the mid 19th century, the industrial revolution had taken hold in the United States and was beginning to see early signs of development within central Canada. After confederation in 1867, the nation continued to export natural resources and agricultural products, but began a period of development by using trade protection to promote development of an indigenous manufacturing sector. Canada was not unique, and with the exception of Britain, most countries had highly protectionist regimes covering their manufacturing sectors, and in some cases agriculture and natural resources.

However, the costs of trade protection and its negative impacts on economic development became more widely appreciated by the end of the 19th century and a period of limited trade liberalization covering manufactured goods began. This process came to a brutal halt in the 1920s, and with the beginning of the Great Depression the modern world saw a dramatic shrinkage in international commerce as countries pursued beggar-thy-neighbour policies of trade protectionism. High rates of unemployment, falling incomes, and general

---

[1] See Cameron and Cross (1999) for one such calculation. One has to net out imported inputs necessary for exports to do this calculation.

12

economic misery were the consequence. It would be fair to say that the lessons learned from the Great Depression serve today as the intellectual and political foundations upon which the modern system of a rules-based international trading system evolved. Post World War II, the multilateral international trading system was fostered with the established of the General Agreement on Trade and Tariffs (the GATT) subsequently replaced by the World Trade Organization (the WTO). The last 50 years has seen a steady erosion of trade barriers, and subsequently barriers to investment. Within the last 20 years, two important developments occurred. First, there were deeper regional trade integration agreements, of which the Canada-US Free Trade Agreement (FTA) and its successor the North American Free Trade Agreement (NAFTA), are important examples. Regional integration agreements (RIAs) have become more common as volumes of trade between close neighbouring nations accelerated, and frameworks for covering these close economic ties became easier to negotiate among a few parties, rather than the more cumbersome multilateral process under the WTO. In the 1990s this process accelerated dramatically; in 1989 there were seven major RIAs—by 1998 there were 84. The other development has been the gradual inclusion of developing countries within the GATT-WTO system. As imports from developing countries have surged, however, fears of low wage competition have become probably the single most important concern for those opposed to either WTO-led multilateral liberalization or in many cases regional integration agreements. There remain some sectors in which trade protectionism remains the rule rather than the exception. These include agriculture, textiles, footwear and clothing.

The results of trade liberalization have been nothing short of spectacular. Trade flows since 1950 have grown by more than a factor of 25 while output increased by only a factor of 7.2. International trade has similarly grown steadily in importance to Canada since the end of World War II. These increases in trade have occurred for a number of reasons, including changes in the cost of transport and communication, the end of the Cold War, economic and political developments in developing countries, and the success of market oriented domestic reforms in a number of countries, which contributed to a greater receptiveness to openness. Nevertheless it is universally recognized that policies by government towards reducing barriers to trade and investment have played a major role in these developments. Canada steadily liberalized its trade in the series of GATT rounds, taking a number of important unilateral initiatives. One of the more important developments within Canada was the 1964 Auto Pact between Canada and the US which led to the subsequent growth in two-way trade in autos and auto parts between the two countries.

Trade liberalization carries with it substantial national benefits. The case for "Free Trade", an ideal state in which there are no policy impediments to trade, is also the basis for the more practical objectives of international agreements which liberalize trade. These benefits generally fall under the following headings:

a) Greater efficiency from the pursuit of national comparative advantage. This basically says that a country should produce what it is best at, and import goods that it is (relatively) inefficient at producing. For the world as a whole, the use of market signals is the method by which a more efficient world allocation of production occurs.

13

b) Increased competition. More open markets increase the level of competition faced by domestic producers. This lowers prices to consumers, improves product quality, and removes monopolistic distortions in the economy.

c) Greater variety in goods consumed, and greater efficiency through specialization in goods produced with economies of scale and product specialization.

d) Productivity gains. Opening markets to international trade promotes innovation, better use and adoption of improved organizational and technological methods, and incentives to shift more generally toward best practice methods, and facilitates the transfer of knowledge between countries.

The liberalization of foreign direct investment helps in the achievement of similar gains. Liberalizing FDI or alternatively removing restrictions to foreign investment is motivated in general by the pursuit of greater gains in efficiency, competition, and productivity enhancement. Most FDI has been liberalized through unilateral policy decisions or bilateral agreements specific to investment. The OECD reports that the 1990s saw over 800 such agreements. Many, if not most, of the Regional Integration Agreements which cover trade also, however, contain specific provisions covering the liberalization of FDI—this was certainly true in the case of the FTA and the NAFTA.

Despite the general case "for" trade and investment liberalization there are a number of economic arguments which have been advanced that suggest more open international markets, or more specifically more imports, are not always a good thing. Two of the most important arguments are: a) the possibility that trade liberalization can create unemployment or permanently destroy jobs, and b) the possibility that income inequality is increased as a consequence of freer trade. These potential "negatives" played a very prominent role in the debate on NAFTA and to a limited extent in the FTA debate. Both of these will be dealt with in this chapter.

The bulk of trade liberalization in the more recent past has occurred in the form of Free Trade Areas or Custom Unions—or more generally Regional Integration Agreements (RIAs). While there has been a great deal of discussion about the WTO since the completion of the Uruguay Round of the GATT in 1994, there has not been another substantial round of multilateral trade liberalization. Much of the hostility towards trade agreements in Canada has focused explicitly on the FTA and NAFTA. On purely economic grounds, multilateral trade liberalization is generally preferred to preferential trade liberalization because there is scope for an RIA to potentially hurt both some member and non-member countries through its *trade diverting impact*. A RIA is not therefore necessarily trade liberalizing, if the net result is less trade than occurred before the agreement. A RIA, by giving preference to member countries, at the expense of non-members, might reduce trade between member and non-member countries. There is a large debate as to how important these effects are, and in the case of NAFTA we will review the evidence on the important question of trade diversion costs and impacts on third parties. The World Bank, in its comprehensive study on RIAs called *Trade Blocs*, comes to the general conclusion that the need for deeper integration on a regional level implies that RIAs are here to stay and if anything will increase in importance. They generally endorse a concept called *open*

14

regionalism. While too lengthy to elaborate here, the basic prerequisites for an RIA to qualify as promoting open regionalism are that: a) it does not lead to serious trade diversion effects, b) it permits deeper integration between members, c) it preserves the effects of previous liberalizations and provides credibility for any subsequent extensions of the RIA, and d) it "support[s] a liberalizing dynamic within member countries and the world trading system as a whole."[2] In practice most RIAs fall short of this ideal.

There are other complex political and social arguments with respect to the impact of recent trade agreements—in particular RIAs. These include issues such as: a) the impact on the environment, b) the impact on labour standards, c) the delivery of social services and other important public goods such as education and health, and d) potential undermining of the multilateral trading system. While important, these are not the subject of the current study which is focused on the economic impact of FTA-NAFTA on the Canadian economy. With the exception of the last issue, which is a fairly trade specific issue, the other issues can be raised with respect to almost any international agreement including those covering taxation, health and sanitary measures, defence, water supplies, etc.

The national interest case for governments to sign binding treaties covering trade and investment rests ultimately on the fact that these agreements are essential to sustaining the current level of income and employment in the economy, and providing a framework which is best suited to promoting future economic growth. They can be viewed in economic terms as a general extension of the rule of law and use of binding contracts in commercial relations. Governments that sign trade agreements voluntarily limit the application of national policy instruments that impact on trade. Most important are restrictions on the use of subsidies, tariffs and other non-tariff barriers to trade such as technical standards. While this represents a "loss" in national sovereignty in that the set of instruments governments may use to impact on the economy has been reduced, the case "for" is based on the evidence that the net impact is beneficial. This is not to argue that all RIAs are beneficial. Those which are poorly designed or give rise to strong trade diverting effects could actually lead to a decline in national economic welfare. Nevertheless, as discussed in the following sections, the available evidence strongly confirms the hypothesis that on economic grounds the FTA and its successor NAFTA have had an overwhelming positive impact on the Canadian economy.

The Economic Impact of FTA and NAFTA on Canada

In this section, we review a number of studies which look at various impacts of FTA and then NAFTA on the Canadian economy. It is first important to highlight a number of important factors that were impacting on the Canadian economy during a period in which economic adjustment to FTA-NAFTA was no doubt also ongoing. Two primary features stand out in this regard: The first was the prolonged economic slowdown in Canada between 1990 and 1992 but from

---

[2] See World Bank (2000), *Trade Blocs*, page 106. There yet is little agreement as exactly how to operationalize these principles.

15

which a true recovery was not witnessed until 1996; The second was the U.S. economic boom that lasted for most of the 1990s.

At about the same time that the FTA was to enter into force, the Bank of Canada announced a significant change in policy direction towards achieving "price stability" (Crow 1998). At about the same time, faced with large deficits and a growing debt, fiscal policy in Canada was also tightening. The result was to cause real interest rates in Canada to exceed those in the U.S. by, on average, more than three percentage points between 1988 and 1996 leading to the 'made-in-Canada' recession of the early 1990s. While the U.S. also suffered a mild slow-down in 1991, the recovery south of the border was much more rapid and was followed by many years of rapid economic growth and productivity improvements. Not unrelated to these events was the depreciation of the Canadian dollar from 89 cents US in 1991 to 62 cents in 2003. It is within this context that the Canada-U.S. FTA entered force on January 1st, 1989.

The main studies used herein are concerned with the impact on Canada, Canada-U.S. or all three NAFTA countries. There are a very large number of NAFTA studies which focus just on the US economy that are not reported unless they bear directly on an issue being discussed. The studies are divided into those focused on: a) trade creation and trade diversion effects, b) foreign direct investment, c) productivity, d) scale and specialization e) jobs and wages, f) product variety and other consumer effects, and g) dynamic effects on innovation, R&D and international technology diffusion. Ideally one would like to explicitly identify the impacts of the trade agreements on the welfare of Canada, Mexico, the United States and other countries. This is often done through the use of applied general equilibrium models which are widely used to evaluate the ex ante effects of trade agreements. However, thus far they have not been used for ex post evaluations of NAFTA. Existing ex post studies focus on specific channels of influence without taking an overall view on the net welfare impact.

Trade Creation and Trade Diversion

As noted in the introduction, the growth in trade volumes between Canada and the United States in the 1990s had been quite strong—extraordinary relative to the past history of Canada-US trade. But, for increased trade volumes to have a welfare enhancing impact, it is important to distinguish between trade creation and trade diversion. The preferential reduction in tariffs within a regional integration agreement (RIA) will induce buyers from one country who are members of the RIA to switch their demand towards supply from partner countries, at the expense of both domestic production and imports from non-members. The former is trade creation and occurs when a high cost domestic source of supply is replaced with a lower cost international source. In some cases trade diversion occurs. This is when a low cost foreign source of supply is replaced with a higher cost source from some country that is a member of the RIA. Trade creation is beneficial, but trade diversion may be costly.

The net impact of trade creation benefits less trade diversion costs on national income may be positive or negative, depending on the costs of alternative sources of supply and on trade policy towards non-member countries. Simply looking at shifts in trade volumes, the best of all possible worlds is when trade

16

between all countries rises—both members and non-members of the RIA. However, some substitution of trading partners is a predictable effect of an RIA; these shifts do not necessarily result in trade diversion.

Three studies exist which attempt to control for the impact of the trade agreement through detailed comparisons of the sectors for which NAFTA resulted in significant trade liberalization as measured by tariff reductions in comparison with other sectors in which trade was already liberalized or, for practical purposes, barrier free. They also look at trade with non-NAFTA partners as another set of benchmarks. The first study was by Schwanen (1997) and the second by Clausing (2001). Schwanen (1997) looks at Canada-US trade from 1985 to 1995 with a focus on total bilateral trade across 18 product groups. Schwanen found that in those sectors in which the FTA liberalized trade, Canada-US bilateral trade volumes grew by 139 percent versus 64.5 percent for those not liberalized. He excluded autos and crude oil trade in these calculations because both of these sectors were not significantly impacted by the FTA. This calculation strongly suggests that the growth in trade (total trade creation) between Canada and the United States was strongly linked to the FTA. To check on this explanation, he then examines Canada's non-US trade. Bilateral trade with countries other than the US, in the FTA liberalized sectors, grew by 34.7 percent compared to growth of 53.6 percent in those sectors not liberalized by the FTA. The comparison suggests that the FTA worked in those sectors in which liberalization was significant. Note the latter numbers do not provide conclusive evidence on the trade diversion effects of the FTA since they only show that trade with all countries grew, although the fact that the liberalized sectors grew faster for the FTA members, but slower for non-members may indicate some trade diversionary effects. Schwanen also does a comparison of pre- and post-FTA data using 1981-88 as the pre-period. He finds that there was a greater acceleration in the FTA liberalized group than the non-liberalized group. This was true for both exports and imports, but the effect was greater for exports.

Clausing (2001) takes a similar approach but used much more detailed US trade data. She examines US imports in approximately 8000 10-digit commodity groups as classified by the Harmonized Classification System using US census data from 1989 to 1994. She constructs a partial equilibrium supply and demand model and derives a reduced form expression for the change in US imports from Canada as a function of the initial Canadian import share in the US market, the level of US tariffs against Canadian imports, and time dummies to control for cyclical, exchange rate and other macroeconomic factors. Her results were quite striking. She found that the elimination of US tariffs had a statistically significant, positive, and large effect on imports from Canada. Each one percentage point reduction in tariffs is associated with a 9.6 percent increase in imports from Canada. For the United States, her estimates imply that total imports from Canada were 26 percent higher owing to FTA than they would have been otherwise. In terms of the growth of US imports from Canada between 1989 and 1994, this implies that over half (54 percent) of the $42 billion increase in US imports from Canada was due to the FTA.

The Clausing (2001) study is also notable in that it is the only one available which used detailed product line comparisons to explicitly check for

17

trade diversion within the US due to more liberal trade with Canada. She does this by estimating an equation which explains US imports from countries other than Canada as a function of tariff liberalization of the US with Canada, average tariff liberalization with other countries, the initial share of Canadian imports, and time dummies to control for macroeconomic effects. If the Canada-US trade agreement were trade diverting from the US perspective, one should find that reductions in US tariffs on Canadian imports actually lowered imports from other countries. What she found was that in all cases, the coefficients on the variables indicating tariff liberalization on Canadian goods were statistically indistinguishable from zero. There was no discernible relationship between the extent of tariff liberalization on Canadian produced goods and import growth in the US from countries in the rest of the world.

A more recent study by Romalis (2005) uses a similar approach to Schwanen and Clausing but estimates demand and supply elasticities on trade volumes and prices using six-digit HS classifications. He finds that the Canada-U.S. FTA increased bilateral trade between Canada and the U.S. by 5.35% while NAFTA resulted in a 24% increase in trade between Canada and Mexico. However, Romalis also found that there were minimal impacts from either trade agreement on welfare due to the small reduction in prices largely being offset by reduced duties collected. Furthermore, contrary to the findings of Clausing, Romalis finds support for some trade diversionary effects under both the FTA and NAFTA.

A second category of studies use the gravity model of international trade to impute the impact of the FTA-NAFTA for Canada. The main variables used to explain trade are GDP levels, real exchange rate variables, and distance between country pairs. The popularity of this approach is primarily explained by the relative ease with which one can obtain the data necessary to implement a statistical model of bilateral trade. One estimates the model across a number of countries over time and adds a dummy variable intended to pick up the introduction of the trade agreement. Since the estimation includes countries both in and out of the agreement, the potential variation between these groups ought to help explain the added effect on trade that can be attributed to the existence of a RIA after controlling for the other variables. This approach has yielded almost no consistent results. Coefficients are highly unstable, insignificant, and often of the wrong sign, and very sensitive to the data period chosen. However if one has to conclude, almost all these studies find no impact of FTA-NAFTA on trade volumes. The major problem with this particular approach is the high degree of correlation between a number of macro variables and the introduction of the FTA, as has already been discussed. Estimating a model ex post over this period, most studies find that US income and the exchange rate changes "explain" most of the growth in Canada-US trade. The variable capturing the introduction of FTA-NAFTA actually does very little to add explanatory value. Other problems, as discussed by Frankel (1997), include the small number of observations and the fact that GDP and trade are both endogenous to the overall economic system. Examples of this type of approach include Frankel (1997), Krueger (2000), Gould (1998) and Soloaga and Winters (2000). Acharya, Sharma and Rao (2001) pursue a variant of this approach but are even more limited in that they look only at

18

bilateral Canadian-US trade by sector and thus have no non-NAFTA countries for purposes of comparison. They estimate a time series model of Canadian export growth to the US from 1980 to 1998, finding that growth in Canadian exports to the US is largely explained by US income and the depreciation of the Canadian dollar. Their estimates suggest that of the total increase in exports, only 8 percent is due to the FTA. A close examination of their parameter estimates reports a US income elasticity for Canadian exports of 2.7—a highly implausible number. The results largely follow from the limited manner in which the impact of FTA-NAFTA are imputed.

Some of these studies focused on the issue of trade diverting effects of NAFTA from a US perspective including Canadian trade. Both Krueger (2000) and Soloaga and Winters (2001) are largely concerned with this issue and both focus on the US-Mexico aspect of NAFTA. Krueger claims to find no evidence of trade diversion and Soloaga and Winters find some mild evidence of trade diversion within NAFTA—largely these effects hinge on a shift towards Mexican produced goods at the expense of goods from East Asia.

A recent variant on the trade diversion argument has found its way into the Canadian policy debate following the release of John McCallum's (1995) study on international versus interprovincial trade using pre FTA data. It is well known that, subsequent to the FTA, there was a substantial increase in international trade, while there was a mild decline in interprovincial trade. From 1988 to 2000 interprovincial trade declined as a percentage of GDP from 27 percent to around 20 percent. Is it the case that "trade diversion" has occurred within Canada so that north-south Canada-US trade is replacing east-west interprovincial trade as a consequence of FTA? There are two points to make about this type of trade share shift analysis. First, and most important, the fall in the share of interprovincial trade cannot be trade diversion in the traditional sense. Trade diversion, which is income reducing, only occurs if a low cost source of imports is replaced with a high cost source of imports. In the absence of internal tariffs on trade between provinces, if a province shifts its source of imports from another province to a source outside of Canada, it cannot result in trade diversion There remains, however, the possibility that trade patterns shift and that clearly seems to have occurred in the data. Not surprisingly, the removal of barriers on international trade, with no barriers to interprovincial trade, led to an increase in international relative to interprovincial trade. Helliwell, Lee and Messinger (1999) use a gravity model to infer the extent of the shift in trade. Their estimates suggest that in 1996 interprovincial trade would have been 13 percent higher if the pre-FTA trade structure had remained in place *and* Canadian and US GDP by state and province were the same as actually existed in 1996. In the case of Canada, the latter assumption is highly implausible given the income creating effect of trade with the US that occurred over that period.

Foreign Direct Investment

The impact of trade agreements on FDI flows and stocks remains in general a contentious area. Unlike trade, the impact of increased outward and inward FDI is theoretically ambiguous with respect to its ultimate effects on economic performance. There are a variety of potential channels at work when a

19

free trade agreement comes into place. Inward FDI could rise or fall depending upon the location effects of the trade agreement. Canada could be a more desirable place for foreign firms to undertake production for both domestic and export purposes as trade barriers are reduced, with the implication that increased trade and inward FDI occur simultaneously, or are complementary to one another. On the other hand, a reduction in trade barriers could lower FDI in some sectors if firms no longer need to locate within the Canadian market in order to serve Canadian demand. In the latter case, FDI and trade would be viewed as substitutes as trade barriers are removed. With NAFTA, firms can produce from a US or Mexican base and then export to Canada. With respect to outward FDI there are similar tradeoffs from the point of view of Canadian multinational firms. Canadian outward FDI may transfer low-wage, low-skill production to other countries, and at the same time increase the production of high value-added goods to be exported, thus causing an increase in high-paying, high-skill jobs in Canada. Thus, it may be that higher outward FDI in one industry causes exports to increase in other industries. Even if one finds the intra-industry relationship between trade and FDI to be one of substitutes, they may be complements when considering inter-industry links. Some outward Canadian FDI may also simply reflect the attempt by Canadian firms to avoid trade harassment in the US market. On theoretical grounds, there are no strong a priori expectations as to the effect of FTA-NAFTA on FDI patterns other than an expectation that two-way flows would rise.

Given that there is potential two way causality running between trade and FDI, one would in principle like to know what aspects of the agreement might have spurred additional FDI in the absence of trade liberalization. The Canada-U.S. FTA included a number of provisions which reduced discrimination against bilateral foreign direct investment, including the extension of rights-of-establishment and national treatment. A range of prominent sectors, such as basic telecommunications, was excluded from coverage under the investment liberalization provisions of the Agreement and Canada's existing foreign investment screening procedures were left in place (Globerman and Walker, 1993). Nevertheless, the thrust of the investment provisions of the FTA was clearly to expand the legal scope for bilateral direct investment. Moreover, the inclusion of a relatively robust dispute resolution procedure arguably reduced the risks of either government acting in a discriminatory manner towards investors from the other country.

Independent of its relationship to trade liberalization, there is quite a large literature which establishes that FDI promotes competitiveness through increased innovation, technology transfer and international knowledge spillovers (Caves, 1974; Globerman, 1979; Blomstrom and Persson, 1983; Blomstrom and Wolff, 1989; Xu, 2000). Some of these studies will be reviewed later in this chapter when the growth and dynamic effects are discussed. The literature on these effects however is largely international in nature; no specific FTA studies deal with the issue directly.

There are also relatively few studies which attempt to isolate the impact of the FTA-NAFTA on FDI patterns or relate them to shifts in trade patterns. But, those that do, generally come to similar conclusions. Schwanen (1997) looks at

20

the period from 1989 to 1995. He noted that while the level of FDI in Canada was increasing, Canada's relative share of global FDI was falling due to an explosion of FDI elsewhere. He also notes there was a trend toward Canadian FDI going to destinations other than the U.S. Similar results are found in a case study of three regional integration agreements. Magnus Blomstrom and Ari Kokko (1997) look carefully at the Canada-U.S. FTA. They suggest that the effects of liberalizing investment on Canada would be expected to be modest at best. Looking at the data from 1983 to 1995 they conclude that bilateral direct investment has increased since the early 1990s. However, before that, the relative importance of bilateral direct investment changed erratically, and it is difficult to discern a consistent pattern in FDI flows that would clearly be related to the FTA. Inward direct investment from countries other than the United States exhibits no consistent pattern over the period studied, although the largest inflows took place between 1988 and 1990, right after the implementation of the FTA. However, like Schwanen, they note an increasing share of Canadian outward FDI going to places other than the US after 1990. They argue that the profitable opportunities encouraging a redirection of Canadian direct investment outflows were not related to FTA, although it may have played an important role in that it guaranteed access to the US market, so that available FDI resources within Canadian firms could instead be utilized to establish Canadian presence in other markets.

More recently, there have been some econometric studies which take up these issues. Globerman and Shapiro (1999) estimate capital inflows to Canada and capital outflows from Canada for the period 1950-1995. The dependent variables used are FDI in Canada and Canadian FDI abroad, with explanatory variables including Canadian GDP, GDP abroad (US and UK), relative costs (Canada-US, Canada-UK), exchange rates, investment climate (investment to GDP ratio in Canada), Canadian imports and exports. They estimate two equations, one for inbound foreign investment into Canada (FDI) and one for outbound foreign investment from Canada (ODI). The results suggest that FIRA (the Foreign Investment Review Act) had little influence on either FDI or ODI. On the other hand, trade liberalization agreements (NAFTA, FTA) had statistically significant impacts on gross FDI and ODI flows with a net bias toward ODI.

Hejazi and Safarian (1999) analyze the impact of outward (inward) FDI on the economy, specifically on trade (imports, exports) using a gravity model of bilateral trade. Using bilateral trade and FDI data between Canada and 35 other countries over the period 1970-96, the paper establishes that trade and FDI are complementary.[3] The results indicate that outward (inward) FDI increases exports (imports) and the size of the impact of inward FDI on imports is one-third that of outward FDI on exports. Over the period 1970-1996, the stock of inward FDI was larger than the stock of outward FDI. The ratio of the stock of inward FDI to GDP fell from about 30 percent in 1970 to 20 percent in the early 1990s and increased

---

[3] This study also looks at more detailed industry level links between trade and FDI for Canada, the United States, the United Kingdom and Japan. They find overall that outward FDI and exports are complementary rather than substitutes. For inward FDI they find that inward FDI tends to increase imports.

21

to about 25 percent in 1996. The ratio of the stock of outward FDI to GDP increased from about 7 percent in 1970 to 22 percent in 1996. That is, in 1996 Canada had about the same stock of outward FDI as inward FDI. They make no attempt to link these results directly to NAFTA. However, the timing suggests that FTA and NAFTA were at least partially responsible for these trends, and the news is certainly not bad. Generally, greater outward FDI tends to encourage exports and thus is trade creating. This type of result is now more common in the international literature. A recent OECD study by Fontagne (1999) using a large data set on FDI flows within the OECD finds complementarity between trade and FDI. He concludes that for each additional dollar of outward FDI around two dollars of additional exports are created. It appears therefore in the modern period, outward FDI has become a powerful trade creating mechanism.

Jobs, Wages and Employment

The argument that trade should be limited because imports destroy jobs is probably the oldest and most frequently advanced in public policy debates on trade and globalization. The argument was heard both in the public debate leading up to the FTA and in the NAFTA debate. It played a much larger role in US public discussion on NAFTA than was the case in Canada, however, likely due to the closer proximity to Mexico. Given the export-oriented nature of the Canadian economy, it may also be the case that most Canadians are aware that exports create jobs. In the short to medium run, following a shift in trade policy, it is possible a trade deficit or surplus may arise, and thus jobs created by exports may be more or less than offset through jobs destroyed by increased imports. But in the long run these ought to balance out. Most economists argue that movements in the rate of employment and unemployment have far more to do with macroeconomic factors and shifts in labour force participation rates than they do with trade policy. To quote trade historian Douglas Irwin:

In fact, the overall effect of trade on the number of jobs is best approximated as zero. Total employment is not a function of international trade, but the number of people in the labour force. (Irwin 2002, page 71)

Nevertheless there are a large number of studies in the US that attempted to isolate, using various methodologies, the short to medium run impact of NAFTA on US jobs. One study, Hinojosa-Ojeda et al. (2000), looks at the impact in the US labour market of imports from Canada and Mexico over the period 1990 to 1997. Looking just at imports, they estimate that job losses within the US due to imports from Mexico would be 299,000, and would be 458,000 for imports from Canada. That is an average of 37,000 jobs *per year* for Mexican imports and 57,000 *per year* for Canadian imports. As they observe, considering that the US economy creates over 200,000 net new jobs *per month* and causes the separation of about 400,000 workers *per month* from their jobs, the small relative share of potential job impacts from this trade is apparent. This type of argument, however, does not carry as much weight in Canada when a much larger share of the economy is exposed to international trade. One has to deal more directly with the issue of the relative magnitudes of job creation and destruction.

In Canada, it is generally clear from evidence in the 1990s that increased trade exposure of the economy has driven a great deal of job creation, for whatever reasons those trade increases occurred. A central question is whether employment gains in export-oriented and related sectors compensate for employment losses in industries facing import competition, or alternatively whether jobs are reallocated from the tradables sectors—notably manufacturing—toward non-tradable sectors such as services. It is first worth pointing out that a large number of jobs in Canada depend on exports. Gera and Massé (1996) found that the expansion of exports accounted for around 75 percent of new jobs (1.4 million) between 1971 and 1991. A Statistics Canada study (1999), estimates that in 1995 around one in five jobs in Canada was directly or indirectly related to exports. On balance, the available evidence suggests that the net impact of trade on employment has been positive. Gera and Massé (1996) found that, despite the negative employment impact of imports, trade accounted for 23 percent (719,000) of net new jobs in Canada between 1971 and 1991. However, during the second half of the 1980s, trade had a small net negative impact on employment.

As in the last section in which the question is more specifically focused on the impact of a particular trade agreement on jobs, it becomes more difficult to make a definitive assessment. In the 1970s and 1980s, there were a large number of studies on the labour market adjustments required by trade liberalization. The OECD (1989) conducted a number of studies on the employment effects of trade liberalization and summarized the evidence available at that time. It concluded that the net impact of trade liberalization on employment is in general small relative to that occurring for other reasons, such as technological change. It is commonly argued that trade amongst OECD countries can be characterized as intra-industry (i.e. trade in similar products). Adjustment in this case involves shifting employment and other factors of production within a firm to new production lines, or shifts within an industry. As the bulk of trade liberalized under the FTA was characterized as intra-industry rather than inter-industry trade it was argued that labour adjustment under the FTA would be less of a problem.

The emergence of the deep and long recession that began in 1989 led many to associate job losses in the recession with the implementation of the FTA. What is apparent is that the recession and the FTA simultaneously led to large pressures for structural adjustment in the economy. There are a number of Canadian studies which look at the impact of the FTA on employment through a comparison of high and low protection sectors.

a) Gaston and Trefler (1997), argue that the FTA was not the primary cause of most of the job losses in the Canadian manufacturing sector during the 1989-1993 period. According to the authors, FTA tariff cuts account for no more than 15 percent of employment losses. They find that most of the employment losses were due to the recession of the early 1990s, which they attributed to the Bank of Canada's fight against inflation, a consequence of which was high domestic interest rates and a strengthened Canadian dollar.

b) Schwanen (1997) argues that the FTA did not contribute to Canada's employment problems in the early 1990s in any significant way. Sectors most

23

sensitive to the FTA do not appear to have fared worse than manufacturing as a whole. Moreover, he argues that the poor employment performance of some sectors was primarily due to factors other than the FTA—for example, import competition from non-US sources (leather and electronics products), the recession (construction materials), or long-term decline not related to trade (fish products, shipbuilding).

c) Trefler (1999) finds that the FTA reduced employment in manufacturing by about 5 percent over the 1988-1996 period while industries exposed to large tariff cuts experienced relatively large employment declines of about 15 percent over that period.

d) Beaulieu (2000) distinguishes between skilled and less-skilled workers using production and non-production works as proxies for each group respectively. He finds that the FTA lowered employment among less-skilled workers but had no impact on skilled workers.

Another aspect of trade liberalization that has received a lot of attention is its potential impact on the distribution of income and wages. There is a school of thought that argues that the rising inequality between the skilled and unskilled in OECD countries is due to increased competition from low wage unskilled labour in developing countries. The available evidence suggests trade is not the answer, and most analysts have come to the conclusion that technological change, which is biased against employment of low skilled workers, has been the major cause. Slaughter (1999) provides a useful summary of this debate.

In Canada, the trade and wages debate, as it is known, has been quite muted. This is for the simple reason that Canada has not experienced the same rise in skill premia that occurred in the United States and other countries although the same general trend has been observed here. In the case of the FTA, the argument was clearly less relevant as opening up Canadian markets to US imports was a case of opening up the economy to high wage, not low wage competition. On the other hand, the FTA might have hastened a process of structural change that was under way, leading to job losses or wage losses for unskilled workers. Total manufacturing employment in Canada declined from 2,130,000 to a low of 1,786,000 (or 16.1 percent) between 1989 and 1993. Job losses among production workers was larger in percentage terms than among non-production workers. However, manufacturing employment, in absolute size, has actually increased since then and surpassed 2,300,000 in 2002. As noted by Curtis and Sydor (2005), Canada has been one of the few industrialized countries to have increased total manufacturing employment over this period and trade has played an important role in this.

There are only a few studies on the link between the FTA and the relative wages of low-skilled workers in Canada. These focus on the manufacturing sector only and offer somewhat conflicting evidence. Some find a positive impact of trade on the relative wages of low-skilled workers in Canada. For example, Trefler (1999) finds that the FTA increased the wages of production workers relative to non-production workers in manufacturing. Gu and Whewell (2000) report that imports to Canada are in fact more skilled-labour-intensive than Canadian manufacturing exports and suggest that increased trade has not hurt the wages of unskilled versus skilled workers. In contrast, Baldwin and Rafiquzzaman (1998) find a direct link between increases in the wage premium of skilled workers and changes in trade intensity. Sectors where import competition increased the most (labour-intensive, product-differentiated and natural resources sectors) also saw the largest increases in the wage premium of non-production workers. However, these results are not directly comparable to those above, as the authors examine changes in relative wages at only a sectoral level and do not provide evidence for manufacturing as a whole.

Schwanen (1997) finds some evidence that, in the immediate post FTA period, manufacturing wages grew faster those sectors that had previously been open while sectors newly exposed to the FTA did not fare as well. Beaulieu (2000), on the other hand, while finding an effect on employment finds no evidence of any impact on earnings for either skilled or less-skilled workers. Townsend (2004), using micro-level data and controlling for worker's characteristics such as education and experience, explores a number of questions relating to the impact on workers of the FTA. He finds that relative wages fell in those industries faced with the deepest tariff cuts, and tended to be low-end manufacturing workers. Lemieux (2005) explores a slightly nuanced version of this question asking whether wages rates in Canada and the U.S. have converged post FTA. He finds that wage rates between the two countries were quite comparable in 1984 but have diverged to some degree since then, most notably in the wage premium associated with higher education rising much more in the U.S. than in Canada.

On balance, one could conclude that the FTA contributed mildly to job losses in Canada in the early 1990s, but the overall effect was relatively modest and was likely off-set by employment gains elsewhere in the economy. Similarly, while there may have been some skill bias in wages resulting from the FTA, this effect too was not overly pronounced and likely relatively small compared to other changes ongoing in the economy at the time.

Productivity

The productivity effects of the FTA have been the most controversial of the ex post FTA results after employment. Many ex ante studies of the FTA, including my own (Harris 1984), suggested the FTA could significantly raise productivity in Canadian industry through a variety of channels—improved scale economies, longer production runs, improved resource allocation across sectors due to better exploitation of comparative advantage, and increased competition due to more open markets. The debate on productivity effects was given added impetus by an increase in the labour productivity gap between Canada and the US, which accelerated after 1994 as discussed by Bernstein, Harris and Sharpe (2002). From 1977 to 1994 the Canada-US gap in output per hour in manufacturing averaged 14 percent. Since 1994, however, Canada's relative gap has risen 20 percentage points from 12 percentage points in 1994 to 32 percentage points in 2001. Output per hour in Canadian manufacturing fell from 88 percent of the US level in 1994 to 68 percent in 2001. Clearly productivity did not increase as was expected, but worse, it actually declined in the latter part of the 1990s. The determinants of productivity growth are quite complex, and the story of the late 1990s is as much about the acceleration of US productivity growth and the US technology boom as it is about the situation in Canada after the introduction of free trade. The debate on the situation in the late 1990s has tended to cloud what more direct evidence is available on the impact of the FTA on productivity. The studies that do attempt to isolate the impact of the FTA generally indicate that it was a positive impact on productivity.

Trefler (1999) is the most detailed study on the productivity effects of FTA for the manufacturing sectors during the 1989-96 period. The impact of tariff cuts is estimated for manufacturing as a whole and for the most affected industries (the industries faced with tariff cuts greater than 8 percent). The data covers the years 1980-96 and is mostly at the 4-digit SIC level (213 manufacturing industries). He looks at the average annual change of average labour productivity in each industry over the pre-FTA period and over the FTA period. The analysis includes as explanatory variables the differences over the two periods for the following variables: (i) the average annual change of the preferential tariff concession extended to the US (the difference between the Canadian tariff against the US in each industry and the Canadian tariff against the rest of the world in each industry, and (ii) a control variable for supply-demand changes and technological changes. He estimates the change in the growth of productivity due to the FTA tariff concessions in the manufacturing as a whole and in the most protected industries (tariff cuts larger than 8 percentage points over the FTA period analyzed, 1988-96). The tariff cuts raised labour productivity at a compound rate of 3.2 percent per year (out of 3.5 percent) for the most impacted industries and at 0.6 percent per year (out of 2.5 percent) for manufacturing as a whole. The study strongly supports the view that high rates of domestic protection contributed to large productivity losses relative to the situation with free trade. Even the aggregate numbers are significant. Cumulating the estimated FTA effects over the eight-year period, total productivity in manufacturing would have been 5 percent less by 1996 without the FTA than with it.

Acharya, Sharma and Rao (2001) estimate the impact of intra-industry trade, inter-industry trade, firm size, capital intensity, and the FTA on the level of labour productivity using data on 84 Canadian manufacturing industries with 15 years of data (from 1984 to 1997). Their results suggest that increases in intra-industry trade raised labour productivity. Employment per establishment is positive and significant, indicating that the larger the size of the firm, the higher will be labour productivity. Both of these effects are consistent with the view that scale and intra-industry adjustment were the major sources of adjustment precipitated by the FTA—to be discussed in the next section. Nevertheless, having controlled for these variables, they find that the FTA had a significant and positive impact on labour productivity levels in Canadian manufacturing. Their parameter estimates imply that the FTA raised labour productivity in 1997 by about 18 percent relative to what would have occurred without the FTA. However, given their identification of the FTA with a post 1988 dummy variable, it is possible the attribution is overstated. On the other hand, the fact that they control for both the level of intra-industry trade specialization and firm size, suggests they may have understated the total impact of the FTA on productivity.

The above studies do not attempt to isolate the factors by which more liberalized trade raises productivity. In the next two sections, we consider studies

26

which look at the issue in more detail and try to isolate some channels through which this might occur. It is important to remember, however, that productivity growth is a complex process determined by the interaction of many different factors. While the evidence suggests that the FTA contributed positively to productivity growth in the manufacturing sector, there are clearly a number of other factors at work. Nevertheless, as Trefler (1999) notes, it is remarkable to find government policies which yield productivity benefits of this magnitude.

Specialization and Scale

Of the possible sources of increased productivity that come from increased openness, and one of the most debated prior to the FTA, was the potential for firms to achieve greater scale and more efficient specialization across product lines. A long history of analysis of Canadian industrial development had suggested that Canadian producers were generally too small and operated plants that were too diversified with relatively short production runs.[4] The strong gains in productivity in automotive plants which were achieved by product line rationalization after the 1964 Canada-US Auto Pact were suggestive of what might occur under free trade with the United States. At the same time, studies on European integration had suggested that trade liberalization in manufacturing was largely precipitating adjustment within industries leading to increased *intra-industry trade* and increased *intra-industry specialization*. Intra-industry specialization implies countries specialize within industries in particular product niches. Economies of scale and specialization are the technological factors which drive this type of specialization when markets open to greater international competition. Opening the Canadian market to competition on a priori grounds should have induced this type of specialization after the FTA. There are two factors mitigating against this type of efficiency gain: very large transport costs, and industries that are heavily reliant on natural resource inputs. If either of these forces is strongly present, then intra-industry specialization is less likely. What impact did FTA have in this regard?

By and large, the studies generally are indicative that the specialization and scale effects that were predicted have subsequently taken place. One factor which may well have significantly slowed the adjustment process in intra-industry specialization, as suggested by some commentators, was the depreciation of the Canadian dollar during the 1990s. Exchange rate depreciation would tend to provide import competing manufacturing with an increased margin of protection as tariff walls came down. This exchange rate protection effect would certainly have reduced the incentives for Canadian producers to make the type of adjustments in the organization of plants that the intra-industry specialization argument would have suggested, and thus delayed the adjustment process to free trade with the United States.

Head and Ries (1999) document that the scale of the average manufacturing firm increased by 34 percent from 1988 to 1994. The number of establishments over the same period declined by 21 percent. In contrast, from 1980 to 1988, output per plant increased by 3 percent. These numbers probably

---

[4] See Eastman and Stykolt (1967), Harris (1982) and Wonnacott and Wonnacott (1967).

27

overstate the scale growth post FTA because of undercounting in the Statistics Canada data of small firms. Head and Ries argue these increases were largely to due to US tariff reductions and not Canadian tariff reductions. Gu, Sawchuk and Whewell (2002) look at the dynamics of this process by focusing on increased firm turnover as the source of FTA-induced productivity benefits. Tariff reductions expose firms to increased global competition, which tends to drive out the less efficient firms, giving rise to increased firm turnover. The decline in the number of less-efficient firms in the economy contributes to overall productivity growth. To test the importance of the above two explanations for productivity growth, they examine whether the reduction in Canadian tariffs since the implementation of the FTA has had a significant effect on firm size, firm entry rates, and firm exit rates using a database that provides comprehensive coverage of firms across 81 manufacturing industries from 1983 to 1996. They suggest that while there was no evidence that the that FTA-related tariff cuts led to an increase in *average* firm size in Canadian manufacturing, they did find two interesting impacts of tariff reductions. First, tariff reductions forced the exit of the least productive manufacturing firms. Second, they found quite robust evidence that that the FTA tariff cuts had a positive and significant effect on the exit rate of Canadian manufacturing firms. Their calculation shows that the tariff cuts in the FTA period increased the exit rate by 0.7–2.0 percentage points for the most-affected industries. It appears, therefore, that trade liberalization was having a strong rationalization effect.

One of the difficulties with these studies is that firm size, their measure of scale, does not correspond to what most pre-FTA industry studies focused on, which was production runs on individual product lines within plants. The reason most authors used value of firm shipments as an output measure was simply data availability. Recent efforts by Statistics Canada have rectified the situation; there are now new data sets which allow specific examination of product line specialization within plants. Baldwin, Beckstead and Caves (2001) use longitudinal data on all plants in Canadian manufacturing over the period 1973-1997. They are also able to match plants to firms so they can distinguish between plant level and firm specialization across detailed product groups. Their findings are striking. They find that there has been a general increase in specialization of both firms and plants. But the most significant trend was within plants in a given industry—what they refer to as "commodity specialization". Commodity specialization at the plant level emerged late in their data period, around the time of implementation of FTA. Moreover they also find that plant specialization increased most in those plants that moved most strongly into export markets.

> But in contrast to firm-level diversification, the decrease in plant level diversification has a discontinuous break around the time of the Free Trade Agreement between Canada and the United States. Product line specialization increased dramatically just before the FTA and this increase continued well into the 1990s. As a result, product-run length within plants increased dramatically over the period before and after the FTA. The evidence shows that product

28

specialization increased more than industry level specialization in the late 1980s. (Baldwin, Beckstead and Caves 2001, p. viii)

The study then goes on to check whether this break in specialization patterns can be specifically related to trade liberalization. They find a strong relationship between the export intensity of a plant and its specialization. Plants that export more of their sales are likely to be more specialized. They also find that during the transition period from the late 1980s to the early 1990s, those plants that increased their export intensity increased their plant specialization. The timing is strongly suggestive of the proposition that the FTA induced the rationalization within plants. To date, this is the only study available on the issue of product line specialization but it is strongly supportive of the arguments advanced by economists prior to the FTA on the likely impact. Overall, these effects should have raised plant level efficiency and ultimately should be reflected in plant level productivity data. The data on industry level productivity discussed previously suggests this is exactly what has occurred.

A different perspective on the specialization issue is provided by intra-industry trade statistics. These types of indexes attempt to show whether intra- or inter-industry trade specialization has any particular pattern, and its likely effects. Both history and theory suggest that the FTA should have increased intra-industry trade (usually identified in the literature as IIT). Three studies have looked at this issue. Harris and Kherfi (2000), Andressen, Harris and Schmitt (2001), and Achayra, Sharma and Rao (2001). Harris and Kherfi found evidence of general increases in intra-industry trade from 1988 to 1995. Looking at productivity dynamics over the pre and post 1988 period, they found that increases in Total Factor Productivity were significantly and positively affected by intra-industry specialization.

Achyra, Sharma and Rao (2001) compute a different specialization index using trade flows with the US for 84 manufacturing industries for 15 years of data from 1983 to 1997. They confirm that intra-industry trade (IIT) increased relative to inter-industry trade over the period by a factor of approximately two. They undertake to try to explain the growth of intra-industry trade by a few variables but their results are generally inconclusive. However, both they and Trefler (1999) are unable to detect a significant FTA effect using time dummy variables as an FTA proxy.

Andressen, Harris and Schmitt (2001), using much more detailed trade data, argue that the overall trends on intra-industry trade are sensitive to the index used. By some methods, IIT rose and by others it remained relatively stable over the period. Two significant problems occur within the aggregate trends. First is the importance of the auto industry where IIT was quite high prior to the FTA. The second problem is the role of resource prices and comparative advantage trade. The aggregate trends include resource trade and are sensitive to shifts in natural resource prices such as fluctuations in oil prices. One could argue that since there was no predicted impact on specialization within these sectors they should be excluded when judging the specialization effects of the FTA. When one removes these sectors, the increase in IIT is much greater. On balance, however, one would

29

have to say there is no definitive proof that the FTA was responsible for these developments although the timing is suggestive.

Variety and Price of Goods and Services

Trade liberalization has as one of its major benefits lower prices for consumers and increased availability of goods and services. Lower trade barriers and more open markets both induce firms to lower prices and to increase the range of products supplied. Despite these widely recognized benefits, it has proven extremely difficult to quantify these effects. Even the most basic price impacts on consumers remains an area in which the absence of reliable data has made progress in this area almost impossible.

There are a couple of studies which at least bear on the issue. Head and Ries (2001), using some estimates of demand price elasticities in conjunction with actual tariff and import data, calculate the loss in consumer welfare that would come from imposing 1988 level Canadian tariffs on US imports in 1998 (by which time all such tariffs had in fact been removed) for each 3-digit industry. Summing across all manufacturing industries, they find the tariff imposition on imports from the US would cost Canadian consumers C$7.86 billion in lost surplus. This is 4.1 percent of their 1998 expenditures on US-made manufactured goods. They note that this loss would be partially offset by increases in government duty revenue of C$6.56 billion. Thus, the net benefit to Canadians of implementing the FTA tariff reductions appears to be C$1.29 billion. This works out to about $40 per person per year.[5]

The availability of new goods and services is also potentially a major source of increased consumer welfare. While putting a dollar number on this benefit is difficult to quantify, there has been some effort on identifying the extent to which the increase in NAFTA trade is associated with trade in new goods. A study by Russell Hillberry and Christine McDaniel (2002), using very detailed US trade data, decomposes the growth in the value of US trade between its NAFTA partners from 1992 to 2001 into price, volume and a "variety of good" effects. This latter effect looks at the change in trade values due to trading more or fewer goods as classified in the Harmonized Tariff Schedule. Of their measured 35 percentage point increase in US exports to Canada, 3.4 points of these represent trade in new goods as measured in the HTS schedule. The interpretation of this number is that Canadian imports from the US would have gone up by 3.4 percentage points holding the price and quantity of other pre-existing trade constant due to the export of new varieties to Canada. This would be viewed as a gain to consumers in Canada.

This study also provides some evidence on price effects. They report that on average, using the goods traded in 1993, inflation adjusted real prices of US

---

[5] This of course is only one of many effects that real consumers experience as a result of the FTA. This ignores, for example, change in the incomes of consumers dealt with under the productivity issue, and changes in the supply price of both domestic imported and exported goods. The pro-competitive effects of the FTA may well have reduced prices to consumers on a range of domestically produced goods for example although there is no evidence on this in existing studies.

30

exports to Canada fell by 7.1 percent over the period 1992 to 2001. One cannot necessarily attribute these price reductions to the Free Trade Agreement other than to note that had trade volumes been at levels that existed prior to the FTA the beneficial impact of these price reductions to Canadian consumers would have been much less. Ironically, US import prices on goods coming from Canada actually went up 9.7 percent over the same period. Economists refer to the relative difference between changes in export and import prices as the terms of trade. This study seems to suggest that using the goods that were initially traded in 1993, the Canadian terms of trade with the US improved significantly (9.7+7.1=16.8 percent). Further research, however, on this issue would be required to measure to what extent the FTA-NAFTA would be responsible for these effects.

Innovation, International Spillovers, and Technology Transfer

In this section, the "dynamic gains from trade" arguments will be dealt with. These are the growth enhancing effects of trade and trade liberalization which operate through a set of mechanisms related to the international diffusion of technology, innovation, and the production and use of new knowledge. There is a very large literature associated with these potential channels running from trade to economic growth, most of them focused on international comparative experience. The most numerous studies in the area document an empirical statistical relationship running from trade and economic openness to growth.[6] At a practical level, it is often difficult to distinguish between the impact of trade and trade agreements on productivity levels and the impact on growth rates of productivity, which are the primary determinants of the growth in living standards. Most of the productivity issues referred to earlier in this chapter implicitly are concerned with the impact of trade on productivity levels. Generally we think of increased trade as raising the level of income or productivity, but not necessarily having a permanent impact on the growth rate. Evidence on the "dynamic gains from trade" comes from three sorts of studies: i) the impact of the level of trade (measured relative to GDP on growth of per capita incomes, ii) the role of imports and FDI in facilitating the international diffusion of technology or what are known as R&D spillovers, and iii) the impact of exports on productivity growth. In each case, the literature tends to be fairly general, that is covering a wide range of countries, and does not relate specifically to the NAFTA case.

Evidence linking trade and economic growth, as measured by changes in per capita incomes, comes primarily from comparison of growth across a large number of countries in the post-war period known as the country-growth regression literature. The majority of these studies find strong evidence linking openness to economic growth—countries that have degrees of openness or lower barriers to trade tend to have higher growth rates of per capita income. Other important variables in these studies include investment, levels of education, and the starting level of income. One of the major problems, however, is that

---

[6] Levine and Renelt (1992) is the most frequently cited study in this area. There are literally dozens of other growth regression studies which document this link. Harris (2002) discusses these and their interpretation for a country such as Canada which is both open and high income.

investment and trade are very highly correlated across countries and therefore it is difficult to disentangle the separate effects of trade and investment on income. Secondly, there is another problem in distinguishing cause and effect; trade affects income and income affects trade, especially in smaller countries, holding trade policy constant. Ideally one would like to measure the impact on income of exogenous or policy induced changes in trade. More recent research has attempted to correct for this ambiguity by looking at sources of variations in trade not due to income. In a study by Frankel and Romer (1999), they focus on that portion of trade which is driven by geography and therefore not by income. Redefining what they call geographically determined trade, they find a very large impact of this type of trade on per capita income levels—a one percentage point increase in the trade share or openness ratio, raises income by between one half and two percent. This is a very large effect. To put this in perspective, since the Canadian trade share has risen from about 0.50 to 0.80 or 30 percentage points since the inception of the FTA in 1988, this parameter estimate would suggest Canadian per capita income increases due to trade over the period would be anywhere between 15 and 60 percent! From 1989 to 2001, GDP per hour worked in Canada actually grew at an annual rate of 1.54 percent, or 21 percent over the entire period. No doubt some of that increase can be attributed to the increase in the trade share of the Canadian economy. Unfortunately these types of studies only provide a general indication of the direction of trade on income, and the variation across countries is likely to be large. The dynamic gains from trade have probably been substantial but measuring them with any precision is not possible.

Any one small country produces only a small share of the world's leading edge technology. Growth in Canada depends crucially on the diffusion of technology developed abroad to Canada. It has long been argued that trade facilitates or is an important mediator of the pace at which international technological diffusion occurs. There is a large set of studies which attempt to measure these "technological spillovers" and the role that trade plays. This was first done by measuring the impact of R&D expenditures undertaken in one country on productivity growth in another country. For example, Coe and Helpman (1995) and Coe, Helpman and Hoffmaister (1997), construct an index of total knowledge capital in each industrial country, and assume that trading partners get access to a country's stock of knowledge in proportion to their imports from that country. They find that access to foreign knowledge is a statistically significant determinant of the rate of total factor productivity growth within a country. The most obvious interpretation of this finding is that technological knowledge is diffusing from one country to another. The estimated effects are very large. In a widely-cited study, Keller (2001) estimates that diffusion from the G-5 countries to nine other small OECD countries contributed almost 90 percent of total effect of R&D on productivity growth. When one accounts for the fact that trade patterns impact on whose R&D knowledge flows to whom, the potential role for trade to increase productivity growth becomes important. These results imply for example that Canada, as a large trader with the US, benefits from US R&D. Bayoumi, Coe and Helpman (1999) estimate the cumulative effect of permanently increasing the share of GDP devoted to R&D by 0.5 percent in selected countries and then looking at the macroeconomic effects over a 75-year period. In the case of the United States, for example, this would amount to about a 25 percent increase in R&D spending. Their simulations show this would produce a 6.8 percent increase in Canadian output.

In a related study that pertains directly to Canada, Keller (2001) looks at the role of distance, trade, FDI and language similarity as a propagation mechanism for international technological diffusion. Looking at distance effects, he finds that the average value of a dollar of US R&D in Canada is 78 percent of the value of a domestic dollar of Canadian R&D. Given that US R&D spending is about 40 times that of Canada, this explains the importance of US technological development to Canadian growth. However, he then goes on and attempts to measure the impact of other mediation channels—the combined roles of trade, FDI flows, and language similarity—on technological diffusion. The level of technology is approximated in an industry by the level of total factor productivity. The contribution of each OECD countries' own R&D on Canadian productivity growth is estimated. Keller then, measures the strength of bilateral technology diffusion across different country pairs by showing the share of a sender country in a given technology recipient's total technology inflows relative to distance. He finds that for many countries the distance effect on diffusion can be better explained by a combination of trade, FDI, and language factors. In the case of Canada, he estimates that 69 percent of total world technology diffusion to Canada originates from US R&D, while the share originating in the UK for example is much lower, equal to 13.5 percent. The combined results show that distance and low trade volumes reduce technological diffusion spillovers dramatically. The clear implication of these results are that: (a) Canada depends heavily on technological diffusion from the US, (b) bilateral increases in trade and FDI increase the magnitude of the impact of R&D conducted in other countries on Canadian productivity growth, and (c) given Canada's lack of proximity to other major industrial countries, there are no serious alternative countries as sources of technological spillovers. To the extent that FTA-NAFTA led to growth in trade and FDI, one can therefore conclude Canada's access to global technological spillovers increased as a direct consequence of these trade agreements and productivity growth subsequently benefited.

Lastly, there is a large literature on exporting and productivity. While there is general agreement that trade and growth seem to be related, more specific hypotheses have been tested with respect to the role of exports in contributing to productivity growth. Generally, the evidence on international data appears to be mixed. In a study on US productivity, Bernard et al. (2000) found that exporting did not explain productivity growth but that productivity growth seems to explain exporting. But in a large number of other cases it seems to go in the opposite direction. What Canadian evidence we have on this issue is more positive. However, most of it pertains specifically to data covering the early 1990s. It is therefore difficult to distinguish the transitional impact on productivity due to a shift towards export orientation from what might ultimately be longer-term growth effects. Gu and Whewell (2000) and Baldwin and Gu (2002), for example, found evidence that export-producing industries and firms experienced faster productivity growth following the FTA.

In conclusion, we can be sure there were undoubtedly dynamic growth effects from FTA and NAFTA. The Frankel-Romer estimates are probably an upper bound on this number, but even considerably more modest magnitudes suggest considerable growth benefits have been derived from these agreements.

Market Access and Dispute Settlement

In the debate leading up to the Canada-US free trade agreement, much of the public and business attention was focused on trade disputes which had taken place with the United States during the early and mid 1980s. Canadian firms became concerned with the increasing application of US domestic trade law with respect to anti-dumping, countervailing duties, and the use of "safeguard" import relief measures. Given that the US even then accounted for over 70 percent of the market for Canadian exports, it seemed that the economic risk to Canada posed by US protectionism was substantial and any reduction in this risk would be of great economic value. Canadian negotiating objectives were the complete elimination of these trade risks from US unfair trade law; the initial objective was to replace both Canadian and US laws on unfair trade with an agreement for common rules on subsidies, and a common antitrust policy on predatory pricing. The US, however, was not willing to go this far and the end result was the establishment of a binational dispute resolution process. Most of these arrangements are in place in Chapters 19 and 20 of the NAFTA agreement. Together with the reduction in US tariff and non-tariff barriers to Canadian imports, these were the parts of the CUSFTA which were intended to increase market access. Achieving more secure and predictable access to the US market for Canadian firms was a major objective of the Canadian government in signing the Canada-US free trade agreement.

There are also a number of investment provisions in Chapter 11 of the North American Free Trade Agreement covering investment, which are analogous to those covering goods and services. Their intention was to create more favourable and secure access on the part of any NAFTA based business wanting to invest in each of the three partner countries. Under the agreement, countries are obliged to accord national treatment and most favoured nation (MFN) treatment to foreign investors. This chapter also includes a dispute settlement mechanism. The chapter is unique as 'the first comprehensive international trade treaty to provide to private parties direct access to dispute settlement as of right' (Trebilcock and Howse 2001, page 355). The overall effect was intended to increase investment by reducing barriers, eliminating discriminatory behaviour by governments against investors, and generally to create expectations of regime and rule stability with respect to investment in all three countries.

Given the close interaction between trade and investment, those aspects of the agreement which tended to reduce uncertainty of future government interventions in either trade or investment flows are generally viewed by economists as having contributed to an increase in effective market access. Measuring the impact of these provisions though is considerably more difficult than, for example, measuring the impact of tariff reductions.

At one level, given the volume of trade between Canada and the US, one would certainly expect trade disputes. Between 1989 and 1994, there were a total of 57 disputes under Chapter 18 (5 cases) and Chapter 19 (52 cases) of the

Canada-U.S. FTA. The Chapter 19 (AD-CVD) disputes affected around US$ 7 billion in trade (the lumber dispute accounted for almost US$ 6 billion). On average during this period, the United States and Canada traded US$ 185 billion annually. Therefore, disputes affected less than 4 percent of two-way trade. Under the NAFTA, between January 1994 and 2001, there were a total of 96 disputes (including Mexico) under Chapter 11 (12 cases), Chapter 19 (80 cases), and Chapter 20 (4 cases) of the NAFTA. The Chapter 19 dispute cases involving Canada and the United States between 1994 and 1999 affected US$ 11 billion in trade out of an average annual trade of over US$ 303 billion—again under 4 percent of total trade.[7] These figures suggest trade disputes, while important, appear to be relatively minor against the backdrop of the volume of overall trade. Nevertheless, these disputes are politically very visible and legitimacy of the overall trade agreement is clearly heavily impacted by perceptions as to the efficacy and fairness of the process. The single largest "failure" has been the ongoing Softwood Lumber dispute between Canada and the United States.

Economic evidence on either the impact or effectiveness of dispute resolution mechanisms is relatively scarce. Most of the literature on these issues is either legal or political in nature. There are a couple of studies, however, which provide some insight as to the significance of both trade disputes, and the value of reducing the number of disputes. Jones (2000) looks at the data covering antidumping (AD) and countervailing duty (CVD) unfair trade cases in Canada and the United States from 1980 to 1997. In the pre-Canada-U.S. FTA period he notes that US firms filed an average of 2.8 AD cases per year against Canada, while in the post CUSFTA period AD filings dropped to 1.6 percent. This occurred despite a dramatic increase in the level of imports going into the US from Canada. Furthermore, the annual share of filings against Canada as a proportion of all filings dropped from an average of 7.4 percent to 3.9 percent between the two periods. Jones notes that the upshot of Chapter 19 is that it has changed the expectation of future benefits that US firms achieve by filing an unfair trade petition, and possibly altered the way in which US agencies administer US trade law. Of the 62 panel reviews up to November of 1998, 33 involved challenging US government agency decisions and 29 challenged Canadian government agency decisions. Of the 33 challenges to US decisions, the panels affirmed 6 of the original decisions, 10 were withdrawn or terminated, and 8 resulted in partial remands that did not result in overturning the original agency determination. However, in 7 of the unfair US trade cases, the dispute panel decisions resulted in significant changes relative to the initial agency determination. Looking at a statistical analysis of the data, Jones used the number of cases filed annually as the variable to be explained and controlled for a number of macroeconomic variables (exchange rate, unemployment etc.), a dummy variable to control for the steel industry in 1992, when there was a concrete joint effort by the US steel industry to file complaints against all steel supplying countries, and some dummy variables to capture the Canada-U.S. FTA. The results were estimated separately for AD and CVD cases, as well as jointly. In the case of AD actions, the Canada-U.S. FTA variable was highly significant. The

---

[7] These estimates are drawn from a variety of sources.

estimated coefficient indicated that the FTA reduced AD filings in the US against Canada from 5.9 to 4.1 annually. In the case of CVD, he finds the impact of the Canada-U.S. FTA appeared only after the first Chapter 19 decisions came out against the US. Correcting for this, he finds the Canada-U.S. FTA reduced CVD filings against Canada from 4.3 to 2.4 per year. He emphasizes it was clear in this case that US firms filing unfair trade actions were only impacted significantly after a "demonstration effect" on the effectiveness of the panels. Jones concludes:

> *In summary the results suggest a robust inverse relationship between the introduction of Chapter 19 and unfair trade petition filings. The impact of chapter 19 appears to have been relatively quick, beginning soon after the introduction of the CUSFTA or after the first panel decisions, leading to a uniform shift in diminished filing incentives.* (Jones 2000, page 155)

The evidence, therefore, is that the Canada-U.S. FTA and NAFTA significantly reduced the incentives for US firms to file unfair trade petitions against Canadian firms exporting to the US market. Was this of significant value? The data suggests that, even given the relatively small trade volumes subject to trade disputes, this may be the case. Unfair trade laws are thought to have two effects. First, if the petition is successful, they result in the application of duties and a reduction in imports. However, even if they are not successful, the simple act of filing has an important *trade harassment effect*. As noted by many trade scholars, one of the principal values to domestic firms having access to unfair trade laws is the ability to harass actual and potential competition. A study done a number of years ago Staiger and Wollack (1994) found that the mere investigation launched under an AD action tended to sharply reduce imports the year after the filing. This tends to have a deterrent effect in that those firms impacted either reduce their imports in anticipation of being harassed, or raise their prices. It is only recently that economists have quantified these effects.

Prusa (1992), (1997) conducted two important studies on these issues in the case of the application of US unfair trade law on the effectiveness of AD actions. Using a data set based on the line-item tariff codes identified in the cases documentation, he examines the imports from both countries named in the petition and those countries not subject to the investigation. Several important finding emerge:

First, AD duties substantially restrict the volume of trade from *named countries*, especially for those cases with high duties. His best estimates imply that imports fall by 50 percent in each of the three years following an affirmative finding. Actions that are settled reduce imports by 60 percent. Second, AD actions that are rejected still have an important impact on named country trade, especially during the period of investigation. Third, there is substantial trade diversion from named to non-named countries and the diversion is greater the larger is the estimated duty. Because of the diversion of imports, the overall volume of trade continues to grow—even for those cases which result in duties.

Prusa's work shows that actual and potential market restricting effects of AD actions on countries impacted is very substantial. While there is no comparable work on CVD cases the economic logic is the same. In conjunction with the work of Jones, the two sets of results suggest that the reduction in the application of unfair trade laws against Canada in the US market has had a substantial impact on Canada's exports to the United States. Unfortunately one of the negative aspects of preferential trade has come into play. Prusa's results on trade diversion suggest that undoubtedly suppliers from Canada and Mexico have had their sales increase in response to AD actions against non-NAFTA suppliers.

In summary, the evidence that exists suggests Canada has received substantial benefits in terms of increased trade through the dispute settlement process covering Chapter 19 actions. Other than the case studies on the legal aspects of Chapter 11 disputes, there is no economic evidence available. As of July 2002, there have been 23 cases under Chapter 11 and only 5 have led to arbitral decisions. The relatively small number of cases simply makes a statistical analysis of the impact of the chapter on investment flows impossible. As noted earlier, the overall impact of NAFTA on FDI has been positive. The economic value to resolving disputes more effectively constitutes one of the factors contributing to the larger bilateral FDI flows within NAFTA.

Conclusion

The overall impact on Canadian prosperity of the Canada-U.S. FTA and the NAFTA has been significant. In virtually all domains in which economic measurement is possible—trade flows, investment, employment, consumer benefits, productivity growth, improved competition in product markets and reduced exposure to protectionist actions in the US export market —there have been important measurable and positive impacts of this agreement.

Nations sign trade agreements first and foremost to secure economic benefits. There is virtual universal agreement among economists that a stable rules based trading system is the foundation on which international commerce has expanded and contributed to a remarkable period of rising world prosperity. For smaller and medium sized countries such as Canada, growth through international integration has become increasingly important. Moreover as Canada has shifted from the extraction of natural resource products to a manufacturing exporter, global market access has become a crucial determinant of Canadian employment and living standards. Since the end of World War II, Canada has secured its access to global markets as a participant in a number of multilateral, bilateral and regional agreements covering both trade and investment. In most instances, these agreements have been trade liberalizing. Undoubtedly the most important of these agreements were those under successive rounds of the GATT up to and including the Uruguay round and the FTA. Given the very large importance of the US market, however, the landmark Canada-US Free Trade Agreement stands out as the most significant in terms of its direct positive economic impact on Canada within the last two decades.

Bibliography

Acharya, Ram C., Prakash Sharma, and Someshwar Rao. (2003) "Canada's Trade and Foreign Direct Investment Patterns with the United States." In Richard G. Harris , ed. *North American Linkages: Opportunities and Challenges for Canada* Calgary: University of Calgary Press, pp 13-88.

Addison, John, Douglas Fox, and Christopher Ruhm. (1995) "Trade Displacement in Manufacturing." *Monthly Labor Review,* 118, pp 58-67.

Andressen, Martin, Richard Harris, and Nicolas Schmitt. (2001) "Canada-U.S. Intra-Industry Trade Patterns." Presented at a Festschrift in Honour of Jim Melvin, University of Western Ontario, September 20.

Arndt, Sven, and Alex Huemer. (2001, 2002). "North American Trade After NAFTA: Part I, Part II, and Part III." *Claremont Policy Briefs.* Issue No. 01-01, 01-02, and 02-01. Claremont Graduate University.

Baldwin, John, Desmond Beckstead, and Richard Caves. (2001) "Changes in the diversification of Canadian manufacturing firms and plants (1973-1997): A move to specialization," Analytical Studies Branch, Statistics Canada: Research Paper no. 179.

Baldwin, J., T. Gray, and J. Johnson. (1997) "Technology-Induced Wage Premia in Canadian Manufacturing Plants During the 1980s." Analytical Studies Branch, Statistics Canada: Research Paper No. 92.

Baldwin, John, and Wulong Gu. (2002) "Plant turnover and productivity growth in Canadian manufacturing." OECD, STI Working Papers 2002/2.

Baldwin, J., and M. Rafiquzzaman. (1998) "The Effect of Technology and Trade on Wage Differentials between Nonproduction and Production Workers in Canadian Manufacturing." Statistics Canada, Analytical Studies Branch: Research Paper No. 98.

Baldwin, John R., and David Sabourin. (2001) "Impact of the Adoption of Advanced Information and Communication Technologies on Firm Performance in the Canadian Manufacturing Sector." Statistics Canada, Analytical Studies Branch: Research Paper No. 174.

Bayoumi, T., D. Coe, and E. Helpman. (1999) "R&D Spillovers and Global Growth." *Journal of International Economics* 47: 399-428.

Beaudry, P., and D. Green. (2000) "Cohort Patterns in Canadian Earnings: Assessing the Role of Skill Premia in Inequality Trends." *Canadian Journal of Economics* 33(4)

Beaulieu, Eugene. (2000) "The Canada-U.S. Free Trade Agreement and Labour Market Adjustment in Canada." *Canadian Journal of Economics* 33(2): 540-63.

Bernard, Andrew B., Jonathan Eaton, J. Bradford Jensen, and Samuel Kortum. (2000) "Plants and productivity in international trade." NBER Working Paper no. 7688.

Bernstein, J., R. Harris, and A Sharpe. (2002) "The Widening Canada-US Manufacturing Productivity Gap." *The International Productivity Monitor*, Number Five, Fall 2002.

38

Blomström, Magnus, and Ari Kokko. (1997) "Regional Integration and Foreign Direct Investment: A Conceptual Framework and Three Cases". The World Bank Policy Research Working Paper Series, No. 1750.

Blomstrom, Magnus, and Hakan Persson. (1983) "Foreign Investment and Spillover Efficiency in an Underdeveloped Economy: Evidence from the Mexican Manufacturing Industry." *World Development* 11(6): 493-501.

Blomstrom, Magnus, and Edward Wolff. (1989) "Multinational Corporations and Productivity Convergence in Mexico." NBER Working Paper no. 3141.

Cameron, G., and P. Cross. (1999) "The Importance of Exports to GDP and Jobs." *Canadian Economic Observer*, Statistics Canada, November.

Trade Update 2002: Third Annual Report on Canada's State of Trade, Department of Foreign Affairs and International Trade, Canada.

Caves, Richard. (1974) "Multinational Firms, Competition and Productivity in Host Country Markets," *Economica*, 41(162): 176-93.

Caves, Richard. (1982) *Multinational enterprise and economic analysi*s. New York: Cambridge University Press.

Clausing, Kimberly. (2001) "Trade Creation and Trade Diversion in the Canada-United States Free Trade Agreement." *Canadian Journal of Economics* 34(3): 677-96.

Coe, David T., and Elhanan Helpman. (1995) "International R&D Spillovers." *European Economic Review* 39(5): 859-87.

Coe, D.T., E. Helpman, and A.W. Hoffmaister. (1997) "The North-South R&D Spillovers." *The Economic Journal* 107: 134-149.

Cox, D., and Richard Harris. (1985) "Trade liberalization and industrial organization: Some estimates for Canada." *Journal of Political Economy* 93: 115-145.

Crow, John. (1988) "The Work of Canadian Monetary Policy." Bank of Canada Review (February):3-17.

Curtis, John M. and Aaron Sydor. (2005) « L'ALENA et le changement structurel dans l'économie canadienne » L'ALENA: Le libre-échange par défaut sous la direction de Dorval Brunelle et Christian Deblock.

Dungan, Peter, and Steve Murphy. (1999) "The Changing Industry and Skill Mix of Canada's International Trade." Industry Cnada: Perspectives on North American Free Trade Series, No. 4.

Dunning, John. (1981) International Production and the Multinational Enterprise. London: George, Allen & Unwin.

Eastman, Harry C., and Stefan Stykolt. (1967) *The Tariff and Competition in Canada*. Toronto: Macmillan.

Fontagne, Lionel. (1999) "Foreign Direct Investment and International Trade: Complements or Substitute?" OECD; Directorate for Science, Technology and Industry" STI Working Papers 1999/3.

Fortin, Pierre. (1996) "The Great Canadian Slump." *Canadian Journal of Economics* 29(4): 761-87.

Frankel, Jeffrey. (1997) *Regional Trading Blocs in the World Economic System*. Institute for International Economics, Washington, DC.

Frankel, Jeffrey, and David Romer. (1999) "Does Trade Cause Growth?" *American Economic Review* 89(3): 379-399.

Fukao, Kyoji, Toshihiro Okubo, and Robert M. Stern. (2003) "Trade Diversion under NAFTA." In Robert M. Stern, ed. *Japan's Economic Recovery: Commercial Policy, Monetary Policy, and Corporate Governance.* Cheltenham, U.K.: Edward Elgar Publishing, Ltd.

Gaston, N., and D. Trefler. (1997) "The Labour Market Consequences of the Canada-U.S. Free Trade Agreement." *Canadian Journal of Economics* 30(1): 18-41.

Gera, S., W. Gu, and Z. Lin. (1999) "Technology and the Demand for Skills: An Industry-Level Analysis," Industry Canada, Working Paper No. 28.

Gera, S., and P. Massé. (1996) "Employment Performance in the Knowledge-Based Economy." Industry Canada, Working Paper No. 14.

Gestrin, Michael, and Alan Rugman. (1994) "The North American Free Trade Agreement and Foreign Direct Investment." *Transnational Corporations* 3(1): 77-95.

Globerman, S. (1979) "Foreign direct investment and "spillover" efficiency benefits in Canadian manufacturing industries." *Canadian Journal of Economics* 12: 42-56.

Globerman, Steven, and Daniel M. Shapiro. (1999) "The Impact of Government Policies on Foreign Direct Investment: The Canadian Experience." *Journal of International Business Studies* 30(3): 513-32.

Globerman, S., and M. Walker. (1993) *Assessing NAFTA: A Trinational Analysis.* Vancouver: The Fraser Institute.

Gould, David M. (1998) "Has NAFTA Changed North American Trade?" Federal Reserve Bank of Dallas Economic Review - First Quarter.

Graham, Edward, and Paul Krugman. (1995) *Foreign Direct Investment in the United States.* 3rd edition, Washington: Institute for International Economics.

Graham, Edward, and Christopher Wilkie. (1994) "Multinationals and the Investment Provisions of NAFTA." *International Trade Journal* 8: 9-38.

Gu, Wulong, Gary Sawchuk, and Lori Whewell. (2002) "The Effect of Tariff Reductions on Firm Size and Firm Turnover in Canadian Manufacturing." Mimeo Industry Canada, July.

Harris, Richard. (1984) "Applied general equilibrium analysis of small open economies with scale economies and imperfect competition." *American Economic Review* 74: 1016-1032.

Head, Keith, and John Ries. (1999) "Rationalization effects of tariff reductions." *Journal of International Economics* 47: 295-320.

Hejazi ,Walid, and A. Edward Safarian. (1999) "Modeling Links Between Canadian Trade and Foreign Direct Investment" Industry Canada: Perspectives on North-American Free Trade Series, Working Paper, No. 2.

Helliwell, John, Frank C. Lee, and Hans Messinger. (1999) "Effects of the Canada-United States Free Trade Agreement on Interprovincial Trade." Industry Canada: Perspectives on North-American Free Trade Series, Working Paper, No. 5..

Hillberry, Russell, and Christine McDaniel. (2002) "A Decomposition of North American Trade Growth Since NAFTA." U.S. International Trade

Commission: *International Economic Review*. Publication 3527. May/June,

Irwin, Douglas A. (2002) *Free Trade Under Fire*. Princeton University Press, Princeton, New Jersey.

Hinojosa-Ojeda, Raúl, David Runsten, Fernando De Paolis, and Nabil Kamel. (2000) "The U.S. Employment Impacts of North American Integration After NAFTA: A Partial Equilibrium Approach." North American Integration and Development Center, School of Public Policy and Social Research, Working Paper Series UCLA.

Jones, Kent. (2000) "Does NAFTA Chapter 19 Make a Difference? Dispute Settlement and the Incentive Structure of U.S./Canada Unfair Trade Petitions." *Contemporary Economic Policy* 18(2); 145-58.

Karemara, David, and Kalu Ojah. (1998) "An Industrial Analysis of Trade Creation and Diversion Effects of NAFTA," *Journal of Economic Integration* 13: 400-25.

Keller, Wolfgang. (2001a). "International Technology Diffusion." NBER Working Paper # 8573.

Keller, Wolfgang. (2001b) "Geographic Localization of International Technology Diffusion." *American Economic Review* 92(1): 120-142.

Krueger, Ann O. (2000) "NAFTA's Effects: A Preliminary Assessment" *World-Economy* 23(6): 761-75.

Lemieux, Thomas. (2005) "Trade Liberalization and the Labour Market" in *Social and Labour Market Aspects of North American Linkages* Edited by Richard G. Harris and Thomas Lemieux, University of Calgary Press 119-146.

Levine, R., and D. Renelt. (1992) "A Sensitivity Analysis of Cross-Country Growth Regressions." *American Economic Review* 82(4): 942-963.

McCallum, John. (1995) "National Borders Matter: Canada-U.S. Regional Trade Patterns." *American Economic Review* 85: 615-23.

NAFTA. (1993) North American Free Trade Agreement between the Government of the United States of America the Government of Canada and the Government of the United Mexican States, vol.1, Washington: U.S. Government Printing Office.

NAFTA. (2001) NAFTA – Chapter 11 – Investment Notes of Interpretation of Certain Chapter 11 Provisions, Washington: NAFTA Secretariat, United States National Section.

OECD. (1998) "Open Markets Matter: The Benefits of Trade and Investment Liberalization," Paris.

Ortiz, Antonio. (2001) "Dispute Settlement in NAFTA: The Challenges Ahead": Paper presented at NAFTA in the New Millennium Conference, University of Alberta, May.

Prusa, T. J. (1992) "Why are so many antidumping petitions withdrawn?" *Journal of International Economics* 33: 1-20.

Prusa, Thomas J. (1997) "The Trade Effects of U.S. Antidumping Actions" in Robert C. Feenstra,(ed.) *Effects of U.S. Trade Protection and Promotion Policies,*(Chicago: University of Chicago Press) 191-213.

Romalis, John. (2005) "NAFTA's and CUSFTA's Impact on International Trade" NBER Working Paper 11059.

Schwanen, D. (1997) "Trading Up: The Impact of Increased Continental Integration on Trade, Investments and Jobs in Canada." C.D. Howe Institute Commentary No. 89.

Sharpe, Andrew. (2002) "Recent Productivity Developments in the United States and Canada: Implications for the Canada-U.S. Productivity and Income Gaps," *International Productivity Monitor* 4: 3-12.

Slaughter, Matthew. (1999) "Globalisation and Wages: A Tale of Two Perspectives." *The World Economy* 25(5): 609-630.

Soloaga, Isidro, and L. Alan Winters. (2001) "Regionalism in the Nineties: What Effect on Trade?" *North American Journal of Economics and Finance* 121:1-29.

Staiger, R., and J. Wollack (1994) "Measuring Industry Specific Protection: antidumping in the United States." Brookings Papers on Economic Activity, Microeconomics, 51-103.

Teece, David. (1977) Technology Transfer by Multinational Firms: The Resource Cost of Transferring Technological Know-how." *Economic Journal* 87: 242-61.

Townsand, James. (2004). "Do Tariff Reductions Affect the Wages of Workers in Protected Industries? Evidence from the Canada-U.S. Free Trade Agreement" University of Winnipeg, Mimeo.

Trebilcock, Michael, and Robert Howse. (2001) *The Regulation of International Trade*. University Press, Cambridge 2nd ed., New York: Routeledge.

Trefler, D. (1999). "The Long and the Short of the Canada-U.S. Free-Trade Agreement." Industry Canada, Perspectives on North-American Free Trade Series, Working Paper, No. 6.

Trefler, Daniel. (2001) "The long and short of the Canada-U.S. Free Trade Agreement." NBER Working Paper No. 8293.

Wall, Howard J. (2002) "Has Japan Been Left Out in the Cold by Regional Integration?" Federal Reserve Bank of St. Louis, *Review* 84: 25-36.

Wonnacott, Ronald J., and Paul Wonnacott. (1967) *Free Trade Between the United States and Canada: The Potential Economic Effects*. Cambridge: Harvard University Press.

World Bank. (2000) *"Trade Blocs"* World Bank Trade Policy Report, Washington: World Bank.

Xu, Bin. (2000) "Multinational enterprise, technology diffusion and host country productivity growth." *Journal of Development Economics* 62: 477-493.

The Variety Effects of Trade Liberalization

Shenjie Chen
Foreign Affairs and International Trade Canada

Introduction

This paper assesses the variety effects of trade liberalization in the context of the Free Trade Agreement between Canada and the United States. Since the Canada-U.S. FTA was implemented 15 years ago, a large body of ex post empirical analyses has emerged to study the resulting economic impact. Most of these analyses follow the standard welfare interpretations of trade, seeking the expected relative price and quantity changes following upon the Canada-U.S. FTA. While relative price and quantity changes are likely the primary benefits of trade liberalization, liberalization also yields gains by enhancing consumers' and producers' access to new varieties in each country, which is also important to a nation's welfare. Unfortunately, there are few available studies that allow the strength of such an argument to be evaluated on empirical grounds in the Canada-U.S. FTA context. This paper attempts to fill this research gap by presenting the latest empirical evidence on the variety gains that accrue from trade liberalization under the Canada-U.S. FTA.

There has been well-established literature on the role of "variety" or "product differentiation" in international trade. Much of this literature is motivated by the observation that large volumes of intra-industry trade take place between countries with similar factor endowments, while the traditional factor-endowment-based explanation of trade predicts large inter-industry trade between countries with different factor endowments. The monopolistic competition trade model, or the so-called "love of variety" approach, which was introduced in Krugman (1979, 1980) and Helpman (1981), and consolidated in Helpman and Krugman (1985), represents one of many intellectual efforts to address this empirical puzzle by emphasising product differentiation and economies of scale as alternative sources of trade. They have successfully shown how product differentiation and increasing returns to scale in production could give rise to trade between similar countries in the absence of comparative advantage.

The product differentiation explanation of trade claims that many varieties of a product exist because producers attempt to distinguish their varieties from rivals' in the minds of consumers in order to achieve brand loyalty, or because consumers demand a wide spectrum of varieties. Although countries without substantial cost differences are not specialized at the industry level in international trade, they are, nevertheless, specialized in the different varieties of a product within the same industry, resulting in intra-industry trade. Product differentiation, reinforced by brand-specific economies of scale, gives rise to large volumes of trade between similar countries.

The product differentiation explanation of trade suggests a completely different empirical framework for assessing the impacts of trade liberalization. In

43

the world of comparative advantage, gains from trade would be evaluated in terms of increases in allocative efficiency arising from the reallocation of resources across industries, while in the product differentiation framework, gains from trade would be reflected in the availability of new varieties following upon trade liberalization. With the opening of trade, each country increases its exports of varieties to other countries, at the same time, it faces competition from foreign varieties produced by foreign firms. As a result, a country under free trade is expected to produce fewer domestic varieties due to foreign competition, but it would have a wider range of available varieties through imports. In addition, there is a price effect associated with trade liberalization and increases in competition, which lowers the price for each variety, thereby increasing consumers' and producers' affordability and access to new varieties. Consequently, the sum of varieties under freer trade would exceed the number of varieties available before the opening of trade (Feenstra, 2001)[1].

Product differentiation typically involves brand-specific economies of scale. However, Helpman (1998) downplays the significance of economics of scale, because product differentiation might limit the scope for economics of scale. As the number of varieties increases, the output of each individual variety necessarily falls. He stresses that what matters is that there exists economies of scale, not their size[2]. Feenstra also finds that several country empirical studies fail to find any significant scale effects following upon trade liberalization (Feenstra, 2001)[3]. Feenstra argues that if the elasticity of demand for product varieties is constant, consumption of each variety is likely to fall under free trade because individuals are spreading their expenditures over more product varieties. Under such a circumstance, firms' scale will not change at all, though the number of varieties consumed will increase due to increasing imports.

In the context of the Canada-U.S. FTA, extensive policy discussions in the half-century or more leading up to the Canada-U.S. FTA argued that Canadian firms would benefit from unrestricted access to the U.S. market. It was believed that the Canadian market was too small to allow manufacturing industries to operate at a minimum efficient scale. Indeed, this was the principal reason that Canada entered into a free trade agreement with the U.S. in 1989. However, with more than a decade since the Canada-U.S. FTA has been in effect, the expected scale effect has not been borne out empirically. Head and Ries (1999) examined the impact on the plant scale in the six years following the Canada-U.S. FTA, using plant level data for a sample of 230 Canadian industries. They found that tariff reduction in the U.S. increased the Canadian plant scale by 10% on average, but this was largely offset by an 8.5% reduction in plant scale due to the reductions in Canadian tariffs. On balance, the Canada-U.S. FTA had only a marginal impact on scale[4]. This disappointing result suggests that economists

---

[1] Feenstra, Robert C. (2001) "Advanced International Trade: Theory and Evidence", Princeton University Press, forthcoming. Chapter 5.
[2] Helpman, Elhanan (1998) "The Structure of Foreign Trade", NBER Working Paper 6752.
[3] See Head, Keith and John Ries, (1999) on Canada, Tybout and Westbrook (1995) on Mexico, and Tybout, de Melo and Corbo (1991) on Chile.
[4] Head, Keith and John Ries, (1999) "Rationalization Effects of Tariff Reductions", *Journal of International Economics*, 47(2), April, 295-320.

might have misunderstood the nature and dynamism of North American trade. Given the fact that bilateral trade between Canada and the U.S. has been dominated by trade in differentiated products within the same industry (this will be explained below), access to new varieties is perhaps a more important source of gains from trade than the scale effect.

There have been some empirical studies emerging in the past decade which attempt to establish the link between changes in trade policy and an increase in the availability of new varieties from the perspective of consumer welfare. Many of these studies argue that growth in the availability of new varieties is more valuable to economic welfare than growth in quantity. Romer (1994) shows that lower tariffs increase demand for foreign varieties, allowing more of them to enter the local market, and sell enough units to cover local fixed costs; as a result, welfare gains would be 10% of GDP, compared to 1% of GDP in more standard models, in response to a 10% tariff reduction on all imports[5].

Russel Hillberry and Christine McDaniel (2002), using very detailed U.S. trade data, identified the extent to which the increase in NAFTA trade was associated with trade in new varieties. They decomposed the growth in the value of U.S. trade with its NAFTA partners from 1992 to 2002 into price, volume, and variety effects. The latter effect was measured by the change in trade values due to trading more or fewer goods as classified in the Harmonized Tariff Schedule. They measured the increase in US exports to Canada as 35% and the increase in Canadian exports to the US as 69% between 1993 and 2001. Of the 35% increased US exports to Canada, only 3.4 percentage points of these represented trade in new varieties. They concluded that most of the post-NAFTA changes in U.S. trade patterns were increases in the quantity of goods traded in HS lines that were already traded in 1993. They found only a marginal variety effect[6].

While most of available empirical studies of what variety gains might follow from trade liberalization uses growth in the number of the HS lines with positive trade as an indicator of increases in variety. a paper by Haveman and Hummels is an important exception to this. They calculated the number of exporters from whom the importer purchased that good for each importer and good, and then expressed this as a ratio over the total number of exporters in that good. If an importer did not purchase a good from any exporter, the ratio is zero. Their calculations showed that importers purchased a very small fraction of available varieties. The zero values represented fully 22% of the distribution. Conditional on importing the good from at least one exporter, they found that, in nearly half of these cases, importers bought from fewer than 10% of available exporters. Indeed, the most common situation was that countries traded a particular 4-digit HS good with only one partner. Haveman and Hummels suspected that the fraction of available varieties that were actually imported was even lower than their figures suggested, because they did not have direct evidence

---

[5] Romer, Paul (1995) "New Goods, Old Theory, and the Welfare Costs of Trade Restrictions," *Journal of Development Economics*, vol. 43, 1995, pp. 5-38.
[6] Hillberry, H. Russell and Christine A. McDaniel (2002) "A Decomposition of North American Trade Growth since NAFTA", International Economic Review, Many/June 2002, U.S. International Trade Commission.

on the full set of varieties produced. Based on their findings, they concluded that the existing trade models such as the monopolistic competition model might considerably overstate either the extent of product differentiation (incomplete specialization) or the degree to which consumers value that differentiation[7].

Caves (1981) has made an important observation about product differentiation. According to him, product differentiation does not necessarily lead to greater intra-industry trade. If product differentiation is due to the complexity of the characteristics of the product, it should stimulate intra-industry trade. On the other hand, if product differentiation has a strong information component, requiring substantial advertising by the firm in order to inform customers of its product's uniqueness, language and cultural barriers to advertising in a foreign country might make product differentiation a hindrance to intra-industry trade[8].

Most of what is available in the literature to date involving the measurement of the variety effects of trade liberalization suffers a fundamental weakness: HS lines considerably underestimate the number of varieties traded across countries. For instance, there are many car models produced in North America and imported from abroad, but only one HS code that covers them all. A full examination of the variety of trade requires evidence on the full breadth of varieties produced.

This study contributes to recent empirical literature on trade in varieties in the following two areas. First, it uses the World Intellectual Property Office (WIPO)'s cross-country trademark registration statistics to measure recent trends in global trade in variety. It confirms Haveman and Hummels' suspicion that nations are trading far fewer varieties than commonly supposed, and there is a strong "home bias' in the global production and consumption of differentiated products. It also finds evidence that supports Caves' hypothesis that languages and culture constitute important barriers to trade in differentiated products, while at the same time trade liberalization helps to facilitate trade in varieties. Second, this study uses the Canadian Intellectual Property Office's and U.S. Intellectual Patent Office's trademark databases to track bilateral trade in varieties between Canada and the U.S. at detailed industrial levels to determine whether the Canada-U.S. FTA has enhanced each country's access to varieties.

The paper is organized as follows: the following section will set the stage for the analysis by outlining the economics of trademarks, section three will describe global trade in varieties from the early 1980s through 2002 using WIPO's cross-country trademark registration statistics. Section four will present the econometric results, while the theoretical framework that underpins the econometric estimation is included in the appendix. Section five will outline the changes in North American trade pattern, the variety gains under the Canada-U.S. FTA, and the industry-level regression analysis detailing the variety-enhancing effect of the Canada-U.S. FTA. The final section will summarize the results.

---

[7] Jon Haveman and David Hummels (1999) "Alternative Hypotheses and the Volume of Trade: Evidence on the Extent of Specialization".

[8] Caves, Richard E. (1981), " Intra-Industry Trade and Market Structure in the Industrialized Countries", Oxford Economic Papers, 33 (July):203-223.

Why trademarks?

Before presenting the detailed trademark statistics, one needs to know what trademarks are. Why are trademarks being used in this context in the first place? And, do the trademark statistics match what the differentiated product trade model describes?

According to the Canadian Intellectual Property Office's definition, a trademark is a word, a symbol, a design, or a combination of these features to distinguish the goods or services of one person or organization from those of others in the marketplace. Trademarks come to represent not only actual goods and services, but also the reputation of the producer. As such, they are considered as valuable intellectual property. A registered trademark can be protected through legal proceedings from misuse and imitation[9].

In general, a trademark performs the following four main economic functions:

1) A trademark is one means of achieving product differentiation. As Chamberlin (1947) explained a half century ago, a product is differentiated if any significant basis exists that helps a consumer to distinguish the goods or services of one seller from those of another, leading to a preference for one variety of the product over another. Such a basis could be found in certain characteristics of the product itself, such as exclusive patented features; trademarks, trade names; peculiarities of the package or container; or singularity in quality, design, colour or style[10].

2) By distinguishing the source, origin, and quality of particular products from other similar products, the trademark protects the public against confusion and deception, as well as the trademark owner's trade and business and the goodwill that is attached to the trademark. The rationale for patent protection is quite different from that of a trademark. Patents are granted to encourage inventions by private enterprises or individuals, and to encourage prompt and adequate public disclosure of a new technology. Unlike patents and other intellectual properties, the trademark is the only instrument in the differentiation process that receives specific legal protection for unlimited time. Registrations are usually valid for a limited time period, but trademark holders have the option of renewing their registrations.

3) A trademark gives market power to the businesses that own them. In the case of patents, a grant of a monopoly for a certain period of time is in itself an indicator of market power, while in the case of trademarks, the market power of a specific product is achieved through the development of brand loyalty. Brand loyalty constitutes a barrier to the entry of new competitors into the market, making more difficult not only actual but also potential competition.

4) A trademark is a prime instrument in advertising and selling differentiated products. Although advertising need not be brand specific, the advertising effort is chiefly concentrated on the promotion of a particular trademark. Trademarks tend to proliferate among those products such as apparel,

---

[9] Canadian Intellectual Property Office (2002), "A Guide to Trade-Marks".

[10] E. H. Chamberlin, *The Theory of Monopolistic Competition: A re-orientation of the Theory of Value*, 5th ed. (Cambridge, Mass., Harvard University Press, 1947, p.56

cosmetics, and toilet preparation products for which the advertising effort is highest and most persuasive. They are a basic element in the persuasive content of advertising messages aimed at influencing consumers' purchase behaviour. In addition, brand specific advertising is an important factor in the creation of market power. High levels of advertising create an additional cost on any new entrant into the industry. If, at the same time, economies of scale exist in advertising, new entrants not only have to reach the average level of advertising existing in the industry, but they also have to achieve a high volume of sales to enjoy all the benefits from the advertising expenditure.

Overall, the economic rationale of having trademark protection is to help the business achieve product differentiation, to protect the trademark owner's business from unfair competition as well as the public against confusion in the market place. In reporting the bill that became the United States Federal Trademark Act of 1946 (Lanham Act), the Senate Committee on Patents pointed out the fundamental basis for trademark protection:

> *Trademarks, indeed, are the essence of competition, because they make possible a choice between competing articles by enabling the buyer to distinguish one from the other. Trademarks encourage the maintenance of quality by securing to the producer the benefit of the good reputation which excellence creates. To protect trademarks, therefore, is to protect the public from deceit, to foster fair competition, and to secure to the business community the advantages of reputation and good will by preventing their diversion from those who have created them to those who have not. This is the end to which this is directed.[11]*

Because of the nature of trademarks, the trademark registration statistics offer more information on the availability of varieties than any other statistics that have been used in empirical studies to date. Each trademark represents a unique variety, which distinguishes itself from others by its own designs, technologies, concepts, or ideas. In addition, the registration statistics contain other useful information for research and analysis such as the registration number, industrial classes, the name and address of the applicant, the owner of the trademark, the nationality of the owner, the date of registration, etc...

However, several problems are encountered in interpreting the trademark registration statistics published by the WIPO:

1) The registration statistics adequately capture the number of new products being introduced into the market, but they fail to reflect the number of trademarks withdrawn from the market. Since the cost of registration is relatively low, many firms prefer to renew the existing registrations to prevent others from using them, even though these trademarks are no longer being used. Therefore, using the stock number of registrations would significantly inflate the actual number of varieties in the market.

---

[11] J.T. McCarthy, op.cit., vol. 1, p. 54.

2) Some countries' registration statistics include both new registrations and renewals; as a result, their figures are higher than those that separate new registrations from renewals.

3) Some countries such as Canada, the U.S. and many other English-speaking countries allow multiple-class applications in the sense that one registration can be applied to several industrial classes, (for instance, a Disney trademark can be used for a T-shirt as well as for a cup, while a T-shirt and a cup belong to different classes of industries), while other countries, such as Mexico, allow only single-class applications. Consequently, the number of trademark registrations in Mexico could be higher than those in Canada, but in reality, new products introduced in Canada are not fewer than those in Mexico.

4) The standards for accepting trademark applications vary by country. In Canada and other advanced industrialized countries, the ratio of registrations over applications is about 50 percent; while in many less developed countries, that ratio is more than 90 percent. As a result, registrations in some less developed countries are substantially higher than in many industrialized countries.

5) With respect to cross-country registrations of trademarks, a problem might arise in so far as there are cases where corporations that are actually controlled by foreigners might appear as national entities. Under these circumstances, the trademarks registered by these corporations appear in the statistics as nationally owned. However, the underestimation of the ownership of trademarks by foreigners is not likely to be a serious distortive factor because the current international legislation is not biased against foreign registrations and generally the owners of trademarks prefer to have them registered in their own names.

Because of these reasons, the trademark registration statistics should be used with caution. Nevertheless, the cross-country trademark registration statistics still provide rich and useful information on global trade in varieties. The following will present some stylized facts of trade in varieties in the global and North American context using the WIPO's cross-country trademark registration statistics.

North American trade in variety in a global context

Table 1 reports average annual new trademarks for selected source countries (including the U.S., Canada, the U.K., Japan, German, Spain, Switzerland, China, and India) in a list of host countries for the period between 1990 and 2000. Wherever the cell points to, the source countries refers to average annual domestic registrations in these countries. For instance, the average annual new trademark registrations by U.S residents in Canada between 1990 and 2000 were 4,647, while the corresponding figure for U.S. residents in the U.S. was 73,686. Similarly, the average annual new trademark registrations by Canadians in the U.S. were 2,535, while the corresponding figure for Canadian domestic registration was 8,416.

The second to last row sets out the average annual trademark registrations summing over all host countries by source country. For instance, the average annual trademark registrations by U.S. firms in all host countries were 3,051 between 1990 and 2000, while the similar figures for Canada and the U.K.

49

were 205, and 688, respectively. The last row is the ratio of the average annual registrations in all host countries over the average annual domestic registrations. This ratio indicates the extent of "home bias" in the production of varieties. For instance, the average annual trademark registrations in foreign countries by U.S. firms accounted for only 4 percent of domestic registrations in the U.S. between 1990s and 2000, while the corresponding figure for Switzerland was 12.8 percent, and for China was 0.1 percent.

Table 1. Annual Average Cross-Country Trademark Registration, 1990-2000.

	U.S.	Canada	U.K.	Japan	Germany	Spain	Swiss	China	India
China	3625	125	685	1952	1905	255	956	77102	30
India	307	5	108	91	140	12	62	5	4565
Japan	6193	188	1077	131073	1430	171	755	97	7
Korea	3145	84	496	1840	710	56	425	38	7
Canada	4647	8416	311	336	379	64	200	37	7
Austria	874	28	253	134	2127	154	873	30	3
Finland	968	23	287	129	1279	107	433	25	2
France	5092	209	1069	810	4504	879	2039	92	7
Germany	2592	99	826	567	22958	276	1091	69	8
Ireland	1235	20	952	115	755	124	240	14	3
Italy	3415	91	1120	692	2258	385	1203	93	9
Norway	1297	30	399	158	1624	151	492	32	3
Portugal	1884	39	770	287	2198	1101	920	62	4
Spain	2748	61	943	472	1291	53172	598	60	5
Sweden	1264	36	393	185	1392	123	479	27	4
Swiss	1561	53	414	235	2231	188	5301	44	3
UK	5266	278	23142	1028	3083	385	1167	77	32
Australia	4008	171	1028	582	724	74	417	47	12
N.Z.	2604	82	717	304	435	38	296	36	13
Brazil	1985	45	295	252	466	85	272	16	6
Argentina	5957	133	968	558	1118	564	810	32	9
Mexico	6448	174	464	356	757	360	462	30	5
USA	73686	2535	1556	1285	1887	296	722	110	39
Av. For Reg.	**3051**	**205**	**688**	**562**	**1486**	**266**	**678**	**49**	**10**
Ratio of For. Over Dom. Reg. (%)	4.1	2.4	3.0	0.4	6.5	0.5	12.8	0.1	0.2

Source: Author's calculation based on WIPO's Industrial Property Annual Statistics

Examining Table 1, several interesting trends stand out, and each is discussed in turn below:

1)   The data strongly confirms Haveman and Hummel's suspicion that nations are trading far fewer varieties than is commonly supposed. Importers purchase only a very small fraction of available varieties from foreign countries. There is a strong "home bias' effect in the production of varieties. This is even after taking account of natural and policy barriers to trade such as language, distance, and regional preferential trade arrangements. For instance, between 1990 and 2000, the annual average domestic registrations in the U.S. were 73,686, implying about 73,686 new products, concepts, and ideas were introduced into the U.S. market annually during that period. However, over the same period, the annual average registrations by US residents in Canada, the U.K. and other English speaking countries (assuming English-speaking industrializing countries are more likely to accept U.S. varieties than other countries) were around 4-5000, which was 5-6% of average domestic registrations in the U.S.

This trend is not unique to the U.S. It applies to other advanced industrialized countries as well. By way of illustration, the annual average domestic registrations in Japan between 1990 and 2000 were 131,073, but the average Japanese registrations in foreign countries over the same period were only 1,285 in the U.S., 1,028 in the U.K., and 567 in Germany. In Germany, the annual average domestic registrations were 22,958, but the registrations by German residents in the U.S. were 1,887; and 3,083 in the U.K., and 4,504 in France.

Switzerland, however, is an exception. Relative to other countries, Switzerland's varieties are widely accepted in many parts of the world, particularly in its neighbouring countries. As indicated at the last row of Table 1, Switzerland was leading the industrial countries in terms of exports of varieties; its foreign registrations accounted for 12.8 percent of domestic registrations, compared to 6.5 percent for Germany and 4.1 percent for the U.S.

2)   Nations that share the same language exchange more varieties between them. For instance, English-speaking countries traded more varieties among themselves than with non-English-speaking countries. The same is the case for Spanish and German speaking countries. This lends support to Caves' hypothesis that if product differentiation has a strong information component, requiring substantial advertising, countries that speak the same language and share the same culture would be more likely to trade their varieties among themselves. On the other hand, for the countries that are not part of language and cultural traditions, language and culture constitute a barrier to trade in differentiated products.

3)   Trade in varieties is more likely to take place in less distant economies. The distance effect of bilateral trade is one of the clearest and most robust findings in empirical trade literature. With respect to trade in varieties, distance matters perhaps even more than trade in quantity. Table 1 shows that nations that shared the common border were trading far more varieties than those located far apart.

4)   Higher income countries tend to trade more varieties between themselves than with lower income countries. A possible explanation is that higher income countries are the producers of most of the varieties in the world,

and their rich consumers can afford, and are willing to pay more, than poor consumers for the first unit of each variety.

Low-income countries export far fewer varieties than high-income countries. As indicated in Table 1, trademark registrations between low-income and wealthy industrialized countries were very asymmetric. For instance, the annual average trademark registrations by U.S. residents in China and India were 3,625 and 307, respectively, while the corresponding registrations by Chinese and India residents in the U.S. were only 110 and 39, respectively. This implies that despite rapid export growth from China and India to industrialized countries, and rising skill levels in these two countries, their exports were driven more by the increases in the quantity of trade, than by the increases in the variety of trade. The bulk of their exports to rich countries represented "process trade", outsourced by industrialized countries that own the intellectual properties of the products. China and India manufactured these products without developing their own products, concepts, and ideas, or creating their own brand royalties in rich countries.

5)   Nations that have formed regional trading arrangements tend to trade more varieties among themselves. Trade liberalization is playing a facilitating role in global trade in varieties. Lowering tariff barriers increase demand for foreign varieties, allowing more of them to enter the local market, thereby increasing the range of products supplied in the domestic market and enhancing consumers' access to foreign varieties.

6)   Canada is not a heavyweight in global trade in varieties. Between 1990 and 2000, the annual average registrations by Canadian residents in all foreign countries were 205, compared to 3,051 for the U.S., and 1,486 for Germany, and 688 for the U.K. Further, Canadian foreign registrations are almost exclusively concentrated in the U.S. market with U.S. registrations totalling 2,535, compared to only 278 registrations in the U.K., and 209 registrations in France. The U.S. is the single largest supplier of differentiated products in the world. Its annual average trademark registrations in foreign countries totalled 3,051.

The picture painted above suggests that the product differentiation model, which is based on the very strict assumptions of complete specialization and identical consumer's preferences, is not what one observes in a real world. Consumers' preferences for different varieties are far from identical. Product differentiation is strongly influenced by language, distance, culture, and historical ties. A theoretical framework that is developed by incorporating some of these elements discussed above is included as an appendix. The empirical investigation on the determinants of global trade in variety is presented below.

Estimation results

The gravity-type equation that is presented below is derived from the theoretical model explained in the Appendix. The equation attempts to investigate the determinants of global trade in variety, and it is specified as follows:

$$\ln v_{ij} = \eta_1 \ln y_i + \eta_2 \ln y_j + \eta_3 \ln py_i + \eta_4 \ln py_j + \eta_5 \ln Dis_{ij} + \eta_6 t_{ij} +$$
$$+ \eta_7 Lan_{ij} + \eta_8 \phi_i + \eta_9 \phi_j + \varepsilon_{ij} \tag{1}$$

The variables are defined next. Subscripts i and j represent the source and target country, respectively.

v_{ij} is the number of trademarks registered by country i in country j,

y_i represents source country i's GDP,

y_j represents the target country j's GDP,

py_i is source country i's per capita GDP,

py_j is target country j's per capita GDP,

Dis_{ij} is the distance between the source country i and the target country j, using Haveman's bilateral distance calculation[12],

t_{ij} is a binary dummy variable, which is unity if both source and target countries belong to the same regional trade agreement and zero otherwise,

Lan_{ij} is a binary dummy variable that is unity if two countries have a common language and zero otherwise,

ϕ_i is the source country fixed effect, representing a country's propensity to export its varieties abroad. It equals to one if the country is exporting and 0 otherwise,

ϕ_j is the target country fixed effect, representing a country's propensity to import the varieties from its trading partners. It equals to one if the country is importing and 0 otherwise,

ε_{ij} is the stochastic error term, representing other influences on cross-country trademark registrations.

The dependent variable, trademark registrations by non-residents in the regression analysis, are taken from the WIPO's Industrial Property Annual Statistics for the following 33 countries: Argentina, Australia, Bulgaria, Brazil, Canada, Switzerland, China, Czechoslovak, Germany, Denmark, Spain, Finland, France, the U.K., Greece, Hungary, Ireland, Israel, India, Italy, Japan, Korea, Mexico, Norway, New Zealand, Poland, Portugal, Romania, Sweden, Russia, Turkey, the U.S., and South Africa. This is the cross-section regression. The numbers in the registrations are annual averages for the entire period of 1990-2000 so as to eliminate the yearly fluctuations, as registrations often fluctuate with business cycles and merger and acquisition activities. GDP and population data are taken from the Penn World Tables.

Table 2 reports the estimation results of (1). The estimation results confirm several observations mentioned earlier. First, the estimated coefficients for both source- and target-country GDP are significant and positive, with the

---

[12] http://www.macalester.edu/research/economics/PAGE/HAVEMAN/
Trade.Resources/TradeData.html

source-country GDP effect dominating. The statistical significance of both source- and target-country GDP effects suggest that the size of the economy matters: "larger" economies supply and demand more varieties than "smaller" ones. "Larger" economies specialize in everything, while "smaller" countries specialize in a few things.

Second, source-country per capita GDP is estimated to have a significant and positive effect on the cross-country registrations of trademarks. This is consistent with the conventional wisdom that wealthy industrialized economies have a comparative advantage in producing brand-name differentiated products; as such, they are the main suppliers of differentiated products in the global market. On the other hand, it is surprising to see that per capita GDP for target country is negatively correlated with registrations as wealthy industrialized countries are expected to have a high propensity to import the differentiated products from abroad due to the income effect. The possible explanation for this result is that several low-income countries started to introduce new trademark registration systems into their countries during the 1990s in compliance with the new Trade-related Intellectual Property Agreement concluded at the Uruguay Round trade negotiations, resulting in a surge in foreign trademark registrations in these countries.

Third, the estimated coefficient for distance has the expected negative sign, which indicates that trade in variety is more likely to take place between less distant economies. The estimated coefficient for the "language" dummy is significant with a positive sign. This confirms Caves' hypothesis that product differentiation has a strong information component; countries that share the same language and culture are more likely to appreciate the uniqueness of their own products, and more likely to develop the brand-name loyalty for their own products. Regional trade agreements are estimated to have a significant and positive impact on cross-country trademark registrations, suggesting that trade liberalization is contributing positively to global trade in variety. However, the estimated effect of "regional trade liberalization" appears far smaller than that of "language". The estimated coefficient for "language" is 0.8 compared to only 0.22 for "regional trade liberalization". This raises a question as to how effective trade liberalization is in facilitating global trade in variety. However, caution should be taken in interpreting these regression results since many regional trading partners share the same border and language; as such, the distance and language effects might dilute the effect of trade liberalization.

Fourth, with respect to the source-country fixed effects, several source countries are estimated to have a relatively high propensity to export their varieties, most notably the U.S., Germany, France, the U.K., Switzerland, and Italy. The estimated fixed country effects range from 2.529 for the U.S., 1.913 for Germany, to 1.5061 for Italy. On the other hand, India, China, and Mexico have fewer varieties available for their foreign customers. The source-country effects for Australia, Canada, and Finland are statistically insignificant.

The overall target-country effects appear weaker than the source-country effect. The economies of the U.S., Australia, China, and the U.K. are relatively open to foreign varieties, while India and Brazil are relatively restrictive with

54

respect to foreign varieties. The target-country effects for Canada, Switzerland, Germany, Spain, Finland, Korea, and Mexico are statistically insignificant.

Table 2. The Determinants of Global Trade in Variety

Variables	Parameter Estimates	t-statistics	Variables	Parameter Estimates	t-statistics
Constant	-14.03528	-9.832357	py_i	0.706213	20.05190
y_i	0.365454	8.532996	py_j	-0.105936	-3.013511
y_j	0.245630	5.788625	Dis_j^i	-0.541819	-16.90024
Lan_j^i	0.802707	7.921156	t_j^i	0.217310	2.736747
ϕ_i Australia	0.144272	0.953675	ϕ_j Australia	0.722609	4.786037
ϕ_i Brazil	0.293154	1.757711	ϕ_j Brazil	-0.549002	-3.240389
ϕ_i Canada	0.124041	0.803184	ϕ_j Canada	-0.237624	-1.543223
ϕ_i Switzerland	1.574166	10.54413	ϕ_j Switzerland	0.025581	0.171540
ϕ_i China	0.485852	12.42470	ϕ_j China	0.700212	3.514917
ϕ_i Germany	1.913054	10.30381	ϕ_j Germany	0.035565	0.192720
ϕ_i Spain	1.096261	7.122069	ϕ_j Spain	0.178654	1.164607
ϕ_i Finland	-0.217976	-1.533044	ϕ_j Finland	-0.224229	-1.576640
ϕ_i France	1.847351	10.61162	ϕ_j France	0.531485	3.038636
ϕ_i UK	1.532777	9.135715	ϕ_j UK	0.422334	2.528291
ϕ_i India	0.087257	5.580154	ϕ_j India	-1.985353	-9.890453
ϕ_i Italy	1.506131	9.066492	ϕ_j Italy	0.302856	1.831600
ϕ_i Japan	0.682604	3.296985	ϕ_j Japan	0.356332	1.734706
ϕ_i Korea	0.610631	4.030031	ϕ_j Korea	0.177119	1.172584
ϕ_i Mexico	0.405210	2.617597	ϕ_j Mexico	0.233299	1.511967
ϕ_i US	2.528950	11.54231	ϕ_j US	0.638620	2.938193

$R^2 = 0.85$ N = 1105

The variety gains under the Canada-U.S. FTA

To have a better picture of the variety-enhancing effect of trade liberalization, the following uses the Canadian Intellectual Property Office's and U.S. Intellectual Patent Office's trademark databases to track bilateral trade in variety between these two countries at the detailed industrial level over the past several decades. The advantages of using these two countries' trademark data are twofold: 1) these two countries have better-quality trademark registration statistics, and they have very similar trademark registration and enforcement systems; 2) by focusing on these two countries' registrations statistics, one could further isolate the trade liberalization effect by removing the language and distance effects from the regression analysis, as these two countries share the same border, culture, and language.

Changes in Canada's merchandise trade pattern

Prior to examining the variety effects of the Canada-U.S. FTA, it might be helpful to highlight the changes in the bilateral trade pattern between Canada and the U.S. in past decades. During this time, the bilateral merchandise trade pattern between Canada and the U.S. experienced profound changes. The most significant was the rapid expansion of Canada's exports of differentiated products, resulting in a steady rise in the share of differentiated products in Canada's total merchandise exports to the U.S[13]. As illustrated in Figure 1, the share of differentiated products in Canada's merchandise exports reached 70 percent in the late 1990s, up from 50 percent in the early 1980s; while the corresponding share of homogenous products fell to 14 percent from more than 20 percent over the same period. The increases in Canada's exports of differentiated products to the U.S. were partly attributed to the 1965 Auto Pact between Canada and the United States. However, from the mid-1980s onward, a noticeable trend emerged; the significant expansion of Canada's exports of non-auto differentiated products to the U.S. The share of non-auto differentiated products in Canada's total exports of differentiated products to the U.S. increased to nearly 60 percent in the late 1990s from just above 40 percent in the mid-1980s, while the corresponding share for auto products went down to nearly 40 percent from 57 over the same period. The rising exports of machinery and equipment were largely responsible for the shift in the composition of Canada's exports of differentiated products to the U.S. (See Figure 2).

On the imports side, the U.S. has always been Canada's main supplier of differentiated products. Imports of various types of differentiated products from the U.S. consistently dominated Canada's merchandise import pattern, accounting for 85 percent of total Canada's merchandise imports from the U.S. This trend has changed little over the past several decades.

---

[13] Merchandise trade data are grouped into three categories according to the classification by Rauch (1999). These groups are: (1) homogeneous, which refers to products traded on organized exchanges; (2) differentiated, which refers to products that are "branded"; and (3) referenced, which refers to those that are "in-between", whose prices are often quoted in trade publications.

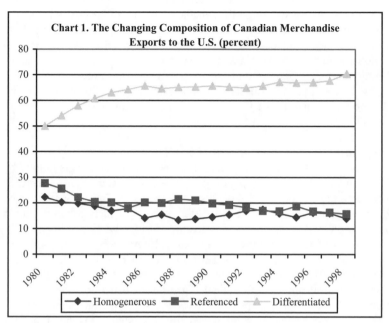

Chart 1. The Changing Composition of Canadian Merchandise Exports to the U.S. (percent)

Source: Authors' calculations based on Statistics Canada data

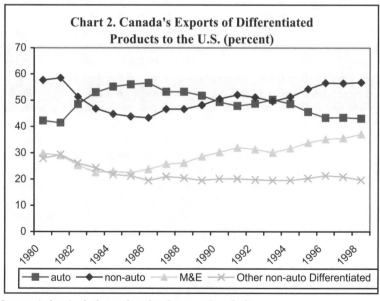

Chart 2. Canada's Exports of Differentiated Products to the U.S. (percent)

Source: Authors' calculations based on Statistics Canada data

The changes in the bilateral merchandise trade pattern described above indicate that while homogeneous products remained significant in Canada's total exports to the U.S., the recent surge of Canada's exports to the U.S. was almost exclusively explained by increased exports of differentiated products, particularly non-auto differentiated products. This fact underlies the need to use the product differentiation framework to explain and understand the nature and dynamism of bilateral trade between Canada and the U.S. Access to more varieties and enhancing the levels of product differentiation are the key benefits of the Canada-U.S. FTA. The following will use Canadian and U.S. trademark statistics to verify this hypothesis.

The variety gains under the Canada-U.S. FTA

Tables 3 and 4 present average annual new trademark registrations by U.S. residents in Canada and corresponding registrations by Canadians in the U.S. by product over the periods of 1980s-90s. As shown in Tables 3 and 4, the increased access to different varieties of differentiated products following upon trade liberalization was a distinguishing feature during the Canada-U.S. FTA period[14]. By way of illustration, the average annual new trademark registrations for differentiated products by U.S. residents in Canada rose from 4,342 in the 1980-89 period to 7,018 in the 1990-02 period, an increase of 2,676 annually. This can be compared to an increase in annual registrations of 61 for homogeneous products and 581 for referenced products over the same period. Similarly, the average annual new trademarks registered by Canadians in the U.S. for differentiated products increased by 1,432 between the 1980s and 1990s, compared to only 46 for homogeneous products and 316 for referenced products. The figures based on the number of registrations per billion dollars of imports show a similar picture: one billion dollars of Canadian imports of differentiated products from the U.S. contained 97 new trademarks (if the auto products were excluded, that figure increased to 126), compared to 25 for homogenous products; similarly, there were 38 varieties embedded in every billion dollars of Canadian exports of differentiated products to the U.S. (if the auto products were excluded, that figure rises to the 55), compared to only 5 varieties for homogenous products. These figures confirm that trade in homogeneous products is driven by changes in quantity within a narrow set of varieties; while trade in differentiated products is determined by changes in the number of varieties. The actual traded quantities for each variety could be relatively small. Given the fact that the recent surge of Canada's exports to the U.S. was driven mainly by exports of differentiated products, examining the gains from variety--the increased numbers of Canadian varieties sold in the U.S. and the availability of U.S. varieties sold in Canada will feature prominently in the remaining analysis of this chapter.

---

[14] Trademarks are registered based on the product classification. When the product classification is converted into the industry-based classification such as North American Industry Classification System (NAICS), the total number of registrations summing over all industries might be larger than that of original registrations as both Canadian and the U.S. allow multiple-class registrations, which means that one trademark could be registered under different industries.

Table 3. The Annual Average Trademark Registrations by U.S. Residents in Canada and Canada's Imports from the U.S. by Product, 1980-02

	1980-89	90-02	Change	Growth (%)	Imports (Can$ Billion) (90-02)	Number of Trademark per Billion of Imports
Homogeneous Products	185	246	61	33.5	10	25
Referenced Products	974	1555	581	59.7	9.8	158
Differentiated Product	4342	7018	2676	61.6	72.5	97
Differentiated Product without Auto Products	4041	6550	2509	62.1	51.9	126
Goods	5501	8820	3319	60.3	92.3	96
Services	930	2402	1472	158.4	31.5	76
Total	6431	11222	4791	74.5	123.8	90.6

Source: Author's calculation from the data listed at the CIPO trademark database, and the U.S. Bureau of Economics Analysis.

Table 4. The Annual Average Trademark Registrations by Canadian Residents in the U.S. and the U.S. Imports from Canada by Product, 1980-01

	1980-89	90-01	Change	Growth (%)	Imports (U.S$ Billion)	Number of trademark per billion of imports
Homogeneous Products	48	94	46	97.2	17.3	5.4
Referenced Products	210	526	316	151	16.5	31.9
Differentiated Product	864	2296	1432	165.6	60.3	38.1
Differentiated Product without Auto Products	804	2142	1338	166.5	38.8	55.2
Goods	1122	2916	1794	166.5	94	31
Services	265	902	637	240.6	13.2	68.3
Total	1387	3818	2431	175.3	107.2	35.6

Source: Author's calculation from the data listed at the U.S IPO trademark database, and the U.S. Bureau of Economics Analysis.

Tables 3 and 4 also show that Canada's access to U.S. varieties was almost three times more than what the U.S. obtained from Canada. During the 1990s, the average annual trademark registrations by U.S. residents in Canada amounted to 11,222, compared to 3,818 by Canadian residents in the U.S. The number of varieties embedded in every billion dollars of imports was also much

59

higher in the case of Canada's imports from the U.S. versus U.S. imports from Canada. For instance, Canada's imported 91 varieties for every billion imports from the U.S., compared to 36 for every billion U.S. imports from Canada. This asymmetric pattern of registrations was particularly pronounced in the case of differentiated products. Canada obtained 126 varieties for every billion dollars of imports of differentiated products from the U.S.; on the other hand, Canada provided only 38 varieties in every billion dollars of exports of differentiated products to the U.S. The asymmetric pattern of registrations suggests that the size of the market matters with respect to the availability of varieties. The number of varieties is likely greater in large economies, both for consumer and intermediate goods, as larger markets allow more units for each variety to be sold in the local market to cover fixed costs. Large economies specialize in everything, while smaller countries specialize in a few things. As such, when trade is liberalized, a medium-size country like Canada would gain more by expanding its trading relationship with the U.S., not only because trade liberalization gives Canada an opportunity to expand the volume of trade, but also because it enhances its access to varieties that are more available in large economies.

Across industries, those in which Canada has had the most increase in variety from the U.S. were those that experienced the most rapid technology changes, and those in which many new ideas, new concepts, and new products proliferated. These industries, including computer and electronic products, chemical products, as well as machinery, topped the new trademark registrations by U.S. residents in Canada. Food, apparel, and toilet preparation products that were subject to heavy advertisements to influence consumers' purchase behaviour also saw heavy new registrations (See Table56).

Table 5. Annual Average Registrations of Trademarks by U.S. Residents in Canada, 1980-02

NAICS	Industries	1980-89	1990-02	Growth (%)
334	Computer & Elec. Products	463	981	111.8
339	Miscellaneous Manu.	587	868	47.8
325	Chemical Products	641	864	34.7
311	Food	364	572	57.2
333	Machinery	392	571	45.6
332	Fabricated Metal Product	391	571	46.0
323	Printing	275	561	103.8
336	Transportation Equipment	301	469	55.5
315	Apparel	282	465	64.9
326	Plastics & Rubber Products	288	444	54.5

Source: Author's calculation from the data listed at the CIPO trademark database.

Canada's leading exports of varieties to the U.S. were also found in the same category of industries as in the case of the U.S., though the number of Canadian registrations in each category was fewer than the corresponding U.S. registrations in Canada (See Table 6). This result is consistent with what the product differentiation model predicts, trade in differentiated products between similar countries often takes places in the same industry, which results in intensive intra-industry trade. However, it is important to note that although the number of Canadian registrations in the U.S. was trailing U.S. registrations in Canada, average annual Canadian registrations in the U.S. reported stronger growth in the 1990s, increasing by 175 percent over the 1980s, outstripping U.S. registrations in Canada that grew by 75 percent over the same period. The growth of Canadian registrations in the U.S. was particularly pronounced in the computer and electronic product industry, which increased by 239.6 percent over the 1980s. This was followed by the apparel industry that increased by 193 percent, and by the plastics and rubber product industry that increased by 170.5 percent.

Table 6. Annual Average Registrations of Trademarks by Canadians in the US, 1980-02

NAICS	Industries	1980-89	1990-02	Growth (%)
334	Computer & Electronic Products	116	394	239.6
339	Miscellaneous Manufacturing	112	266	137.9
325	Chemical Products	85	207	144.7
311	Food	78	198	152.5
332	Fabricated Metals	81	196	140.6
333	Machinery	78	191	146.7
323	Printing	69	175	152.5
326	Plastics & Rubber Products	58	158	170.5
315	Apparel	53	156	193.8
336	Transportation Equipment	61	153	153.1
335	Electrical Equipment	52	131	151.4

Source: Author's calculation from the data listed at the U.S IPO trademark database.

To examine the variety effects of the Canada-U.S. FTA, Table 7 presents the Canadian *ad valorem* duty rates for its imports from the U.S. and the corresponding U.S. rates for U.S. imports from Canada by product during the Canada-U.S. FTA period. Overall, the Canadian rates were higher than the U.S. rates before the Canada-U.S. FTA. Throughout the 1990s, the overall duty rates for Canadian merchandise imports from the U.S. fell by 2.92 percentage points, while the U.S. duty rates fell by a one-percentage point. Across products, duty rates for resource-based homogeneous goods were low even before the Canada-U.S. FTA in both countries. Thus, progressively reducing or eliminating tariffs for differentiated and referenced products was the focus of trade liberalization under the Canada-U.S. FTA. Between 1989 and 2001, the Canadian tariff rates for imported U.S. differentiated products fell by 2.88 percentage points (If auto products were excluded, the rate fell by 3.92 percentage points). Similarly, the U.S. tariff rates for imported Canadian differentiated products declined by 1.26 percentage points (if auto products were excluded, the rates fell by 2.19 percentage points) over the same period. Overall, these tariff changes occurred in parallel with the broad changes in the bilateral trade pattern between Canada and the U.S. since the Canada-U.S. FTA came into effect--the rising share of differentiated products, particularly of the non-auto differentiated products in total Canada's exports to the U.S. The tariff reductions at the both sides of the border stimulated greater trade in differentiated products between the two countries, reflected in the increases in the volume and varieties of trade of differentiated products.

Table 7. Canadian and the U.S. tariff ratios by Products, in selected years

	Homogeneous		Referenced		Differentiated		Differentiated without Auto		Total	
	Can	US	Can	US	Can	US	Can	US	Can	US
1989	1.66	0.72	4.99	0.92	3.01	1.34	4.08	2.26	3.03	1.10
1995	0.57	0.27	1.18	0.37	0.70	0.43	0.93	0.57	0.74	0.39
2001	0.01	0.02	0.06	0.04	0.13	0.08	0.16	0.07	0.11	0.06
89-01	-1.65	-0.70	-4.93	-0.88	-2.88	-1.26	-3.92	-2.19	-2.92	-1.04

Source: Authors' calculations from the data listed in Statistics Canada

Tables 8 and 9 presents the links between Canada-U.S. FTA tariff reductions and changes in trademark registrations between the two countries at the detailed industry level. Table 8 reports that the industries that had the deepest Canadian tariff reductions during the Canada-U.S. FTA period had the strongest growth of imported U.S. varieties. For instance, compared to the 1980s, industries such as beverage and tobacco, apparel and textile products that had the Canadian tariff reductions by a range of 10-25 percent reported, a 69.7 percent increase of average annual U.S. registrations in Canada during the Canada-U.S. FTA period. This was compared to a 59.2 percent increase for the industries with 1-10 percent tariff cuts, and a 57.2 percent increase for the industries with 0-1 percent tariff cuts.

A similar but more pronounced trend can be found in Canadian registrations in the U.S. During the Canada-U.S. FTA period, in the industries that had 1-10 percent U.S. tariff reductions, the average annual registrations of Canadian trademarks in the U.S. increased by 160.6 percent over the 1980s. This was followed by a 144.2 percent increase for the industries with the U.S. tariff reductions of 0.1-0.99 percent, and a 56.4 percent increase for the industries with no tariff changes (See Table 9). It appeared that Canadian registrations were more sensitive to the tariff reductions in the U.S. than U.S. registrations to the tariff reductions in Canada.

Services trade is considerably more restricted than goods trade. As a result, bilateral registrations of service trademarks were far smaller than those of goods. For instance, the average annual goods registrations by U.S. residents in Canada during the 1990s was 8,820, more than triple their service trademark registrations. The Canadian registrations of service trademarks in the U.S. relative to their registrations in goods were of a similar order.

62

Table 8. Changes in the Annual Average Registrations of U.S. Trademark in Canada and in the Canadian Tariffs on Imports from the U.S. by industry

		Trademark			Tariffs		
NAICS	Industry	1980-89	1990-02	Growth (%)	1989	2001	Change
312	Beverage & Tobacco	84	146	73.4	38.97	14.08	-24.89
315	Apparel	282	465	64.9	19.09	1.17	-17.92
313	Textile Mills	119	190	59.2	14.25	0.25	-14.00
314	Textile Products	98	176	80.5	13.93	0.73	-13.20
337	Furniture	74	138	86.4	11.99	0.26	-11.73
	Subtotal	**658**	**1116**	**69.7**			
316	Leather Products	183	317	73.7	9.82	2.42	-7.40
323	Printing	275	561	103.8	7.37	0.09	-7.28
335	Elect. Equipment & Appliance	265	412	55.2	6.55	0.20	-6.35
326	Plastics & Rubber	288	444	54.5	5.94	0.13	-5.81
339	Miscellaneous Manufacturing	587	868	47.8	4.97	0.21	-4.76
322	Paper Products	216	364	68.1	4.48	0.01	-4.46
325	Chemical Products	641	864	34.7	4.54	0.10	-4.44
332	Fabricated Metal Products	391	571	46.0	4.45	0.14	-4.31
327	Non-metallic Mineral Products	131	196	49.2	4.03	0.10	-3.93
321	Wood Products	133	207	56.2	3.30	0.06	-3.24
311	Food	364	572	57.2	3.20	0.09	-3.11
331	Primary Metals	92	113	22.8	2.82	0.02	-2.81
333	Machinery	392	571	45.6	2.29	0.05	-2.24
334	Computer & Elect. Products.	463	981	111.8	1.74	0.02	-1.72
	Subtotal	**4422**	**7042**	**59.2**			
324	Petroleum & Coal Products	82	108	32.7	0.60	0.01	-0.59
336	Transportation Equipment	301	469	55.5	0.62	0.14	-0.48
114	Fishing, Hunting & Trapping	1	2	90.0	0.06	0.00	-0.06
212	Mining (except Oil and Gas)	2	3	80.3	0.01	0.00	-0.01
115	Support for Agri. & Forestry	2	4	92.5	0.00	0.00	0.00
221	Utilities	11	26	148.9	0.00	0.00	0.00
211	Oil & Gas Extraction	1	4	187.5	0.00	0.00	0.00
111	Crop Production	2	3	36.4	0.00	0.00	0.00
113	Forestry & Logging	2	4	73.9	0.00	0.00	0.00
210	Other Mining	4	9	128.1	0.00	0.00	0.00
310	Other Manufacturing	15	33	122.5	0.00	0.00	0.00
	Subtotal	**423**	**664**	**57.2**			

Table 9. Changes in the Average Annual registrations of Canadian Trademarks in the U.S. and U.S. Tariffs against the U.S. Imports from Canada

		Trademark			Tariffs		
NAICS	Industry	1980-89	1990-02	Growth (%)	1989	2001	Change
315	Apparel	53	156	193.8	10.87	0.39	-10.48
313	Textile Mills	26	56	113.0	9.34	0.06	-9.29
316	Leather Products	32	86	170.2	6.67	0.28	-6.39
314	Textile Products	17	48	180.3	4.80	0.44	-4.36
326	Plastics & Rubber Products	58	158	170.5	3.66	0.03	-3.63
325	Chemical Products	85	207	144.7	2.88	0.10	-2.78
337	Furniture	19	56	194.3	2.56	0.00	-2.56
339	Miscellaneous Manufacturing	112	266	137.9	2.61	0.05	-2.56
335	Elect. Equip. & Appliance	52	131	151.4	2.66	0.17	-2.49
332	Fabricated Metal Products	81	196	140.6	2.42	0.09	-2.33
311	Food	78	198	152.5	2.39	0.14	-2.24
327	Non-metallic Mineral Prod.	23	69	197.4	1.79	0.02	-1.76
111	Crop Production	1	2	80.0	1.63	0.01	-1.61
333	Machinery Manufacturing	78	191	146.7	1.56	0.06	-1.50
312	Beverage & Tobacco Products	28	63	127.4	1.27	0.01	-1.26
334	Computer & Electronic Prod.	116	394	239.6	1.22	0.02	-1.19
331	Primary Metals	24	44	83.1	1.09	0.01	-1.07
	Subtotal	**831**	**2165**	**160.6**			
324	Petroleum & Coal Products	18	37	107.1	0.87	0.06	-0.81
321	Wood Products	36	78	116.8	0.44	0.01	-0.43
322	Paper Products	44	113	159.6	0.40	0.00	-0.40
114	Fishing, Hunting & Trapping	1	1	40.0	0.35	0.00	-0.35
323	Printing	69	175	152.5	0.34	0.01	-0.33
211	Oil & Gas Extraction	1	2	114.3	0.25	0.00	-0.25
336	Transportation Equipment	61	153	153.1	0.30	0.10	-0.20
	Subtotal	**230**	**561**	**144.2**			
113	Forestry & Logging	2	3	100.0	0.00	0.00	0.00
212	Mining (except Oil and Gas)	2	4	75.0	0.00	0.00	0.00
110	Other Agr., For. & Fishing	1	2	120.0	0.00	0.00	0.00
115	Support Activities for Agr.	1	2	50.0	0.00	0.00	0.00
210	Other Mining	3	3	27.3	0.00	0.00	0.00
213	Support Activities for Mining	2	2	0.0	0.00	0.00	0.00
	Subtotal	**10**	**15**	**56.4**			

Industry-level regression analysis

The disaggregated industry-level trademark statistics allow one to test whether the observed trend in bilateral trademark registrations are systematically related to the tariff reductions that occurred over the Canada-U.S. FTA period. The following panel specialization will be estimated:

$$\ln V_{it}^{k} = \alpha_i^k + \beta_t^k + \eta \ln \tau_{it}^k + \varepsilon_{it}^k \tag{2}$$

The variables are defined next. The subscript i represents host country, Canada or the U.S., and t represents year. Superscript k denotes the type of products, namely, homogeneous, referenced, and differentiated products. V_{it} is the number of trademarks registered by source country at the host country i in year t. α_i^k are the industry fixed effects, and β_t^k are the year effects. τ_{it}^k are host country i's tariff rate for the product k in year t. ε_{it}^k is the stochastic error term, representing other influences on bilateral trademark registrations.

Equation (2) is applied to Canadian and U.S. data separately, and is estimated for each of three groups: differentiated products, referenced products, and total products for the period of 1980 and 2002. Homogenous products are excluded from the estimation since the product differentiation model is only applied to differentiated products,

Table 10 reports the estimated effects of Canadian tariff reductions on Canada's imports of U.S. varieties for three product groups: differentiated products, referenced products and total products. Differentiated products had the strongest variety-enhanced effect with the estimated tariff coefficient coming to − 0.1023; this was followed by total products of –0.0601, and referenced products of –0.0307. This result is to be expected as trade in homogeneous products is driven by changes in quantity within a narrow set of varieties; while trade in differentiated products is driven by changes in varieties with a wider range of selections. Table 11 confirms the same trend based on U.S. data. The estimated coefficient for U.S. tariffs on U.S. imports of differentiated products from Canada was -0.1018, while that for total products and referenced products were –0.0765 and –0.0417, respectively. Overall, the variety-enhanced effect of tariff reductions was slightly higher in the case of the U.S. imports from Canada relative to Canada's imports from the U.S. The estimated tariff coefficient for the U.S. total imports of Canadian varieties was -0.0765, compared to the corresponding Canadian figure of –0.0601. This is consistent with what has been discussed above, based on Table 6, that gives an account of stronger growth of Canadian registrations in the U.S. relative to U.S. registrations in Canada during the Canada-U.S. FTA period.

To control the effect of business cycles, in particular the recession in the early 1990s on the imports of varieties, the estimation of (2) includes a fixed time-effect represented by a dummy variable "90". For the Canadian data, the estimated time-effect had the expected negative signs. They were significant for both total products and referenced products, but were less significant in the case of

65

differentiated products (negative and significant at the 10 percent level). This implies that business cycles, or economic downturns in Canada, had a negative impact on Canada's imports of varieties for both homogeneous and referenced products from the U.S. But, in the case of differentiated products, Canada's imports of variety appeared less sensitive to economic downturns. The estimated time-effects were even weaker in the U.S. data as reported in Table 11. The estimated time effects for both total products and referenced products were negative but significant only at the 10 percent level, while that for differentiated products was statistically insignificant.

The estimation results reported at Table 10 also takes account of strong industry-effects, reflected in large and positive estimated coefficients for computer, chemical, food, and apparel industries. This is consistent what has been reported in Table 5, that Canada had the most variety gains from the U.S. in the sectors that experienced the most rapid technology changes and the sectors that were subject to heavy advertisements. The estimation results based on the U.S. data also report the similar strong fixed industry-effects in the industries of computer, chemical, food, and apparel products.

Table 10. The estimated effects of Canadian tariff reductions on U.S. trademark registrations in Canada by product

	Total imports	Differentiated products	Referenced products
Tariffs	-0.0601	-0.1023	-0.0307
Apparel	0.7751	0.7014	
Chemical	1.2661		
Computer	1.276	1.0613	
Electrical prods.	0.5363		
Fabricated medal	0.8367		
Food	0.8726	0.7104	
Plastics	0.6111		
Printing	0.7788	0.5991	
Textile products	-0.2955		0.1721
Transportation	0.5407		
90	-0.2451	-0.1153*	-0.315
N	311	198	86
Adjusted R-square	0.5325	0.3968	0.8936

* Statistically significant at the 10 percent level.

Table 11. Effects of U.S. tariff reductions on Canadian trademark registrations in the U.S. by product

	Total imports	Differentiated products	Referenced products
Tariffs	-0.0765	-0.1018	-0.0417
Apparel	0.8363	0.9496	
Chemical	0.9391		
Computer	1.508	1.5497	
Electrical prods.	0.552	0.6236	
Fabricated medal	0.9163	0.9823	
Food	0.9423	1.0081	
Machinery	0.8249		
Plastics			
Printing	0.6023	0.6044	
Textile products			0.1951
Transportation			
90	-0.2309*	-0.1836**	-0.2542*
N	273	171	78
Adjusted R-square	0.5085	0.7425	0.844

* Statistically significant at the 10 percent level.
** Statistically insignificant.

Conclusions

Nations are trading far fewer varieties than is commonly supposed, and there is strong "home bias' in the global production and consumption of differentiated products. This is true even after taking account of language, distance, and regional preferential trade arrangements that are commonly seen as major factors explaining global trade and production patterns.

Language, trade liberalization, distance, and per capita income matter in the context of global trade in variety. Nations that share the same language and culture are more likely to trade their varieties among themselves. This is because product differentiation often has a strong information component, requiring substantial advertising by the firm in order to inform customers of its product's uniqueness. Low-income countries produce far fewer varieties than high-income ones. This implies that the recent export expansion from China, India, and other low-income countries to industrialized countries was mainly driven by "process trade" or "outsourcing" by firms in industrialized countries with little contribution of intellectual property from these low-income countries.

Trade liberalization has contributed significant variety-enhancing effects to both Canada and the U.S. The underlying premise is that there are fixed costs to importing a variety, so that tariffs limit the imports of varieties by shrinking the market for each variety, while free trade expands the size of the market and enhances access to varieties by lowering the fixed costs of importing a given product from other countries.

Canada's access to U.S. varieties was three times more than what the U.S. obtained from Canada. This asymmetric pattern of exchange in varieties suggests that the size of the market matters with respect to the availability of varieties. When trade is liberalized, a medium-size country like Canada gains more by expanding its trading relationship with a larger one than vice-versa, not only because trade liberalization gives Canada an opportunity to increase its volume of trade, but also because it enhances Canada's access to varieties that are often more available in large economies. Under the Canada-U.S. FTA, Canada has increased its annual access to U.S. new varieties (goods) by 60 percent, or average annual gains of 3,319 new varieties during the period of 1990-2002.

Appendix: The theoretical framework

Consider a representative consumer's utility in country j is portrayed by a CES utility function with a preference that is allowed to vary across countries. Consumers in country j maximize

$$\left[\sum_i \omega_i^{-\beta} \left(\alpha_{ij} q_{ij} \right)^{\beta} \right]^{1/\beta}, \qquad \beta = \left(1 - \frac{1}{\sigma} \right), \qquad \sigma > 1,$$

(A1)

subject to the budget constraint

$$\sum_i p_{ij} q_{ij} \leq y_j$$

(A2)

Here q_{ij} is country j's imports of all varieties from country i, p_{ij} is the price of country i products for country j consumers, y_j is the country j's normal income, ω is a parameter, σ is the elasticity of substitution between varieties, and α_{ij} is the preference intensity of country j's consumers over the varieties produced by country i. The preference parameter varies across countries according to the similarity (or differences) in cultures, languages, distances, and preferential trade arrangements between nations as discussed above. If j country consumer's preference over the varieties produced by country i is high, a larger share of j country consumer's income (higher α_{ij}) will be spent on those varieties; otherwise, a smaller share spent on those varieties. By allowing α_{ij} varying across countries, this preference structure accommodates that fact that importers value and therefore will purchase only their preferable varieties.

The first-order condition that satisfying maximization of (A1) subject to (A2) is

$$\Psi^{(1/\beta)-1} \omega_i^{-\beta} \alpha_{ij}^{\beta} q_{ij}^{\beta-1} = \lambda \, p_{ij},$$

(A3)

Here λ is the marginal utility of income and $\Psi = \sum_i \omega_i^{-\beta} \alpha_{ij}^{\beta} q_{ij}^{\beta}$. Rearrange the terms in (A3) to give

69

$$q_{ij} = (\lambda)^{1/(\beta-1)} \left(\frac{\omega_i^{\beta} p_{ij}}{\alpha_{ij}^{\beta}} \right)^{1/(\beta-1)} \Psi^{1/\beta}$$

(A4)

Multiple both sides of (A4) by p_{ij}, sum up the condition for all varieties, and make use of the budget constraint to give

$$I_j = (\lambda)^{1/(\beta-1)} \sum_i \left[\frac{\omega_i p_{ij}}{\alpha_{ij}} \right]^{\beta/(\beta-1)} \Psi^{(1/\beta)}$$

(A5)

Substitute (A5) into (A4) to yield j country consumers' demand for the varieties produced by country i,

$$q_{ij} = \frac{\left(\dfrac{\omega_i t_{ij} p_i}{\alpha_{ij}} \right)^{1-\sigma}}{\sum_i \left(\dfrac{\omega_i t_{ij} p_i}{\alpha_{ij}} \right)^{1-\sigma}} I_j$$

(A6)

Here, p_i denotes the exporter's supply price, and t_{ij} is the importing country's tariffs. Thus, $p_{ij} = t_{ij} p_i$. Following Deardorff's approach (1998), namely, using the market clearance to solve for the coefficient ω_i while imposing the choice of units such that all supply prices equal to one and then substituting into the import demand equation, one will get,

$$q_{ij} = \frac{y_i y_j}{y_w} \left(\frac{t_{ij}/\alpha_{ij}}{P_i P_j} \right)^{1-\sigma}$$

(A7)

where y_w is normal world income, P_j is the price index of country j, given by

70

$$P_j^{1-\sigma} = \sum_i P_i^{\sigma-1} \frac{y_i}{y_w} \left(\frac{t_{ij}}{\alpha_{ij}} \right)^{1-\sigma}$$

(A8)

Further, assuming the consumers' preference, α_{ij}, is influenced by languages and distances,

$$\ln \alpha_{ij} = \rho_1 \ln d_{ij} + \rho_{ij} \ln l_{ij}$$

(A9)

(A7) can be rewritten as,

$$\ln \alpha_{ij} = c + \ln y_i + \ln y_j + (1-\sigma)\ln t_{ij} - (1-\sigma)\rho_1 \ln d_{ij} -$$
$$(1-\sigma)\rho_2 \ln l_{ij}$$
$$-(1-\sigma)\ln P_i - (1-\sigma)\ln P_j$$

(A10)

Assuming the same quantity for each variety imported by country j, the number of varieties can be obtained by dividing (A10) with the standard quantity for each variety, this will give rise to

$$\ln v_{ij} = c + \ln y_i + \ln y_j + (1-\sigma)\ln t_{ij} - (1-\sigma)\rho_1 \ln d_{ij} - (1-\sigma)\rho_2 \ln l_{ij}$$
$$-(1-\sigma)\ln P_i - (1-\sigma)\ln P_j$$

(A11)

where c is a constant, and v_{ijz} is the number of varieties that country j imports from country i. Using the source-country fixed effect, ϕ_i and the target-country fixed effect, ϕ_j, to capture the multilateral resistance terms P_i and P_j as Anderson and van Wincoop (2003) suggested, one gets the following equation,

$$\ln v_{ij} = c + \ln y_i + \ln y_j + (1-\sigma)\ln t_{ij} - (1-\sigma)\rho_1 \ln d_{ij} - (1-\sigma)\rho_2 \ln l_{ij}$$
$$-(1-\sigma)\ln \phi_i - (1-\sigma)\ln \phi_j$$

(A12)

(A12) forms the basis for the econometric estimation used in Section 4 to investigate the determinants of global trade in variety.

Bibliography

Anderson James, E. and Eric Van Wincoop (2003) "Gravity with Gravitas: A Solution to the Border Puzzle," American Economic Review, March 2003, 93, 170-192.

Canadian Intellectual Property Office (2002), "A Guide to Trade-Marks".

Caves, Richard E. (1981), " Intra-Industry Trade and Market Structure in the Industrialized Countries", Oxford Economic Papers, 33 (July):203-223.

Chamberlin, E. H. (1947) *The Theory of Monopolistic Competition: A re-orientation of the Theory of Value*, 5th ed. Cambridge, Mass., Harvard University Press.

Deardorff, Alan V. (1998) "Determinants of Bilateral Trade: Does Gravity Work in a Neoclassical World?" in J. A. Frankel, ed., *The regionalization of the world economy*, Chicago: University of Chicago Press, pp. 7-22.

Feenstra, Robert C., Dorsati Madani, Tzu-Hayn Yang, ChiYuan Liang (1997) "Testing Endogenous Growth in South Korea and Taiwan," NBER Working Paper Series 6028.

Feenstra, Robert C. (2003) "Advanced International Trade: Theory and Evidence", Princeton University Press. Chapter 5.

Head, Keith and John Ries, (1999) "Rationalization Effects of Tariff Reductions", Journal of International Economics, 47(2), April, 295-320.

Haveman, Jon and David Hummels (1999) "Alternative Hypotheses and the Volume of Trade: Evidence on the Extent of Specialization".

Helpman, Elhanan (1998) "The Structure of Foreign Trade", NBER Working Paper 6752.

Hillberry, H. Russell and Christine A. McDaniel (2002) "A Decomposition of North American Trade Growth since NAFTA", International Economic Review, Many/June 2002, U.S. International Trade Commission.

Romer, Paul (1995) "New Goods, Old Theory, and the Welfare Costs of Trade Restrictions," *Journal of Development Economics*, vol. 43, 1995, pp. 5-38.

Specialization in NAFTA Partner Countries: What Factors Explain the Observed Patterns?

Ram C. Acharya
Industry Canada

Introduction

There are three principal theories of why countries trade: the Ricardian model, the Heckscher-Ohlin model and increasing returns to scale.[1] In the Ricardian model, comparative advantage comes from technological superiority; countries concentrate output in those sectors in which they have a technological advantage. Heckscher-Ohlin (HO) theory, on the other hand, suggests that all countries have access to the same technologies, and comparative advantage comes from the relative abundance of factors. Hence, countries relatively rich in capital or other resources will have output mixes shifting in favour of those sectors that use these abundant resources intensively. The increasing returns to scale model suggests that trade could take place even if the economies have identical tastes, technology and factor endowments, since economies of scale would generate comparative advantage and strengthen the tendency to specialize.

There is a considerable amount of research which empirically tests the importance of these theoretically established reasons in explaining trade flows. To cite a few of them, Leamer (1984), Harrigan (1995) and Bernstein and Weinstein (2002) estimate the relevance of the HO model using trade and production data. Bowen et al. (1987), Trefler (1993, 1995), Davis et al. (1997) and Harrigan (1997) use models where technological differences across countries are introduced, thereby incorporating both Ricardian and HO aspects. Davis and Weinstein (1999, 2003) assess the relative importance of comparative advantage and increasing returns in accounting for production structure and trade. Recently, Antweiler and Trefler (2002) developed a methodology for estimating returns to scale using a data set consisting of a large number of countries.

Researchers have realized that for a model to be realistic, it should be able to integrate all key determinants of trade and specialization into a single coherent framework. However, both in theory and empirical work, this realization has not met with much success. As far as the study of specialization is concerned, Leamer (1997) is the only paper that combines two variables, the Ricardian and the HO, in determining specialization in OECD countries. Due to data limitation,

---

[1] The other potential reason, the supply by oligopolists in each others' markets, as developed by Brander (1981), is not considered a significant factor for trade. All these theories are based on the supply side of the economy. The demand side, differences in tastes, can also lead to trade, but has only rarely been analyzed as a source of comparative advantage (an exception is Markusen, 1986 and Hunter and Markusen, 1988).

however, he has to make some compromises. First, his model does not directly incorporate an HO variable. For this purpose, Leamer op. cit. uses a common country factor as a proxy for all industries, instead of a more direct measure such as factor endowment and intensity. Second, he does not allow for effects other than the Ricardian and the HO to play any role in specialization. Third, his model is a cross-country examination with one year of data and hence cannot capture the dynamics of change over time.

In order to fill this gap, this paper incorporates all theoretical determinants of trade to evaluate specialization that has taken place in North America (Canada, the United States and Mexico) from 1980 to 2000. It decomposes the relative importance of Ricardian, HO, increasing returns and trade policy in determining the specialization patterns in 23 manufacturing industries. By doing so, it indirectly evaluates the conjecture made by Leamer (1993) more than a decade ago that economies of scale may play an important role in the regional division of manufacturing between Canada and the United States, whereas the factor proportion effect would capture most of the effect for Mexico.

The North American market consists of the world's most productive and capital intensive country (the United States), a relatively poor labour intensive country (Mexico), and Canada in between these two extremes. The huge differences in productivity, factor proportion and market size among these three countries make North America a good laboratory to study the relative importance and mutual interaction of these factors in setting up specialization. Furthermore, at the time of signing of Canada-United States Free Trade Agreement (FTA) in 1988 and the North American Free Trade Agreement (NAFTA) among Canada, United States and Mexico in 1993, it was considered that these agreements would lead to more specialization in production. NAFTA was also supposed to be a facilitator in technology transfer from an advanced to a less advanced partner country. This paper sheds light on whether these expectations have been realized.

The results show that the level of specialization in NAFTA countries has increased for some industries and decreased for others, but there is no discernable trend for many industries. On balance, the overall specialization is slightly up. Obviously, some industries are more concentrated than others. The most concentrated industries are the building of ships and boats, leather products and aircraft and spacecraft, whereas the least concentrated industries are rubber and plastics, electrical machinery and chemicals. On average, high-tech industries are more concentrated than others. Further, all the high-tech industries are over-represented in the United States and most of them are under-represented both in Canada and Mexico. The prediction is that at least in one high-tech industry, office accounting and computing machinery, the United States might capture an even larger share over time.

Somewhat counter-intuitively, for the last two decades Canada has remained the least specialized country in North America. The regionalization index shows that in terms of employment structure, Canada and the United States have become more similar (diversified) over time, whereas both of them have become more dissimilar (specialized) to Mexico. Interestingly, the United States has a larger than expected size of all five high-tech sectors, whereas Canada barely maintains its share in only one high-tech industry.

74

Out of 23 industries, the Ricardian variable (revealed labour productivity advantage) has a significant role in explaining specialization in 21 industries, the HO variable (capital-labour ratio) in 17 industries and the increasing returns to scale variable (R&D intensity) in eight industries. Food and beverages, textiles, chemicals and miscellaneous manufacturing are the only Ricardian sectors. The value added of the first three industries is predicted to become concentrated in the more productive country, whereas miscellaneous manufacturing is predicted to locate in the less productive country. For the other eleven industries, the Ricardian variable determines specialization along with the HO variable. They include industries like machinery and equipment, metal, wood, pharmaceuticals, petroleum, apparel and rubber and plastics. Except apparel, the Ricardian effects reveal that all of them tend to locate in the country with higher labour productivity, whereas the HO effect states that all of them tend to locate in the low capital intensive country.

The locations of the production of leather and motor vehicles are driven by both Ricardian and increasing returns variables. Leather tends to be concentrated in a highly productive and less R&D intensive country, whereas motor vehicles tend to be concentrated in the highly productive and high R&D intensive country. Electrical machinery, the only industry where the Ricardian variable has no effect, is a HO and increasing returns to scale sector, indicating that having higher productivity and a higher capital-labour ratio is the reason for concentration in this industry. For all the remaining five industries, which contribute more than a quarter of value added in total manufacturing in NAFTA countries, the production location is determined by all three factors. These five industries include three of the five high-tech sectors, namely aircraft and spacecraft, radio, television and communication equipment, office accounting and computing machinery. The other two industries in this category are pulp, paper, printing and publishing and tobacco products. The prediction is that these five industries tend to be over-represented in a country with high productivity, low capital intensity (except office accounting and computing machinery) and high R&D intensity.

Even though the specialization patterns in NAFTA countries are driven by all three factors, the role of the Ricardian variable is more important not only in terms of number of industries in which this variable is significant, but also in terms of the value added that these industries contribute. The predominant role of Ricardian effects suggests that technological differences are substantial among NAFTA countries. It also suggests that if there is a convergence of productivity levels, it is rather slow. Otherwise, there should not be such a significant impact of the productivity variable in determining production locations in the two decades of data.

Results show that the role of NAFTA is not very important in determining specialization. NAFTA affected specialization in only three industries, raising it in one industry (refined petroleum) and reducing it in two industries (motor vehicles and radio, television and communication equipment).

Since the Ricardian and HO effects generate somewhat opposite effects in countries with very different factor endowments and technology, the findings of interplay of these two effects in many industries suggest that the adjustment in

North America was moderate, as was the pace of specialization. There probably was some technology transfer and wage increase in the less developed countries as the Ricardian model would indicate; there probably was a bit of wage pressure on unskilled workers in more developed countries and some advantage of specialization in all countries as the HO model would predict. The role of increasing returns to scale in shaping the North American manufacturing sector is important mostly in the high-tech sectors. Among eight industries where the increasing returns to scale variable is significant along with other variable(s), five are high-tech and medium-high tech industries.

NAFTA Trade and Specialization

Both export orientation and import penetration of the manufacturing sector in all three NAFTA countries have increased over time (Table 1). In 2000, together these countries exported more than one-fifth of their manufacturing gross production and imported more than one-quarter of their consumption, an increase of about ten percentage from a decade ago. Among them, Canada is the most open economy, with about 53 percent of its manufacturing production (consumption) exported (imported) in 2000.

Table 1. Manufacturing Trade Orientation of NAFTA Countries (Percent)

	Export Orientation			Import Penetration		
	1990	1995	2000	1990	1995	2000
NAFTA	13.2	17.4	21.5	16.4	21.1	26.5
Canada	36.2	50.2	52.7	37.4	49.5	52.6
U.S.	11.1	13.6	16.8	14.5	18.0	22.6
Mexico	10.2	39.6	43.3	15.6	39.0	46.4

Source: OECD, Structural Analysis (STAN) and Bilateral Trade (BTD) databases.
Note: Export orientation is defined as the share of exports in gross production and import penetration is defined as the share of imports in consumption, which in turn is calculated as gross production *less* exports *plus* imports. The trade data in the OECD database are in U.S. dollars, and gross production data for Canada and Mexico were converted to U.S. dollars using average annual market exchange rates for national currencies.

The detailed account of intra-NAFTA trade is provided in Table 2. Looking across the first row, it is clear that in 1990 the share of NAFTA countries in Canada's total manufacturing exports was about 80 percent (79.2 percent for the United States and 0.5 percent for Mexico), which increased to 88 percent in 2000. Similarly, NAFTA countries' share of U.S. exports increased from about 30 percent in 1990 to about 38 percent in 2000. The fastest intra-region export growth occurred for Mexico from 76 percent in 1990 to 92 percent in 2000. As a result of this intra-regional export growth, 55 percent of NAFTA countries' manufacturing exports were destined to their own markets in 2000. On the import side, the intra-regional integration is less pronounced. For NAFTA as a whole, the share of NAFTA partners in its total manufacturing imports increased from 33 percent in 1990 to about 41 percent in 2000.

Table 2. Share of Intra-NAFTA Trade in Manufacturing (in Percent)

	1990				2000			
	Canada	U.S.	Mexico	NAFTA	Canada	U.S.	Mexico	NAFTA
Exports								
Canada	-	79.2	0.5	79.7	-	87.6	0.5	88.0
U.S.	22.2	-	7.5	29.7	23.3	-	14.4	37.7
Mexico	1.2	75.1	-	76.4	2.1	90.2	-	92.3
NAFTA	16.4	20.5	5.7	42.6	15.7	29.9	9.6	55.2
Imports								
Canada	-	66.9	1.3	68.2	-	66.9	3.5	70.4
U.S.	18.1	-	5.1	23.1	17.7	-	11.1	28.7
Mexico	1.1	66.8	-	67.9	1.8	79.3	-	81.1
NAFTA	14.0	15.3	4.1	33.4	13.1	19.5	8.6	41.2

Source: OECD, Bilateral Trade Database (BTD).
Note: For the export part of the table, the country as column heading indicates the source, and the country as row heading shows the destination. However for the import part, the country as column heading indicates the destination, whereas the country as row heading indicates the sources.

The increase in the shares of intra-NAFTA exports in three countries' exports by more than 12 percentage points and of imports by 8 percentage points in a period of one decade is a reflection of a deeper product market integration that is taking place among these three countries. Of course, the degree of integration varies a great deal by industry. For example, in 2000 the share of intra-NAFTA imports in total NAFTA imports ranged from 72 percent in pulp, paper, printing and publishing to only 16 percent in pharmaceuticals. Now the question is, how has this increased integration affected the specialization pattern? This subject is discussed in the rest of this section. As in Leamer (1997), specialization is measured using revealed comparative advantage (RCA), after correcting for country size and for industry size using the following formula:

$$(1) \qquad RCA_{ij} = \frac{\left[v_{ij} / \left(v_i - v_{ij} \right) \right]}{\left[v_j / \left(v - v_j \right) \right]},$$

where v_{ij} = value added in industry i for country j, $v_i = \sum_j v_{ij}$ = total NAFTA countries' value added in industry i, $v_j = \sum_i v_{ij}$ = total value added in country j and $v = \sum_i \sum_j v_{ij}$ = total NAFTA value added.[2]

As in Leamer, we use the rest-of-NAFTA and rest-of-industry value added instead of total NAFTA and total manufacturing value added to correct for country-size

---

[2] We have used value added data rather than trade data to compute RCA. We could have used gross production data rather than value added. Again, if the proportion of intermediate inputs used in gross output is not very different among countries (which we assume to be the case), the relative RCA among countries will be the same whether we use gross production or value added data.

effects, which spreads the magnitude of RCA.[3] The results on the extent of specialization using value added data by country and industry for two time periods (1980-1981 and 1999-2000), are given in Table 3, where industries are ordered based on international system of industrial classification (ISIC) codes. The detailed list of ISIC codes and industry names is given in Appendix 1. We have used data for 23 manufacturing industries, most of them at the 2-digit level, with three industries at the 3-digit level, and one industry at the 4-digit level.[4]

The revealed comparative advantage of the first industry for Canada in 1980-1981 is 1.31, meaning that Canada had 31% more value added in the food and beverages industry than would have predicted based on the size of this industry in NAFTA and the size of Canada. Based on RCA in 1999-2000, the only sectors that are larger than expected in Canada are wood products with RCA of 2.26 (2.26 times or 126% larger than what is expected), railroad and transport equipment (89% larger than expected), basic metals, motor vehicles and trailers, and pulp, paper, printing and publishing. During this period, the biggest negative RCA for Canada is in office and computing machinery, with RCA of 0.23 (a size of only 23% of what is predicted based on country and industry size). The other two very small sectors in Canada are pharmaceuticals, with RCA of 0.33, followed by refined petroleum, with RCA of 0.52.

For the United States, some of the larger than expected sectors are the building of ships and boats, aircraft and spacecraft, tobacco, radio TV and communication equipment, pharmaceuticals, machinery and equipment, refined petroleum, electrical machinery and apparatus, fabricated metal and office and computing machinery. The aircraft and spacecraft industry is twice as large as expected, and miscellaneous manufacturing is 2.17 times larger than expected.[5] The relatively smaller sectors in the United States, to name a few, are leather (RCA of 0.34), food and beverages (RCA of 0.5) and motor vehicles and trailers (RCA of 0.56).

---

[3] The control of industry and country effects in the formula does not alter the value of RCA from more than one to less than one or vice versa from the RCA if it were calculated using the regular formula without any correction. What the correction does is that it raises (lowers) the value of RCA in those industries which would have RCA greater (smaller) than one if calculated using the regular formula. In other words, the correction increases the range of RCA.

[4] The industry-wide data on value added in national currencies were converted to U.S. dollars by using GDP purchasing power parity exchange rates given by the OECD. This implicitly assumes that relative prices are the same in different industries; to the extent that they are not, output comparison will be distorted. The use of PPP for GDP will overestimates the value of the industries whose relative prices are falling and underestimate the value of those whose relative prices are rising.

[5] Miscellaneous manufacturing is predominantly medical, precision and optical instruments. In addition, it also includes furniture and fixtures, recycling and other manufacturing which are not included elsewhere. Hence, the result for the United States is driven by its unusually high share of value added in medical, precision and optical instruments.

78

Table 3. Specialization by Country and Industry

Industry	Canada		U.S.		Mexico	
	1980-1981	1999-2000	1980-1981	1999-2000	1980-1981	1999-2000
Food and beverages	1.31	0.99	0.52	0.50	2.28	2.81
Tobacco products	0.64	0.72	1.79	1.97	0.52	0.36
Textiles	0.68	0.65	0.57	0.66	2.71	2.34
Wearing apparel	1.32	1.49	0.75	0.65	1.27	1.45
Leather products	1.04	0.73	0.39	0.34	3.69	4.91
Wood products	1.60	2.26	0.63	0.65	1.44	0.78
Pulp, paper, print & publishing	1.70	1.42	0.94	1.19	0.50	0.35
Refined petroleum	0.47	0.52	1.28	1.44	1.11	0.92
Chemicals excl pharma	1.02	0.79	1.02	1.21	0.95	0.89
Pharmaceuticals	0.63	0.33	1.10	1.73	1.20	0.88
Rubber and plastics	1.05	1.18	1.01	1.08	0.94	0.71
Other non-metallic mineral	1.02	0.76	0.55	0.62	2.42	2.40
Basic metals	1.11	1.69	1.02	0.64	0.87	1.28
Fabricated metal	0.96	0.97	1.40	1.38	0.52	0.53
Machinery and equipment	0.76	0.87	1.77	1.64	0.42	0.41
Office account. & computing mach.	0.22	0.23	6.03	1.31	0.15	1.39
Electrical m. and apparatus	0.78	0.70	1.27	1.13	0.82	1.09
Radio, TV & commu. equipment	0.95	0.67	1.23	1.85	0.72	0.47
Motor vehicles and trailers	0.97	1.56	0.75	0.56	1.62	1.74
Building of ships & boats	1.67	0.71	1.21	2.88	0.16	0.06
Aircraft and spacecraft	0.77	1.02	2.55	2.00	0.11	0.09
Railroad and transport equip.	2.07	1.89	0.42	0.88	2.33	0.53
Miscellaneous manufacturing	0.53	0.59	2.34	2.17	0.37	0.38

Note: In the manufacturing sector, there are altogether 23 industries at ISIC 2-digit level. Among them, we took 16 industries as they are; combined two 2-digit industries (ISIC 21: pulp, paper and paper product and ISIC 22: printing and publishing) into one. We also combined other three 2-digit industries (ISIC 33: medical, precision and optical instruments; ISIC 36: manufacturing not elsewhere mentioned and ISIC 37: recycling) into another and called it miscellaneous manufacturing. Furthermore, we split one 2-digit industry (ISIC 24: chemicals) into two (24: chemicals excluding pharmaceuticals, and ISIC 2423: pharmaceuticals) and another 2-digit industry (ISIC 35: other transport equipment) into three 3-digit industries (ISIC 351: building and repairing of ships and boats; ISIC 353: aircraft and spacecraft; ISIC 352 *plus* ISIC 359: railroad equipment and transport equipment). This leaves us with the total of 23 industries as the sample for the study. The number in parentheses behind the industry name in the table represents the ISIC code.

For Mexico, the larger than expected sectors are leather products (almost 400% larger than expected), food and beverages, non-metallic minerals, textiles, motor vehicles and trailers, apparel, office accounting and computing machinery,

79

basic metals and electrical machinery. On the other hand, Mexico has only 9 percent of its expected size of value added in the aircraft and spacecraft industry.[6] Mexico has an even lower share of expected size for the building of ships and boats.

Table 4. Country Distribution of Concentrated Industries by Technology Definition

Technology Classification	Number of industries	Share in value added in 1999-2000	Number of larger than expected industries in 1999-2000		
			Canada	U.S.	Mexico
High-tech manufactures	5	24.7	1	5	1
Medium-high-tech manufactures	5	26.4	2	3	2
Medium-low-tech manufactures	6	20.2	2	4	2
Low-tech manufactures	7	28.7	3	2	4
Total	**23**	**100**	**8**	**14**	**9**

Note: In the column entitled "number of industries", the number reported is based on our scheme of aggregation rather than on the ISIC industry count that falls into a certain classification. For example, based on ISIC codes there are six industries in medium-high-tech manufacturers. However, since we have aggregated ISIC 352 and 359 into one industry in this study, we count the industry number as five not six. Also note that in Table 3, the ISIC 33 is aggregated with ISIC 36, and 37 and we count the aggregate of 33, 36 and 37 as high-tech, as ISIC 33 is a predominant sector in terms of value added.
In terms of ISIC codes, the four categories of technology classification consists of following industries:
High-tech manufactures: 2423, 30, 32, 33 and 353
Medium-high-tech manufactures: 24 excluding 2423, 29, 31, 34, 352 and 359
Medium-low-tech manufactures: 23, 25, 26, 27, 28 and 351
Low-tech manufactures: 15-22, 36 and 37

Based on the data in Table 3, we present the country distribution of specialization by the OECD's technology classification in Table 4. The first column provides the four technology classifications, and the second column lists the respective ISIC codes for industries which fall under each category, the names of which can be read both from Table 3 and Appendix 1.

The five high-tech manufacturing industries which contribute more than a quarter of manufacturing value added in NAFTA are concentrated in the United

---

[6] In Canada, out of 23 industries, the RCA remained larger than one in six industries in both periods. RCA changed from being greater than one to less than one in five industries and vice versa in two industries. For the remaining 10 industries, Canada's RCA was lower than one in both periods. For the United States, there were 13 industries whose RCA was greater than one in both periods. There was only one industry each which changed from being greater than one to less than one and vice versa, while the remaining eight industries had RCA less than one. In the case of Mexico, the RCA was greater than one in six industries in both periods. For four industries, the RCA changed from greater than one to less than one, whereas for three industries the case was reversed. The remaining 10 industries had RCA less than one.

States. Canada's shares in all these sectors are far smaller than expected (ranging from 23 percent to 79 percent), except in aircraft and spacecraft, in which Canada just maintains its share. Mexico has larger than expected value added in office accounting and computing machinery (39 percent larger than expected), which comes at Canada's cost.

Industry and Country Specialization

Based on the results given in Table 3, we compute cumulative industry specialization indices across NAFTA countries which are reported in Table 5. These indices are value added weighted averages of the absolute values of the RCA. The industry specialization index is computed using the following formula:

$$s_i = \sum_j \log_2 \left| RCA_{ij} \right| w_j, \qquad \text{where } w_j = \sum_i v_{ij} \Big/ \sum_i \sum_j v_{ij}$$

The weight is country j's share of total value added in NAFTA.[7]

What is clear from Table 5 is that some industries have highly specialized production patterns, while others are more uniformly distributed. The most highly concentrated industry in 1999-2000 is the building of ships and boats, followed by leather products and aircraft and spacecraft. On the other hand, the least concentrated industries are rubber and plastics, electrical machinery and chemicals. The index for the most concentrated industry (building of ships and boats) is almost three times higher than that of the least concentrated, rubber and plastics. The industries with low specialization indices are the ones that are distributed more or less symmetrically relative to the size of the country.

---

[7]To compute the specialization index in Tables 5 and 6, we converted the specialization index in Table 3 into base 2 logarithmic function (log 2 forms), then computed the weighted index and converted it back to level form to report in this table. Since we have to weight RCA in three countries to arrive at the industry cumulative index for NAFTA, the results differ depending on whether RCA value is used in level form or in log 2 form. And for the weighted average of this nature, log 2 form is a better form to adopt because it allows equal chance for each country to influence the index whether the country has larger than or smaller than expected size of industry. That is not the case if RCA is used in level form. For example, suppose that in a particular industry two countries have RCA = 2 and RCA = 0.5 in level forms. If we convert it into log 2 forms, they will have RCA = 1 and RCA = –1 respectively. Now in the weighting scheme, if we use the level form, the country with RCA = 2 will dominate the results, whereas if we use absolute value of log 2 form, both countries will have equal chance of affecting the cumulative specialization index. Leamer (1997) justifies the use of log 2 forms. The similar rationale applies for computing the country cumulative index.

Table 5. NAFTA Specialization by Industry

	Value added using PPP exchange rates			Specialization index with value added weights		
	Total (billions)	Share (%)	Per worker ($'000)			
	1999-2000	1999-2000	1999-2000	1980-1981	1988-1989	1999-2000
Rubber and plastics	71	3.9	53	1.01	1.06	1.11
Electrical machinery and apparatus	47	2.6	54	1.27	1.34	1.15
Chemicals excl. pharmaceutical	125	6.7	133	1.02	1.15	1.21
Pulp, paper, printing, publishing	194	10.7	67	1.14	1.17	1.30
Railroad and transport equip.	10	0.6	61	2.38	1.98	1.31
Fabricated metal	125	6.9	64	1.40	1.34	1.39
Refined petroleum	40	2.4	210	1.31	1.26	1.43
Office and computing machinery	41	2.1	135	5.90	3.83	1.46
Wearing apparel	26	1.4	27	1.32	1.28	1.54
Basic metals	67	3.6	78	1.05	1.70	1.54
Wood products	57	3.0	47	1.57	1.25	1.57
Textiles	39	2.1	36	1.78	1.54	1.58
Machinery and equipment	134	7.5	58	1.77	1.93	1.65
Other non-metallic mineral	55	3.0	69	1.78	2.11	1.65
Pharmaceuticals	69	3.9	189	1.13	1.13	1.75
Motor vehicles and trailers	165	9.0	99	1.33	1.52	1.75
Radio, TV & commu. equipment	146	8.4	101	1.23	1.92	1.84
Food and beverages	188	10.0	71	1.89	1.92	1.96
Tobacco products	22	1.3	449	1.78	1.60	1.97
Misc. manufacturing	129	7.3	58	2.33	2.45	2.16
Aircraft and spacecraft	56	3.0	92	2.64	4.58	2.22
Leather products	6	0.3	32	2.48	2.81	2.91
Building of ships & boats	8	0.4	41	1.38	2.02	3.14
Total manufacturing	**1,820**	**100.0**	**72.2**			

Source: OECD, STAN Database

Note: The data are in U.S. dollars using purchasing power parity (PPP) exchange rates. The list of industries is sorted by the specialization index of 1999-2000 (the last column) from least to most specialized.

Figure 1. Specialization and Total NAFTA Value Added, 1999-2000

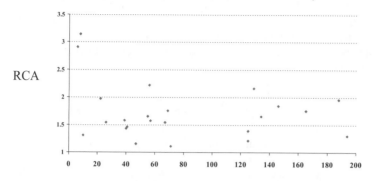

NAFTA value added per worker (in thousands of U.S. $)

Figure 2. Specialization and NAFTA Productivity, 1999-2000

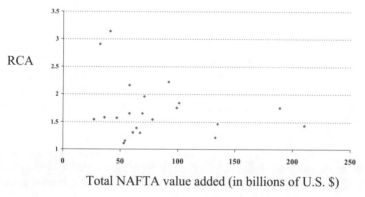

Total NAFTA value added (in billions of U.S. $)

It is also obvious that the relative ranking of specialization across industries is changing over time. For example, in 1980-1981 the most specialized industry was office and computing machinery, whereas in 1988-1989 it was aircraft and spacecraft, and yet in 1999-2000 it was the building of ships and boats. Also in some cases, we see that the RCA of an industry fluctuates without a clear trend. There are 13 industries whose RCA in 1988-1989 rose (fell) from the level in 1980-1981 and fell (rose) in 1999-2000. The reversal of specialization patterns implies that there is a continuous restructuring going on across industries in NAFTA countries. Therefore, the results might be misleading if one relies only on few years of data. This is one of the reasons why data for 21 years (1980-2000) in the econometric study in Section 4 has been used.

We can employ data in Table 5 to study the relationship of specialization with total value added and labour productivity. The association of the specialization index and total NAFTA value added by industry is shown in Figure 1. The plot shows that there is no association between these two variables, which

83

is a comforting result, especially because a negative relationship would suggest that the specialization index is very much influenced by the level of data aggregation.

Even though looking at the endpoints on the left hand side, suggests that there is a negative relationship, that is not the case for most of the industries. For example, the third smallest industry, railroad and transport equipment, is the fifth least specialized industry, whereas the second largest, food and beverages, is the sixth largest specialized industry.

The relationship between specialization and labour productivity shown in Figure 2 is slightly negative. This could be suggestive of the fact that the labour productivity differences among NAFTA countries might be larger for those industries whose overall labour productivity levels are low compared to those whose labour productivity levels are high. Put differently, technological catch up or convergence is probably faster in sectors with higher labour productivity levels, so that productivity differences are not very effective in affecting RCA in these industries, thereby keeping their specialization index low.

Next, we compute the country specialization index using the following formula:

$$ s_j = \sum_i \log_2 \left| RCA_{ij} \right| w_i, \qquad \text{where } w_i = \sum_j v_{ij} \bigg/ \sum_i \sum_j v_{ij} $$

The weight is industry i's share in NAFTA. The results for the country specialization index are given in Table 6, where we have also provided total value added and the share of value added for all three countries based on two different data sources. The first set of results presented under the column heading "at the two-digit level" use the same data source that we have used so far in this paper, the OECD's STAN database. According to this data, Canada and Mexico have comparable manufacturing sizes, and they have gained shares over time.

The results for the specialization index show that Mexico is the most specialized country, with an index of 2.06 in 1999-2000; Canada is the least specialized one, with the United States in the middle. Since the specialization index could be sensitive to the level of data aggregation, the country specialization index using ISIC 3-digit data with 59 manufacturing industries is also calculated. The results are reported under the column heading "at the 3-digit level" in Table 6. Since the historical data are not available at this level, the index was computed only for the years 1997 and 1999. As the data on 2-digit and 3-digit levels use different sources, these two estimates are not perfectly comparable. However, comparing the results allows us to make a point that even at 3-digit level, Mexico is the most specialized country, followed by the United States and then Canada.

It is clear from Table 6 that all three countries became more specialized in 1999-2000, compared to the situation in 1980-1981. However, all of them had reached a higher level of specialization previously, in 1988-1989. To understand the dynamics of specialization over time, Figure 3 plots specialization indices (based on 2-digit data) in the three countries for 21 years. The country specialization rose in the 1980s and started falling in the 1990s but did not fall all the way to the level from where it had started in the early 1980s. Put differently, the three NAFTA countries grew dissimilar in the decade of the 1980s, raising

84

their specialization level, but reversed this trend in the 1990s by becoming more similar (diversified) in their production structure.

Table 6. Specialization by Country

		At the two-digit level			At the three-digit level	
		1980-1981	1988-1989	1999-2000	1997	1999
Value added in billions of U.S.$	Canada	45,735	82,779	157,799	150,887	183,531
	U.S.	619,849	998,788	1,500,802	1,825,688	1,962,644
	Mexico	49,670	88,410	161,584	83,503	89,792
Share of value added (%)	Canada	6.40	7.08	8.67	7.32	8.21
	U.S.	86.67	85.37	82.46	88.62	87.78
	Mexico	6.93	7.56	8.88	4.05	4.02
Specialization index	Canada	1.36	1.47	1.44	1.58	1.67
	U.S.	1.51	1.63	1.58	1.67	1.70
	Mexico	1.91	2.10	2.06	3.62	3.78

Note: The data at the two-digit level are from the STAN database and those for the three-digit level are from Structural Statistics for Industry Services (SSIS) database of the OECD. These data are based on two different sources. SSIS uses data collected through annual industrial or business surveys supplementing them with censuses and with administrative sources. STAN attempts to provide data consistent with annual National Accounts using a wide range of data sources such as annual business surveys and/or censuses, as well as labour force surveys, business registers, income surveys, I/O tables. As a result, there is a difference in coverage between these two data sets. Some of these differences are as follows. Business surveys typically cover establishments and/or enterprises above a certain size limit (with more than a certain number of employees). Establishments with no employees are generally not covered. On the other hand, in National Accounts, attempts are made to get a more complete picture of industrial activity consistent with other accounts through the use of data coming from a variety of alternative sources mentioned above. However, adjustments and estimations carried out in countries may differ. Nevertheless, National Accounts (hence, STAN database) are traditionally considered more internationally comparable.

Figure 3. Country Specialization Indices

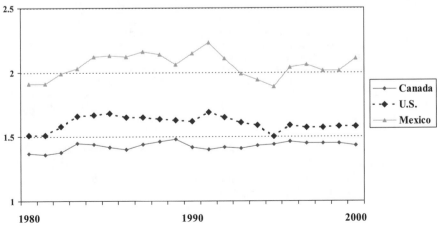

It is rather surprising that Canada has remained less specialized than the United States throughout the last two decades. This result is contrary to the generally held perception that bigger countries are less specialized. When looked at in the context of NAFTA, it makes sense why Canada is the least specialized country. In terms of productivity, the capital-labour ratio, skill intensity and R&D intensity Canada remains mainly in the middle, with United States as the leader in all indicators and Mexico is at the bottom. Hence it is not generally the case that industries will concentrate largely in Canada, unless natural resources are a factor in location, as in wood products where Canada has twice the size of its economic share (Table 3).

The above discussion helps to explain the specialization evident in manufacturing industries in three NAFTA partner countries. However, it does not explain how the bilateral production structure of these countries is changing. To assess this bilateral specialization index for these three countries, we use Krugman's index of regional specialization (RS). For a pair of countries j and j' it is defined as follows:

$$(2) \quad RS_{jj'} = \sum_{i=1}^{n} \left| \frac{e_{ij}}{e_j} - \frac{e_{ij'}}{e_{j'}} \right|,$$

where e_{ij} is the employment in industry $i = 1, ..., n$ for country j, e_j is total employment in country j and similarly for country j'. The index ranges from zero to two. If the index between countries j and j' is equal to zero, then the two countries are completely diversified; if the index is equal to two, then the countries are completely specialized. Using data at both 2-digit and 3-digit levels, we present the Krugman's index in Table 7.

Table 7. Krugman's Index of Regional Specialization

	ISIC 2-digit				ISIC 3-digit		
	1980	1990	1994	2000	1997	1998	1999
Canada-U.S.	0.31	0.28	0.29	0.27	0.33	0.32	0.36
Canada-Mexico	0.44	0.46	0.48	0.60	0.71	0.70	0.71
U.S.-Mexico	0.53	0.55	0.53	0.63	0.76	0.75	0.75

Source: OECD, STAN Database for the 2-digit level and SSIS Database for the 3-digit level.
Note: For the 2-digit level, the employment data for Mexico is headcounts of total employees, so it excludes the self-employed and unemployed family workers. For Canada, the data are number of jobs engaged in domestic production rather than headcounts. Therefore, Canadian employment data have both employed, self-employed and unpaid contributions but people with more than one job (full- or part-time) are counted more than once. For the United States, the employment data are total head counts of all persons who are engaged in domestic production. At the 3-digit level, there are altogether 59 industries. The employment data are in number of employees for Canada and the United States and total employment for Mexico.

Comparing the degree of specialization between Canada and the United States at the 2-digit level, we see that the two countries are becoming slightly more similar, as the specialization index fell from 0.31 in 1980 to 0.27 in 2000. However, Canada and Mexico and the United States and Mexico are becoming more dissimilar as the indices between this pair of countries rose over time.[8] Both levels of data show that among these three countries, the most similar ones are Canada and the United States, followed by Canada and Mexico, and by United States and Mexico.

Explanation of Specialization

So far, we have analyzed the specialization pattern that is taking place across industries and countries in the North American market. The next question is what is shaping this specialization pattern? What are its determinants? As discussed in Section 1, there are basically three trade theories, Ricardian, Heckscher-Ohlin, and increasing returns to scale that explain specialization across countries. In this section, we conduct an econometric test integrating all these three factors to determine their relative role in explaining specialization patterns in North America in the last two decades.

The variable suggested by the Ricardian model is relative technological differences across sectors in different countries. Since the data on technological differences are not available, differences in labour productivity are used to compute the Ricardian variable — revealed productivity advantage (RPA) — which is defined as follows.

$$(3) \qquad RPA_{ij} = \frac{y_{ij}/(y_i - y_{ij})}{y_j/(y - y_j)},$$

where $y_{ij} = v_{ij}/e_{ij}$ value added per employee in industry i for country j,

$y_i = \sum_j y_{ij} / \sum_j e_{ij}$ is NAFTA's value added in industry i;

$y_j = \sum_i y_{ij} / \sum_i e_{ij}$ is value added per employee in the manufacturing sector as a whole in country j; y is per employee value added for NAFTA (aggregate of all industries and countries).[9] As in RCA, we take out the industry and country size effects while computing RPA. Using this index, a country is said to have a Ricardian technological advantage in a sector if its productivity in that sector is high after adjusting for the sector and the country's general level of productivity. In a world of incomplete specialization, loosely speaking, this theory predicts that when a country becomes relatively more productive compared to other countries in a particular sector, the more productive country will increase its production share in that sector.

According to the Heckscher-Ohlin model, comparative advantage comes from the abundance of factor endowments. The theory states that, *ceteris paribus*, if a country is capital abundant (has a higher capital-labour ratio compared with another country), it will produce more of those goods which are more capital intensive in production. So a capital abundant country will have a higher

---

[8] The 3-digit level data show a somewhat different trend. But since there is no time lag in these data, we find 2-digit data more reliable to study changes over time.

[9] In this computation, I combine the value added and employment data that were used separately in the previous sections.

87

proportion of those goods which use capital more intensively and a labour abundant country will have more labour intensive goods. Among other things, a variable suggested by this theory is the capital-labour ratio, which we use in this paper (data-description is provided in Appendix 4).[10] Leamer (1997) estimates a similar model but using a country's overall value added per worker adjusted for the composition of output for the HO variable. He considers it an uncomfortable way of representing the HO model and suggests the capital-labour ratio as a better representation.

In addition, R&D intensities (share of business R&D expenses in gross output) are employed as another explanatory variable. The hope is that once the technological differences and factor abundance effects are controlled, whatever is left over to explain in the pattern of international specialization can be attributed to returns to scale. According to this theory, since average cost falls with the level of production, a country with a larger domestic market can produce at lower costs. And when opened for trade, the country with the larger domestic market will have a comparative advantage in foreign markets. Even in a free trade regime, as long as there are transport costs, there will still be a tendency for production to concentrate in a country where domestic markets are large. In NAFTA's context, it is probably the United States for which size might be a more helpful factor in raising industry concentration than for other countries.

There is not a single convincing way to represent the presence of increasing returns in an empirical test. There are studies using a measure of intra-industry trade as a proxy for it. However, Davis (1995) shows that intra-industry is also consistent with Ricardian and Heckscher-Ohlin explanations. In a series of papers, Davis and Weinstein (1999, 2003) run regressions for the share of a country's production on the share of its demand and interpret that if there were increasing returns to scale, there should be more than a one-for-one response in production as a result of a change in demand.[11] The method suggested by Davis and Weinstein (op cit.) could be a reasonable way of introducing returns to scale,

---

[10] Alternatively, we could have used the total manufacturing capital-labour ratio instead of industry-wide, but we opted for the latter hoping that this might capture the effects of both factor abundance and factor intensity differences.

[11] The more than proportionate change in production as a result of a change in demand occurs in a model of increasing returns to scale with transport costs. The argument goes as follows. In a world with increasing returns, typically each good is produced in only one location. When there are transport costs, a country with unusually strong demand for a good makes an excellent site for production. In order to save transport cost and enjoy the benefit of declining average cost with production, firm will be established in the market with relatively higher demand and export to the market where demand is relatively low. Thus if there are increasing returns to scale and transport costs, a strong demand can lead that country to export the good. However, in the traditional comparative advantage model, a strong demand leads to the imports of that good. To explain how it happens, let us take an extreme case of two countries with similar size, endowment and technology, but with different demand condition, one country consuming more of a good than the other country. The similarity of size, endowment and technology will dictate the country to produce the same goods in the same proportion in two countries. Hence, the country which have higher demand for one good should import that good from the country which have lower demand for it.

but it is not helpful for the present purpose. The reason is that with the data available, it is possible to have the estimate either for each industry (by pooling data over years) or for each year (by pooling data over industries). It is not possible to have both industry and year dimensions in the estimation, which are essential for this study.

In a recent paper, Antweiler and Trefler (2002) approach the problem using the factor content of trade. This is a novel approach; however, it requires input-output tables comprising all industries and years, which is not possible due to data limitations. Because of these difficulties with other approaches, R&D intensity is used as a proxy for increasing returns. Moreover, since the data on R&D expenses are not available for Mexico by industry, their total economy-wide R&D to GDP ratio is used to compute R&D expenses for each industry, such that industry R&D expenses are a constant fraction of its GDP (see Appendix 4 for data description).

We saw that specialization varies across countries and over time, so the model of cross-country variation in specialization should allow for country effects and time trends. We assume that there are industry specific time trends which are common across countries. In this case, pooling observations across countries is an efficient estimator. Using i to denote country, j to denote industry and t to denote time, and assuming that specialization patterns are log-linear, we have

$$
\text{(4)} \quad \ln\left(RCA_{ijt}\right) = \beta_{0j} + \beta_{1ij} + \beta_{2j}\, t + \beta_{3j} \ln\left(RPA_{ijt}\right) + \beta_{4j} \ln\left(k_{ijt}/l_{ijt}\right) + \beta_{5j} \ln\left(r_{ijt}/q_{ijt}\right) + \beta_{6j} NAFTA + u_{ijt}
$$

where β_{0j} is the intercept, β_{1ij} is fixed country effect, β_{2j} is coefficient for time trend, k is capital stock, l is labour employment, r is business expenditure on R&D and q is gross output. With data on RCA, RPA, capital-labour ratio, and R&D intensity, this equation is estimated over a panel of countries and years for industry j. For reference, the data on these explanatory variables for year 2000 are presented in Appendix 2. NAFTA is a dummy variable, which take the value of zero from years 1980 to 1993 and value of one from 1994 to 2000.

The estimates of equation (4) are reported in Appendix 3. The industries are sorted into five subgroups depending on the statistical significance of t-values of the Ricardian (RPA), Heckscher-Ohlin (k/l), and increasing returns to scale (R&D intensity) variables. First, there are four Ricardian industries with t-values significant only for the Ricardian variable. Then there are 11 industries with t-values significant for both the Ricardian and HO variables. The third subgroup consists of two industries with statistically significant impacts of the Ricardian and the increasing returns variables, which is followed by one HO and increasing return industry, the fourth subgroup. Finally, for the fifth subgroup of the remaining five industries, all three variables have significant effects on specialization. Within each subgroup, commodities are ordered by the adjusted R^{2}.[12]

---

[12] The high R^2 value in time series data indicates that there could be a unit root in the data series. Indeed, data series in many industries had unit roots suggesting that the data were nonstationary. They were stationary at the first difference, but since we wanted to check the regression results at the level form rather than at the first difference, we checked whether these series were cointegrated. We found that they were cointegrated and hence there was

The sectors which are only Ricardian are food and beverages, miscellaneous manufacturing, textiles and chemicals. For food and beverages, the coefficient for RPA is 0.58, meaning the value added of this sector rises by 0.58 percent with 1-percent increase in revealed labour productivity. Hence, if one moves from a less productive to a more productive country, the value added of this sector rises by 0.58 percent of the revealed labour productivity differences in the two countries. Similarly, for the other two industries (textiles and chemicals) the comparative advantage rises by moving from the less productive to more productive country. The elasticity of 1.23 for chemicals predicts that the value added of this industry rises by 23 percent more than the difference in labour productivity, as we move from a country with low labour productivity to the one with high productivity. For miscellaneous manufacturing, the comparative advantage runs in the opposite direction; it tends to be located in less productive countries.[13] This is a bit counterintuitive considering the fact that it consists mainly of medical and precision instruments.

Both the Ricardian and the HO factors have significant impact on specialization in eleven industries. The list includes: (1) machinery and equipment (2) non-metallic minerals (3) ship buildings (4) rubber and plastics (5) apparel (6) refined petroleum (7) fabricated metal (8) wood (9) railroad and transport equipment (10) pharmaceutical and (11) basic metals. The coefficients for the Ricardian variables are positive for 10 industries except apparel. Hence these 10 industries are expected to be concentrated in the more productive country; that is, the Ricardian comparative advantage rises from the low productive to the high productive country, except for apparel whose size falls as productivity rises. On the other hand, the negative coefficients on the capital-labour ratio for all 11 industries predict that these products are under-represented in countries with higher capital-labour ratios (HO effect).

This is an interesting result; the increase in labour productivity and capital intensity play opposite roles in determining the sizes of these industries in a country. Other things being the same, when we move from a more productive country (for example the United States) to a low productive country (for example

---

no spurious correlation. All industries passed the cointegrating regression Durbin Watson test, as computed DW statistics were higher than the critical value at the 5% level, thereby validating our estimation approach.

[13] If we look at RCA for 2000 in Table 3, Mexico is over-represented in food and beverages and textiles, whereas the U.S. is under-represented in both. However, in chemicals, it is the U.S. which has the larger than expected sector. Looking at Appendix 2, in absolute terms the U.S. is the most productive country in food and beverages, and chemicals and Canada in textiles. And according to the coefficients reported in Annex 3, all three sectors are predicted to concentrate in the more productive country. Then why are food and beverages not concentrated in the U.S. and textile in Canada rather than in Mexico? There are two possible reasons for this seemingly contradictory result. First, the results are driven not only by year 2000 but all 21 years of data. Second and more important, what matters is not the absolute sectoral productivity differences across countries, rather it is relative productivity differences across sectors compared with other countries. For example, even though Mexico is not the most productive country in food and beverages and textiles, it could be relatively more productive in these sectors compared with other sectors. Appendix 2 somewhat confirms this line of argument.

90

Mexico) the sizes of these sectors will fall, yielding higher (lower) than expected sizes for the United States (Mexico). On the contrary, as we move from a high capital intensive country such as the United States to a low capital intensive country such as Mexico, the prediction is that the sizes of all these sectors rises from its initial position causing under-representation in the United States and over-representation in Mexico. In the end, the equilibrium level of specialization would be determined out of these two conflicting forces — the Ricardian and the HO — one counterbalancing the other. On average, the most productive country, the United States, is also the most capital intensive, while the least productive country, Mexico, is also the least capital intensive. Since productivity and capital intensity have opposite effects cancelling each other, the restructuring of the industries is somewhat locked in without much effect in any country. That could be the reason why the specialization has not changed rapidly in North America.

Combined Ricardian and increasing returns variables have influenced two industries: leather and motor vehicles. The Ricardian effects state that for both sectors, the value added rises in more productive countries. However, R&D intensities show that leather tends to be located in a country with a low level of R&D intensity, whereas motor vehicles tend to be located in a high R&D intensive country. The location of production of electrical machinery and apparatus is driven by both HO and increasing returns. The value added of this sector increases by 13 percent if capital intensity rises by 100 percent and by 4 percent if R&D intensity rises by 100 percent.

All the three variables are significant in determining the production location of the remaining five industries, namely: (1) pulp, paper, printing and publishing (2) aircraft and spacecraft (3) radio, television and communication equipment (4) office and computing machinery, and (5) tobacco products. Based on the sign of prediction, these industries are expected to concentrate in the more productive, less capital intensive country (except for office and computing machinery) and high R&D intensive countries.

Note that among the five high-tech manufacturers listed in Table 4, the specialization in three industries (aircraft and spacecraft; radio, television and communication equipment; and office and computing machinery) is determined by all three factors. For the other two, the production location of medical, precision and optical instruments is determined by the Ricardian variable, and that of pharmaceuticals is determined by both Ricardian and HO variables.

In sum, out of 23 industries in the manufacturing sector, there is only one industry, electrical machinery, where the Ricardian variable is not statistically significant in determining production location. Among the 22 industries where revealed comparative advantage has significant effects, productivity superiority of a country leads to higher value added in all these industries except in miscellaneous manufacturing and apparel. The Heckscher-Ohlin model is statistically significant in a total of 17 industries. Out of these, having a higher capital-labour ratio leads to larger value added in only two industries, electrical machinery and apparatus and office and computing machinery. In all the other 15 industries, the predicted sizes fall with the increase in capital intensity. The third factor — R&D intensity — is statistically significant for eight industries, with positive effects in seven and negative in leather products. Out of these seven industries, five are high-tech and medium-high-tech sectors.

The results also show that there are no industries whose production location is determined either only by the HO effect or only by the increasing returns to scale effect. Office accounting and computing machinery is the only industry for which all three variables are positively statistically significant. Since the United States is the most productive, most capital intensive and most R&D intensive in this industry (Appendix 2), the prediction is that this industry will concentrate more in the United States; Canada and Mexico might further loose their shares with respect to this industry.

The NAFTA dummy is significant only for three industries, positively for refined petroleum and negatively for motor vehicles and trailers and radio, television and communication equipment. The NAFTA coefficient of 0.15 in refined petroleum means that NAFTA led to a one time 16 percent $\left(= e^{0.15} - 1\right)*100$ increase in specialization in this industry, whereas NAFTA decreased specialization in motor vehicles by 8 percent and in radio, television and communication equipment by 12 percent. Therefore, once we control all other gravitas of specialization, NAFTA did not have much additional impact. Trefler (1999) has reached a similar conclusion regarding the impact of the 1988 Free Trade Agreement on Canadian specialization. His study was not specially designed to estimate specialization, but he does it for Canada at the aggregate level (without any industry dimension) by computing the Herfindahl index.

Next, we look at the economic significance of these three factors in determining the specialization by computing the *beta* coefficient for each. Even though the elasticities (the coefficients in the log-linear model) are not susceptible to the units of measurements of the dependent and independent variables, we cannot rank the importance of the explanatory variables simply by comparing them. The reason is that the magnitude of change in the dependent variable due to change in an independent variable depends both on the coefficient and the *range* of data. A beta coefficient takes both these factors into account and tells the number of standard deviation changes in the dependent variable induced by a one standard deviation change in an independent variable. These statistics are useful in answering questions regarding which independent variables are important in determining movement in the dependent variable. The beta coefficient for an independent variable is obtained by multiplying its coefficient by the ratio of its standard deviation to the standard deviation of the dependent variable.

The beta coefficients are presented in Table 8, and the industries are reported in the same order as in Appendix 3. Comparing the absolute magnitude of beta coefficients of three variables, it is evident that the Ricardian model is the most important explanatory variables for eight industries, the HO for 11 industries and R&D intensity for the remaining four industries. Furthermore, the Ricardian model is the second most important explanatory variable for 12 industries, the HO for eight industries, and R&D intensity for the remaining three industries.

The last two columns of Table 8 rank the relative importance of three variables in determining specialization in each industry. Next, using the magnitude of beta coefficients of a variable across industries from this table, we can sort an industry list according to the importance of this variable in determining specialization in each industry. For example, the 10 industries which have the largest Ricardian impacts are: (1) refined petroleum (2) tobacco (3) chemicals (4) radio, TV and communication equipment (5) basic metals (6) rubber and plastics (7) pharmaceuticals (8) motor vehicles (9) other non-metallic metal, and (10) wood products. For all these industries, the beta coefficient for the Ricardian variable is larger than 0.5, with the highest at 1.16 for the refined petroleum industry. It means that if the standard deviation of labour productivity in refined petroleum increases by one standard deviation, the predicted value added of this industry rises by 1.16 standard deviation. This list shows that these are the industries whose production location is most responsive for a given change in the Ricardian variable. However, it does not necessarily mean that the Ricardian variable is the most important factor in determining specialization in these industries, compared to other variables.

Similarly, the 10 industries with largest HO effects are: (1) refined petroleum, (2) wood products (3) radio, TV and communication equipment (4) railroad and transport equipment (5) tobacco (6) apparel (7) pharmaceutical (8) chemicals (9) basic metals, and (10) fabricated metals. Note that seven of these industries also made the list of 10 industries which have the largest Ricardian effects. Similarly, the top five industries with highest increasing returns to scale are: (1) motor vehicle (2) aircraft and spacecraft (3) office accounting and computing machinery (4) radio, TV and communication equipment, and (5) chemicals.

With this discussion, the analysis of empirical results is complete. Based on the above results on specialization, we can now make some inference about the adjustment process that has taken place in North America. The nature of industrial restructuring and adjustment differs according to each country's economic structure and the forces that are at play. If the forces were only Ricardian in nature, the signing of NAFTA would not have had much benefit to a more productive country and would have had moderate adjustment costs for low skilled workers in such a country. In this case, the less productive country would be expected to have benefited from superior technology in partner countries helping wage convergence from below, but would not have been expected to benefit from its endowment differences. On the other hand, if the adjustment were only HO, there would have been a great gain from exchange, but also potentially great pressures on wages of the unskilled workers in the capital abundant country, the United States in this case. The poor country (Mexico) would have benefited from being able to expand output in low skilled intensive sectors, but with less benefit from potential technology transfer. Finally, if internal market size were the only determinant of production location, the United States would have attracted most of the production.

Table 8. Beta Coefficients and Determinants of Specialization

	Ricardian model (RPA)	HO model (k/l ratio)	IRS model (R&D intensity)	Important determinants of specialization	
				First	Second
Food and beverages	0.12	0.09	0.05	R	HO
Misc. manufacturing	-0.05	0.00	0.19	IRS	R
Textiles	0.32	0.11	0.04	R	HO
Chemicals excl. pharma	1.13	-0.50	0.71	R	IRS
Machinery and equipment	0.23	-0.28	-0.03	HO	R
Other non-metallic mineral	0.53	-0.20	0.05	R	HO
Building of ships & boats	0.34	-0.35	0.02	HO	R
Rubber and plastics	0.81	-0.44	0.23	R	HO
Wearing apparel	-0.25	-0.76	0.10	HO	R
Refined petroleum	1.16	-2.28	-0.12	HO	R
Fabricated metal	0.47	-0.45	0.24	R	HO
Wood products	0.52	-2.20	-0.10	HO	R
Railroad and transport equip.	0.36	-0.99	0.22	HO	R
Pharmaceuticals	0.71	-0.72	0.13	HO	R
Basic metals	0.85	-0.48	-0.21	R	HO
Leather products	0.13	0.14	-0.10	HO	R
Motor vehicles and trailers	0.55	0.01	1.26	IRS	R
Electrical machinery and apparatus	0.16	0.45	0.28	HO	IRS
Pulp, paper, printing and publishing	0.13	-0.34	0.33	HO	IR
Aircraft and spacecraft	0.21	-0.26	1.08	IRS	HO
Radio, TV & commu. equipment	0.92	-1.04	0.77	HO	R
Office and computing machinery	0.39	0.21	1.01	IRS	R
Tobacco products	1.15	-0.88	0.47	R	HO

R: Ricardian model
HO: Heckscher-Ohlin model
IRS Increasing returns to scale model

In other words, as Leamer (1997) has explained for advanced countries, the Ricardian framework is less robust with respect to explaining the economic gains but more so with respect to the adjustment problems. For less productive countries, this framework is more promising on the potential benefit of technology transfer, but less so on endowment benefit to them. On the other hand, the HO effect predicts larger economic gains and somewhat severe adjustment problems in developed countries. For a less developed country, it predicts benefits from the endowment effect without any possibility of technology transfer.

The interplay of these three factors in determining specialization, especially of Ricardian and Heckscher-Ohlin effects, indicates that the adjustment process of NAFTA was moderate; the end result fell somewhere between the two extremes suggested by the Ricardian and HO models. There were some benefits to reap from specialization for all countries as shown by the HO model; there were benefits from technology transfer; after all these factors are taken into account, there are only a few industries where size mattered.

Conclusions

We have measured the pattern of international specialization in 23 manufacturing industries that has taken place in the last two decades in the North American Free Trade Agreement (NAFTA) partner countries, Canada, the United States and Mexico. Results show that the degree of specialization varies across industries and countries. Some industries have become more concentrated, while others have become more uniformly distributed. But the patterns of specialization have no clear trend in many industries, indicating continuous dynamic forces at play.

Among the 23 manufacturing industries, except for electrical machinery, the Ricardian variable (represented by revealed productivity advantage) explains production location for all other 22 industries, the Heckscher-Ohlin (HO) (represented by capital-labour ratio) for 17 industries and increasing returns (represented by the ratio of R&D to gross production) for eight industries. For four industries, the specialization patterns are predicted only by the Ricardian variable, whereas for 19 other industries they are predicted either by two or all three variables. Among them, the specialization of 11 industries is the combined effects of the Ricardian and HO variables. Furthermore, Ricardian and increasing returns to scale variables predict the production location of two other industries. The production location of electrical machinery is determined jointly by HO and increasing returns to scale variables. For the remaining five industries, all three factors are significant in shaping specialization patterns. There is no industry whose production location is explained either only by HO or only by increasing returns to scale.

Except for apparel and miscellaneous manufacturing, the Ricardian effects are positive for all 20 industries indicating that these industries tend to concentrate in more productive countries. On the other hand, the HO effects are negative for 15 industries and positive only for two, electrical machinery and office accounting and computing machinery. It means that except for these two industries, the other 15 industries tend to be under-represented in more capital-intensive countries. Out of these 15, 10 are the industries whose specialization was determined also by the Ricardian variables, indicating that these sectors tend to concentrate in more productive countries. Among the eight industries where R&D intensity has played a role along with other variables in influencing production location, except in the case of leather products, the prediction is that having higher R&D intensity leads to higher value added in a country. Out of eight industries where R&D intensity is significant, five are high-tech and medium-high-tech sectors.

The Ricardian model is either the first or the second main determinant of specialization in 20 industries; the similar number for HO is 19 and for R&D intensity seven. Hence all three variables are effective in determining specialization patterns in NAFTA countries, which confirms Leamer's (1993) conjecture that both factor proportion and increasing returns to scale variables should be operative in the NAFTA countries. The NAFTA impacted the specialization patterns of only three industries, one positively and two negatively.

The impact of industrial restructuring differs among countries depending on productivity and capital intensity levels and the nature of forces that are driving the change. Ricardian and HO models generally predict opposite effects. Hence, the interplay of all three factors, especially of Ricardian and HO, in determining specialization indicates that the adjustment process of NAFTA was moderate, one factor lessening the effect of other. The impact fell somewhere between the two extremes suggested by the Ricardian and HO models. As a result, there were some benefits to reap from specialization for all countries as shown by the HO model; there were potential benefits to achieve from technology transfer as shown by technology differences as a very important factor for specialization in many industries. As the Ricardian effect counterbalanced this effect, there were not severe consequences on low paid workers in developed countries the HO model would suggest.

Even though all three variables affected specialization, in terms of industry counts and the level of value added the industries contribute, the Ricardian variable seems to be the most important. The predominant role of productivity differences in explaining specialization indicates that there are huge technological differences among NAFTA countries. And, even if there were convergence to productivity levels, it is probably slow. Had it not been so, productivity differences should not have had the enormous impact in determining the production location in so many industries for such a long period of time.

Bibliography

Antweiler, Werner and Trefler Daniel. (2002) "Increasing Returns and All That: A View from Trade." *American Economic Review*, March 2002, 92(2), pp. 93-119.

Bernstein, Jeffrey R. and Weinstein, David E. (2002) "Do Endowments Predict the Location of Production? Evidence from National and International Data." *Journal of International Economics*, January 2002, 56(1), pp. 55-76.

Bowen, Harry; Leamer, Edward E. and Sveikauskas, Leo. (1997) "Multicountry, Multifactor Tests of the Factor Abundance Theory"*American Economic Review*, December 1997, 77(5), pp. 791-809.

Brander, James A. (1981) "Intra-Industry Trade in Identical Products." *Journal of International Economics*, February 1981, 11(1), pp. 1-14.

Davis, Donald R. (1995) "Intra Industry Trade: A Heckscher-Ohlin-Ricardo Approach." *Journal of International Economics*, November 1995, 39(3-4), pp. 201-26.

Davis, Donald R. and Weinstein, David E. (2003) "Market Access, Economic Geography and Comparative Advantage: An Empirical Investigation." *Journal of International Economics*, January 2003, 59(1), pp. 1-23.

Davis, Donald R. and Weinstein, David E. (1999) "Economic Geography and Regional Production Structure: An Empirical Investigation." *European Economic Review*, February 1999, 43(2), pp. 379-407.

Davis, Donald R.; Weinstein, David E.; Bradford, S.C. and Shimpo, K. (1997) "Using International and Japanese National Data to Determine When the Factor Abundance Theory of Trade Works." *American Economic Review,* June 1997, 77(5), pp. 791-809.

Harrigan, James. (1997) "Technology, Factor Supplies, and International Specialization: Estimating the Neoclassical Model." *American Economic Review*, September 1997, 87(4), pp. 475-494.

_____. (1995) "Factor Endowments and International Location of Production: Econometric Evidence for the OECD, 1970-1985." *Journal of International Economics*, August 1995, 39(1-2), pp. 123-41.

Hunter, Linda C. and Markusen, James R. (1988) "Per Capita Income as a Determinant of Trade," in Robert C. Feenstra ed., *Empirical Methods for International Trade*. Cambridge: MIT Press, 1988, pp. 89-109.

Leamer E. Edward. (1997) "Evidence of Ricardian and Heckscher-Ohlin Effects in OECD Specialization Patterns," in Keith E. Maskus ed., *Quiet Pioneering: Robert M. Stern and His International Economic Legacy*. Ann Arbor: University of Michigan Press, 1997, pp. 11-35.

_____. (1993) "Factor-Supply Differences as a Source of Comparative Advantage." *American Economic Review,* May 1993, 83(2), 436-39.

_____. (1984) *Sources of International Comparative Advantage: Theory and Evidence*. Cambridge, MA: MIT Press, 1984.

Markusen, James R. (1986) "Explaining the Volume of Trade: An Eclectic Approach." *American Economic Review*, December 1986, 76(5), pp. 1002-11.

Trefler, Daniel. (1999) "The Long and Short of he Canada-U.S. Free Trade Agreement" Perspective on North American Free Trade, Industry Canada Research Publication, No 6, 1999.

_____. (1995) "The Case of Missing Trade and Other Mysteries." *American Economic Review*, December 1995, 85(5), pp. 1029-46.

_____. (1993) "International Factor Price Differences." *Journal of Political Economy*, December 1993, 101(6), pp. 961-87.

Appendix 1

International System of Industrial Classification (ISIC), Revision 3

ISIC Codes	Industry	ISIC Codes	Industry
15	Food products and beverages	28	Fabricated metal
16	Tobacco products	29	Machinery and equipment
17	Textiles	30	Office, accounting and computing machinery
18	Wearing apparel, dressing and dying of fur	31	Electrical machinery and apparatus
19	Leather, leather products and footwear	32	Radio, TV & communication equipment
20	Wood and products of wood and cork	33	Medical, precision and optical instruments
21	Pulp, paper and paper products	34	Motor vehicles, trailers and semi-trailers
22	Printing and publishing	35	Other transport equipment
23	Coke, refined petroleum products and nuclear fuel	351	Building and repairing of ships & boats
24 excl. 2423	Chemicals excluding pharmaceuticals	353	Aircraft and spacecraft
2423	Pharmaceuticals	352 + 359	Railroad equipment and transport equipment
25	Rubber and plastics products	36	Manufacturing, not elsewhere counted
26	Other non-metallic mineral products	37	Recycling
27	Basic metals	15-37	Total manufacturing

Appendix 2

The Values of Ricardian, Heckscher-Ohlin and Increasing Returns to Scale Variables in 2000

	Revealed productivity advantage (RPA)			Capital labour ratio (in thousands of US $ at PPP exchange rates)			Share of R&D in gross production (%)		
	Canada	U.S.	Mexico	Canada	U.S.	Mexico	Canada	U.S.	Mexico
Food and beverages	61	74	60	63	105	18	0.115	0.318	0.132
Tobacco products	323	605	76	130	289	38	0.005	0.009	0.002
Textiles	53	42	24	62	60	9	0.054	0.024	0.024
Wearing apparel	39	38	10	12	26	1	0.065	0.028	0.010
Leather products	32	48	20	28	39	4	0.006	0.002	0.006
Wood products	73	46	24	73	37	1	0.056	0.037	0.013
Pulp, paper, print and publishing	64	72	35	94	79	25	0.170	0.637	0.020
Refined petroleum	140	306	73	876	778	8	0.056	0.243	0.011
Chemicals excl. pharmaceutical	115	142	83	234	235	66	0.313	1.719	0.032
Pharmaceuticals	100	212	117	121	234	80	0.947	2.669	0.018
Rubber and plastics	62	58	24	49	70	16	0.102	0.349	0.015
Other non-metallic mineral	75	69	67	98	103	28	0.016	0.183	0.034
Basic metals	101	71	128	264	194	130	0.235	0.129	0.024
Fabricated metal	63	70	28	31	61	9	0.163	0.400	0.020
Machinery and equipment	71	62	30	31	67	15	0.392	1.395	0.017
Office and computing machinery	69	150	90	59	120	34	0.622	2.128	0.015
Electrical m. and apparatus	57	69	19	28	36	9	0.313	0.789	0.015
Radio, TV & commu. equipment	96	128	21	47	141	1	5.594	5.319	0.021
Motor vehicles and trailers	112	117	53	109	102	26	0.492	3.832	0.080
Building of ships & boats	44	45	5	54	65	5	0.100	0.100	0.000
Aircraft and spacecraft	109	94	44	44	81	0	1.257	2.128	0.001
Railroad and transport equip.	78	62	56	43	71	16	0.028	0.265	0.002
Misc. manufacturing	45	65	29	17	55	5	0.407	4.118	0.016
Total	**73**	**80**	**41**	**96**	**142**	**17**	**1.319**	**3.039**	**0.112**

Appendix 3

Estimates of the Specialization Equation, dependent variable log of specialization, 1980-2000

Independent variables	Constant	RPA	k/l ratio	R&D intensity	NAFTA	Adj. R^2	Best Model	
Food and beverages	1.24 (3.12)**	0.58 (5.23)**	0.05 1.40	0.06 1.19	-0.02 -0.94	0.99	R	
Misc. manufacturing	-0.30 -0.40	-0.11 (-2.57)*	0.00 -0.13	0.07 0.87	0.04 1.11	0.99	R	
Textiles	1.20 1.65	0.78 (3.90)*	0.06 0.85	0.07 0.89	0.02 0.30	0.97	R	
Chemicals excluding pharmaceuticals	0.45 0.87	1.23 (10.0)*	-0.05 -1.19	0.06 0.99	0.00 0.14	0.69	R	
Machinery and equipment	-0.86 (-3.59)**	0.89 (13.7)**	-0.12 (-12.1)**	-0.01 -0.44	0.00 0.01	0.99	R HO	
Other non-metallic mineral	1.30 (2.85)**	1.01 (5.79)**	-0.20 (-2.23)*	0.04 0.71	-0.01 -0.11	0.98	R HO	
Building of ships & boats	-1.47 (-3.13)**	0.54 (5.76)**	-0.31 (-4.47)**	0.01 0.30	0.15 1.55	0.97	R HO	
Rubber and plastics	0.24 1.03	0.89 (19.4)**	-0.06 (-3.73)**	0.03 1.07	0.00 0.37	0.96	R HO	
Wearing apparel	0.28 0.65	-0.28 (-6.54)**	-0.15 (-2.82)**	0.03 0.84	0.04 1.55	0.94	R HO	
Refined petroleum	0.72 1.93	0.91 (16.9)**	-0.42 (-7.28)**	-0.03 -0.81	0.15 (2.40)*	0.94	R HO	
Fabricated metal	0.36 0.92	0.90 10.04	-0.12 -5.96**	0.07 1.71	-0.04 -1.30	0.98	R HO	
Wood products	-0.67 (-3.23)**	0.93 (9.30)**	-0.41 (-4.81)**	-0.05 -1.88	0.08 1.40	0.90	R HO	
Railroad and transport equip.	0.94 1.72	0.35 (2.64)*	-0.35 (-8.98)**	0.08 1.50	0.07 0.89	0.89	R HO	
Pharmaceuticals	1.36 1.46	0.97 (8.24)**	-0.39 (-3.17)**	0.02 0.24	-0.04 -0.78	0.88	R HO	
Basic metals	-0.08 -0.10	0.58 (5.11)**	-0.22 (-2.59)*	-0.07 -0.86	-0.02 -0.37	0.88	R HO	
Leather products	-0.64 -0.69	0.82 (6.89)**	0.10 1.35	-0.23 (-2.56)*	-0.02 -0.40	0.99	R	IRS
Motor vehicles and trailers	3.11 (5.45)**	1.27 (17.1)**	0.00 0.05	0.30 (4.52)**	-0.08 (-2.07)*	0.96	R	IRS
Electrical m. and apparatus	0.11 0.67	0.11 0.75	0.13 (2.13)*	0.04 (2.08)*	0.00 -0.04	0.89	HO	IRS

101

Pulp, paper, printing and publishing	0.67 1.88	0.87 (10.1)**	-0.18 (-4.55)**	0.13 (3.15)**	0.03 1.24	0.99	R HO IRS	
Aircraft and spacecraft	2.72 (2.86)**	0.67 (6.10)**	-0.10 (-3.71)**	0.48 (5.78)**	0.10 1.12	0.99	R HO IRS	
Radio, TV & commu. equipment	1.70 (4.02)**	0.96 (12.7)**	-0.40 (-8.37)**	0.19 (4.43)**	-0.11 (-2.80)**	0.98	R HO IRS	
Office accounting and computing machinery	4.12 (3.27)**	0.94 (6.84)**	0.18 (3.11)**	0.47 (4.01)**	0.03 0.37	0.97	R HO IRS	
Tobacco products	4.56 (4.50)**	0.64 (9.49)**	-0.30 (-3.39)**	0.38 (4.34)**	0.01 0.14	0.94	R HO IRS	

There are 21 years (1980-2000) of data for each industry in each country. The three countries are pooled together; as a result the total number of observations is 63 for each regression. The dependent variable is the measure of specialization as defined by equation (1). The independent variables are revealed productivity advantage (RPA) as defined by equation (3), the capital-labour ratio (k/l ratio) in thousands of U.S. dollars at purchasing power parity exchange rates, and the ratio of R&D to gross production (R&D intensity). The dependent and these three independent variables are in log forms. The model was estimated using country dummies and a time trend, but theirs results are not included to conserve space. NAFTA is used as a dummy variable.

R: Ricardian model
HO: Heckscher-Ohlin model
IRS Increasing returns model

The t-values are given in parentheses
** indicates significant at 1 percent level
* indicates significant at 5 percent level

Appendix 4: Data Description

Capital stock

The capital stock data for Canada are taken from Statistics Canada's series on "fixed non-residential capital, geometric infinite year end net stock at current price" at North American industrial classification system (NAICS) and converted to the international system of industrial classification (ISIC) codes using NAICS to ISIC concordance given in OECD's database. The data are converted from Canadian dollars into U.S. dollars using purchasing power parity exchange rates.

For the United States, the capital stock data are from Table 3.1ES "Current-Cost Net Stock of Private Fixed Assets by Industry, year end estimates" of the Bureau of Economic Analysis (BEA)'s home page. These data were in U.S. SIC87, and we transferred them into ISIC Revision 3 using concordance given in OECD's structural analysis (STAN) database. For some industries that we are interested in, the BEA did not have separate data; sometimes two industries were aggregated into one. In that case, we used data on gross fixed capital formation (GFCF) in STAN database (which have all industries that we are using in this study) as a guideline to separate the combined capital stock data of BEA into two industries. For example, the capital stock data corresponding to industries ISIC-17 and ISIC-18 were combined in the BEA data set. However, these industries have separate data on GFCF in the STAN database. Using these STAN data, we computed the total GFCF of these two industries and their shares in this total. And according to these shares, we distributed the combined capital stock data of BEA into ISIC-17 and ISIC-18 industries. A similar approach was adopted for ISIC industries 29 and 30, industries 31 and 32.

For Canada we use data on *non-residential* series and for the U.S. we use data on private capital. Even though *private* capital includes both residential and non-residential capital in the private sectors, in terms of manufacturing, the private capital stock is equal to non-residential capital stock, as there is no residential capital in manufacturing industries. Therefore, the two series that we have used for Canada and the U.S. are comparable for manufacturing industries. Furthermore, in manufacturing sectors, all capital stock data are private, as the government sector has no capital stock in manufacturing.

The capital stock data for Mexico is computed using data on GFCF from World Bank's "Trade and Production Database" from 1976 to 1991 and beyond 1991 we use data on investment from the OECD's structural statistics for industry and services (SSIS) database. The data on SSIS were in Mexican Pesos and were converted into U.S. dollars using purchasing power parity exchange rates. To generate capital stock data from GFCF and investment, we use the following method. For example, the net capital stock in base year 1976 (subscript of zero) is calculated using the following mechanism:

$$k_0 = I_0/(\delta + g),$$

where g is the average growth rate of investment over the entire period, δ is the depreciation rate, k_0 is the capital stock at base year 1976 and I_0 is the

103

investment in base year 1976. For the subsequent years, the data are computed using the following formula:

$k_t = I_t + (1 - \delta)k_{t-1}$, where t runs from year 1977 to 2000.

R&D Data

For both Canada and the U.S., the R&D data are obtained from OECD's analytical business enterprise research and development (ANBERD) database from 1987 to 2000. However, for years 1980 to 1986 we use data from U.S. National Science Foundation (USNSF) for the U.S. and Statistics Canada for Canada. Since the USNSF data were in U.S. SIC87 codes and Canadian data were in Canadian SIC81, they were converted into ISIC revision 3.

However there were some industries which did not have data and were aggregated with other industries. For example, for the U.S., for ISIC 15 and 16 industries, the data were aggregated for some years and were given separate for other years. We decompose the data that were in aggregate using the proportion of data from the year they were given separately. A similar approach was adopted for ISIC industries 17, 18 and 19 and for ISIC industries 20 whose data were given along with industries ISIC 21 and 22. The data on ISIC 351 was appropriated as the difference of R&D value on aggregate manufacturing and the R&D sum of all other industries. A similar approach was adopted for Canada.

For Mexico, there were no industry R&D data. I took the share of economy-wide R&D to GDP ratio from the OECD's main science and technology indicator (MSTI) and computed the total R&D by industry simply by multiplying this ratio by industry GDP.

For the study, all R&D data were converted to the same unit of measurement using purchasing power parity exchange rates.

104

The Effect of Trade on Productivity Growth and the Demand for Skilled Workers in Canada

Wulong Gu	&	Lori Whewell Rennison
Statistics Canada		Department of Finance

Introduction

The last two decades have witnessed growing trade integration between Canadian industries and those in the United States and elsewhere. The ratio of exports to gross domestic product in the Canadian business sector rose from 35.3 percent in 1981 to 52.6 percent in 1997, while the ratio of imports to gross domestic product increased from 37.2 percent to 51.3 percent. Most of the increase in trade integration occurred in the 1990s after two major policy developments: the implementation of the Canada-U.S. Free Trade Agreement (FTA) in 1989, which led to the gradual removal of trade barriers between Canada and the United States, and the North American Free Trade Agreement (NAFTA) in 1994, which expanded the free trade area to Mexico.

In this paper, we examine the implications of this marked increase in trade integration on productivity and the demand for skilled workers in Canada over the past two decades. Increased trade integration institutionalized and expanded by the FTA were expected to significantly improve Canadian productivity — as industries benefited from further specialization and economies of scale and as resources were reallocated to more efficient industrial pursuits. Similarly, the increased volume of international trade with low-wage countries was expected to increase the demand for skilled workers relative to unskilled workers as the production of less skill-intensive goods shift to the low-wage countries. In this study, we examine the extent to which these effects have taken place.

To examine the effect of trade integration on productivity growth, this study departs from most previous empirical studies. Typically, empirical studies on trade and productivity capture only the productivity impacts on export and import industries. However, trade integration affects more than just the productivity of industries directly involved in trade. It also affects supplier industries. To properly assess the impact of trade integration on productivity growth requires the analysis of productivity impacts at all stages of production. For this reason, we use the effective rate of productivity growth to examine the relationship between trade integration and productivity growth.

---

* We would like to thank John Baldwin, Gary Sawchuk and an anonymous referee for their helpful comments. This paper reflects the views of the authors and not those of Statistics Canada or of the Department of Finance.

The effective rate of productivity growth in exports and imports captures the direct productivity gains of sectors involved in trade as well as those associated with industries that supply intermediate inputs to export and import industries. The concept of an effective rate of productivity was introduced by Sraffa (1960) and has been used by Rymes (1972), Hulten (1978), and Wolff (2003). De Juan and Febrero (2000) argue for the use of the effective rate of total factor productivity growth to better measure competitiveness.

To examine Canada's comparative advantage in international trade and the effect of trade on the demand for skilled workers, we follow the factor content of trade approach. We use an input-output model to determine how much skilled and unskilled labour Canada uses in producing its exports, and how much labour would have been used had its imports been produced in Canada. The difference between the skilled and unskilled labour content of exports and imports provides a measure of the impact of trade on the demand for skilled and unskilled workers.

The share of skilled workers in Canada's exports relative to that in imports also sheds light on where Canada's comparative advantage lies in international trade. According to the Heckscher-Ohlin-Vanek model, trade specialization and comparative advantage result from relative factor abundance (Vanek, 1968; Deardorff, 1982). A country will export products that use intensively those factors in which it is relatively abundant and import those products that use intensively those factors in which it is relatively scarce. It is thus believed that Canada has a comparative advantage in goods and services intensive in natural resources. However, Canada also has the highest share of workers with post-secondary education among the OECD countries (OECD, 2004). The share of Canadians with a university degree is below that of the U.S., its major trading partner, but Canada exceeds all other countries once other forms of post-secondary education are included. Thus, human capital might also be expected to be a growing source of Canada's comparative advantage.

Review of Previous Empirical Literature

A large number of studies have examined the effect of trade on productivity growth. The studies using aggregate data demonstrate that access to foreign intermediate inputs and capital goods through imports is associated with higher productivity (e.g., Eaton and Kortum, 2001; Gera, Gu and Lee, 1999). This evidence supports the view that imports act as a conduit for knowledge transfer across countries. However, most of these studies focus on imports and use the black-box approach that relies on aggregate data.

A number of recent empirical studies use micro data to examine the effect of exports on productivity growth. These studies provide mixed evidence. While Bernard and Jensen (2004) find that there is little to suggest that exports have a positive effect on productivity growth in U.S manufacturing plants, Baldwin and Gu (2001, 2004), however, show that exports lead to productivity improvements in Canadian manufacturing plants.

A number of studies in Canada have examined the effect of trade liberalization and increased trade integration on productivity growth (Trefler, 2004; Baldwin, Caves and Gu, 2005). Trefler (2004) finds that the Canada-U.S. FTA increased labour productivity in the Canadian manufacturing sector. He

106

shows that those industries with the largest tariff cuts experienced the greatest increases in labour productivity growth during the post-FTA period. Baldwin, Gu and Caves (2005) show that Canadian plants became more specialized in output as a result of trade liberalization. The increased product specialization and the exploitation of scale economies are an important source of productivity gains from the FTA.

The issue of whether increased trade with low-wage countries has hurt unskilled workers has become a topical area of research in Canada and other developed countries. Wood (1991) argues that increased trade with developing countries is the main cause of the widening wage gap between skilled and unskilled workers in developed countries. Sachs and Shatz (1996) conclude that trade with developing countries has reduced the demand for unskilled workers. In a survey of empirical evidence, Baldwin (1995) finds that domestic factors have been much more important in accounting for changes in total employment in Canada than changes in the demand for imports. However, he concludes that increased imports were a major factor in accounting for employment declines in such low-technology industries as textiles, clothing, footwear, wood and furniture.

Regarding skills and human capital as a source of comparative advantage for developed countries, Lee and Schluter (1999) use an input-output model and occupational data to estimate the skill content of U.S. trade over the period 1972-1992. They find that the ratio of high-skilled to low-skilled workers was greater for exports than for imports, although the difference between the ratios was unchanged over the period. Moreover, the difference between the skilled and unskilled employment content of exports and imports was quite small suggesting that trade was not a contributing factor to changes in the demand for skilled and unskilled workers in the U.S.

Wolff (2003) also examined skill content and comparative advantage in U.S. international trade for the period 1947-1996 using input-output data and an occupation-based measure of skill. He finds that U.S. exports have a high content in cognitive and interactive skills relative to imports, and a low content in motor skills. In contrast to Lee and Schulter (1999), the analysis shows that the skill gap between exports and imports has widened over time, primarily due to changes in the composition of U.S. exports and imports. The results suggest that the U.S. comparative advantage in international trade lies in cognitive and interactive skill-intensive products, and the comparative advantage in cognitive and interactive skills increased over time. Wolff (2003) further found that imports are more capital-intensive and R&D-intensive than exports. However, in the case of capital intensity, he finds that the difference has decreased over time. This suggests that there has been a gradual shifting of U.S. comparative advantage toward capital-intensive goods.

Webster (1993) looked at the skill content and comparative advantage in U.K. international trade. He found that the U.K. tended to export goods and services that are intensive in non-manual skills (professional occupations). This indicates that skills and broad levels of human capital are an important source of the UK's comparative advantage. Driver et al. (2001) used an input-output model to examine the effect on employment of various changes in trade structure in the U.K. They found that radical changes in the U.K. trade pattern (e.g. adopting the

107

trade pattern of West Germany) would lead to large employment gains. Engelbrecht (1996) estimated the skill content of German exports and imports in 1976, 1980 and 1984. In contrast to the evidence for the U.K (Webster, 1993), he concluded that comparative advantage for Germany resulted more from specialization in particular skill types than from the overall level of human capital. Germany tended to export goods and services intensive in skilled manual occupations.[1]

While there is a considerable empirical literature for the U.S. and other countries, there is little recent empirical evidence on the skill content and comparative advantage in Canada's international trade. This paper provides such evidence.

Methodology

Our method for calculating the factor content of trade is based on an input-output model. The method dates back to the work of Leontief (1956, 1964) and continues to be a standard method for examining the factor content and comparative advantage in international trade (Wolff, 2003; Webster, 1993; and Hans-Jurgen, 1996). In this section, we first present the method for estimating the factor content of Canadian exports and imports. The method is based on the total (direct plus indirect) factor requirements of exports and of the domestic substitutes for imports. We then use the total factor requirements of exports and imports to calculate the effective rate of partial factor and total factor productivity in export and import industries.

The starting point for the construction of the factor content of trade is the fundamental input-output relationship:

(1) $\quad X = BX + C + E - M$.

The column vector $X = \lfloor X_j \rfloor_{N \times 1}$ represents the gross output of industry j, where N denotes the number of industries. The input-output matrix $B = \lfloor b_{ij} \rfloor_{N \times N}$ denotes the quantity of goods in industry i used in the manufacturing of one unit of output in industry j. The vector $C = \lfloor C_j \rfloor_{N \times 1}$ is domestic consumption of the output of industry j and includes personal consumption, fixed investment and government consumption. Industry exports and imports are shown by the export and import vectors $E = \lfloor E_j \rfloor_{N \times 1}$ and $M = \lfloor M_j \rfloor_{N \times 1}$.

In equation (1), column vector BX is the intermediate input demand for an industry's output. The remaining terms on the right-hand side are the final domestic demand for the industry output.

To determine the gross output of Canadian industries for a given level of final demand, we take into consideration "import leakages." These are leakages from final demand that occur when some final demand is met from imports

---

[1] A number of studies have also estimated the factor content of trade for emerging economies (e.g. Ohno, 1988).

108

instead of domestic production. To do so, we assume that imports of an industry are proportional to domestic production less exports:[2]

(2) $M = m(X - E)$.

A typical element m_j of the diagonal matrix $m = diag(m_j)$ gives the ratio of imports to domestic production net of exports in industry j.

Therefore, equation (1) may be re-written as

(3) $X = BX + C + E - m(X - E)$.

Solving for gross output X, we have:

(4) $X = (I - B + m)^{-1}(C + (1+m)E)$,

where I is an identity matrix. X in Equation (4) is the gross output levels that are required to satisfy final demand. Let us define:

$k = [k_1, k_2, ..., k_N]$ = row vector of capital coefficients, where k_j is total capital per unit of output in industry j,

$l = [l_1, l_2, ..., l_N]$ = row vector of labour coefficients, where l_j is the total labour per unit of output,

$s = [s_1, s_2, ..., s_N]$ = row vector showing natural-resource intermediate inputs per unit of output,

$w = [w_1, w_2, ..., w_N]$ = row vector showing labour compensation in 1992 dollars per unit of output.

The total capital, labour and natural resource content of final demand is calculated as:

(5) $K = k(I - B + m)^{-1}(C + (1+m)E)$,

(6) $L = l(I - B + m)^{-1}(C + (1+m)E)$, and

(7) $S = s(I - B + m)^{-1}(C + (1+m)E)$.

The total labour compensation in final demand is calculated as:

(8) $W = w(I - B + m)^{-1}(C + (1+m)E)$

On the basis of the total capital and labour contents in exports, we can estimate the effective rate of capital and labour productivity in export industries. The effective rate of capital productivity in exports is defined as output per unit of total capital requirements in exports. It is given by

---

[2] Previous studied have used alternative assumptions about imports. Lahr (2001) and Jackson (1998) assumed that imports are proportional to the sum of domestic production and net imports. St. Louis (1989) assumed that imports are proportional to the sum of domestic production and total imports. We have used these two alternative assumptions about imports in our empirical analysis. Our findings on the sources of comparative advantage and the effect of trade on productivity and the demand for skilled workers are robust to these alternative assumptions.

$E / \left[k \left(I - B + m \right)^{-1} \left((1 + m)E \right) \right]$. The effective rate of labour productivity in exports is defined as output per unit of total labour requirements in exports, and is given by $E / \left[l \left(I - B + m \right)^{-1} \left((1 + m)E \right) \right]$. The effective rate of total factor productivity in exports is calculated as a weighted sum of capital and labour productivity using the share of capital and labour in total income as weights.[3]

To examine the comparative advantage in Canada's international trade, we need to calculate the factor content of imports. To do so, we require the input-output matrices of the import-producing countries. However, those matrices are not available. As in most previous studies, we instead use the Canadian input-output matrices to estimate the factor content of Canadian imports. The estimated factor content of Canadian imports thus measure how much capital and labour would have been required if the imported goods had been produced in Canada.

Data

The data for the analysis consist of input-output tables, capital stock and labour inputs from Statistics Canada. The original input-output tables are 147-sector input-output tables in nominal dollars for the years 1981, 1989 and 1997. The tables are aggregated to 123 business sector industries to be consistent with the industry aggregation for data on capital and labour inputs. We have chosen those three years so as to compare the factor content of trade and productivity growth between pre-FTA period 1981-1989 and post-FTA period 1989-1997.

Capital stock figures represent net capital stock in 1992 dollars, start-of-year estimates. It is calculated using a perpetual inventory method and geometric depreciation pattern (for details, see Statistics Canada, 1994). Data on the labour input include hours worked and labour compensation at the 123 industries of the business sector. They are derived from the labour input database in the Statistics Canada productivity account (see, Gu et al., 2003). The data base classifies workers by four educational attainment levels: 0-8 years of schooling, high school, post-secondary and university or above. We will use this classification to measure the skill content of Canada's international trade.

The Composition of Canada's international trade

The percentage composition of Canada's exports and imports is shown in Tables 1A and 1B. In general, Canada's international trade has been shifting away from primary industries toward manufacturing and services over the past several decades. Manufacturing increased from 65% of total exports in 1981 to 71% by 1997, as services' share rose from 14% to 18%. As a result, the share of exports in primary industries fell from 21% to 11%. Similar shifts were observed in imports.

---

[3] For the remainder of the paper, all references to productivity rates refer to effective rates.

110

Table 1A: Percentage Composition of Canadian Exports

	1981	1989	1997	Change, 1981-1997
Primary	20.72	13.32	11.43	-9.30
Manufacturing	65.11	70.89	70.93	5.82
Services	14.17	15.78	17.65	3.48
By detailed industry (ranked by change over 1981-97)				
Transportation equipment	17.41	24.42	23.47	6.06
Electrical & electronic products	3.36	5.34	6.63	3.27
Business services	1.56	1.99	3.10	1.54
Wholesale	2.33	3.15	3.69	1.36
Wood	4.00	4.12	5.24	1.24
Chemical & chemical products	3.20	3.45	4.14	0.94
Plastic	0.41	0.68	1.21	0.80
Finance & insurance	1.44	2.25	2.21	0.77
Furniture & fixtures	0.35	0.53	0.84	0.49
Clothing	0.43	0.44	0.81	0.39
Rubber	0.61	0.77	0.93	0.32
Printing & publishing	0.27	0.46	0.54	0.27
Primary textile	0.35	0.35	0.62	0.27
Textile products	0.19	0.27	0.36	0.17
Retail	0.08	0.16	0.20	0.12
Non-metallic mineral products	0.57	0.75	0.68	0.11
Other services	3.38	3.72	3.46	0.08
Transportation services	3.59	3.13	3.64	0.05
Leather & allied products	0.14	0.14	0.16	0.01
Construction	0.03	0.03	0.01	-0.02
Tobacco	0.16	0.09	0.10	-0.06
Fabricated metal	3.00	2.32	2.93	-0.07
Fishing, logging & forestry	0.35	0.29	0.25	-0.10
Beverage	0.42	0.32	0.32	-0.10
Other manufacturing	1.96	1.69	1.70	-0.25
Communication & other utilities	1.76	1.37	1.35	-0.41
Machinery	3.73	2.71	3.29	-0.45
Food	4.22	3.42	3.61	-0.61
Refined petroleum & coal	2.29	1.26	1.27	-1.02
Crude petroleum & natural gas	7.50	4.88	5.47	-2.04
Primary metal	8.80	8.32	5.89	-2.92
Paper & allied products	9.22	9.04	6.17	-3.05
Agriculture & related services	6.36	2.98	3.03	-3.33
Metal mines & other mines	6.51	5.18	2.67	-3.83

Table 1B: Percentage Composition of Canadian Imports

	1981	1989	1997	Change, 1981-1997
Primary	14.22	6.08	5.19	-9.03
Manufacturing	72.80	78.74	79.07	6.27
Services	12.98	15.17	15.74	2.76
By detailed industry (ranked by change over 1981-97)				
Electrical & electronic products	8.49	12.51	13.58	5.09
Transportation equipment	19.87	22.91	21.83	1.97
Chemical & chemical products	4.38	4.84	6.22	1.84
Finance & insurance	2.14	3.08	3.29	1.15
Communication & other utils.	0.51	1.22	1.29	0.78
Plastic	1.02	1.44	1.50	0.49
Other services	4.20	4.96	4.68	0.48
Business services	2.71	2.75	3.10	0.38
Clothing	1.46	2.23	1.82	0.36
Paper & allied products	1.46	1.56	1.76	0.31
Rubber	0.85	1.08	1.15	0.30
Printing & publishing	1.07	1.67	1.35	0.29
Food	2.99	2.92	3.05	0.06
Textile products	0.81	0.77	0.86	0.05
Furniture & fixtures	0.59	0.82	0.64	0.05
Tobacco	0.07	0.10	0.12	0.04
Wood	0.71	0.66	0.75	0.03
Transportation services	2.36	2.13	2.39	0.03
Wholesale	0.89	0.88	0.91	0.02
Beverage	0.33	0.33	0.31	-0.02
Retail	0.12	0.11	0.09	-0.04
Construction	0.05	0.04	0.01	-0.04
Leather & allied products	0.85	1.04	0.76	-0.09
Fishing, logging & forestry	0.36	0.23	0.25	-0.11
Non-metallic mineral products	1.16	1.33	1.03	-0.13
Refined petroleum & coal	1.24	1.46	1.04	-0.19
Fabricated metal	5.18	4.22	4.97	-0.21
Primary textile	1.55	1.27	1.12	-0.43
Other manufacturing	4.25	3.80	3.66	-0.58
Agriculture & related services	1.97	1.42	1.12	-0.85
Primary metal	5.53	4.17	4.34	-1.19
Metal mines & other mines	2.82	1.98	1.27	-1.55
Machinery	8.96	7.58	7.22	-1.75
Crude petroleum & natural gas	9.06	2.45	2.54	-6.52

Transportation equipment was the most important traded good in Canada over the 1981 to 1997 period by a large margin, accounting for more than 20% of both exports and imports. Moreover, its share of exports increased by more than any other industry over the period. While four of the top five leading Canadian exports in 1981 were also among the top five in 1997 (transportation equipment, 23%; paper and allied products, 6.1%; primary metals, 5.9%; and crude petroleum and natural gas, 5.5%), there were two notable shifts over the period. First, the biggest gains (after transportation equipment) were made by electrical and electronic equipment, from 3.4% to 6.6%, becoming one of Canada's top five exports by 1989. Business services, wholesale, and wood industries also increased their share of total exports by more than a percentage point over the 1981-1997 period. Second, mining and agricultural industries were among the leading exports in 1981 but have steadily declined in importance, losing approximately half of their share of total exports by 1997. Mining industries fell from 6.5% to 2.7%, while agriculture and related services dropped from 6.4% to 3%. Other industries which lost significant share over the period included crude petroleum and natural gas, primary metals and paper and allied products. Nevertheless, these three industries remained among the most important Canadian exports in 1997.

Turning to imports, the leading imports in 1997 after transportation equipment (21.8%) were electrical and electronic equipment (13.6%), machinery (7.2%), and chemicals and chemical products (6.2%). Electrical and electronic products made the biggest gains, growing from 8.5% of total imports in 1981 to 13.6% in 1997. Significant gains were also made in chemicals and chemical products and in finance and insurance. The industry that lost the largest share over the period was crude petroleum and natural gas, as imports fell from 9.1% in 1981 to 2.5% in 1997 (with the shift occurring between 1981 and 1989).

In summary, the composition of Canada's international trade, in the period under review, has shifted away from primary industries toward manufacturing and services. The auto sector accounted for the largest share of Canadian exports and imports throughout the 1981 to 1997 period, and the electrical and electronic products industry became an increasingly important part of both Canada's exports and imports. The change in export and import composition was similar across the period; the correlation between 1981 and 1997 export and import shares is 0.94 and 0.93 respectively.

Skill Composition of Canada's Exports and Imports

Based on the methodology described in Section 3, we now examine the factor content of Canadian exports and imports. The results for skill composition, shown in Table 2, are a bit surprising. Based on our measure of skills (educational attainment), the data suggest that human capital is not a source of comparative advantage in Canada's international trade. Rather, skill composition over the period 1981-1997 is similar for exports, imports and the total business sector. In particular, Canadian exports were not more skill-intensive than Canadian imports over this period. For instance, in 1997, the share of workers with bachelor degrees or above in exports was 15 percent, and the share of those workers in imports was 16 percent. When we include those workers with other types of post-secondary tertiary education, we find that that the share of more educated workers in exports was 56 percent, compared with 57 percent in imports.

Moreover, the share of workers with some form of post-secondary education in Canadian exports and imports showed similar increases over the 1981-1997 period, those in exports increased from 39 percent to 56 percent, and in imports increased from 41 percent to 57 percent.

Table 2: Skill Content of Canadian Exports and Imports

	1981	1989	1997	Change, 1981-1997
A. Share of hours with less than high school (%)				
Exports	16.26	10.49	6.09	-10.18
Imports	14.67	10.02	5.69	-8.98
Difference	1.60	0.47	0.40	
Business Sector	14.27	9.09	5.13	-9.14
B. Share of hours with high school (%)				
Exports	45.00	44.69	37.72	-7.27
Imports	44.40	44.27	36.94	-7.46
Difference	0.60	0.43	0.79	
Business Sector	46.30	44.85	37.06	-9.24
C. Share of hours with post-secondary education (%)				
Exports	30.70	34.01	41.00	10.30
Imports	31.90	34.33	41.58	9.69
Difference	-1.20	-0.32	-0.59	
Business Sector	31.38	35.15	42.63	11.25
D. Share of hours with university or above (%)				
Exports	8.04	10.80	15.19	7.15
Imports	9.04	11.37	15.79	6.75
Difference	-1.00	-0.57	-0.60	
Business Sector	8.05	10.91	15.18	7.14

The results stand in sharp contrast to those reported in similar studies for the U.S. and the U.K. where skills and human capital are identified as sources of comparative advantage (Lee and Schulter, 1999; Wolff, 2003; Webster, 1993), in the case of the U.S. the comparative advantage in skill-intensive industries increased over time (Wolff, 2003). However, there are several things to bear in mind in interpreting these results. First, other studies measure skills based on occupation rather than on educational levels as we do in this paper. For example, Wolff (2003) uses occupation data which allows him to distinguish between substantial complexity, interactive and motor skills – these results need not be the same as those based on education levels which have been rising among workers in all sectors over the past two decades. Indeed, when Wolff (2003) measures skills by mean educational attainment he finds that the U.S. comparative advantage in skill-intensive industries has been constant since 1950, contrary to his results based on occupational data. Wolff suggests that this might be explained by the fact that schooling levels among the United States' trading partners have increased faster than the cognitive skill content of their exports to the United States.

Second, the composition of Canada's international trade is different from that in the United States, and has evolved differently over time. While Canada's exports have been shifting away from natural resources toward manufacturing and services, primary industries continue to represent a larger share of Canada's exports than in the United States. The share of workers with post-secondary education in hours worked tend to be lower in these industries – 42% versus 67% for manufacturing industries such as electrical and electronic products which comprise a larger share of U.S. exports. Moreover, less knowledge-intensive industries such as clothing and textile products represent a larger share of U.S. imports than Canadian imports, which lowers the skill content of their imports relative to their exports.

Despite these differences, the finding that Canada has a comparative disadvantage in skills may simply reflect the fact that Canada has a smaller pool of workers with a university degree. Despite the larger share of those with other forms of post-secondary education in Canada, the U.S. studies may be capturing skills that require university education in specific knowledge fields which are less prevalent in Canada. In this sense, it wouldn't be surprising that the U.S. has a comparative advantage in skills while Canada does not; rather, it would be consistent with the view that comparative advantage stems from relative factor abundance.

Capital Intensity of Canada's Exports and Imports

Panel A of Table 3 shows the capital intensity of Canadian exports and imports. The results show that Canadian exports were more capital intensive than were Canadian imports over the period 1981-1997. In 1997, the capital intensity of Canadian exports was 53 percent higher than that of Canadian imports. This suggests that the comparative advantage in Canada's international trade has been in capital-intensive industries, and that capital is a source of comparative advantage for Canada.

It must be noted, however, that over the period 1989-1997, the capital intensity of exports relative to imports declined from 1.7 to 1.5. This indicates a gradual shifting of Canada's comparative advantage away from capital-intensive goods and services in the 1990s. For the period 1981-1989, there was little change in the relative capital intensity of exports and imports.

Panels B, C and D of Table 3 show results for total net capital stock of equipment and structures per hour worked. We find that Canada tended to export goods and services that were more intensive in both equipment capital and structure capital. This means that equipment capital and structure capital are sources of comparative advantage for Canada. In 1997, the capital intensity of exports relative to imports was 1.5 for equipment capital, 1.1 for building structure, and 1.7 for engineering structure.

While Canada's comparative advantage in capital-intensive industries declined in the 1990s, comparative advantage in engineering structure capital increased during the period. The results in Panel D of Table 3 show that the

115

engineering-structure intensity of exports relative to imports increased from 1.70 to 1.74 during the period 1989-1997.

Table 3: Capital Intensity of Canadian Exports and Imports

	1981	1989	1997	Ratio of 1997 to 1981
	A. Total capital (in 1992 dollar) per hour worked			
Exports	65.80	74.41	75.06	1.14
Imports	48.72	51.19	53.75	1.10
Ratio	1.71	1.72	1.53	
Business Sector	38.45	43.17	49.02	1.27
	B. M&E capital (in 1992 dollar) per hour worked			
Exports	17.86	20.52	21.00	1.18
Imports	12.97	15.22	17.03	1.31
Ratio	1.80	1.77	1.52	
Business Sector	9.91	11.61	13.80	1.39
	C. Building structure capital (in 1992 dollar) per hour worked			
Exports	15.33	17.33	17.70	1.15
Imports	12.92	14.44	15.87	1.23
Ratio	1.19	1.20	1.12	
Business Sector	11.30	13.04	14.89	1.32
	D. Engineering structure capital (in 1992 dollar) per hour worked			
Exports	32.61	36.56	36.35	1.11
Imports	22.82	21.52	20.85	0.91
Ratio	1.43	1.70	1.74	
Business Sector	17.24	18.52	20.33	1.18

Our results are consistent with the results for Canada of ten Raa and Mohnen (2001), who suggest that Canadian exports were more capital intensive than imports and Canada was a net exporter of capital service (Table 2 in ten Raan and Mohnen, 2001). These results for Canada differ from the results for the U.S. reported in Wolff (2003). He found that U.S. exports are less capital-intensive than U.S. imports over the period 1947-1996. This suggests that while capital is a source of comparative advantage for Canada, it is source of comparative disadvantage for the U.S. However, there was a gradual shifting of U.S. comparative advantage back toward capital-intensive goods and services over the period 1977-1996. Over that period, Wolff (203) finds that the capital intensity of U.S. exports relative to U.S. imports increased from 0.67 to 0.91.

Natural Resource Intensity
We have classified natural resources into: (1) agriculture, forestry and fishery products, (2) metal mines and other mines and (3) crude petroleum and natural gas. Webster (1993) and Hans-Jurgen (1996) used a similar classification in their natural-resource content of trade calculation for the U.K. and Germany. It

116

is widely believed that Canada's comparative advantage in international trade lies in natural-resource-intensive industries. Canada tends to export goods and services that are intensive in natural resources and import goods and services that are less intensive in natural resources.

The results in Table 4 confirm this view. We find that Canadian exports have higher natural-resource content per unit of output than Canadian imports. All three types of natural resources are a source of comparative advantage for Canada. In 1997, the ratio of natural-resource content in exports relative to imports was 1.5 for agriculture, forestry and fishery products, 1.4 for metal mines and other mines and 1.2 for crude petroleum and natural gas.

There was a decline in Canada's comparative advantage in agriculture, forestry and fishery products and crude petroleum and natural gas over the period 1981-1997. On the other hand, Canada's comparative advantage in metal mines and other mines showed little change. Over the period 1981-1997, the ratio of natural-resource content in exports relative to imports declined from 1.8 to 1.5 for agriculture, forestry and fishery products. The ratio declined from 1.4 in 1981 to 1.2 in 1997 for crude petroleum and natural gas, and remained unchanged for metal mines and other mines.

Table 4: Natural Resource Intensity of Canadian Exports and Imports

	1981	1989	1997	Ratio of 1997 to 1981
	A. Agriculture, forestry and fisheries			
Exports	0.060	0.042	0.041	0.684
Imports	0.033	0.030	0.027	0.823
Ratio	1.818	1.425	1.512	
Business Sector	0.054	0.040	0.041	0.765
	B. Metal mines and other mines			
Exports	0.060	0.055	0.032	0.532
Imports	0.040	0.032	0.022	0.553
Ratio	1.488	1.747	1.432	
Business Sector	0.040	0.032	0.022	0.553
	C. Crude petroleum and natural gas			
Exports	0.087	0.038	0.034	0.394
Imports	0.062	0.035	0.029	0.473
Ratio	1.412	1.080	1.175	
Business Sector	0.034	0.020	0.025	0.728

Wages and Productivity of Exports and Imports

Panel A of Table 5 shows that average wages in export industries were similar to those in import industries. Over the period 1981-1997, wages in export industries relative to import industries showed little change. Panel B of Table 5 shows that the level of labour productivity (defined as value added per hour) in export and import industries was also similar during the period. This suggests that the average labour costs (defined as the ratio of real wages to labour productivity) in exports was similar to the average labour costs in imports. The results are

117

surprising and differ from the prediction of Ricardian trade theory. According to Ricardian trade theory, a country will export those products whose cost is relatively low and import those products whose cost is relatively high.

Panel C of Table 5 shows the results for total factor productivity. Total factor productivity (TFP) is constructed as a weighted sum of capital and labour productivity using the share of capital and labour in total nominal income as weights.[4] We find that the level of TFP in export industries was 12 percent lower than in import industries in 1997. The relative TFP level of export and import industries did not change over the period 1981-1997. However, during the same period, export and import industries had faster labour productivity growth and faster TFP growth than the total business sector. Over that period, annual labour productivity growth was 2.7 percent in exports, 2.5 percent in imports and 1.3 percent in the total business sector. Annual TFP growth was 2.4 percent in exports, 2.3 percent in imports and 0.8 percent in the total business sector.

In Table 6, we consider average wages and productivity of exports and imports in the manufacturing sector. We find that export industries in manufacturing paid wages that were about 5 percent higher than import industries. Export industries in manufacturing had labour productivity that was similar to that in import industries, but had lower TFP. Over the period 1981-1997, labour productivity and TFP grew faster in the export and import component of manufacturing than in the overall manufacturing sector.

Table 5: Labour Costs and Productivity of Canadian Exports and Imports

	1981	1989	1997	Ratio of 1997 to 1981
	A. Real wage (of 1992 dollars per hour)			
Exports	17.49	18.18	18.36	1.05
Imports	17.47	17.60	18.14	1.04
Ratio	1.00	1.03	1.01	
Business Sector	16.35	16.64	17.18	1.05
	B. Labour productivity (GDP per hour, 1,000s of 1992 dollars)			
Exports	34.66	40.37	53.14	1.53
Imports	36.84	41.20	54.55	1.48
Ratio	0.94	0.98	0.97	
Business Sector	22.02	24.28	27.28	1.24
	C. Total factor productivity			
Exports	9.87	11.08	14.55	1.47
Imports	11.48	12.65	16.51	1.44
Ratio	0.86	0.88	0.88	
Business Sector	7.37	7.85	8.49	1.15

---

[4] We have chosen the capital share of income to be 0.3 and the labour share to be 0.7 for calculating TFP.

Table 6: Labour Costs and Productivity of Manufacturing Exports and Imports

	1981	1989	1997	Ratio of 1981 to 1997
	A. Real wage (1992 dollars per hour)			
Exports	19.32	19.61	19.72	1.02
Imports	18.45	18.56	19.02	1.03
Ratio	1.05	1.06	1.04	
Manufacturing Sector	18.99	19.27	19.92	1.05
	B. Labour productivity (GDP per hour, 1,000s of 1992 dollars)			
Exports	38.59	43.70	61.49	1.59
Imports	38.73	44.18	61.46	1.59
Ratio	1.00	0.99	1.00	
Manufacturing Sector	23.53	27.33	34.22	1.45
	C. Total factor productivity			
Exports	11.39	12.37	17.31	1.52
Imports	12.60	13.73	18.73	1.49
Ratio	0.90	0.90	0.92	
Manufacturing Sector	8.36	9.25	10.95	1.31

The Effect of Trade on Productivity Growth

Our finding that export and import industries had faster productivity growth than the total business sector is consistent with the view that trade is linked to higher productivity growth. But the faster productivity growth in exports and imports relative to the business sector might reflect a more rapid pace of technical progress that is taking place in export and import industries, and thus it should not be attributed solely to the effect of trade.

To estimate the effect of trade on productivity growth, we should control for the productivity growth that would have taken place in trade industries without trade. To that end, we compare the change in productivity growth in trade industries between the periods 1981-1989 and 1989-1997 with the change that occurred in the total business sector. If the productivity growth of export and import industries relative to the total business sector widened in the 1989-1997 period, we interpret this as evidence that trade is linked to higher productivity growth. The underlying assumption behind this difference-in-differences approach is that the productivity growth difference between traded industries and the business sector should remain unchanged if trade has no effect on productivity growth.[5]

Panel A of Table 7 shows that labour productivity growth increased for exports, imports and the total business sector in the period 1989-1997 vis-à-vis the period 1981-1989. But the increase was much faster in export and import

---

[5] It could be argued that the deep recession in the early 1990s could affect the extent to which a comparison of the two periods reflects only the effects of trade. However, if we assume the recession has a similar effect on productivity growth in the trade sector and the business sector, the difference-in-differences approach would control for such an effect (Trefler, 2004).

119

industries than in the business sector. This is consistent with the view that trade is linked to high labour productivity growth.

Between the periods 1981-1989 and 1989-1997, labour productivity growth in export industries increased from 1.9 percent per year to 3.4 percent per year, representing an acceleration of 1.5 percent per year between the two periods. For import industries, there was an acceleration of 2.1 percent per year: 1.4 percent per year in the period 1981-1989 versus 3.5 percent per year in the period 1989-1997. For the business sector, the labour productivity acceleration was much smaller (estimated to be 0.2 percent per year).

Panel B of Table 7 shows the results for TFP growth. The results suggest that trade is linked to high TFP growth. TFP growth in export and import industries was faster than in the business sector during the period 1981-1989. It became even faster in the 1989-1997 period, suggesting that trade is linked to high TFP growth.

Table 8 shows the results on the effect of trade on productivity growth in the manufacturing sector. Consistent with the view that trade has a positive effect on productivity growth in the manufacturing sector, the results show that export and import industries in the manufacturing have increased productivity growth relative to the total manufacturing sector over time.

Table 7: The Effect of Trade on Productivity Growth in the Business Sector

	1981-1989	1989-1997	Changes in two periods	Changes in two period relative to the business sector
A. Labour productivity growth (% per year)				
Exports	1.91	3.44	1.53	1.29
Imports	1.40	3.51	2.11	1.87
Total business sector	1.22	1.46	0.24	
B. Total factor productivity growth (% per year)				
Exports	1.44	3.40	1.96	1.76
Imports	1.21	3.32	2.11	1.92
Total business sector	0.79	0.98	0.20	

Table 8: The Effect of Trade on Productivity Growth in the Manufacturing Sector

	1981-1989	1989-1997	Changes in two periods	Changes in two period relative to the business sector
A. Labour productivity growth (% per year)				
Exports	1.55	4.27	2.71	1.77
Imports	1.65	4.13	2.48	1.54
Total manufacturing	1.87	2.81	0.94	
B. Total factor productivity growth (% per year)				
Exports	1.03	4.21	3.18	2.34
Imports	1.07	3.88	2.81	1.97
Total manufacturing	1.27	2.11	0.84	

The Effect of Trade on the Demand for Skilled Workers

Table 9 shows the skilled and unskilled labour requirements of Canadian exports and imports in 1997. The main result is that trade had little effect on the demand for skilled and unskilled workers in Canada. In 1997, output of Canadian exports required 816 million hours of work from workers with bachelor degree or above compared with 842 million hours of work implicit in imports. This resulted in a net trade loss of 26 million hours of work from those workers. The effect of net trade on employment of those workers was small as the net trade loss accounted for 0.9 percent of total hours worked from those workers.

Table 9: The Effect of Trade on Demand for Skilled and Unskilled Workers, 1997

	Exports	Imports	Net trade (1000 hours)	Total	Net trade (%)
Less than high school	326874	-303428	23446	1043617	2.2
High school	2026281	-1970165	56116	7540693	0.7
Post-secondary education	2202108	-2218120	-16012	8674273	-0.2
University or above	815952	-842371	-26419	3089005	-0.9
Total	5371216	-5334084	37132	20347588	0.2

The results in Table 9 show that trade increased the demand for unskilled workers (with less than post-secondary education) and reduced the demand for skilled workers. But the effect of trade on the demand for skilled and unskilled workers was small. We have also calculated the skilled and unskilled labour requirements of net trade for the years 1981, 1989 and 1991. The results are similar. Trade was found to have had little effect on the demand for skilled and unskilled workers in Canada.

Conclusion

In this paper, we have used an input-output model to examine the effect of trade on productivity growth and the demand for skilled workers in Canada. We have also examined the sources of comparative advantage in Canada's international trade. Our main findings are as follows:

First, we find that trade is linked to high labour and total factor productivity growth. For the period 1981-1997, productivity growth was faster in export and import industries than in the total business sector; this productivity growth gap has widened over time.

Second, we find that trade has little effect on the demand for skilled and unskilled workers. The skilled and unskilled labour requirements of net trade are small share of their total employment.

Third, Canada has comparative advantage in capital- and resources-intensive industries. While, comparative advantage in equipment and building structure capital-intensive industries declined over the 1990s, the comparative advantage in engineering structure capital increased over the period. Canada's comparative advantage in agriculture, forestry and fishery products and crude petroleum and natural gas has also fallen over time. Metal mines and other mines continue to be a main source of comparative advantage for Canada and have shown little change over time.

Fourth, despite a high share of more educated workers in Canada compared with the U.S. and other developed countries, we find that skills and human capital are not a source of comparative advantage in Canada's international trade. For the period 1981-1997, the skill composition is similar between exports and imports. In contrast, U.S. studies such as that by Wolff (2003) show that skills and human capital are sources of comparative advantage for the U.S., while physical capital (equipment and structure) is a source of comparative disadvantage in U.S. international trade.[6] It is interesting to note that while Wolff's study shows that the U.S. has a comparative advantage in human capital, it also shows that their R&D advantage has declined over time, such that the U.S. now has a comparative disadvantage in R&D. An examination of the R&D intensity of Canada's international trade is an interesting avenue for future research.

---

[6] Wolff (2003) did not calculate the natural resource content of U.S. trade.

Bibliography

Aulin-Ahmavaara, P. (1999) "Effective rates of sectoral productivity change" *Economic Systems Research*, 11(4), pp. 349-363.

Baldwin, J.R. Caves, R.E. and Gu, W. (2005) "Responses to trade liberalization: changes in product diversification in foreign- and domestic-controlled plants", in Eden L. and W. Dobson (eds.) Governance, Multinationals and Growth, Edward Elgar.

Baldwin, J.R. and Gu, W. (2003) "Participation in export markets and productivity performance in Canadian manufacturing" *Canadian Journal of Economics*, 36(3) 634-57.

Baldwin, J.R. and Gu, W. (2004) "Trade liberalization: export-market participation, productivity growth, and innovation", *Oxford Review of Economic Policy*, 20(3). 372-392.

Baldwin, R.E. (1995) "The effects of trade and foreign direct investment on employment and relative wages", *The OECD Jobs Study Working Paper Series*, No. 4, Paris, OECD.

Bernard, A. B. and Jensen, J.B (2004)."Exporting and productivity in the U.S". *Oxford Review of Economic Policy*, 20(3), 343-357.

De Juan, O. and Febrero, E. (2000) "Measuring productivity from vertically integrated sectors", *Economic Systems Research*, 12(1), pp. 65-81

Deardorff, A.V. (1982) "The general validity of the Heckscher-Ohlin theorem" *American Economic Review*, 72, pp. 683-694.

Driver, C., Kilpatrick, A. and Naibitt, B. (1985) "The employment effects of changes in the structure of UK trade" *Journal of Economic Studies*, 12, pp. 19-38.

Dungan, P. and Murphy, S. (1999) "The changing industry and skill mix of Canada's international trade" *Industry Canada Research Series on Perspectives on North American Free Trade*, Ottawa, Canada.

Eaton, J. and Kortum S. (1999) "International Technology Diffusion" *Journal of International Economics*, 40(3), 537-70.

Engelbrecht, H. (1996) "The composition of the human capital stock and the factor content of trade: evidence from West(ern) Germany", *Economic Systems Research*, 8, 271-297.

Gera, S., Gu, W. and Lee, F.C. (1999) "Information technology and labour productivity growth: empirical evidence for Canada and the United States" *Canadian Journal of Economics*, 32(2), 384-407.

Gu, W., Kaci, M., Maynard, J.P and Silamaa, M. (2003) "Changing composition of the Canadian workforce and its impact on productivity growth", in: Baldwin, J.R. and Harchaoui (eds.) *Productivity Growth in Canada*, Statistics Canada Catalogue, 15-204.

Helpman, E. (1999) "The structure of foreign trade" *Journal of Economic Perspective*, 13, pp. 121-44.

Hulten, C. R. (1978) "Growth accounting with intermediate inputs" *Review of Economic Studies*, 45, pp. 511-518.

Jackson, R.W. (1998) "Regionalizing national commodity-by-industry accounts" *Economic Systems Research*, 10, pp. 223-238.

Lahr, M L. (2001) "Reconciling domestication techniques, the nation of re-exports and some comments on regional accounting" *Economic Systems Research*, 13(2), pp. 165-179.

Lee, C. and Shluter, G. (1999) "Effect of trade on the demand for skilled and unskilled workers" *Economic Systems Research*, 11(1), pp. 49-65.

Leontief, W. (1956) "Factor proportions and the structure of American trade: further theoretical and empirical analysis", *Review of Economics and Statistics*, 38(4), pp. 386-407.

Leontief, W. (1964) "International comparison of factor cost and factor use" *American Economic Review*, 54, pp. 335-345.

Organization for Economic Co-operation and Development (2004) Education at a Glance, OECD, Paris.

Ohno, K. (1988) "Changes in trade structure and factor intensity: a case study of the Republic of Korea", *The Developing Economies*, 26. pp. 367-385.

Rymes, T. K. (1972) "The measure of capital and total factor productivity in the context of Cambridge theory of capital" *The Review of Income and Wealth*, 29, pp. 297-316.

Sachs, J. and Shatz, H. (1994) "Trade and jobs in U.S. manufacturing" *Brookings Papers on Economic Activity*, 2, pp. 1-84.

Schwanen, D. (1997) "Trading up: the impact of increased continental integration on trade, investment, and jobs in Canada" *C.D. Howe Institute Commentary, No. 89.*

Sraffa, P. (1960) Production of Commodities by Means of Commodities (Cambridge: Cambridge University Press).

St. Louis, L. V. (1989) "Empirical tests of some semi-survey update procedures to rectangular input-output tables", *Journal of Regional Sciences*, 29, pp. 373-385.

Statistics Canada (1994) "Fixed Capital Flows and Stocks", Catalogue 13-568 Occasional.

ten Raa, T. and Mohnen, P. (2001) " The location of comparative advantages on the basis of fundamentals only", *Economic Systems Research*, 13(1), pp. 93-108.

Trefler, D. (2004) "The long and short of the Canada-U.S. free trade agreement", *American Economic Review*, 94(1), 870-895.

Vanek, J. (1968) "The factor proportions theory: the N-factor case" Kyklos, 21(4), pp. 749-756.

Webster, A. (1993) "The skill and higher educational content of UK net exports", *Oxford Bulletin of Economics and Statistics*, 55(2), pp. 141-159.

Wolff, E.N. (1985) "Industrial composition, inter-industry effects, and the U.S. productivity slowdown", *Review of Economics and Statistics*, 67, pp. 268-277.

Wolff, E.N. (2003) "Skills and changing comparative advantage", *The Review of Economics and Statistics*, 85(1), pp. 77-93.

Wood, A. (1991) "The factor content of North-South trade in manufacturing Reconsidered", Weltwirtschaftliches Archiv, pp. 719-743.

Ten Years After: An Assessment of the Environmental Effectiveness of the NAAEC

John Kirton[1]
University of Toronto

Introduction

The January 1, 1994 advent of the North American Free Trade Agreement (NAFTA), its accompanying North American Agreement on Environmental Co-operation (NAAEC) and the Commission for Environmental Cooperation (CEC) brought a revolution in North American governance. It was a transformation with potentially significant implications for environmental policymaking, policy and performance in the member countries of Canada, the United States and Mexico. NAFTA brought Mexico "in" to the free trade relationship enjoyed by Canada and the United States since the Canada-US Free Trade Agreement (CUFTA) of 1989. NAFTA further marked the world's first full free trade agreement equally joining countries of the developed north and developing south. NAFTA introduced pioneering provisions for investment protection and, above all, environmental protection and the promotion of sustainable development. NAFTA and its accompanying NAAEC and North American Agreement on Labour Co-operation (NAALC) introduced the first major trilateral interaction and institutions to Canada and its two North American partners. These joined Canada to Mexico in a much broader, deeper and more permanent way than the almost exclusively bilateral or broadly multilateral Canada-Mexican relationship had before. Above all, the NAAEC and CEC brought to North America its first regional international organization, with substantial resources to facilitate environmental co-operation among the three member governments and their citizens, with direct access for civil society in environmental governance and dispute resolution, and with a regional secretariat with autonomous powers all its own.

After ten years of operation, how effective has this innovative NAAEC and its CEC been in meeting their environmental objectives, as well as the integrally linked environment-economy goals that brought this pioneering North American environmental regime to life? To help address this question, this study undertakes, from a Canadian perspective, a retrospective assessment of the implementation, effectiveness and utility of the NAAEC and CEC, and their

---

[1] The author gratefully acknowledges the research assistance of Caitlin Sainsbury, the support of Environment Canada, and the financial support for relevant research from the Social Sciences and Humanities Research Council of Canada through its strategic grant to the projects on "EnviReform" and on "Trade, Environment and Competitiveness" at the University of Toronto.

impact on Canadian environmental and environment-economy policy, policymaking and performance during the ten years up to January 1, 2004. While the North American environmental regime can be legitimately assessed according to its contribution to global environmental governance and impacts, to processes and outcomes within its United States and Mexican members, and to the values of the transnational trade and environmental communities across the North American region, this analysis is grounded in the objectives of the government and interested citizens of Canada, both at the outset of the regime and as those objectives evolved during the NAAEC's first ten years.

This study thus focuses on identifying the overall impact, effectiveness and utility of the NAAEC in and for Canada after ten years of experience. It looks back at the original assumptions and expectations of this agreement, the actual experience in implementation, and the conclusions that can be drawn. It analyzes which of the measures in the agreement have worked well, poorly or not at all in terms of environmental protection in Canada, and what the result has been in Canada in terms of new environmental regulations, activities and programs. It seeks to provide an analytical foundation for drawing lessons that can be learned, particularly lessons of relevance to the government of Canada, for the future of this agreement, and to identify which features would or would not be useful to include in other agreements.

The Approach

As the NAAEC was negotiated in parallel with NAFTA and the two agreements have been, and will continue to be, viewed as a package, the few analyses produced from a Canadian perspective over the years have concentrated on the structure and potential, or a restricted range of high-profile components of the NAAEC and linked NAFTA environmental provisions, rather than the overall agreement and organization itself (Winham 1994, Munton and Kirton 1994, Richardson 1994, Swenarchuck 1994, Bennett 1994, Johnson and Beaulieu 1996, Blair 2003). This more comprehensive review from a Canadian perspective will thus highlight the longer term effectiveness of the NAAEC in meeting the distinctive, enduring and evolving objectives of Canada and Canadians. It will also serve as an analytical foundation to assist Canadian governments and other stakeholders in the important task of building the North American community in the decade ahead.

Drawing in the first instance upon the liberal-institutionalist approach to international regimes in political science, this study explores the autonomous impact of the NAAEC regime and CEC institution on the policymaking process, the resulting policies and actions of the government of Canada and other key actors within Canada, and thus on the state of the environment within Canada. Its vision is consequently broader than the important but narrower question of the extent to which various actors have complied with the legal provisions of the NAAEC itself (Johnson and Beaulieu 1996). It is also more focused and grounded than the larger issue of who has benefited or lost most from the overall NAFTA regime, or whether the NAAEC is adequate to address the actual environmental challenges Canadians and other North Americans will face in the decade ahead.

126

The judgments and conclusions in this study rest primarily on overall analyses of the broad patterns of NAAEC-created activity, critical cases in the life of the NAAEC and CEC, and the degree to which the NAAEC's successes and shortcomings are currently recognized and valued by the Canadian government itself. In addition to aggregate analysis of shifting objectives, agendas, activities and cases, the study draws on interviews with selected high-level officials and individuals conducted by the author or his scholarly colleagues from 1995 to the present day. It is also enriched by the author's personal involvement with the NAAEC, from the earliest civil society design efforts in the 1980s and intergovernmental negotiations in the early 1990s through to the spring of 2003 (for details see Appendix A).

Canadian Objectives for the NAAEC

Initial Objectives

The negotiators of the NAAEC equipped this agreement with innovative measures intended to promote an environmentally positive relationship among the three countries of North America in the context of NAFTA-induced and -guided trade liberalization. Since January 1994, North America has been seen as a "regional experiment" for testing the utility of the various new provisions and processes intended to have positive impacts for the environment. Canadian participation in this experiment was guided by five seminal objectives: making the CEC work effectively; putting the environment first in the NAFTA era; bringing citizens into a North American community and its governance; securing expanded environmental resources in an age of austerity; and fostering an independent Secretariat at the CEC.

Canada's most central and enduring objective in negotiating, accepting and operating the NAAEC was to make NAFTA work. More specifically, it was to ensure the passage and effective operation of NAFTA itself, by reinforcing the environmental provisions of the free trade agreement, by providing an assured mechanism for their realization and implementation, and by creating a centre for broader and expanding environmental co-operation to ensure that any unforeseen environmental opportunities or costs of NAFTA trade and investment liberalization would be, respectively, realized and controlled. To be sure, by the late 1980s there had arisen strong functional ecological grounds for creating what was initially termed a North American Commission for the Environment (NACE) to deal with common trilateral environmental issues, quite apart from any negotiated economic integration that might take place. But it was NAFTA that was the necessary condition for giving birth to the CEC. Equally and reciprocally necessary were the environmental provisions of the draft NAFTA, and the addition of the NAAEC, to bring NAFTA as a full free trade agreement to life.[2] In the true spirit of sustainable development, each agreement was thus equal in value

---

[2] This was certainly true in the US and arguably true in Canada as well, given the skepticism of the Chretien government that assumed office in the autumn of 1993, and that of the Canadian public as a whole (see below).

127

to, and integrally necessary for, the realization of the other, and rooted in a deep belief that there were important mutually reinforcing synergies to be realized by doing them together in both a temporal and institutional way.

It is thus both the NAFTA-related provisions of the NAAEC, notably those of Article 10(6), and the NAAEC's more stand-alone provisions on ecological co-operation, that have equal value in assessing the effectiveness of the NAAEC's performance during its first ten years. Proactively, in particular, it is the ability of the NAAEC to enhance environmental quality through mobilizing the power of more open trade, investment, technology, social interaction, and regional community and capacity building that is the Canadian standard by which the NAAEC's effectiveness should be judged. Defensively, it was and is to ensure that Part Five of the agreement, which allows the United States and Mexico to impose trade sanctions on each other for environmental purposes, would not only legally exempt Canada as the NAAEC did, but also would never be applied at all or become embedded in agreements elsewhere, and would thus recede as a consideration in stakeholders' approach to the overall regime.

The second Canadian objective, integral to the realization of the first, was to convince Canadians that the environment mattered centrally in the NAFTA age. Specifically, it was to persuade Canadians and others in the embryonic North American community that the parties were indeed deeply committed to environmental and sustainable development values, and were faithfully operating an effective regime and organization to ensure that such values were being realized. This objective was particularly important in the year leading up to the acceptance of the agreement, given the deep dislike of many Canadians at the time for NAFTA itself and for the preceding CUFTA, and the campaign commitment of the new Canadian government of Prime Minister Jean Chrétien to accept the NAFTA-NAEEC package only with new assurances of additional protections in several areas, including the environmental and sustainable development ones of water and energy.

Yet this objective was much broader, deeper and more durable than just that. Since the late 1980s, almost all Canadians, when asked about their priority values for Canadian foreign policy, have placed "global environmental protection" and natural resource conservation first, and always well ahead of trade liberalization as a goal. Moreover, by the autumn of 2003, the environment was the policy area where Canadians (along with Americans and Mexicans) most strongly wished to develop policies, not in a "more independent fashion" but to "develop integrated North American policies." Environmental protection in its outward orientation is the one value that enduringly unites all Canadians. Canadians now wish to develop environmental policies (at home and abroad) on a completely integrated (70%) or somewhat integrated (an additional 14%) North American basis (Graves 2003).

A third Canadian objective was to bring citizens into the NAFTA regime. Specifically, it was to assure Canadians that they had a meaningful influence in the ongoing operation and governance of the new North American regime. This influence was both for the defensive task of controlling any NAFTA-induced pressure for reduced domestic environmental enforcement or addressing priority environmental problems, and for the offensive task of reaping sustainable development synergies and strengthening the sustainable development values of open, transparent, accountable, broadly multistakeholder, consensus-oriented decision-making. Here the central NAAEC measures were the Joint Public Advisory Committee (JPAC), the trilateral working groups joining government and non-government stakeholders across a wide range of CEC program areas, and the participation of Canadians in the Article 14-15 citizens' submission process.

A fourth Canadian objective was to secure additional resources, beyond those of the Canadian government, to address Canada's domestic and regional environmental objectives. The NAAEC and CEC were born at a time of substantial and sustained fiscal consolidation within the Canadian government. This process was to lead Environment Canada and several provincial environment departments to suffer budget reductions of about 35% and substantial reductions in expert personnel as well. At the same time, the advent of a regional organization in the form of the CEC brought additional central infrastructure costs, beyond those of actual NAAEC programs themselves. Canada thus supported the initial compromise that gave the CEC Secretariat an annual budget of US$9 million, composed, unusually for international organizations, of three equal national contributions of US$3 million each.

A fifth Canadian objective was to have a strong, visible, independent CEC Secretariat. In part this was driven by Canada's sense of ownership of the Secretariat, as its "own" international organization located in Montreal. The Secretariat thus served as a visible symbol of the unifying values that all Canadians shared. In part it was motivated by Canada's confidence, given its successful multilateral environmental leadership in the early 1990s "Rio" era, that effective international institutions would naturally bring to life Canada's environmental priorities and Canadians' environmental convictions.

Evolving Objectives

Over the years of the NAAEC's operation, the Canadian government developed additional objectives. The four most important were: preserving balance by emphasizing co-operation; facilitating intergovernmental co-operation; advancing domestic strategy; and employing the CEC's trade-environment work

The first two were aimed at preserving the initial balance in the face of unexpected developments in the CEC's life. The first of these additional objectives was containing the growing centrality of the Article 14-15 process in the CEC Council, Secretariat, JPAC, and in the lives of the government and the public. From the start, there had been a senior-level view at Environment Canada that the CEC was to be a "Commission on Environmental Cooperation," and not a "Commission on Environmental Enforcement." Indeed, this was a strong Canadian government position, as chief Canadian NAFTA negotiator John Weekes had opposed the unduly "prosecutorial and adversarial" approach of the initial American draft of the NAAEC (Winham 1994: 41). Canada's approach prevailed in the naming of the new entity, as the initial US proposed term of a North American Commission for the Environment, was replaced by the agreed upon name of CEC and NAAEC, with the work "co-operation" added to, and prominently featured in both, the agreement and the organization it established.

Canada's emphasis on co-operation was reinforced when the early years brought a heavy and unexpected number of submissions against Canada, and a consequent "legalization" of the CEC's work. The Canadian government became concerned that this trend would detract from the limited resources available to the CEC for its other programs, particularly those aimed at direct environmental improvements in Mexico. In addition, the growth of a litigious, adversarial approach to the CEC's work and culture was inconsistent with Canada's preferred approach, indeed unifying cultural commitment, to broad, multistakeholder-based, scientifically grounded, consensus-oriented decision-making.

The second additional objective was ensuring that the CEC served as a facilitator of co-operation and even co-ordination among the three national governments of North America, as opposed to its strong contribution as an independent provider of policy development, initiative, and policy direction. In the early years, the latter role had quickly acquired prominence as a result of several factors. These included the strong independence of the CEC's first Executive Director, the expectations surrounding this novel regional organization, the need of the Secretariat to establish relations with, and secure the confidence of, the broader stakeholder and civil society community, the innovative nature of many of the CEC's projects and the absence in most areas of established intergovernmental networks or relationships among the three North American governments. Over time, however, the Canadian government developed expertise in many project areas, such as the environmental assessments of trade liberalization agreements, and the habit of successful trilateral intergovernmental co-operation developed. The demand thus grew for a greater emphasis on the CEC's role as a responsive intergovernmental facilitator, as opposed to that of an independent institutional initiator.

A third evolving objective was to tie the CEC's work more closely to Canada's domestic policy priorities, and to use the former as a strategic instrument for realizing the latter. At the start, due to the novelty of the CEC and Canadian respect for the Commission's independence, Canada's approach had been largely a matter of general attitude and senior-level emphasis, centered on a feeling that the CEC's primary purpose was to build environmental capacity in Mexico. Since 1999, there has been a shift to the point where all proposed CEC activities are, as a routine, systematically and thoroughly assessed according to their ability to forward Canada's domestic environmental priorities and Canada's management of its relationship with the US. The objective is to ensure that Canada's main priorities are reflected in the CEC work program, while respecting the need for the CEC, as an autonomous institution, to engage in activities that are not necessarily current Canadian priorities. Part of this shift has been to involve more senior individuals in Environment Canada in the work of the CEC through briefing senior officials on CEC activities as well as soliciting their views on more high level issues, for example at ADM/DM meetings. The major thrust has been an attempt to involve more departments within the Canadian government in the work of the CEC.

A fourth evolution has been a significant shift in Canada's attitude to the value of specific CEC programs. A leading example is the Environment, Economy and Trade Program, which both Environment Canada and the Department of Foreign Affairs and International Trade (DFAIT) had been skeptical about when the emphasis was on developing a method to assess NAFTA's environmental effects on an ongoing basis, pursuant to the mandatory provision of Article 10(6)D. While doubt still exists in some places about how the resulting research can be transformed into visible benefits, there is now considerable enthusiasm at both Environment Canada and DFAIT for the assessment and other trade-environment work of the CEC.

The NAAEC and Its Institutions

The NAAEC established the tripartite Commission for Environmental Cooperation (CEC) to address regional environmental concerns, help prevent potential trade and environmental conflicts, and promote the effective enforcement of environmental law. The NAAEC, in Article 1, lists ten objectives, which can be summarized as follows:

NAAEC Objectives:
1. Protect and improve the North American environment for the present and future.
2. Promote sustainable development through co-operation and mutually supportive environmental and economic policies.
3. Increase co-operation for environmental enhancement, including wild flora and fauna.
4. Support the environmental goals and objectives of NAFTA.
5. Avoid creating trade distortions or new trade barriers.
6. Co-operate to develop and improve environmental laws, regulations, procedures, etc.
7. Enhance compliance and enforcement.
8. Promote transparency and public participation.
9. Promote economically efficient and effective environmental measures.
10. Promote pollution prevention.

These objectives were followed, in Article 2, by six specific obligations, which can be summarized as follows:

NAAEC Obligations:
1. General commitments regarding public state of the environment reporting, emergency preparedness, scientific research and technology development, environmental impact assessment, economic instruments and export prohibitions regarding pesticides and toxics.
2. High levels and continuous improvement of environmental laws.
3. Publication and comment on environmental laws.
4. Specific procedures to enhance government environmental enforcement.
5. Private access to remedies;

131

6. Procedural guarantees.

Any overall assessment of the effectiveness of the NAAEC in fulfilling these objectives and obligations must be made against this particular configuration of specified goals. First, the NAAEC included a very broad range of environmental and linked economic goals. Second, as the Objectives indicate, the NAAEC was designed as much as a sustainable development agreement linking the economy and the environment as an agreement for stand-alone environmental co-operation. Third, its goal, beyond the first general objective, was to increase co-operation and to promote and to enhance processes, rather than to secure specified outcomes or solve designated problems. Fourth, very few of the economy-environment objectives were carried into the specific obligations. Moreover, the latter concentrated heavily on specified legal and political processes, rather than defined ecological results.

At the most general level, the NAAEC can be judged as effective in meeting its specified Objectives and Obligations. The parties, through the CEC or directly, have undertaken programs, projects and activities that embrace virtually all specified areas, have fostered trilateral interaction and co-operation in virtually all of these, and have helped foster or reinforce ongoing legal and political processes and environmental capacity in Mexico — where they were seen at the time to be most needed.

The NAAEC has further demonstrated its value in the critical domain of sustainable development, and the trade-environment link. This is clear from an analysis of cases of "environmental regulatory protection," defined as intergovernmental activity on issues directly involving both trade and environmental values taking place between or among the three NAFTA parties from 1980 to 1998. The outcomes of these 84 cases, when completed, increasingly favour the interests of Canada, the North American environmental community and, above all, the three countries and two communities together, as the NAFTA era takes effect, as the NAFTA institutions are used and as cases are processed through the CEC (Kirton 2003b, 2002d, Rugman, Kirton and Soloway 1999). In short, NAFTA in general, and the CEC in particular, has helped Canada realize its national objectives, and helped ensure that all North Americans "win together" in the trade-environment field.

The NAAEC's sustainable development success is further evident, on a broader plane, in the way in which Canada's trade policy community, centered in DFAIT, has come to view the CEC's added value. That community regards its work as a useful, if modest, contribution, to Canada's trade goals. Its members judge the CEC to be an effective organization. Since the start of NAFTA, the trade community has sought to assure often skeptical environmentalists that NAFTA was not creating economic pressures that would unwittingly or unknowingly damage ecological capital and concerns. They see the CEC doing a credible job in meeting that core goal. In particular, they value the CEC's contribution in evaluating trade-related impacts and identifying trade-related problems, in environmental co-operation, environmental management, and Mexican environmental capacity building.

Most generally, the NAFTA-NAAEC model for incorporating into trade agreements environmental provisions that do not restrict trade has given Canada experience in, and a valuable model for, building environmental mechanisms into its subsequent trade agreement in ways that are tailored to each country case but that provide an overall coherence among them. It thus serves the larger strategic objective of having a cumulatively compatible set of full bilateral and regional trade agreements on a NAFTA foundation, and of guiding Canada's approach to the multilateral negotiations in the Free Trade Agreement of the America (FTAA) and the Doha Development Agenda of the World Trade Organization (WTO) (Kirton 2003a).

In general, amidst the comprehensive array of NAAEC goals and implementing activities, Canada can find in the first decade a record of visible and valuable activity on its priority concerns. At the same time, legitimate questions of emphasis and balance arise. Some may question whether critical Canadian concerns at the outset, such as emergency preparedness and pollution prevention action, have received sufficiently robust budget attention, for example, in regard to the threat to coastal waters from land-based, maritime and other threats to fragile oceanic ecosystems. Other areas, such as environmental impact assessments, have proved difficult to secure progress on through the CEC. Most generally, the NAAEC has been more clearly successful in its more limited, procedurally focused Obligations than on its broader and more ambitious Objectives, especially those in the economy-environment domain. The CEC Secretariat budgetary resources devoted to the Environment, Economy and Trade Program, while substantial, do not fully reflect the emphasis accorded to these linkages in the Objectives themselves. Such observations fuel questions about whether the spirit of the initial economy-environment bargain that brought NAFTA into being is fully respected as the first decade ends.

At the same time, while forward looking in several ways, both the Objectives and Obligations remain very much a reflection of the ecological and political world of the early 1990s rather than of the twenty-first century that lies ahead. For example, their attention focuses exclusively within the North American region and the transborder issues among its countries, rather than on the common North American needs in, or interdependencies with, the wider world. Current issues such as the relationship of the environment with human health, particularly children's health, the link between the environment and food safety, the environment-security relationship and the precautionary principle are not directly addressed in the Objectives and Obligations. These statements also remain weak in regard to voluntary standardization, technology transfer and capacity building more generally. The NAAEC of 1994 is heavily attached to national sovereignty to a degree no longer reflected in Canadians' public opinion attitudes about the need for "integrated" approaches to North American environmental policymaking. Nor is there any open-ended provision to allow or induce the parties to modernize the Objectives or Obligations periodically and thus better focus the NAAEC regime on the ever evolving contemporary and emerging set of environmental and environment-economy challenges the parties collectively face. In short, the NAAEC has worked relatively well for its first decade in the world of the 1990s. Whether it is an optimal or even adequate platform for its second decade in the twenty-first century is a separate question that warrants serious reflection and review.

The Commission for Environmental Cooperation (CEC)

Budget

Assessments of the NAAEC's utility and effectiveness must be made not only in reference to the "constitutional" Objectives and Obligations specified in the agreement, but also against the resources provided to meet these and other defined goals. These resources include the investment of the time, managerial capacity and political capital of the ministers in the CEC Council, the resources of their departments and governments they mobilize to meet CEC-related needs within their national bureaucracies at home, and the resources which civil society brings to the task. Yet at the centre of the available resources stands the CEC Secretariat, with an annual budget of US$9 million, contributed, as noted above, equally by the three parties and fixed in nominal terms since the start.

The effectiveness and "value for money" of the Canadian contribution to the CEC, and the CEC as a whole, should be assessed against three criteria, each of which relate to a distinct CEC role. The first is the intended purpose of the CEC as a facilitator of intergovernmental and other trilateral co-operation, as policy advisor to governments on innovative and emerging issues, and as an auditor of what its member governments do. These minimalist roles of "intergovernmental facilitator" are distinct from the more ambitious roles of program deliverer, capacity builder or community creator for environmentalists and indeed all citizens across North American society as a whole. Even with this first, minimalist conception of the CEC's proper role, the legal obligation to respond to Article 14-15 submissions whose number and complexity are not controlled by the CEC — together with the existence of the Secretariat's Article 13 power, which the Canadian government now values highly — could fuel a future requirement for resources more robust than the mainstream minimalist conception suggests.

The second referent is the cost and value of the products the CEC directly builds in house, or buys from consultants outside. Here the key test, as the Canadian government's current vision recognizes, is the distinctive added value as a "capacity contributor" to North American's environmental concerns. Is the CEC pioneering ambitious instruments or analysis that other actors have not done, are not doing and cannot do as well? Are the CEC's products ones that influence, or are adopted by, outsiders once they are done? Here, as the analysis below suggests, there are several instances where this has been the case, such as the NAFTA Environmental Effects project, the increasingly trilateral *Taking Stock* and the recent work on renewable energy, where the CEC fills an important gap. The Article 13 and 14-15 instruments are also of central importance here.

The third criterion is the process the NAAEC-CEC has fostered for meeting its primary goals of enhancing and promoting co-operation, doing so on a balanced trilateral and economy-environment basis, and doing so in a way that fosters multistakeholder public participation throughout the North American community as a whole. This third role of North American "community creator" is perhaps the most important one in the years ahead.

Central to the NAAEC was a conception of North America as an expansive community of governments, other stakeholders and interested citizens, a community that would radiate outward from the annual Council meetings and Montreal Secretariat to increase the awareness, engage the interest and mobilize the talents of North Americans as a whole. Here it has been strikingly successful, as the systematic evidence from an early review of its operation confirms. Yet it remains the case that the CEC has found it difficult to attract regular senior level participation from the corporate and economic community, which has limited its ability to influence the powerful national departments for trade, finance, agriculture and energy, and the international organizations and institutions they control.

Despite these successes, there are several trends that raise the question of whether the existing resources, frozen in nominal terms at US$9 billion per year since the CEC's inception a decade ago, are adequate to sustain its success in the years ahead. One is the way in which the "partnership path" diverts CEC attention to fundraising and may dilute its distinct priorities, or give rise to image problems, especially when private sector organizations offer to provide financial assistance. A second is the recent significant fall in the value of the US dollar, which reduces the available resources to the CEC Secretariat for operations in Montreal, Mexico City, and Canada and Mexico as a whole. A third is the value that CEC work has come to possess for the wider, multilateral, environmental community and the added expenses involved in ensuring a CEC contribution, on behalf of North American expertise and interests, in global debates. A fourth is the significant expansion in the North American population, economy and environmental challenges over the first ten years. Together these suggest that the issue of the adequacy of the CEC's budget in the future may warrant an architectural and strategic, as well as an incremental response, with resources provided that are appropriate to the tasks assigned to the CEC in the decade ahead.

Council

The CEC Ministerial Council came to a North America that had previously had virtually no trilateral ministerial institutions or widespread interaction, and where the joint ministerial committees established between Canada and the United States had often quickly fallen into disuse. A detailed examination of the Council's agenda provides an indication of the high-level collective political will and direction it injects into the NAAEC regime. This examination shows several patterns. First, the Environment and Trade Program has been the most consistently, indeed almost continuously, discussed topic, reflecting faithfully the emphasis given to this subject in the overall Objectives of the NAAEC. In second place has come Canada's central priority of Sound Management of Chemicals (SMOC), an indication of Canada's influence in keeping the Council focused on core Canadian concerns. A third area of consistent emphasis, and one that again well reflects the NAAEC Objectives, is public participation (see Appendix B).

The agenda also shows some Council concern with proactive, strategic planning, as delivered through its NAAEC Progress Reviews, CEC Three-Year Planning and the NAFTA Ten-Year Retrospective. Moreover, it displays an outward-looking orientation, not mandated in the NAAEC itself, to address Regional Action on Global Issues and Cooperation on Global Agreements, and the World Summit on Sustainable Development (WSSD). Finally, it is developing direct high-level links with other international institutions through its 2002 joint meeting with the IJC and the International Boundary and Water Commission (IBWC). It is a sign of sound, high-level, political leadership that the ministers in the Council are going beyond the increasingly dated specifications of the agreement through which it was created.

What is particularly striking about the Council's agenda is the large number of new items that have been taken up in the second five-year period from 1999 to 2003. In itself, this shift shows flexibility, innovation and responsiveness to the North America public's and government's priority concerns.

A further sign of the Council effectiveness comes from its internal process of decisionmaking, beyond the agenda formation stage. The Council has displayed its autonomous value-added by altering, rather than merely approving, Secretariat advice, as in the case of Article 14-15 recommendations, including that on Quebec hogs. Within the Council, the available evidence points to a dominant pattern of flexible alignment and mutual adjustment, rather than a permanent majority prevailing over a recurrent loser, or a larger United States regularly inducing Canada and Mexico to follow its lead. One sign of collective Council solidarity is the reluctance of a member to be visibly outvoted on an issue, with the result that unanimous decisionmaking usually comes. Canada has been able to prevail where key national interests, related to national unity, have been relevant, as the Quebec hogs case suggests. Moreover, Canadian ministers have been willing to use their Council participation to further Canada's broader objectives in the overall management of its relationship with the United States, by providing support for U.S. Council initiatives, in part to offset the disagreements between the two countries on key multilateral environmental issues such as climate change.

There are, however, still limits to the effectiveness of the CEC. The three ministers have not intensified the pace of their meetings, by holding more frequent regular sessions, calling ad hoc issue or theme-specific meetings, or regularly caucusing on the margins of large multilateral environmental meetings that they all attend. Nor have they succeeded in attracting their ministerial counterparts in other portfolios, starting with trade but potentially embracing energy and health, to hold a joint session with them to discuss common concerns. And individual ministers who have stepped down from the environment portfolio have not remained actively engaged in the life of the NAAEC.

Secretariat

The work of the CEC Secretariat can also be judged a success. The position of Executive Director has now rotated through incumbents from the

136

three member governments, and thus helped ensure that all three countries' national perspectives have a privileged place in the CEC's life. The CEC quickly established a management model in which the Executive Director was supported by two "national" directors from the other two countries, to help ensure an ongoing balance. On the whole, the most senior staff positions have been occupied by individuals who are regarded as leading environmentalists and respected professionals in the countries from which they come. The location of the headquarters, with the bulk of the staff and activity, in Montreal has made Canada and the Secretariat more easily, affordably and fully sensitive to each others' concerns than might be the case were the dominant centre to be located in a place more geographically, linguistically and culturally distant from Ottawa and Canada's population centres. It has given the Canadian government and all Canadians a particular sense of ownership of, and responsibility for the CEC, and given its work greater Canadian government attention than would otherwise be the case. It has prevented the realization of the powerful initial tendency to regard the NAAEC and NAFTA as arrangements essentially of concern to the US and Mexico alone. At the same time, the opening of the Mexico City regional office has helped ensure the immediacy of the CEC's links with, and sensitivity to, a Mexican government geographically and linguistically far removed from Montreal.

Canada has benefited from having as a senior staff member and the second Executive Director an individual who was intimately involved in advising the Canadian government on the negotiation of NAFTA's environment provisions and who had served as the head of one of Canada's leading mainstream environmental NGOs (ENGOs). Moreover, Canadian nationals have always served as the manager of the Environment, Economy and Trade Program. This helped ensure that Canadian perspectives on this subject of vital interest to an environmentally committed and export dependent Canada have full resonance in the work of the CEC.

Most strikingly, Canada did achieve its initial objective of having the Secretariat led by an individual with a clearly independent approach. Indeed, the independent spirit was exercised in such a fashion that it came to raise Canadian concerns that the Secretariat was pursuing its work in a way that was not adequately sensitive to the larger political context in which all its member governments operated. However, substantive Canadian-specific sensitivities were never at the centre of this concern.

Four features of the Secretariat might have eroded its effectiveness at the margins. First, the scarcity of senior natural or physical scientists or members of the business community among Secretariat staff may have limited its ability to connect or communicate easily with the broader scientific and corporate community and mobilize resources from them. Second, the abrupt termination of senior staff members have led to some disruption in the work of the CEC and concerns, whether justified or not, about national government political interference in the work of what is obliged by the NAAEC to be an independent international body. Third, the recent lengthy reliance on an Acting Executive Director has raised questions in key constituencies as well. Fourth, a question has

137

arisen more recently as to whether the resources available for compensation are adequate to attract the desired individuals to work in the Secretariat.

Article 13

Perhaps the leading NAAEC-codified instrument by which the Secretariat can operate independently is its top-down "roving spotlight" mechanism under Article 13 (Kirton 2002a). This empowers the CEC Secretariat, on its own initiative, to investigate independently and report on any matter related to its extensive co-operative work program. In the initial NAFTA negotiations, Canada supported an Article 13 constructed in such a fashion, particularly in the face of those in the US that wanted a more powerful and independent Secretariat prerogative (Winham 1994). Since that time, Canada has become increasingly enthusiastic about the value of Article 13 as it has been used by the Secretariat. Canada has always, without question, favoured making such reports publicly available, even when discussions take place over issues regarding the Canadian response to the recommendations in the reports. The Canadian government has not been deterred by any fear that the "scientific" Article 13 instrument might move into broad policy and directly trade-related areas, where Canada's preferences could be hurt.

Thus far, there have been five Article 13 cases initiated and four completed, for an average of about one every two years. The initiation of these five reports has been evenly spaced over the first nine years. There is no trend toward making more or less frequent use of this instrument. However, it can take over two years from the start of an investigation to the release of a final report. The elapsed time from initiation to public release is steadily lengthening.

Joint Public Advisory Committee

The JPAC is the leading instrument to ensure the CEC's commitment to inclusiveness, transparency and public participation in CEC governance - all important initial objectives for the Canadian government. In the early years, Canadian JPAC members played valuable roles in establishing open communication and relations of trust with their Mexican counterparts, who were wary of American motives in the CEC.

Canada still values the work of JPAC in making the CEC an institution of citizens and not just of governments. Those in the biodiversity conservation community value its work in raising the profile of the invasive species issue, even if JPAC has not been particularly visible on a broader front. JPAC is also credited, along with the Secretariat, with pointing to the need for a strategic plan for the Enforcement Working Group. Here JPAC has encouraged traditionally closed and cautious enforcement individuals to engage in a more open, outward-looking dialogue, in part through the presence of the JPAC Chair at a meeting of the Enforcement Working Group. The government also accepted seven of the eight recommendations offered by JPAC for the most recent enforcement work plan. JPAC, together with the Council and the Article 13 electricity report, is also credited with creating the CEC working group on air.

On the other hand, there has been a growing ambivalence about JPAC's choice of issues to take up. JPAC's work on the divisive subject of the procedures for dealing with Article 14-15 submissions is seen as having fostered undue attention to this litigious aspect of the CEC's work, at the expense of its co-operative program. More recently, there are doubts about the value of JPAC's work in regard to NAFTA's controversial Chapter 11 on investment disputes. In addition, a JPAC recommendation that the Enforcement Working Group review the factual records made by each country had to be turned down, on the grounds of being too intrusive into national sovereignty. Here Canada and Mexico resisted most, for they, rather than the US, were the subject of the majority of the submissions and factual records. There was also a concern that NGOs and their American industry allies might be using the submission process for protectionist purposes, in a classic tactic of "baptist-bootlegger" or "green-greedy" coalitions. More broadly, there is a sense that JPAC has provided an alternative constituency for the Secretariat that has encouraged it to display its independence and made it less sensitive to the views and context of the parties than it would otherwise have been. A feeling that the Secretariat is less disciplined than that of the Organisation for Economic Co-operation and Development (OECD), for example, stems in part from this orientation toward JPAC and the ENGO community that lies beyond. The work of the Canadian National Advisory Committee, and its role in advising on issues related to the NAAEC, is also relevant in this regard.

Annual Program

A further way of evaluating the CEC's usefulness and effectiveness for Canada is by assessing the components and results of the key aspects of the CEC's annual program covering environment, economy and trade, the conservation of biodiversity, pollutants and health, and law and policy.

Environment, Economy and Trade

The Environment, Economy and Trade Program is composed of activities that assess the environmental effects of trade, trade in environmentally preferable goods and services, financing for environmental protection, energy and carbon sequestration, and the Environment and Trade Officials Group.

At the outset, in defining the first work plan, there was a desire at the official level, from a broadly critical DFAIT, Industry Canada and Environment Canada, to not have the CEC take up trade and environment issues. At the time, the big focus of the economy-environment work was the "NAFTA Environment Effects" project (see below) and the Canadian government had no clear idea of what it wanted out of the CEC in the environment, economy and trade field. Ten years later, there is still a strong view in important quarters in the Canadian government that the CEC should focus on its co-operative agenda, and that the Environment, Economy Trade Program has produced little of practical, visible value thus far. Yet on the whole, the Canadian government's attitude has changed a great deal.

Within Environment Canada, the CEC is now seen as having usefully raised the profile of environmental ministries in North America within their governments in regard to economic decision-making, and in making the environment a more important, integral part of trade negotiations and policy formation. It has helped create a context supportive of the development of a substantial unit within Environment Canada to work on trade-environment issues. It has directly addressed the concern that environmental regulations are intended or unintended barriers to trade. And it has helped promote the message that trade and the environment are mutually supportive, show that environmental measures are good for business, and focused policy thinking on making trade liberalization work for the environment.

The program is further seen as demonstrating the value of the CEC in tackling issues others have not been able to take up because of the number of parties from which the latter must secure permission. The CEC's work on NAFTA Environmental Effects and labeling is cited in this regard. Others see an important research and "think tank" role for the CEC in trade-environment issues. They support the CEC doing more such work and attribute shortcomings to the parties rather than the CEC.

Yet there have also been disappointments. There is an inadequate relationship with trade counterparts in other countries in and through the program. There has not been a strategic plan that would prevent the ad hoc "follow-on" imperative from producing, for example, a proposed project on palm trees that Canada opposed, following the one on shade coffee that the CEC did. Nor has it been possible to attract the trade, or other ministers, to meet with the environment ministers to deal with shared concerns. Moreover, while the CEC is well respected for the quality of its NAFTA Environmental Effects work, it is seen in some places as academic and irrelevant at this stage, even if it will produce results when the methodology is applied. From this perspective the shift from NAFTA Environmental Effects to a broader trade-environment agenda has been a welcome step.

Conservation of Biodiversity

The Conservation of Biodiversity Program consists of activities on conservation strategy, birds, terrestrial species, marine species, marine protected areas, invasive species and biodiversity information.

This program stands apart from the others in that, in the field of biodiversity conservation, there had been considerable interconnected bilateral and trilateral interaction among the three governments and other stakeholders prior to the advent of the NAAEC. This came as a consequence of the 1916 Canada-US Migratory Birds Convention, the North American Waterfowl Management Plan, the Convention on International Trade in Endangered Species (CITES) and the RAMSAR convention on wetlands.[3] This history helps fuel a

---

[3] "The trilateral concept emerged in discussions to involve Mexico in the North American Waterfowl Management Plan (NAWMP). As an alternative, Mexico drafted a Memorandum of Understanding to create a Tripartite Committee" among the countries, which was signed by all three in 1988. The goal of this committee was to develop and design conservation strategies for migratory birds and their habitats. After Mexico became a full partner in NAWMP (in 1994), the role of the Tripartite Committee was less clear.

dominant view in Canada and the trilateral biodiversity conservation community that the CEC should be a facilitator and auditor, rather than a program deliverer or the central management agency through which all trilateral interaction takes place. This is consistent with a seminal high-level Canadian view of the CEC as but one among many mechanisms for trilateral environmental co-operation. It is reinforced by a feeling in the biodiversity conservation community that the CEC, managed in the US by the EPA, will devote insufficient attention to biodiversity conservation, which is entrusted to the Department of the Interior in the US. From this perspective, difficulties have arisen in the CEC's work when the Secretariat has proceeded more rapidly than the emerging consensus among the three governments in regard to implementation, and when it proceeds, as with biodiversity implementation systems, without agreed expectations among them.

Nonetheless, the CEC has made, and is seen to have made, a useful contribution to securing Canadian objectives. It has enhanced the capacity of Mexicans to participate more broadly. It has allowed Canadians to tap into a rich network of Mexican academics. It has provided a forum to explore partnerships on a neutral, third-party ground, without first engaging the formal machinery of all three national governments. It has made it easier to access civil society input at a high level, and thus secure a broader spectrum of ideas than that which emerges when a single agency serves as invitee and host. It also allows for an easier, freer-thinking exchange of ideas, given the prevalence of tightly confined political appointees in the US and Mexican systems and the frequency with which these incumbents change.

At a more concrete level, the CEC has produced useful deliverables on continental ecosystem mapping, forward movement on the North American Bird Conservation Initiative, an agreed work program on species of concern, a biodiversity strategy and a budget to fund projects that adds resources to those otherwise available for biodiversity conservation (Commission for Environmental Cooperation 2003).

Pollutants and Health

The Pollutants and Health Program comprises activities on the Sound Management of Chemicals (SMOC), the North American Pollutant Release and Transfer Register (PRTR), air quality, pollution prevention and children's health.

i. SMOC

The first of these activities, SMOC, is regarded, from the perspective of Environment Canada, the Canadian government, and the broader Canadian community, as by far the most useful and effective CEC program. It is seen as valuable by all, is considered the flagship program and is probably the most visible achievement of the CEC to Canadians as a whole. There are very good

---

The Canadian Wildlife Service suggested revising it with a broader mandate covering all wildlife and its habitat. The new name, the Trilateral Committee for Wildlife and Ecosystem Conservation and Management, reflects this broader mandate." "Migratory Birds Conservation," Environment Canada, http://www.cws-scf.ec.gc.ca/birds/trilat_e.cfm. In addition, 1990 brought a Canada-Mexico Agreement on Environmental Co-operation.

grounds for this highly favourable consensus that SMOC commands. Indeed, so strong, sustained and widespread are SMOC's benefits, both to Canada directly and further afield, that it alone could justify the NAAEC's value for Canada during the Agreement's first ten years.

At the CEC, since the start, Canada has been the only member consistently supporting SMOC. Canada pushed the project and the funding and programs to implement its regional action plans. Within Mexico, the initiative was enthusiastically welcomed by the responsible national official, who used the external support to develop the national program and the capacity that Mexico then almost entirely lacked. The US has been at times reluctant to move ahead rapidly on particular substances, such as benzene, that have been proposed.

SMOC is so highly valued because it is a concrete expression of the larger Canadian desire to have the NAAEC serve as an instrument to build environmental capacity and management at the national level, above all in Mexico.

Above all, SMOC has delivered clear, concrete deliverables that have brought substantial environmental improvement to Canada and to critical Canadian populations, notably indigenous peoples in Canada's Arctic. It has done so by eliminating or reducing in Mexico the use of harmful chemicals that flow north into Canada to do demonstrable damage there. In doing so, it directly saves lives in Canada. Thus far, the first set of "dirty dozen" chemicals have been addressed across North American through action under the program. In particular, the program has eliminated new sources of DDT and chlordane from the environment. It is currently refining its North American Regional Action Plan on lindane and other hexachlorocyclohexanes (HCH).[4]

ii. Pollutants Release and Transfer Registry

The PRTR, with its annual report, *Taking Stock,* is a program for providing rigorously comparable, readily comprehensible, public environmental and pollution information on the industrial release of major toxic pollutants. It is one of the largest programs the CEC has, with a current budget of US$450,000. The PRTR seeks to harmonize national programs, in the limited sense of comparing and informing the public throughout North America, rather than adjusting national programs to operate in the same way. The PRTR was motivated in part by the belief that such standardized public comparisons could help in assessing the environmental impacts of NAFTA-related trade.

When the CEC started the PRTR project, Canada was not particularly supportive. Its first reservation derived from the fact that the project was only a bilateral comparison of releases between Canada and US, rather than a genuinely trilateral activity. Canada's second concern was the CEC's adoption of the US national Toxics Release Inventory (TRI) framework as the model for the PRTR, as opposed to the creation of one that was adapted to include the superior features of Canada's National Pollutants Release Inventory (NPRI). This CEC decision might have been a result of the initial need seen by the CEC for rapid action, and

---

[4] CEC (2004), "Alaskans consulted on lindane action plan," February 12.

of the familiarity of the responsible CEC project manager with the US system. Yet this approach produced considerable Canadian discomfort, on scientific and environmental grounds. The core concern was that because the US method aggregated pollutants in a less sensitive way than Canada's method did, it could mislead the public. The US TRI examined all substances and aggregated them by weight to produce an overall national ranking of the top releasers. In contrast, Canada's NPRI did not aggregate but ranked releasers individually for each of the top ten individual pollutants. The CEC's US-based approach raised concerns for the Canadian government, Canadian industry and some Canadian environmental groups. They felt it was misleading, because an emitter could be ranked low overall even if it had high releases of carcinogens in particular. Canadian firms wrote letters to the Minister of the Environment, expressing concern that their stock price might fall because of the misleading public reports.

Canada brought its concerns to the CEC, which did address some of them. A new CEC project manager examined both the US and Canadian systems thoroughly, and selected what she regarded as the superior features of each. At the same time, Canadian representatives conducted what were, in effect, two parallel dialogues, one with the Mexicans focused on capacity building and one with the Americans focused on transparency and the right to know.

Slowly, the PRTR has become a CEC project that is important to Canada. It is now regarded as an area where the Secretariat has started on the right track, and has now produced a record of useful concrete deliverables. It is one of the CEC projects and publications that has had the most heavy and favourable impact in Canada. In particular, the PRTR has produced a number of clear benefits for Canada.

First, the PRTR has created stronger bilateral relations and results between Canada and the United States. Even though the evolving PRTR framework is still about 80% American in design, every year there is more compatibility and more incremental improvements in information exchange between Canada and the US.

Second, within the Canadian government, the PRTR has influenced Environment Canada's approach to reporting in the NPRI. It tries to see how the NPRI and the TRI can be more compatible, by resolving the areas where comparison is not possible, and perhaps moving toward a system that provides greater comparability. Canada has learned more effective ways from the US to communicate data to the public, such as becoming familiar with tools used by the EPA to work with NGOs in developing maps so citizens can view what is being released in their neighbourhood. It has thus affected the way Canada's national programs work.

Third, the annual PRTR report regularly receives more news coverage in Canada than Canada's own NPRI. This is perhaps because PRTR packages the data more effectively for public release, because of the greater credibility the international CEC source gives it, and because of Canadians' inherent interest in how their country is performing relative to the neighbouring US.

Rather than resisting, Canadian industry is living with the PRTR, responding to it, and trying to get a better performance as a result. Canada's steel companies and others are now issuing reports and press releases highlighting the fact that they have improved or moved up on the PRTR list or explaining their apparently disappointing ranking in the PRTR report.[5] This is a sign that industry is taking the report and its "shaming" effect seriously, and responding in a desirable way. There is a belief that it has also had some impact in reducing toxic emissions in Canada.[6] There is a hope that it might do so for smog and acid rain pollutants, as indicators for these substances are slated to be added to the PRTR list.

Beyond Canada, the Canadian government's commitment to trilateralism is slowly being realized in the PRTR. The CEC brought American and Canadian pressure to bear on Mexico to introduce regulations to require industry to disclose this information to the public. In the face of major resistance from industry in Mexico, much pressure was applied from the EPA Administrator and Canada's Environment Minister. Considerable capacity-building assistance also came from the CEC, and from the discretionary resources of Environment Canada (Kirton 2002a). Mexico has thus increasingly provided data to be incorporated into what is now a trilateral PRTR, if still one heavily oriented to the US and Canada.

Looking ahead, Canada sees PRTR as a concrete expression of Canada's strategic vision to have the CEC focus on activities that it does better than anyone else, and on public accessibility to information, by making available and accessible existing data, rather than by creating new information. Yet there remain several Canadian disappointments in regard to the PRTR. One is the continuing need to promote the PRTR within Environment Canada and other Canadian government departments. The second is to overcome resistance flowing from the fact that PRTR is a self-reporting system with minimal methodological requirements. The third is that media attention on the PRTR, while desirable in itself, has taken attention away from the other accomplishments of the CEC. A fourth is that the CEC did not have its own funding to finance the capacity building required in Mexico to make the PRTR more rapidly a more fully trilateral exercise. Yet together these continuing reservations pale in comparisons to the clear benefits that Canada has secured through the PRTR.

iii. Air Quality

One area where Canada has begun to act more strategically and successfully in recent years is the Air Quality Program. In the past, CEC work in regard to air flowed from Secretariat initiatives such as the Article 13 Report on Continental Pollutant Pathways. It also came from strategic US initiatives, based

---

[5] For example, Noranda (2003), "International Report Demonstrates Importance of Metal Recycling at Noranda," *News Release* April 17, and Francois Blain, Director, media relations, Canadian Pulp and Paper Association, "Letter to the Editor of the Ottawa Citizen, the Globe and Mail, and the Toronto Star, , n.d.

[6] The *Taking Stock* report released on May 29, 2002, containing the first five year trend review, showed a 3% decline in the total of toxic chemicals generated in North America. The report released in the spring of 2003 showed a 5% drop from 1995 to 2000 in North American chemicals released into the environment and shipped for recycling or other disposal, with an 8% drop in air emission in the US and an increase in Canada.

on the US desire to stop dirty air from Mexico entering the US, to create emissions inventories in Mexico that lead to public participation and pressure, and to constitute the foundation for transport modeling.

Canada inspired the creation of a CEC Working Group on Air. This push also came from the Secretariat, JPAC and the CEC's Article 13 report on electricity. The latter confirmed that coal, as a major fuel to generate electricity, had significant smog and acid rain impacts. The Air Working Group first met in June 2003. The Secretariat put existing air-related activity under the heading of the Working Group, and gave it a small amount of money to do air quality monitoring in Mexico. The Working Group then began to develop a strategic plan.

Canada's approach has been to have a focus for the Working Group's work, to avoid duplicating other work that Canada was conducting bilaterally with the US, to have the CEC work on matters, such as emission inventories, that were consistent at both borders, and to take up matters of particular Canadian concern, such as best available technology (BAT) for air pollution control. Within the Canadian government, senior levels have been engaged to examine how to use the trilateral framework to advance Canada's bilateral interests with the US. Canada sees the role of the CEC in air not as setting policy but as building tools to support Canadian interests, notably those on smog and acid rain.

As the same smog and acid rain crosses only one North American border, and is thus physically a bilateral rather than trilateral issue. Canada sees the Air Working Group's role as developing common tools and information on air quality, and on monitoring mechanisms in Mexico to identify air quality for smog. Canada hopes that this work will provide high-quality, detailed data that can be made public, of the sort that Canada lacks at home.

vi. Children's Health

The CEC's work on children's health was a US initiative, led by former EPA administrator Carol Browner and flowing from an EPA priority. Canada gave this initiative strong support. The prevailing view is that the relationship between environment and health needs to be developed in the North American context, if only to better equip Environment Canada for its dialogue with Health Canada, and to develop improved regulatory policies at home.

Canada has suggested that the CEC work on health data and comparability, with some forward-looking assessment included. As the OECD already has work underway in this area, the CEC will focus more narrowly on developing health indicators.

d. Law and Policy

The Law and Policy Program is made up of activities for environmental standards, hazardous waste, enforcement and compliance, as well as freshwater and environmental management systems. Since the start, Canada has viewed the CEC as a way of strengthening the enforcement program, particularly in regard to the import and export of hazardous waste.

Here there have been disappointments. It has not been possible to exchange information on transborder shipments. This is in part for political reasons, due to mistrust between the US and Mexico. It is also due to legal obligations in Canada for the privacy of industry-supplied information and in the US for disclosure. There was a concern that some might use US actors to secure information on Canadian firms that would be confidential under Canadian law at home. Thus far, the CEC has done nothing in the enforcement field with a direct impact on the environment within Canada. One proposal for CEC activity where a specific Canadian interest has been involved — on pollution by maritime vessels — has been difficult to get underway due to budgetary constraints.

Nonetheless the CEC's work as a co-ordinator has been useful in building capacity for Mexican wildlife officers through seminars and training of customs officers. Most recently, the CEC has developed a strategic plan for the Enforcement Working Group. Canada has also successfully avoided being drawn into operational matters where there are sharp US-Mexican differences, as in the treatment of the dumping of tires from the US in Mexico. Most broadly, there has developed a greater willingness by individuals to work together on a common strategic plan, with capacity building in Mexico at its core. Yet here the rapid rotation in personnel on the US and Mexican side has limited progress.

Article 10(6) Trade-Environment

As noted above, the Canadian government trade policy community has a generally and increasingly favourable judgment of the CEC's trade-environment work. This rests on two of the three pillars of the work under NAAEC Article 10(6). These pillars are the Article 10(6)(d) obligation to "assess on an ongoing basis NAFTA's Environmental Effects," the work of the subsequently created "10(6) Working Group on Trade-Environment Linkages" and the desire to express trade-environment integration and equality at the ministerial level through a joint meeting of the CEC Council and NAFTA's Free Trade Commission (FTC).

NAFTA's Environmental Effects

Article 10(6)D imposes on the CEC a mandatory obligation to "assess on an ongoing basis NAFTA's environmental effects." Members of the trade policy community judge the CEC's output under its ensuing Environment, Economy and Trade Program to be balanced and not propagandistic. This judgment applies to such politically charged studies as those on Mexican maize. The work is seen as credible and helpful in showing that trade liberalization under NAFTA is not destroying the environment. DFAIT officials dealing with the trade-environment interface from an environmental perspective also have high regard for the CEC-created framework to assess NAFTA's environmental effects. Indeed, those negotiating Canada's trade agreements have called this breakthrough work from the CEC.

Internationally, the NAFTA Environmental Effects framework, produced by an environmental organization, stands out as being based on an environment-first multidisciplinary approach and on the particular characteristics of North

146

America, including that of its emerging country member Mexico. It thus stands apart from the one major earlier effort, developed by the OECD. This framework, from an economic organization, offered an economy-first framework based on economic methodologies, and reflected the experience of developed countries, largely in the European core. Not surprisingly, the CEC framework has been attractive to ENGOs and developing countries now taking up the task of assessment through organizations such as UNEP. Here the influence of the CEC framework has come less on paper than through people, as those familiar with the CEC framework have moved on to contribute to the task of developing methodologies appropriate on a global scale.

Article 10(6) Working Group on Trade-Environment Linkages

Of less direct benefit thus far has been the Article 10(6) Working Group on Trade-Environment Linkages, a body created once the construction of the NAFTA Effects framework was largely complete. The Working Group has helped Canadian government trade officials become more directly involved in the work of the CEC, and more familiar with, and aware of the value of, the CEC's approach to forging the trade-environment link. These officials have come to regard the annual CEC work program on Environment, Economy and Trade as making a useful contribution.

Yet the Working Group has not led to a similar intra-national integration between the trade and environment communities within the US and Mexico. This has made Working Group discussions somewhat unbalanced. Nor has the Group been able to help with central issues, such as the approach to precaution. In addition, Canada resisted a JPAC proposal that the Working Group take up the question of NAFTA's Chapter 11 investment dispute process, on the grounds that the three governments were already dealing with this issue in another forum under NAFTA itself.

CEC Council–FTC Joint Meeting

Most disappointingly, Canadian officials have been unable to convince their NAFTA partners to proceed with one initiative that would signal the full equality and integration of trade and environment values. This is the proposal to hold a joint meeting of the trade ministers of the NAFTA Free Trade Commission and the environment ministers of the CEC Council. Canada's most recent effort to secure such a meeting was opposed by the US, which feared it would lead to demands that a joint meeting be held for labour as well. Additional concerns relate to the particular agenda, length and prominence of such a meeting, and its symbolic value as a statement of a NAFTA-wide commitment to sustainable trade.

Probably the greatest failure of the NAAEC from a Canadian perspective has thus been the minimal progress made during the first decade in fulfilling the obligation to "cooperate with the NAFTA Free Trade Commission to achieve the environmental goals and objectives of the NAFTA" as specified in Article 10(6) of the NAAEC. To be sure, the emergence of activity in the trade community in the three governments over the NAFTA Environmental Effects project, and the subsequent creation and work of the Environment and Trade Officials Group helped realize the intent of this provision at the working level. But nothing has taken place at senior levels, or in the form of any collective encounter between the trilateral CEC and its trade counterpart, especially at the ministerial level. In part this is because the FTC has not resulted in a trilateral Secretariat that could easily and continuously interact with its CEC counterpart. But, above all, it reflects the inability of the trade and environment communities in all three governments to agree, at the same time, to hold a ministerial or senior-level encounter, and to agree on its purpose, length, format and agenda.

The Canadian government's trade and environment communities are working together to find a way to bring about such a meeting, in recognition of their new enthusiasm for the CEC's trade-environment work, and the sympathy of both Canadian ministers for integrated work on trade and the environment (Kirton 2003a). Yet the experience of the past decade suggests that a top-down injection of political will and a decision of architectural dimensions, rather than incremental, bottom-up consensus, will be required to forge this critical missing link. The similar experience of the CEC and Environment Canada in the field of energy, where NAEWG officials refuse to include the CEC in their meeting, even as the CEC includes NAEWG in its meetings, also shows how difficult the achievement of equal, reciprocal interaction and integration of the economy and the environment can be.

Article 14-15 Citizens' Submission

The NAAEC's Article 14-15 process allows any "interested party" to initiate direct action against governments that are felt to be systematically not enforcing their own environmental regulations (Winham 1994, Raustiala 1995, Markell 2000, Kirton 2002a, Blair 2003, Fitzmaurice 2003). There have been 42 such submissions, or cases, filed from NAFTA's start to the end of 2003. This mechanism, designed largely for the ENGO community, has generated more activity than the NAFTA's Chapter 11 on investment disputes, which was designed for use by firms. Indeed, Article 14-15 has generated almost three times as much activity, if only the 16 environmentally related Chapter 11 cases are included in the count.

Of the 42 cases initiated under the Article 14-15 process to the end of 2003, Mexico was the target of 20, Canada 14 and the United States 8. The overall pattern is not highly unbalanced across the three countries if their relative size is not taken into account. Canada, that is, with one third of the cases directed at it, has not been particularly singled out. When one accounts for the likely capacity of the respective governments to enforce their environmental regulations effectively, it is hardly surprising that a relatively poorer Mexico would be the target of more cases that the richly resourced government of the US.

The balance, however, shifts when one considers only those eight cases that have proceeded all the way to the release of a factual record. Here the distribution is Mexico three, Canada four and the US only one. Of the 11 cases listed as active at the end of 2003, Mexico is the subject of seven and Canada four. The US had no cases under active consideration. However, not all these ongoing cases need end in factual records. Yet when they do, environmentally enhancing change is the major result.

Article 14-15 is operating, as intended, as a mechanism for ENGOs concerned with environmental quality and related social concerns. Most of the cases have been filed by ENGOs. Seven of the eight cases leading to factual records have been submitted by ENGOs. The eighth was submitted by an aboriginal fisheries association in British Columbia. In 1999-2000, firms began to file actions, but the two they mounted were declined on the grounds that they were already the subject of action under NAFTA's Chapter 11. The "process protection" problem for the trade community, in the form of jurisdiction shopping and simultaneously litigating under different mechanisms on the same issue, has thus been contained. Article 14-15 has thus remained a pure mechanism for environmental protection, rather than being mobilized by firms and foreign investors to forward their ultimately commercial concerns. It is also accessible to individuals, who have used it in conjunction with an NGO. The cadence of Article 14-15 usage, with a continuing set of fresh cases initiated each year, and an overall average of four to five cases a year, shows that the ENGO submitter community continues to have faith in the actual and potential impact of the mechanism.

Of the 42 cases initiated to the end of 2003, however, just under 20% have ended in a published factual record. Far more have been terminated, withdrawn, diverted (to an Article 13 investigation) or deferred. Moreover, the CEC's Council has declined a CEC recommendation that a factual record be prepared in two cases.

The Article 14-15 process has served Canadian interests. It has proved to have an embarrassment factor, leading to much questioning within Environment Canada and the government as a whole and from legislators when factual records against Canada are released. It has helped cushion the enforcement resources in Environment Canada against cutbacks at a time of severe departmental downsizing. It has helped Environment Canada more broadly support a strong enforcement process. NGOs are still using the mechanism to launch submissions against Canada, showing the mechanism has value in their judgment. And a CEC study has pointed to the many ecological improvements that have come as a result of the BC Hydro Article 14-15 case (Bowman 2001). In this case, the CEC Secretariat faced little opposition in its recommendation to proceed to a factual record. The US was eager to go forward and Canada did not resist. The record dealt with the strengths and weaknesses of the existing watershed management program and led to better integration on the Watershed Management Plan, in ways that the submitters themselves recognize and approve.

Given its record in Canada, the Article 14-15 model has been regarded as appropriate for — and thus for inclusion in modified form in — the other bilateral free trade agreements that Canada has gone on to negotiate. For example, Canada's agreement with Chile contains an Article 14-14-like clause, with some modifications resulting from the absence of a Secretariat in the Canada-Chile case.

Part 5 Dispute Resolution

The NAAEC Part 5 dispute resolution provisions provided a variable regime. Here the United States and Mexico could sanction each other with trade restrictions at the end of a lengthy process for non-enforcement of environmental regulations. In contrast, under Part 5, Canada could sanction, and be sanctioned by, the US and Mexico only with monetary fines imposed through the Canadian domestic court system. This variable architecture preserved Canada's fundamental objectives. These were to protect the open access to the US market that Canada had secured under CUSFTA and to allow the corporate strategies of Canadian companies to be developed free from fear that that NAFTA, through the NAAEC, would imperil their critical export market access.

Part 5 has remained a dead letter, in that no government has initiated actions that could lead either to trade sanctions or fines. It is widely expected to remain a dead letter in perpetuity, under a *de facto* non-aggression pact in which no country will initiate the first dispute for fear of unleashing a spiral of retaliation under which all would lose. Nonetheless, its very presence and the legal potential for action have substantial negative effects. It has made Canadian provinces more reluctant to accede to the NAAEC. It has made some in the legal and trade community in DFAIT anxious to restrict the Article 14-14 mechanism for fear that the contents of a factual record flowing from it, relating to environmental subsidies with trade effects, could unleash political pressures in the aggrieved country that would induce their government to mount the first Part 5 case. Above all, the presence of Part 5 suggests a continued collective belief in punition and economic protectionism, rather than capacity-building assistance and open commerce and co-operation as the way to secure environmental improvement. It is thus the antithesis of Canada's core sustainable development beliefs. Compounding the costs of Part 5 is the practice of the US government in introducing such provisions into its bilateral trade agreements with other developing countries in the western hemisphere in particular, and thus seeking to legitimize their philosophy of punition in the wider context of the FTAA and WTO. In recognition of its costs and absence of benefits, and knowing that developing countries are strongly opposed to trade sanctions, Canada has eliminated such provisions in its bilateral free trade agreements, and its FTAA and WTO negotiating stance (Kirton 2003a). Indeed, the Canadian government's refusal to accept trade sanctions for environmental reasons is fundamental to its approach to negotiations in the WTO Doha Development Agenda and the FTAA.

There is, at a minimum, no evidence that the presence of either the trade sanctions or fines envisaged by Part 5 have had any deterrent or other psychological effect in inducing improved environmental performance on the part of any of the parties. The absence of Part 5 action during the first decade suggests that no party believes that even the threat of such action would have an environmentally beneficial effect. The absence of any pressure by a civil society actor in any country over ten years to initiate such action suggests that everyone of consequence shares this belief.

Provincial Participation

Ten years after the agreement, little has been accomplished by way of attracting Canadian provinces to participate in the NAAEC. That the two initial leaders were Quebec and Alberta suggests that provincial decisions to participate are more an expression of a political judgment on NAFTA as a whole than of a functional evaluation of the value of the NAAEC and the CEC for this important area of provincial responsibility. Moreover, provinces have been largely uninvolved in the ongoing life of the CEC and its working groups, even in areas such as air quality where they have important concerns.

Although Canadian government officials consider that the greater presence of the provinces in the work of the CEC might strengthen the pan-Canadian voice, they do not see the CEC as a solution for the specific federal-provincial challenges they face. Indeed, in the biodiversity area, the ability of networks outside the CEC to attract state and provincial participation and contributions is one reason why the biodiversity community looks upon the CEC with some wariness.

Specific NAAEC Impacts

It is an analytically challenging task to assess the specific impact of the NAAEC on the way that governments in Canada manage and regulate, and the actual effects on the pressures, supports and the state of the ambient environment that result from the actions of Canadian governments. First, doing so involves specifying the autonomous effect of NAAEC-inspired action, whether through the CEC or outside it, identifying the resulting changes in interaction, institutionalization, learning and altered calculations of interests and conceptions of identity, and then the consequent changes in national government behaviour and the physical transformations in the Canadian ecology. Because the CEC is essentially a policy development facilitator, with virtually no budget for program implementation, the linkages are largely indirect. Moreover, much of the impact of the CEC takes place through nongovernmental mechanisms, through its civil society incubation and participation, and through enhanced public awareness as a whole. Many of the impacts, as with SMOC, have taken place in Mexico, and their effects have then been transmitted back to Canada. And several of the projects of most interest to the Canadian government — including projects now central to Canada's overall strategic vision for the CEC and approach to its work — are of recent origin, with impacts yet to be seen.

Yet several impacts of the NAAEC on the way the Canadian government regulates and manages, and the resulting environmental change in Canada, can confidently be identified at this time. Most broadly, a wide array of officials, from many of Environment Canada's programs and in DFAIT, regularly interact on a trilateral basis, in an increasingly co-operative spirit, through CEC forums. As this is an entirely new experience, outside the biodiversity area, the NAAEC has generated an often intense process of awareness, learning and even embryonic sense of identity on a North American scale. In particular, it has made Mexico a priority and a privileged partner of Canada. And it has strengthened Canada's behaviour abroad, as a member of a North American community, on global

151

debates on sustainability assessments of trade agreements and in securing resources from multilateral organizations to reduce toxic chemicals in Mexico.

Conclusions

During its first decade, the CEC has worked well for Canada. Indeed, it has worked increasingly well as the years have passed. Moreover, it promises to work even better for Canada in the years ahead. This is especially so as and if a more strategic Canadian vision, more continuous Canadian ministerial leadership, and a process of major modification of the CEC and its surrounding architecture are brought to bear.

Key Measures

The NAAEC and CEC represented a revolutionary departure in international governance for Canadians and for their colleagues in the United States and Mexico. Canada's initial aspirations for the new regime, while somewhat reactive, were architectural, ambitious, general and expansive, rather than incremental, modest, narrow in scope and limited in time. Thus, the effectiveness of the NAAEC for Canada should be assessed according to several measures that capture the generality and expansive nature of the great step that Canada made in designing and accepting the NAAEC in 1993. Here the most central measures for identifying success are:

1. Realizing Canada's initial and evolving objectives for the NAAEC and the CEC itself;
2. Forwarding, strategically and otherwise, Canada's national environmental and economy-environment priorities;
3. Engendering a trilateral North American community that fosters an improved environment and more open economy across the inherently integrated region and thus for Canadians living in its Canadian community or the region as a whole.
4. Expressing Canadians' nationally unifying priority for global environmental protection, within North America and on a global scale.

By these broad and ambitious measures, the NAAEC-CEC has, on the whole, served Canada well. A more detailed approach to assessment involves identifying Canada's specific success in achieving its five seminal and four evolving objectives, in securing its approach in each of the CEC's main programs and projects, and obtaining the environmental impacts its desires. Appendix C provides an overall judgment, based on the evidence reported and assessed above, in each of these categories, in regard to the level of Canadian success during the first decade as a whole, the trend over the past decade toward the present, and the prospects for Canadian success in the future should the NAAEC-CEC arrangements and architecture remain essentially the same, in the face of the real environmental and economic changes underway. The overall portrait is one of a medium level of success, a rising trend toward greater success in recent years, and reasonable prospects for success by building on the existing NAAEC-CEC architecture in the years ahead. The major areas of low performance, stagnation, and an uncertain future relate to areas where success is highly dependent on institutions outside the NAAEC-CEC – notably the core NAFTA itself – and where greater resources are required to meet the economic and environmental challenges that lie ahead.

Judgments about present and past success, as well as future prospects, are inevitably related to the investments that have been made. Although the resources available to the CEC are broader than the core funding provided directly to the CEC by the three member governments, this latter contribution is the core resource whose ample provision and wise use is essential for mobilizing the other resources which can come. Here one can compare the Canadian government's annual US$3 million contribution, fixed in nominal dollars at this level since the CEC's start, with a selected array of other international and internationally-oriented environmental institutions that the Canadian government invests in. The results show that the CEC stands as one of the Canadian government's "big four" international environmental institutional investments, as follows: the Montreal Protocol on Ozone at C$10,208,900; the CEC at C$4,650,000; the International Institute for Sustainable Development at C$3,361,000; and UNEP at $2,525,000. The CEC thus emerges as a leading, but not singularly central investment.

Key Impacts

The key impacts of the NAAEC-CEC are best seen in relation to the desired outcome – an enhanced physical environment for Canadians and North Americans to enjoy. Here, as detailed above, there is a substantial legacy of success. It is led by the reductions in toxic chemicals due to SMOC, the containment of air emissions as measured by and in modest part due to *Taking Stock*, prospects for preserving endangered species through regional biodiversity action plans, improved health for vulnerable and regular Canadian populations due to SMOC and PRTR, and a move toward controlling trade in harzardous substances due to the environment, economy and trade work. Demonstrable, physical improvements have thus come across most ambient environmental media, and even, embryonically in the trade-environment realm. Producing similar successes in regard to water, Canada's ice covered regions, and the global community are challenges that await in the next ten years.

Relevance for Other Agreements

The trade-environment achievements raise the central question of whether the revolutionary, pioneering North American regional model of the NAAEC-CEC is appropriate for adaptation and adoption by the global community as a whole. Here it is easy to identify the defects of the NAAEC-CEC architecture and performance, and the distinctiveness in a global context of the North American ecology and economy for which it was designed (Ostry 2002). Yet on the whole the evidence suggests there are good grounds for a more optimistic view (Maclaren and Kirton 2002).

In broad, architectural terms, the NAAEC-CEC model works. It should be strengthened and adapted and adopted on a global scale. Its wider value rests on its unique character as a full free trade regime that normatively, legally and institutionally put the environment in, in a largely integrated and equal way, that

153

did so by bridging countries across the long divisive north-south divide, and that treated equally countries with great diversity in levels of development, economic and social structure, and language, and with little prior social, political or economic connection or sense of community. No other real world model comes close to the NAAEC-CEC's proven record of success in the face of such diversity. Yet as Canada's core recent and prospective trade liberalization agreements will take place across new communities that manifest such diversity in ever larger measure, the NAAEC-CEC model stands as the only proven guide (Kirton 2003a, 2004).

In considering the adaptations required for this outward looking task, there are important issues that arise regarding, *inter alia,* the need to eliminate the impact or existence of the punitive provisions of Part Five, and the need to mobilize the resources required to solve, co-operatively, the environmental problems that the NAAEC's provisions and processes bring to light. Yet beyond the NAAEC-CEC organism and surrounding community lies the broader issue that full free trade agreements have proven to be politically necessary to bring such effective, expanding international environmental communities to life.

Bibliography

Alanis Ortega, Gustavo (2002), "Public Participation within NAFTA's Environmental Agreement: The Mexican Experience," in John Kirton and Virginia Maclaren, eds., *Linking Trade, Environment and Social Cohesion: NAFTA Experiences, Global Challenges* (Ashgate, Aldershot), pp. 183–186.

Audley, John (1997), *Green Politics and Global Trade: NAFTA and the Future of Environmental Politics,* (Georgetown University Press: Washington, D.C.).

Bennett, David (1994), "Harmonization and Risk Assessment in the North American Free Trade Agreement," in Ted Schrecker and Jean Dalgleish, eds, *Growth, Trade and Environmental Values,* (Westminster Institute for Ethics and Human Values: London), pp. 113-122.

Blair, David (2003), "The CEC's Citizen Submission Process: Still a Model for Reconciling Trade and the Environment?" *Journal of Environment and Development* 12 (September): 295-324.

Bowman, Jamie (2001), "Citizen Submission Process Proves Valuable in BC Hydro Case," *Trio* (Fall).

Commission for Environmental Cooperation (2003), *Biodiversity* (Commission for Environmental Cooperation, Montreal).

Commission for Environmental Cooperation (1999), *Assessing Environmental Effects of the North American Free Trade Agreement (NAFTA): An Analytic Framework (Phase II) and Issue Studies* (Commission for Environmental Cooperation, Montreal).

Commission for Environmental Cooperation (1997), *NAFTA's Institutions: The Environmental Potential and Performance of the NAFTA Free Trade Commission and Related Bodies.* Commission for Environmental Cooperation, Montreal.

Fitzmaurice, Malgosia (2003), "Public Participation in the North American Agreement on Environmental Cooperation," *International and Comparative Law Quarterly* 52 (April): 333-368.

Graves, Frank (2003), "Climate Change, The Environment and Continental Policy Convergence," part of the "Rethinking North American Integration" Study, Ekos, Presentation to the Public Policy Forum conference, Ottawa, October 30, 2003.

Hockin, Thomas (2004), "The World Trade Organization, the North American Free Trade Agreement, and the Challenge of Sustainable Development," in John Kirton and Michael Trebilcock, eds., *Hard Choices, Soft Law: Voluntary Standards in Global Trade, Environment and Social Governance* (Ashgate, Aldershot, forthcoming), pp. 261-274.

Hufbauer, Gary, Daniel Esty, Diana Orejas, Luis Rubio and Jeffrey Schott (2000), *NAFTA and the Environment: Seven Years Later* (Institute for International Economics: Washington, DC).

Jacott, Marisa, Cyrus Reed, and Mark Winfield (2002), "The Generation and Management of Hazardous Wastes and Transboundary Hazardous Waste Shipments between Mexico, Canada and the United States, 1990-2000," in Commission for Environmental Cooperation, *The Environmental Effects of*

Free Trade: Papers presented at the North American Symposium on Assessing the Linkages between Trade and Environment (October 2000), (Commission for Environmental Cooperation: Montreal)

Johnson, Pierre Marc and Andre Beaulieu (1996), *The Environment and NAFTA: Understanding and Implementing the New Continental Law* (Island Press, Washington DC).

Kirton, John (2004), "NAFTA for the Next Generation: Lessons Learned and Challenges Ahead," Paper prepared for a workshop on "Regionalism in the 21st Century: A Canada-ASEAN Dialogue as Part of an Opening Up of New Cross Pacific Linkages," ASEAN Secretariat, Jakarta, Indonesia, March 9, 2004. Available at www.envireform.utoronto.ca

Kirton, John (2003a), "Canada's Sustainable Trade Strategy: New Partners, The WTO and Beyond," Paper prepared for a conference on "Canada's Relations with Taiwan and China under the WTO Framework," Centre for WTO Studies, National Chenchi University, Taiwan, December 11–12, 2003. Available at www.envireform.utoronto.ca

Kirton, John (2003b), "NAFTA's Trade-Environment Regime and Its Commission for Environmental Cooperation: Contributions and Challenges Ten Years On," *Canadian Journal of Regional Science* 25:2 (Summer): 135–163.

Kirton, John (2002a), "International Institutions, Sustainability Knowledge and Policy Change: The North American Experience," Paper prepared for the 2002 Berlin Conference on the Human Dimensions of Global Environmental Change, Berlin, Germany, December 6–7, 2002.

Kirton, John (2002b), "NAFTA's Environmental Regime and the CEC: The Canadian Contribution," Paper prepared for a conference on "Canada-US Environmental Relations: From Bilateral Conflicts to Global Alliance?", Universite de Quebec a Montreal, Montreal, November 15.

Kirton, John (2002c), "International Institutions, Sustainability and Policy Change: The North American Experience," In Frank Biermann, Rainer Brohm, Klaus Dingworth, eds., *Proceedings of the 2001 Berlin Conference on the Human Dimensions of Global Environmental Change: Global Environmental Change and the Nations State*: PIK Report 80, Potsdam Institute for Climate Impact Research, December.

Kirton, John (2002d), "Winning Together: The NAFTA Trade-Environment Record," pp. 73–99, in John Kirton and Virginia Maclaren, eds., *Linking Trade, Environment and Social Cohesion: NAFTA Experiences, Global Challenges* (Ashgate, Aldershot).

Kirton, John (1999), "Trade's Benefits and Costs for US and Foreign Environmental Quality," pp. 129-158, in Alan V. Deardorff and Robert M. Stern, eds. *Social Dimensions of U.S. Trade Policies*, Ann Arbor, University of Michigan Press), Studies in International Economics Series.

Kirton, John (1998), "The Impact of Environmental Regulation on the North American Auto Industry Since NAFTA," pp. 184-220 in Sidney Weintraub and Christopher Sands, eds., *The North American Auto Industry under NAFTA* (Washington, D.C.: CSIS Press).

156

Kirton, John (1997), "NAFTA's Commission for Environmental Co-operation and Canada-US Environmental Relations," *American Review of Canadian Studies* 27 (Winter): 459-486.

Kirton, John and Raphael Fernandez de Castro (1997), *NAFTA's Institutions: The Environmental Potential and Performance of the NAFTA Free Trade Commission and Related Bodies* (Montreal: Commission for Environmental Co-operation), 76 pp.

Kirton, John and Virginia Maclaren (2002), "Forging the Trade-Environment-Social Cohesion Link, Global Challenges, North American Experiences," pp. 1-23, in John Kirton and Virginia Maclaren, eds., *Linking Trade, Environment, and Social Cohesion: NAFTA Experiences, Global Challenges* (Aldershot: Ashgate).

Kirton, John and Sarah Richardson (1992) "Canada's Contribution to a New Trade-Environment Regime," pp. 235-264, in John Kirton and Sarah Richardson, eds., *Trade, Environment and Competitiveness: Sustaining Canada's Prosperity* (Ottawa: National Roundtable on the Environment and the Economy).

Kirton, John and Alan Rugman (1999), "Regional Environmental Impacts of NAFTA on the Automotive Sector," *Canadian Journal of Regional Science* 21 (Summer): 227-254.

Logsdon, Jeanne and Bryan Husted (2000), "Mexico's Environmental Performance Under NAFTA: The First Five Years," *Journal of Environment and Development* 9 (December): 370-383.

Maclaren, Virginia and John Kirton (2002), "Conclusions," in , in John Kirton and Virginia Maclaren, eds., *Linking Trade, Environment, and Social Cohesion: NAFTA Experiences, Global Challenges* (Aldershot: Ashgate), pp. 325-331.

Markell, David (2000), "The Commission for Environmental Cooperation's Citizen Submission Process," *Georgetown International Environmental Law Review* 7(3, Spring): 565–574.

Mayer, Frederick (1998), *Interpreting NAFTA: The Science and Art of Political Analysis,* (Columbia University Press: New York).

Munton, Don and John Kirton (1994), "Environmental Cooperation: Bilateral, Trilateral, Multilateral," *North American Outlook* 4 (March): 59-87.

Ostry, Sylvia (2002), "Fix It or Nix It? Will the NAFTA Model Survive?" in , in John Kirton and Virginia Maclaren, eds., *Linking Trade, Environment, and Social Cohesion: NAFTA Experiences, Global Challenges* (Aldershot: Ashgate). pp. 319-324.

Raustiala, Kal (1995), "The Political Implications of the Enforcement Provisions of the NAFTA Environmental Side Agreement: The CEC as a Model for Future Accords," *Environmental Law* 25 (Winter): 31-56.

Richardson, Sarah (2000), "Sustainability Assessments of Trade Agreements: Global Approaches," in John Kirton and Virginia Maclaren, eds., *Linking Trade, Environment and Social Cohesion: NAFTA Experiences, Global Challenges* (Ashgate, Aldershot), pp. 243–263.

Richardson, Sarah (1994), "The Trade-Environment Linkage: Future Challenges of Liberalized Trade and Environmental Compliance," in Ted Schrecker and Jean Dalgleish, eds, *Growth, Trade and Environmental Values,* (Westminster Institute for Ethics and Human Values: London), pp. 11-28

Rugman, Alan and John Kirton (2002), ""NAFTA, Environmental Regulations and Firm Strategies," pp. 130-146 in S. Mansoob Murshed, eds., *Issues in Positive Political Economy,* (Routledge: London and New York).

Rugman, Alan and John Kirton (1999), "NAFTA, Environmental Regulations and International Business Strategies," *Global Focus* 11 (4).

Rugman, Alan and John Kirton (1998), "Multinational Enterprise Strategy and the NAFTA Trade and Environment Regime," *Journal of World Business* 33 (4): 438-454.

Rugman, Alan, John Kirton and Julie Soloway (1999), *Environmental Regulations and Corporate Strategy: A NAFTA Perspective* (Oxford University Press, Oxford).

Rugman, Alan, John Kirton and Julie Soloway (1997), "NAFTA, Environmental Regulations, and Canadian Competitiveness," *Journal of World Trade* 31 (August): 129-144.

Sanchez, Roberto, Konrad von Moltke, Steven Mumme, John Kirton and Don Munton (1998), "The Dynamics of Transboundary Environmental Agreements in North America: Discussion of Preliminary Findings," pp. 32-52, in Richard Kiy and John D. Wirth, eds., *Co-operation and Conflict* (College Station, Texas: Texas A&M University Press).

Spencer, Robert, John Kirton and Kim Nossal, eds. (1982), *The International Joint Commission Seventy Years On* (Centre for International Studies, University of Toronto, Toronto).

Swenarchuck, Michelle (1994), "The Environmental Implications of NAFTA: A Legal Analysis," in Ted Schrecker and Jean Dalgleish, eds, *Growth, Trade and Environmental Values,* (Westminster Institute for Ethics and Human Values: London), pp. 83-112.

Tollefson, Christopher (2002), "Stormy Weather: The Recent History of the Citizen Submission Process of the North American Agreement on Environmental Cooperation," in John Kirton and Virginia Maclaren, eds., *Linking Trade, Environment and Social Cohesion: NAFTA Experiences, Global Challenges* (Ashgate, Aldershot), pp. 153–182.

Vaughan, Scott (2002), "Understanding the Environmental Effects of Trade: Some Lessons from NAFTA," in John Kirton and Virginia Maclaren, eds., *Linking Trade, Environment and Social Cohesion: NAFTA Experiences, Global Challenges* (Ashgate, Aldershot), pp. 225–239.

Weintraub, Sidney (1997), *NAFTA at Three: A Progress Report,* (The Centre for Strategic and International Studies: Washington, D.C.).

Wilson, Serena (2002), "Article 14-15 of the North American Agreement on Environmental Cooperation: Intent of the Founders," in John Kirton and Virginia Maclaren, eds., *Linking Trade, Environment and Social Cohesion: NAFTA Experiences, Global Challenges* (Ashgate, Aldershot), pp. 187–193.

Winham, Gil (1994), "Enforcement of Environmental Measures: Negotiating the NAFTA Environmental Side Agreement," *Journal of Environment and Development* 3 (Winter): 29-41.

Appendix A: Data Sources

The evidence and judgments in this study, where not otherwise identified, are based on two sets of sources. The first are several series of confidential, semi-structural interviews from 1995 to 2003 with relevant stakeholders in all three NAFTA countries, as follows:

1. NAFTA Environmental Effects, Fall 1995–Spring 1996
2. NAFTA Institutions, Summer 1996–Spring 1997
3. IDRC Research (conducted by Julie Soloway), Fall 1997–Winter 1998
4. EnviReform CEC, Autumn 2002–Summer 2003
5. NAAEC@10, Autumn 2003

The second is through the author's "participant observation" involvement in five processes of relevance to the CEC's creation and operation. The first of these was as a member during the late 1980s of an informal multistakeholder group of individuals from the three countries, assembled by Jean Hennessey and Konrad Von Moltke of Dartmouth University, to assess the need for and the design of what was then termed a North American Commission on the Environment (NACE). The second was as a member from 1989 to 1995 of the Foreign Policy Committee of the National Roundtable on the Environment and the Economy with a major role in preparing advice to the Prime Minister of Canada on the environmental and sustainable development dimensions of the NAFTA and NAAEC. The third was a member of the Canadian government's International Trade Advisory Committee from 1995 to 1997. The fourth was as the project team leader of the CEC project on NAFTA Environmental Effects from 1995 to 1998. The fifth was as a member of the CEC's Advisory Committee on NAFTA's Environmental Effects from its inception through the spring of 2003.

It should be added that the community partners of the EnviReform project at the University of Toronto include the CEC, and the following organizations involved in the work of the CEC: Pollution Probe, the Centre patronal de l'environnement de Québec, and the Sierra Legal Defence Fund.

Appendix B: The Council's Agenda, 1995–2003

Issue	95	96	97	98	99	'00	'01	'02	'03
Public Participation	X	X		X			X		
Migratory Bird Deaths in Mexico	X								
Reducing Risks to Human Health through Pollution Prevention Strategies	X								
Wildlife Habitat Protection	X								
Energy Efficiency and Climate Change	X								
Public Access to Environmental Information	X						X		
Transboundary Initiatives (Including Transboundary EIA)	X		X		X		X		
Public Submissions (Article 14 and 15)	X			X		X			X
Enhancing Environmental and Public Health Protection		X							
Environment and Trade		X	X	X	X	X		X	X
Air Monitoring and Modeling/Cooperation on Air Quality Issues		X	X						X
Cozumel Factual Record		X							
North American Pollutants Release Inventory (Pollutant Release and Transfer		X			X	X		X	X

161

Registers)									
Environmental Enforcement and Compliance		X	X		X				X
Green Jobs		X							
Funding Communities		X							
Protection Migratory Species		X							
Evaluating Success of NAAEC/Progress Reviews			X	X					
"A Shared Agenda for Action" CEC 3 year planning				X					
Regional Action on Global Issues and Cooperation on Global Agreements				X			X		
Reducing the Threat of Toxic Chemicals/Sound Management of Chemicals			X		X	X		X	X
North American Bird Conservation Initiative					X		X	X	
Upper San Pedro River Imitative					X				
The Silva Reservoir					X				
Children's Health and the Environment						X	X	X	X
Law and Policy						X			
Biodiversity Conservation						X	X		X
North American Fund for Environmental Cooperation						X			

162

Market Based Approach to Environmental Conservation								X		
CEC Capacity Building								X		
Freight Traffic								X		
Electricity Market								X	X	
Industry Practices								X		
Strengthening CEC's Relationship with Private Sector								X		
Hazardous Waste									X	X
Finance and Environment										
Corporate Environmental Stewardship									X	X
World Summit on Sustainable Development									X	
Joint Meeting with International Joint Commission and International Boundary and Water Commission									X	
Management of Freshwater Resources										X
Renewable Energy										X
Disclosure of Financially Relevant Environmental Information										X
North American Green Purchasing Initiative										X
NAFTA 10 Year Retrospective										X

Prepared by Caitlin Sainsbury, November 14, 2003

163

Appendix C: Canada's Accomplishments at the NAAEC-CEC

Objective/Activity	Level	Canadian Success Trend	Prospects
Canadian Objectives:			
a. Make CEC Work	Medium	Uncertain	Favourable
b. Put Environment First	Medium	Stable	Unfavourable
c. Bring Citizens In	High	Stable	Favourable
d. Expand Resources	Medium	Stable	Uncertain
e. Foster Independence	Medium	Declining	Uncertain
f. Emphasize Co-operation	Medium	Stable	Favourable
g. Facilitate Intergovernmentalism	Medium	Improving	Favourable
h. Forward National Strategy	Medium	Improving	Favourable
i. Employ Trade Work	Low	Improving	Favourable
The NAAEC Institutions:			
a. Preambule Objectives/Obligations	High	Stable	Uncertain
b. CEC Budget	Medium	Declining	Unfavourable
c. Council	High	Improving	Favourable
d. Secretariat	High	Stable	Uncertain
e. Article 13	Medium	Improving	Unfavourable
f. JPAC	Medium	Declining	Stable
g. Environment, Economy and Trade	Low	Improving	Uncertain
h. Conservation of Biodiversity	Medium	Improving	Favourable
i. SMOC	Very High	Improving	Favourable
j. Taking Stock (PRTR)	Medium	Improving	Favourable
k. Air Quality	Low	Improving	Uncertain
l. Children's Health	Medium	Stable	Stable
m. Law and Policy	Low	Stable	Stable
n. NAFTA's Environmental Effects	Medium	Improving	Favourable
o. Article 10(6) Working Group	Low	Improving	Stable
p. A Council–FTC Joint Meeting	Low	Declining	Unfavourable
q. Article 14-15	Medium	Improving	Stable
r. Part 5	Negative	Stable	Unfavourable
s. Provincial Participation	Low	Stable	Stable
Specific NAAEC Impacts			
1. Industrial Pollutants	High	Improving	Favourable
2. Biodiversity	Low	Improving	Favourable
3. Environmental Health	High	Improving	Favourable
4. Water	Low	Improving	Favourable

NAFTA@10

Part 2:

The Way Forward?

MONETARY COOPERATION IN THE NORTH AMERICAN ECONOMY

David Laidler
University of Western Ontario

Asymmetries in North America's Monetary Order

Canadians are sometimes tempted to treat North American economic integration as a project to be pushed forward or resisted, depending on their economic and political preferences, but that is not quite right. Rather, North American economic integration is an already well established fact of life, which has to be managed. Clearly, the way in which it is managed will affect its prospects of deepening or unwinding, but there is no way of avoiding the day by day task of coping with it. It is in this context that Canada's monetary arrangements must be discussed. Even though the Canadian dollar's use is largely confined to Canada, to analyse the country's choice of monetary order from a purely domestic viewpoint is to miss a vital element in the constraints subject to which that choice must be made.

Other facts require attention here too, involving fundamental asymmetries that mark economic relations between Canada and the United States, not to mention Mexico.[1] Among these, the most immediately obvious, namely the relative economic sizes of the three countries, is the least important. Of much greater significance is the matter of their very different economic places in the world economy. To begin with, when it comes to Canada's trade in goods and services, and Mexico's too, the US is, to all intents and purposes, the "rest of the world". In round numbers, a little more than four fifths of the smaller countries' exports, (amounting to about a quarter of GDP in the Canadian case) go to the US. Canada is, to be sure, the US's largest single trading partner, but Asia and Europe are close runners up here, and there is no Canadian, let alone Mexican, dominance in US trade, to match that of the US in Canada and Mexico.

This fact alone implies that, though North American economic relations provide an appropriate context for the analysis of Canada's monetary choices, and of Mexico's too, the relevant background for the US is the international economy taken as a whole. The matter goes much deeper, however. Not only is the US a leading player in the world trading system, but, as McKinnon (2002) has stressed, its currency is dominant as a means of payment, unit of account and store of value for the international economy.

The US dollar is the international economy's money of choice, as well as being a domestic currency, and Benjamin Cohen (2003) has recently pointed out

---

[1] The place of Mexico within North America is an under-discussed topic in the Canadian literature on North American monetary issues. The reader is warned that this paper probably pays too little attention to the issues involved here, which surely require a major study in their own right to bring them into focus.

that this fact creates an important set of opportunities and incentives for the US that it is dangerous to ignore. First of all, the US is able to extract seigniorage, not just from its own citizens, but also from users of the US dollar world-wide, and has no incentive to share this revenue with any other North American country. More importantly, US firms, including financial institutions, gain a competitive advantage in international markets from the latter's reliance on the US dollar. The US government too derives considerable international political influence - soft power - from its ability to affect the international financial climate, and the way in which it impinges on particular countries; and in some rare cases it derives a useful degree of hard power too - Cohen reminds his readers of the case of Panama in the final days of the Noriega regime.

It is also worth recalling that, as with those of any other country, US monetary institutions are the product of a specific history.[2] In this case, a strong strain of monetary populism, that has sometimes taken on nationalist and even isolationist overtones, runs through the history in question. That a nation's monetary system should be organised and run for the benefit of its inhabitants is a difficult idea to object to, and it is deeply embedded in the US political psyche. The importance of this idea helps to explain why the Federal Reserve system, which styles itself as "independent *within* the government" (my italics), routinely operates with one eye firmly fixed on the White House and the Congress.[3] But more important in the current context, it also explains why the United States has long been particularly jealous of its sovereignty in international monetary affairs. This fact was reflected in such important matters as US reluctance to live by the rules of the gold-standard game in the 1920s, and in the design of the White plan that formed the basis for the reconstruction of the international monetary system after the Second World War.

Of less historical importance, but of more immediate relevance, the same quintessential US concern with monetary sovereignty that was at play in these earlier episodes also underlay the sharp and much quoted rebuff administered by Assistant Secretary of the Treasury, Lawrence Summers, in 1999 to Argentina, and by implication to other countries that were considering dollarization at that time, once it became clear that they were also hoping that such a step on their part would lead the US authorities to begin to take their interests into account in future policy decisions.

> . . . it would not be appropriate for the United States authorities to extend the net of bank supervision, to provide access to the Federal Reserve discount window, or to adjust bank supervisory responsibilities or the procedures or orientation of US monetary policy in the light of another country deciding to adopt the dollar. (Summers, 1999)

---

[2]Richard Timberlake (1993) provides an excellent single volume account of the evolution of monetary institutions and monetary policy in the United States from their foundation.
[3]As is evident from the studies of Allan Meltzer (2003) and Thomas Mayer (1999)

168

This was not an isolated remark by a particular official, but rather a statement of the Clinton Administration's policy on this issue, which was re-iterated the following year by the then Assistant Secretary of the Treasury for International Affairs in testimony to the US Senate, as David Howard, Deputy Director of the Division of International Finance the Board of Governors of the Federal Reserve pointed out in (2003). And Howard, speaking for the Federal Reserve System, also remarked at that time, that

> *The decision of a country to dollarise creates no obligations on the part of the Federal Reserve towards that country. In particular, the Federal Reserve is not obliged to act as a lender of last resort to financial institutions of officially dollarised countries, supervise their financial institutions or take into account their economic and financial conditions when setting monetary policy. (Howard, 2003, p. 153)*

These statements do not mean that the US will never take specific monetary measures that are in the interests of other countries. It would obviously do so when such measures were also in its own interests. Furthermore, though Howard (2003) noted explicitly that "there is no reason to think that the Bush Administration has a different view on dollarisation" from that of its predecessor, he was also careful to point out, as befitted a representative of Federal Reserve system, that "US policy on dollarisation could well evolve over time as circumstances change".

Nevertheless, there seems to be no reason to expect an early change of attitude here. The parallels that have sometimes been drawn between possible future US actions, and those of Germany, which surrendered control over its own very successful monetary policy by adopting the Euro, are surely misleading. Substituting the Euro for the Deutschmark was not so much an act of altruism on Germany's part as it was a sacrifice necessary to obtain support and acceptance elsewhere in Europe for its own reunification. Furthermore, European monetary unification is part and parcel of a wider ranging program of economic and political integration that has been going on in Europe since the end of the Second World War, and is driven by profound historical forces whose origins long antedate that war. No similar political dynamic seems to be present in North America, now or in the foreseeable future, that would undermine the United States long standing commitment to putting domestic priorities first in monetary matters.

Recent Canadian Discussions of Monetary Integration

Debate about monetary arrangements has been very much on the agenda in Canada over much of the last decade, with a number of prominent commentators, for example Herbert Grubel (1999) and Thomas Courchene and Richard Harris (1999), advocating the creation of some sort of monetary union in North America, perhaps based on the NAFTA and therefore including Mexico, or perhaps involving only Canada and the United States. Some observers, for example Sherry Cooper (2001), have gone so far as to suggest that such monetary integration is in any event evolving as the irresistible consequence of market forces, that policy measures designed to prevent it are futile, and that a policy of actively embracing the inevitable is to be preferred.

The attention paid to these proposals until quite recently drew some of its energy from a "me too" reaction on the part of some North Americans to the launch of a virtual European currency in 1999 and to the introduction of Euro notes and coins in 2002: if an economically integrated Europe found a common currency desirable, then so perhaps should an economically integrated North America. But their resonance with the Canadian public probably had much more to do with the decline of the Canadian-US dollar exchange rate in the wake of the Asian and Russian crises of 1997-98, which culminated in its reaching an all time low of about 62 cents in 2002. This decline gave forecasts that the Canadian dollar was bound for extinction a superficial claim to plausibility among the public, and ensured that many who remained skeptical about this likelihood nevertheless became concerned about their future living standards.

There is no need here to enter into a long and sustained rebuttal of the case that Canadian proponents of North American monetary integration have advanced. Suffice it to note that many of its elements have failed to stand up to scrutiny. Specifically; it was soon noted that the European Monetary Union was intended by its architects, not as a response to a process of continental economic integration that might bear some resemblance to similar tendencies in North America, but as a means of advancing a project of political integration that had no parallel at all on this side of the Atlantic Anecdotal evidence of a rapid voluntary spread in the use of the US dollar within Canada in traditional monetary roles, furthermore, proved to be false; upon examination of the data, it turned out that dollarization was at a low level in Canada, was growing slowly at best, and not on all measures.[4] As to claims of a dramatic fall in Canadian living standards brought about by a declining currency, these ran into the awkward fact that the latest period of exchange depreciation also saw a rapid and sustained increase in real per capita GDP in Canada, which, over the 1998-2002 period, ran ahead of the United States' performance.

Most important of all, as Cohen (2003) has noted, in recent debates Canadian advocates of North American monetary union paid inadequate attention to the economic, historic and political context in which US monetary decisions are made. They therefore failed to realise that it would not be feasible to eliminate the many economic drawbacks inherent in the unilateral adoption of the US dollar by Canada by negotiating a co-operative arrangement with the US. As Robson and Laidler (2002) showed, the concessions that would have had to be sought in any such negotiations, in order to make dollarization an economically practical and politically acceptable proposition for Canada, coincided almost exactly with those that Assistant Secretary Summers had already explicitly ruled out in 1999.

It is hardly surprising, then, that serious discussions of North American monetary integration had already begun to wind down in Canada, even before the

---

[4]Some of these data, appertaining to the use of the Canadian and US dollars as a unit of account by Canadian firms, were the product of a special survey conducted by the Bank of Canada. Other series, on. for example holdings of US dollar denominated bank deposits by Canadians were already available in regularly published sources. The definitive study of the degree of voluntary dollarization within Canada is Murray and Powell (2002)

recent dramatic rise in the Canadian exchange rate against the US dollar removed a major factor that was, rightly or wrongly, underpinning popular interest in such schemes. Even so, the facts of North American economic integration referred to in the introduction to this paper remain facts, and, in Canada, complaints about the effects of a declining exchange rate among consumers and importers have recently been replaced by complaints about a rising rate among exporters. If North American monetary union is not an option, it does not follow that the monetary status quo in North America is beyond reproach. There are still issues to be addressed.

Co-operation under Current Monetary Arrangements

At present, the three countries which make up the NAFTA area maintain separate currencies and distinct monetary and financial systems, while each of them deploys monetary policy in pursuit of domestic goals. In the United States, the Federal Reserve system is bound by act of Congress to pursue the twin goals of price level stability and high employment, while in 1991 Canada became the second country in the world to adopt formal targets for the inflation rate as the sole goal of monetary policy. Mexico too is nowadays an inflation targeter. Against this background, it is left to markets to determine exchange rates among the three currencies.

These arrangements do not imply, of course, that monetary policies in the other two countries are of no concern to the authorities in any one of them. What happens in the United States is obviously of critical importance to the Bank of Canada. The performance of the economy there affects the demand for Canadian exports, the level of interest rates in international capital markets, not to mention the behaviour of the Canadian/US dollar exchange rate. All of these impinge upon the level of aggregate demand within Canada, which in turn is the proximate determinant of variations in the inflation rate relative to expectations. Thus, what is an appropriate setting for the Bank of Canada's crucial policy instrument, its target range for the overnight interest rate, depends among other things on what is happening in the United States. To a lesser extent, events in Canada form part of the background against which the Fed makes policy, and similar interdependencies exist as far as Mexico is concerned as well.

Nevertheless, so long as the authorities in each country are pursuing purely domestic goals, their prime interest in the overall economic performance of the others, and in their monetary policy in particular, is that these be stable and predictable, and hence not be sources of unexpected shocks that resonate across borders and create problems for domestic policy. A well designed monetary order in any one country contributes to the stability of the others, even if that stability is nowhere among the policy goals that it is pursuing. Canada's success in targeting inflation contributes not just to a satisfactory economic performance in Canada but in North America more generally. Stability in the US is nevertheless much more important to Canada than stability in Canada is to the US. That is both because trade between the two countries is a much more significant for Canada than it is for the US, but also because the place of the US dollar in the international financial system gives monetary instability in the US a potential for disturbing the world economy, and hence by that route the Canadian economy, that has no parallel in the Canadian case.

Even so, current monetary arrangements within North America make an important and positive contribution to the performance of an already significantly integrated regional economy, despite the fact that they are based on national institutions that are firmly tied into domestic political processes. Because it is in their mutual interest to be well informed about the current and likely future performance of each other's economies, moreover, and the domestic policy responses that this might provoke, the three central banks of the region have every incentive to co-operate actively with one another in the creation, transmission, and discussion of relevant information.

This is true not just of North America, of course, but of the international community as a whole. The need for such arrangements was made crystal clear by the monetary chaos that marked the inter-war years, and the lessons learned then have had a lasting influence. Because of the status of the US in the international economy as a whole, moreover, some of the most important institutions that in fact support discussion of North American issues do so as a by-product of their role on this broader stage, though others are specific to the region, and even to bilateral interests within it. Simply to list the formal arrangements that are currently in place (without even referring to the existence of the telephone) is enough to establish that discussions among monetary policy makers are pursued on what is effectively a continuous basis.[5]

Thus: the Bank for International Settlements in Basel provides a venue for the Governors of the central banks of G-10 countries to discuss matters of mutual interest six times a year. Some of these meetings are restricted to G-10 central bank governors, but others meetings have a wider and varying invitation list; Finance Ministers and Central Bank Governors of the G-7 countries meet three times a year, two of these meetings occurring on the margins of the semi-annual meetings of the International Monetary Fund and World Bank; their Deputy Ministers and Deputy Governors accompany them to these meetings and have three other meetings of their own during the year; the G-10 Ministers and Governors also meet on the margins of the IMF-World Bank meetings, and again, their deputies meet separately on three other occasions; there is one meeting per year of G-20 Governors and Ministers, and at least two others of their deputies; central banks of the G-10 countries are also represented at the deputy governor level at 3 meetings a year sponsored by the OECD in Paris, as are those of the G-7 countries at two meetings a year sponsored by the Financial Stability Forum. Within North America, senior representatives of the Bank of Canada participate in an annual meeting with their counter parts at the Federal Reserve Bank of New York, and in another with officials of the Bank of Mexico.

There is also an annual round of conferences attended by central bank representatives of various ranks, one organised by the Bellagio Group, and others by individual central banks or district banks of the Federal Reserve system. Not all

---

[5] I am particularly grateful to John Murray for help in compiling a brief catalogue of these arrangements. He is explicitly absolved of blame for any errors and omissions that might be found in the next few paragraphs.

of these are regularly attended by senior policy makers: the annual conferences sponsored by the Bank of Canada and the Federal Reserve Bank of St. Louis, for example, are dominated by research staff and academics, but the Federal Reserve Bank of Kansas City's annual Jackson Hole conference always attracts its share of Governors and/or their Deputies from around the world. And this is to say nothing of the regular regional academic conferences which central bank and government economists routinely attend, or of the frequent one-off events, organised to discuss particular topics, in which they also participate.

If not all of the above-mentioned conferences involve central bank officials who are directly involved in taking policy decisions, and if not all of them are private, it is still the case that those who make policy receive essentially continuous briefings from the members of their staff who do attend them. More important however, some meetings do routinely involve Governors and/or Ministers and their Deputies, and they do permit frequent, direct and frank exchanges of information and ideas among their participants under conditions of the strictest confidence.[6]

What all this means in practice for monetary policy making in North America (and in the rest of the world for that matter) is that those responsible for it in any one country have access to essentially as many analytic ideas, data sets, forecasts and opinions about the economic outlook for economies that are of particular importance to their own decisions, as do those making policy for the economies in question. And they also have regular opportunities to seek and offer confidential advice to one another about the measures they ought to take, and to argue out the pros and cons of such advice, whenever they think that desirable. Short of senior central bankers having seats and votes on one another's decision making committees, there are no arrangements for facilitating co-operation among monetary policy makers that are not already in place. Nor is it clear that, given current regimes, there would be anything to gain from this last step. Once taken, monetary policy decisions are public information, and the fact that they take effect with long and variable lags is a universally accepted truth. The advance knowledge of any decision that would come with a seat on the relevant committee would only be a matter of a few hours, and would be of little value in helping to make any required response to it (if indeed a response were needed) either more prompt or better calibrated.

To return once more to the basic theme of the foregoing discussion: what any central bank intent on pursuing domestic goals requires above all else of its counterparts in other economies is that their decisions be both predictable and conducive to domestic stability; and this requirement is already largely met in North America. There is, nevertheless, a little room for further improvement. For example, there is a case to be made, and indeed it is currently being made within the Federal Reserve system itself, that the replacement of the qualitative goals currently in place with quantitative inflation targets would create a more

---

[6]One may get some indication of just how frank these discussions can be, and how important therefore it is that their content remains confidential, from the alacrity with which the Bank of Canada (2003a) issued a formal correction when Governor Dodge inadvertently attributed the Bank of Canada's own reading of prospects for the US economy to then Chairman Greenspan.

transparent and predictable monetary environment in the United States.[7] Such a step would have helpful consequences for monetary policy making in other countries, not least those of North America, and if and when the US authorities become convinced that such a change is in the interests of the population they serve, it will be brought about.

Canadian Monetary Policy and the Exchange Rate since 1991

Though not without its problems, the last dozen years has been a period of considerable success for Canadian macroeconomic policy in general, and monetary policy in particular, as Laidler and Robson (2004) have recently documented in some detail. The economy has not been in recession since inflation targets were introduced in 1991, and this resilience was maintained against a background of considerable turmoil on the international scene.

Crucial to the topic of this paper, from 1991 onwards, and particularly after the structural turnaround in the country's fiscal situation that began with the 1995 federal budget, the Bank of Canada found it less and less difficult to ride out pressures on the exchange rate emanating from abroad without countering them with sustained contractionary measures. Though the Asian and Russian crises of 1997-98 were at least as serious as the EMS crisis of 1992, or the Latin American Tequila crisis of 1994, their consequences for the performance of the Canadian economy were more muted. In the late summer of 1998, the Bank of Canada responded to these events, as it had to their predecessors, by raising interest rates, but the response in question was quickly unwound and its domestic consequences were both mild and temporary.[8] When, shortly afterwards, the collapse of the high-tech bubble in the US ushered in a mild recession there, the Bank of Canada was able to keep its eye firmly on the domestic situation and avoid recession.

In short, markets' confidence in the durability of low domestic inflation in Canada has steadily grown since 1991. Before the mid-1990s, financial market participants tended to read a decline in the exchange rate as indicating a weakening of the Bank's anti-inflation stance, and hence as heralding further problems in the foreign exchange market, and there was always a threat that, to use a phrase much favoured by the Bank of Canada in earlier times, expectations of a declining exchange rate might become extrapolative. This risk now seems to

---

[7]Bernanke has supported such a view prior to becoming chairman but, as of yet, has made no explicit move in that direction and there can be no doubt that, given the unpredictability of Congress in monetary affairs, there must be some risk in opening up current arrangements to debate that might lead to new legislation.

[8]The interest rate increase in question came only after large scale intervention in the foreign exchange market, aimed at supporting the Canadian dollar, failed. It is worth noting that in 1998, the policy responses of the world's three major developed economies that are heavily dependent on commodity exports; Australia, Canada and New Zealand, lay along a spectrum, and so did their subsequent performance. Australia allowed its exchange rate to decline without a monetary policy response, and its domestic economy continued to expand, Canada briefly raised interest rates, and the economy subsequently slowed down for a few months, while New Zealand raised rates and held them at a higher level, with a full-blown recession soon following. For a perceptive account of this episode, see Kevin Clinton (2001).

174

have diminished close to a vanishing point. The slow but steady decoupling of domestic inflation expectations from the exchange rate as the 1990s progressed was thus both encouraged and matched by the Bank's paying less and less attention to that variable's behaviour in the conduct of policy.

Early in the decade, it was still sometimes remarked that the exchange rate was the single most important price in the Canadian economy, but a decade or so of successful inflation targeting has ensured that it has now ceded this place to the price of a representative bundle of goods in terms of money, better known as the domestic price level. Even so, the exchange rate is still a very important price for anyone engaged in international trade, or involved in international capital markets, either directly or indirectly, and that means essentially the whole Canadian population. Because it is also a price susceptible to influence by monetary policy, moreover, it is not unreasonable to ask whether some modification to the current monetary order that has room for exchange rate behaviour among its policy goals might be preferable to current arrangements.

It was this basic question that gave intellectual legitimacy to the proposals for the dollarization of the Canadian economy and/or the monetary unification of North America discussed above, because such arrangements, after all, are in some respects analytically equivalent to a limiting alternative to the present monetary order under which an inflation target is replaced by an irrevocably fixed value for the exchange rate as the sole end of monetary policy. And the question remains legitimate even after such proposals have been rejected. If a common currency is not desirable for North America, what about a system of fixed exchange rates? And if a system of fixed exchange rates is not desirable, what about national monetary orders that seek some trade-off between exchange rate and inflation stability? What answers can be reasonably given here hinge upon a logically prior set of issues about what causes the exchange rate to shift under present arrangements, and therefore, what if any would be the consequences of policy intervention to influence its movement.

Purchasing Power Parity and Fundamentals

The Canadian-US dollar exchange rate is simply the price that a Canadian dollar can command in US dollars. It is the price of one financial asset in terms of another. To understand its determination, it is useful to bear in mind two important features of all asset markets: first, they are characterised by an extremely high degree of price flexibility, and second, the current valuations that their participants place upon the items traded in them are dominated by expectations about their future valuations. Significant differences between current prices and expected future prices cannot persist in such markets because the former are free to move, and because if they do not, this would imply the existence of unexploited profit opportunities. Twenty dollar bills, as the saying goes, do not get left lying on the sidewalk for very long.

These features of asset markets in turn yield two implications for asset price behaviour: first, this is likely to display considerable volatility, since all pieces of information that arrive *now* about *any time in the future* affect prices *now*; and second, *after the event,* some price fluctuations will appear to have been unjustified. Information about the future is, after all, likely to be of variable

175

quality and open to misinterpretation; and not everything that looks like a twenty dollar bill turns out to be one upon closer inspection.

We are used to the idea that equity prices, and house prices too, are sometimes subject to *bubbles*, price fluctuations supported not so much by variations in longer term expectations about the evolution of basic economic factors, as by simple extrapolation from the recent behaviour of those prices themselves. We should not rule out *a priori* the possibility that foreign exchange markets display similar characteristics, and yet there are differences here. The occurrence of what might turn out after the event to have been bubbles in stock markets is usually associated with the entry into them of significant numbers of not very well informed non-specialist traders, and it is also of the very nature of housing markets that they mainly cater to just such agents. To a much greater extent, foreign exchange markets are dominated by specialists who are well informed and less error prone than other agents in the economy, and indeed earn their returns precisely from these advantages.

This argument, if accepted, might establish a presumption that variations in foreign exchange rates are less likely to be gratuitous than those in certain other asset prices, but it cannot eliminate the possibility altogether.[9] That is why words and phrases such as "misalignment" and "excess volatility" which figure so prominently in the academic literature dealing with their behaviour need to be taken seriously. In order to draw lessons from that literature, however, it is important to grasp that to characterise an exchange rate as misaligned implies the existence of some base-line, or *fundamental,* value relative to which misalignment can be judged, and that volatility can only be termed "excessive" relative to the volatility of that same fundamental value. It is just as important, moreover, to bear in mind that it is possible for different commentators to base their conclusions on different views about what determines the fundamental value in question.

In recent Canadian debates, criticism of the Bank of Canada's single minded pursuit of stable domestic inflation, and its growing willingness to leave the exchange rate to be determined by markets, has been intimately associated with a particular hypothesis about what determines the long-run equilibrium value of the exchange rate, usually known as *purchasing power parity theory.* Courchene and Harris (1999), for example, systematically used the word "misaligned" to describe any value for the exchange rate that deviated from the value predicted by that theory, and the phrase "excess volatility" to characterise any swings in it that could not be explained by movements in the determinants of its purchasing power parity value.

Given price levels in two countries, the purchasing power parity *value* of the exchange rate between their currencies is simply the one at which a given sum of money can buy the same amount of goods and services on either side of the

---

[9]The idea that markets become more prone to instability unrelated to fundamentals when they attract ill-informed participants is an old one. It was a close to commonplace in the Cambridge tradition of monetary economics that formed the background to the Keynesian Revolution. These issues are discussed in Laidler (1999). Plausible though this idea is, however, I am not aware of any systematic empirical investigations of it in the modern literature.

border.[10] As such, the phrase refers to an economic concept rather than a theory, but purchasing power parity *theory* deploys this purchasing power parity *concept* in a model that predicts: first that, between any two countries, the value of the exchange rate will converge in the long run on its purchasing power parity value; and second that, this long-run equilibrium value of the exchange rate will therefore move in direct inverse proportion to the ratio of the two countries' price levels, so that, for example, a 10 per cent relative increase in the Canadian price level will be associated with a 10 per cent fall in the equilibrium exchange rate. This particular theory of the equilibrium exchange rate is also frequently linked to an explanation of price level behaviour cast in terms of the interaction of the supply and demand for money, and leads naturally to the characterisation of exchange rate movements that cannot be explained by this interaction as "excessive".[11]

Superficial plausibility is lent to this purchasing power parity theory by two circumstances. First, the well known *law of one price* - the proposition that the same good cannot trade for a different price in different parts of the same market - suggests to its advocates that (with due allowance for transport costs and taxation) there are mechanisms that would tend to bring a country's exchange rate back to purchasing power parity after a monetary disturbance that shifts the price level in one country. Thus, they would argue that a higher (lower) price level discourages imports (exports) and encourages exports (imports), and puts downward (upward) pressure on the exchange rate until purchasing power parity is restored. And second, twentieth century economic history has provided two major episodes, in the 1920s, and again from the late 1960s until the early 1980s, in which monetary disturbances of very different orders of magnitude in different countries were prominent features of the international economic landscape, and in which high inflation countries did indeed see their exchange rates fall against those of low inflation countries.

More seriously, formal econometric studies often reveal tendencies for exchange rates to move slowly backwards towards purchasing power parity after disturbances to make it unwise to totally dismiss the theory. However, persistent deviations from purchasing power parity frequently occur, and exchange rate volatility that is excessive relative to the theory's predictions is sufficiently ubiquitous, that it has nowadays become common to follow Kenneth Rogoff (1996) in referring to a "purchasing power parity puzzle": namely, why doesn't the theory work better in explaining the behaviour of exchange rates?

---

[10]The concept is invaluable for such exercises as making international comparisons of living standards. If one wishes to know, for example, whether the median Canadian household enjoys a lower or higher living standard in Canada than its US counterpart does in the US, it is obviously appropriate to convert its Canadian dollar income to US dollars at the purchasing power parity exchange rate in order to make the comparison, rather than at the market rate.

[11]This, for example, is how Robert Flood and Andrew Rose (1998), cited by Courchene and Harris (1999) used the term. In this context, it is interesting that the Canadian-US dollar exchange rate displayed the smallest degree of "excess volatility" of all those that Flood and Rose examined.

Various solutions to this puzzle are on offer, and are conveniently thought of as lying along a spectrum. At one of its extremes lies the possibility that purchasing power parity does indeed characterise exchange rate equilibrium, and that all deviations from it, whether persistent or temporary, reflect a failure on the part of the foreign exchange market to work efficiently. At the other, lies the possibility that the theory is far too simple as an explanation of even long-run equilibrium exchange rate behaviour, that deviations from purchasing power parity reflect the influence of other non-monetary fundamental factors that it neglects, and that exchange rate volatility is simply the result of movements in them. It is extremely doubtful if one could nowadays find any responsible commentator at either of these extremes, but some take up positions much nearer to one of them than do others, and the chosen location bears heavily on how much confidence they then place in the capacity of any monetary order in which the exchange rate figures among the targets of monetary policy to serve the Canadian economy better than current arrangements.

It is obvious that, *other things equal*, exchange rate movements within an already highly integrated North American economy are a considerable and costly nuisance to those routinely involved in cross-border transactions. It is also obvious that, if the central banks of the area are all successfully pursuing similar inflation targets, whether formally or informally, there will be little movement in the values of the purchasing power parity exchange rates among their currencies. If systematic deviations of actual exchange rates from these values, and volatility in them over and above that which can be put down to deviations among the time paths of their price levels, are attributable to chronic inefficiencies in foreign exchange markets, it is also possible for central banks to eliminate these without compromising their inflation goals, and for monetary policy to bring to agents involved in trans-border transactions the same degree of stability that they currently enjoy when they transact domestically. On the other hand, if fluctuations in exchange rates away from purchasing power parity have their roots in shifting fundamentals to which the foreign exchange market is reacting efficiently, then monetary measures taken to smooth them out, though they might be effective in doing so, are going to have consequences elsewhere in the system, which *might* though not *must,* be an even more considerable and costly nuisance than the exchange rate movements in question

Explaining Variations in the Real Exchange Rate

There are many good reasons to believe that there is more to the determination of the equilibrium exchange rate than the purchasing power parity theory would lead one to expect, several of which have to do with the facts that countries do not trade everything that they produce, nor are the bundles of goods that they do trade identical. Both of these facts blunt the capacity of the law of one price - on the assumption that it does indeed hold for individual goods - to pin down and hold the exchange rate at its purchasing power parity level, and open up room for relative price variations among goods, stemming from variations across countries and over time in endowments, tastes, and technology, to affect exchange rates. To put it more precisely, variations in the *nominal* exchange rate, the price of one country's currency in terms of that of another, might sometimes reflect

178

variations in the underlying *real* exchange rate: the relative price of that country's output bundle in terms of that of the other.

For example, differentials in productivity levels and growth rates between countries can affect the real exchange rate and its rate of change too. The so-called Balassa (1964)-Samuelson (1964) effect provides one well-known example of how this can come about. It argues that, in the case of two countries, if there is a larger productivity differential between their tradeables than their non-tradeable sectors, then the currency of the more productive economy will take a value above purchasing-power parity. The law of one price, so it is argued, will tend to keep the prices of tradeables in line, but non-tradeable producers in the higher productivity country will have to pay more for their labour and hence charge a relatively higher price for their output. If productivity growth rates also differ systematically between the two countries, the exchange rate premium in question will also vary over time to reflect this. Should productivity level and growth differentials be greater in the non-tradeables sectors, on the other hand, the signs of these effects will be reversed, with the high productivity country having an exchange rate below purchasing power-parity that will decline over time as the productivity differential opens up.

If the make-up of the bundles of goods traded differs between countries - and if it did not it would be hard to explain why trade would occur in the first place - it is also possible that the price of a representative bundle of one country's imports in terms of a representative bundle of its exports - its *terms of trade* - can vary over time. This effect too can impinge upon both the real and the nominal exchange rate, with the country whose exports are declining in relative price experiencing a definite depreciation of the real rate, and a depreciation of the nominal rate at least relative to whatever time path it was initially following.

Then there is the fact that not all cross-border transactions are in currently produced goods and services, so that capital flows can also affect the exchange rate. A borrowing country must generate an import surplus if the real resource flows that lie behind its financial transactions are to be realised, and this is so whether these originate in the private sector or with the government.[12] Thus, the higher is the rate of capital inflow (and always assuming that there is some difference between the composition of imports and exports), the higher must the country's real exchange rate be to create the matching trade deficit. And stocks of indebtedness can play a role here too: investors hold the liabilities of agents located in any particular country on the basis of expectations about the return to be realised from doing so. The larger is the stock of liabilities to be held, the greater is the risk of their returns being impaired in future, and hence the lower their value

---

[12]Note, however that this conclusion does not necessarily imply that an increase in government borrowing will always tend to appreciate the real exchange rate. That is because so-called "Ricardian equivalence" effect, whereby private agents increase their saving in anticipation of future tax burdens, may come into play, ensuring that extra government borrowing can be financed out of increased domestic saving. Absent Ricardian equivalence, however, increased government borrowing in a fully employed economy does affect capital flows, as either the government itself, or private sector agents who have been "crowded out" of domestic markets, borrow abroad, and, other things equal, it also leads to an appreciation of the real exchange rate.

179

in the present. These stock effects work in the opposite direction to flow effects: borrowing abroad tends to drive a currency up so long as confidence is not impaired, but as debt is thus accumulated confidence effects can come into play to push the currency down. These considerations open up the possibility that capital account activities can be a source of real exchange rate volatility, as the relative significance of opposing forces changes over time.

To say that all of the above factors might compete with purely monetary influences on the nominal exchange rate is not to say that they always will do so, nor is it to say that market adjustments in the nominal exchange rate are the only possible, or always even the best, response to them. But it is to say that it is important to test for their presence before attributing deviations from purchasing power parity and exchange rate volatility over and above what can be explained by monetary factors, to a failure of markets to function efficiently, and to conclude that they can be eliminated by policy without further consequences. The latter phenomena might well be responses to fundamental factors impinging on the real exchange rate. If the nominal rate is prevented by policy from adjusting to them, then other variables will have to.

These considerations are of potentially great importance in the case of Canada within North America, and particularly vis-à-vis the US. Consider: productivity is lower in Canada than in the US, and productivity levels and growth rates continue to differ between the two economies on a sector by sector basis too; Canada is a significant net exporter of primary commodities, and the US is a net importer, their prices are notoriously volatile, and variations in them necessarily affect the Canada-US terms of trade; the two countries' rates of international borrowing and levels of international indebtedness have been on very different, not to mention changing, trajectories for many years. If one is looking for fundamentals whose behaviour might explain why the Canada-US exchange rate has usually differed from purchasing power parity, and has displayed volatility well in excess of what would be predicted by the monetary factors on which that theory of the exchange rate focuses, there is no shortage of candidates.

Empirical evidence, much, but not all of which, is built around what is commonly called the *Bank of Canada Equation*, (See Amano and van Norden, 1993, 1995) at the very least puts the burden of proof on those who would deny that fundamentals in addition to those encompassed by purchasing power parity theory have had a systematic influence on the US Canada exchange rate over the years.[13] This equation's dependent variable is the *real* exchange rate, the market or *nominal* rate adjusted for variations in the price levels of the two countries. One of its basic building blocks is the idea, fundamental to purchasing power parity theory, that the nominal exchange rate does indeed move to offset inflation differentials. However, where purchasing power parity theory has it that the real exchange rate is a constant, the Bank of Canada equation tests the hypothesis that it shifts in response to fundamentals. It postulates, and seems to show, that, in the

---

[13]Neither the studies of Carr and Floyd (2002) of Canada alone, nor of Chen and Rogoff (2002) of Australia, New Zealand and Canada take the Bank of Canada equation as their immediate starting point, though both investigate the role of variables closely related to those that appear in it. Both find that real factors seem to have systematic effects on Canada's real exchange rate, and hence confirm Amano and van Norden's basic results.

Canadian-US case, the real exchange rate's time path is dominated by two sets of variables - in the long run, by movements in world commodity prices, and in the short run by variations in the stance of monetary policy in Canada relative to that of the US, as measured by the short interest rate differential between the two countries.

The latter effect is uncontroversial in the context of this chapter, because advocates of purchasing power parity theory do not expect the exchange rate to be at its long run equilibrium value at every moment, and would regard monetary policy shocks as prime sources of short-term disturbances under a system of flexible exchange rates. They would also argue, correctly, that, had Canada's monetary order made exchange rate behaviour one of the goals of policy over the period to which the Bank of Canada equation has been fitted, the behaviour of this interest differential, which reflects the monetary policy decisions that were actually taken, would probably not have been a source of disturbance. Indeed, they would claim, again correctly, that the fact that monetary policy seems to have a systematic effect on the exchange rate is a point in favour of such a regime, at least to the extent that it suggests that it would be technically feasible.

The long run significance of commodity prices in the equation is problematic for this point of view, however, because it suggests that terms of trade effects are a source of real exchange rate variation whose effects would have to be absorbed elsewhere in the economic system if the nominal exchange rate were less free to adjust to them. This result has, furthermore, stood up to a decade of new Canadian data generated since the equation was first proposed, and also to data generated by those other commodity producing countries Australia and New Zealand (See Ramdane Djoudade et al. 2001).

Even so, the last decade has also seen apparent changes in the factors determining Canada's real exchange rate and in their relative importance. In the original Bank of Canada equation, the commodity prices that were important were those in the non-energy sector. The price index of energy commodities entered either with the "wrong" (negative) sign, or insignificantly, depending upon the particular formulation of the equation and the time period over which it was fitted. More recent work however - for example that reported by Guillemette, Laidler and Robson (2004)- seems to show that energy prices began to enter the equation with a significantly positive sign in the 1990s, while the quantitative importance of non-energy commodity prices declined. These results are consistent with the growing significance of Canada's net exports of energy resources in the 1990s, and with the slow decline in the importance of other commodity exports since the 1970s.

Commodity prices are the only non-monetary variables that have systematically found a place in the Bank of Canada equation from the outset. We have seen, however, that fiscal policy ought to affect the exchange rate, and the relevant variables - government borrowing rates and levels of debt accumulation - have displayed considerable variation over the years in Canada and the US.[14]

---

[14]Once again the reader is warned that this conclusion would not hold if the Canadian economy were to be characterised by "Ricardian equivalence", which it does not seem to be.

Some recent work, for example Murray, Zelmer and Antia (2000) has found a place for them in a version of the Bank of Canada equation, but this result does not seem to be robust against variations in the precise formulation of the effects in question, and in the period to which the equation is fitted. Carr and Floyd (2002) also report problems with fiscal policy variables in their exchange rate equation. Productivity level and growth rate effects were also initially hard to pin down, though Lafrance, Helliwell, Issa and Zhang (2004) have lately found a place for them, albeit not along the lines suggested by the simple Balassa-Samuelson effect discussed earlier.

It is also the case that an exchange rate involves the currencies of two countries, but that the Bank of Canada equation relies heavily on commodity prices, variables which are far more important in Canada than in the US. If real fundamentals are important for the Canada-US exchange rate, one might have expected some specifically US variables to play a systematic role in explaining its behaviour. Furthermore, the appreciation of the Canadian dollar that began in 2003 was somewhat embarrassing for earlier forms of the equation. Commodity prices did begin to rise at that time, to be sure, and a significant short-term interest differential was also in place for a while, so that qualitatively speaking, the equation gave the right prediction. In quantitative terms, however, it failed quite badly: it could explain the direction of the exchange rate's upward movement, but not its magnitude.

It has, of course, been widely and correctly remarked that the behaviour of exchange rates since 2003 has been overwhelmingly a matter of a world-wide depreciation of the US dollar, and that the time path taken by the bilateral Canada-US rate has been mainly a side effect of this broader phenomenon. But this observation simply re-enforces doubts about the Bank of Canada equation's long-standing failure to encompass any important US fundamentals. It does little to excuse its poor performance. Lafrance, Helliwell, Issa and Zhang (2004) as well as Bailliu, Dib and Schembri (2005) have recently confronted this issue, the former by taking account of movements of the US dollar against other currencies, the latter by looking for potential effects stemming from US fiscal and current account imbalances. Both studies have obtained promising results with these variables, in particular they seem to go a long way towards correcting the problems created for earlier formulations of the Bank of Canada by exchange rate behaviour since 2003.

Even so, in all their variations, Bank of Canada style equations are better at explaining long-run trends and broad swings in the exchange rate than shorter term movements. There is a growing body of evidence that when it comes to shorter run but still sometimes significant variations, causation can run from the nominal to the real exchange rate, rather than *vice versa*, and that these effects can perhaps be explained by the presence of price stickiness, particularly in retail markets, that causes the law of one price to fail at this level.[15] Such considerations

---

[15]I conjecture that in the longer run, this result will come to appear unsurprising, once account is taken of the large component of non-tradeable services that are built in to retail prices. This is not to discount the potential significance of "pricing to market" effects that can occur in circumstances where producers are able to price discriminate among national economies.

open up the possibility that a completely clean float for an exchange rate is a second best regime, and that, as for example Devereux and Engel (2004) have argued, there is room in principle for policies designed to eliminate at least some of those variations in it that cannot be attributed to variations in real fundamentals.

The empirical study of Canada's exchange rate is, in short, a work in progress, but economic theory creates a strong presumption that purchasing power parity theory is much too simple; and over a decade of empirical work with the many variants of the Bank of Canada equation has done much to support this view. Even should it turn out that future studies of the type represented by Devereux and Engel (2004) reveal that this work has attributed too much of the exchange rate's variability to movements in real fundamentals (and this is by no means certain), it seems highly unlikely that its basic message about their importance will be undermined. If our knowledge of these matters is still far from complete, then, this conclusion has implications for the design of the monetary order in North America in general and Canada in particular, to which we now turn.

Alternative Monetary Orders

During the recent debate about North American monetary integration, it was sometimes unclear just what form its proponents expected such an arrangement to take, and this occasionally led to a confused discussion. Similar problems can arise in the context of less radical proposals to make the exchange rate an object of policy. A regime under which the behaviour of the exchange rate was added to that of the inflation rate as a policy goal would, for example, have different characteristics to one under which the exchange rate was rigidly fixed. In either case, its performance would be affected by the extent of US co-operation in the system.

It is helpful to begin our discussion of these matters with an arrangement that would involve the smallest movement away from the status quo, namely one under which Canada unilaterally complicates its current regime by making exchange rate behaviour an extra policy goal. Such an approach to policy would be both feasible and preferable to current arrangements if purchasing power parity theory were an adequate explanation of the long run equilibrium exchange rate's behaviour, and if deviations from this benchmark could confidently be put down to inefficiencies in the working of the foreign exchange market. Calls that are currently being heard for the Bank of Canada to "do something" about interest rates and the exchange rate to help exporters, now that inflation is clearly under control, amount to proposals that such a scheme be implemented, at least informally.

The first problem with such proposals is that we can be reasonably confident that purchasing power parity is *not* an adequate theory of Canada's long run equilibrium exchange rate, and the second is that we nevertheless do not know enough to be able to offer advice about how to modify such a scheme in the light of this considerable complication. In principle, to be sure, the solution is straightforward. Instead of a regime under which the Bank of Canada aims at a central inflation target, but also stands ready to iron out "excessive" volatility in the exchange rate around its purchasing power parity level, a scheme could be adopted under which the Bank seeks to eliminate only those fluctuations that can not be attributed to movements in fundamentals, while permitting variation in the inflation rate within a target range to make room for such initiatives. But there is a crucial practical problem here: namely, that, although it would be wrong to argue that such "excessive" fluctuations never occur, it is nevertheless hard to argue that they can be recognised as such, and their order of magnitude determined, with any degree of confidence while they are occurring, let alone that the Bank of Canada has some special knowledge that would enable it to do so with systematically more speed and accuracy than the private sector.

In principle, there might be room for improvement in the conduct of monetary policy along the above lines, but in practice any attempt to realise it is likely to be not just ineffective but positively damaging. At present, agents in the private sector know that the Bank of Canada will always take measures to bring inflation back to a target value of two per cent over an eighteen month time horizon; they combine this information with their own reading of the economy to assess the prospects in their particular line of business, and they then act in accordance with this information. All this is difficult enough, but under the more complicated alternative, they would also have to assess how the Bank was likely to divide up the blame for any current movements in the exchange rate between fundamentals which monetary policy ought to ignore and gratuitous market shocks to which it should respond, decide what its likely actions would imply for inflation, and then factor this information into their decision making. It is difficult to see how all this would make life easier for anyone than it is at present.

The Bank of Canada has worked hard over the last decade to improve the transparency of its policy making. An important step forward here occurred when, in about 1998, it began to de-emphasise the role of the *Monetary Conditions Index* both in its own policy decisions but also, and more importantly, in its attempts to communicate with the public.[16] That index is a weighted average of a representative short-term interest rate and the exchange rate; underlying its deployment was the perfectly correct insight, that, in an open economy, both of these variables impinge upon aggregate demand and hence on the future time path of inflation. The Bank framed its discussions of policy in terms of the interaction between the actual and desired values of this index, the latter depending on, among other things, its assessment of the extent to which fundamentals, as opposed to what it called "portfolio shifts", were moving the exchange rate. It was never able, however, to convince the public to take enough notice of its belief that this desired value would indeed vary over time for these communications to be helpful.[17]

---

[16]Indeed, alongside the reduction in degree of political controversy surrounding monetary policy that took place in the 1990s, for which it was partly responsible, this improvement in the transparency of policy was perhaps the central achievement of Gordon Thiessen's governorship. That this was the result of deliberate policies is evident from Thiessen (1999). Even so, progress here was not always in a straight line. As an anonymous referee points out, the rise as well as the subsequent fall of the Monetary Conditions Index as a guide to monetary policy took place during Thiessen's governorship.

[17]Charles Freedman (1994) provides a clear and thorough description of the role that the Monetary Conditions Index was intended to play in Bank of Canada policy making. The

184

Nor were matters made easier by the fact that, until late 1998, the Bank of Canada routinely intervened in the foreign exchange market, not in order to control the exchange rate's longer run time path, but rather to smooth out its day-by-day fluctuations and to resist sudden movements in the variable. The Bank automatically bought the currency when it was falling, and sold it when it was rising. Difficulties with this procedure came to a head in the summer of 1998. At that time, the Bank's regular interventions failed to prevent to currency's rapid fall, but on the occasional days when this trend was temporarily interrupted, its procedures nevertheless required it to sell the currency at a value at which, only a few days earlier, it had been a buyer. This was bound to confuse markets, and, to add to the Bank's difficulties, when in August 1998 it eventually intervened on an unusually large scale in an effort to drive up the Canadian dollar's value, this influenced the exchange rate only for a day or so. With its credibility in the foreign exchange market on the line, the Bank then had to institute an interest rate rise of one percentage point that was quite unjustified by circumstances in the domestic economy.

The upshot of all this was the Bank's announcement in September 1998 that it would no longer engage in systematic intervention in the foreign exchange market, though it reserved the right to do so in extraordinary circumstances.[18] This announcement, and the Bank's more or less simultaneous de-emphasising of the Monetary Conditions Index in its policy communications, not to mention its rapid unwinding of its August interest rate increase (under the cover of interest rate cuts in the US provoked by the Long Term Capital Management crisis), should be seen as the culmination of a trend away from gearing policy towards the exchange rate that began with the institution of inflation targets in 1991. To modify the current regime to make the elimination of fluctuations in the exchange rate relative to the Bank's assessment of its fundamental value a goal of policy, would be to reverse this development to the point of giving that variable even more prominence in the policy framework than it enjoyed in the mid-1990s. Bearing in mind the problems that were encountered at that time, it is hard to avoid the conclusion that such a step would be destructively retrogressive.

To work well, monetary policy needs to be transparent, and, among other things, the goal of eliminating exchange rate fluctuations relative to a moving time path driven by fundamentals is just too complicated to be easily communicated. One solution here, if the exchange rate is to be re-instated as an object of policy, would be to make the unilaterally chosen target for its behaviour simpler. Perhaps the Bank of Canada should aim to keep the rate in a target zone, or moving along a pre-announced time path, or perhaps the rate should simply be fixed. Though there are many differences among such schemes, they all have one economic characteristic in common, namely that shifts in fundamentals that would take the exchange rate away from its chosen value, or beyond the boundaries of its chosen

---

problem with that role was not any logical flaw in its configuration, but that this proved to be so complicated that it hindered Bank in its efforts to communicate accurately with markets.

[18]In fact, August 1998 remains the last time the Bank has engaged in such activities. A recent Backgrounder (Bank of Canada 2003b) discusses the Bank's current views on intervention in some detail.

range, would have to be accommodated by other variables; it is uncontroversial that among these would be domestic money wages and prices.

When real fundamentals change, it is generally the case that domestic wage and price relativities must respond to them regardless of the exchange rate regime. A flexible exchange rate cannot eliminate this necessity. All it can do, at best, is reduce the amount of nominal variation in domestic variables that is required. How important a factor this is obviously depends on how easy or how difficult it is for such variations to be brought about, and on what side effects they might have. It is a platitude that the more (less) flexible are domestic money wages and prices, the less (more) important is the flexibility of the nominal exchange rate to the economy's performance as it adjusts to real exchange rate shocks, but it does not quite say all that needs to be said on this matter. The monetary authorities, even those of an economy characterised by perfect price flexibility but subject to real exchange rate shocks, would face a choice between maintaining exchange rate and domestic price level stability. The sacrifice of the latter in order to stabilise the exchange rate would not necessarily be without its costs.[19]

To give a concrete example of what might be involved here, it is only necessary to note that wages and prices are generally considered to be rather flexible in an upward direction, and that, on the assumption that the recent world-wide depreciation of the US dollar is largely related to real fundamentals rather than to some failure of the functioning of foreign exchange markets, money wages and prices in Canada would have had to rise by more than 20 per cent to bring about the real exchange rate adjustment that has in fact taken place since the beginning of 2003 under a fixed nominal exchange rate. Had this in fact occurred, then exporters who are currently lamenting the effects of the nominal exchange rate's behaviour on their competitiveness would instead be complaining about domestic wage inflation. Furthermore, to the extent that the behaviour of the price level had been unanticipated, there would have been significant redistributions of wealth within the economy.[20] It is far from clear that all this would have been, , on balance, preferable to what in fact transpired, and it is perhaps worth reflecting on the fact that, in 1950 and again in 1970, the Canadian authorities chose to abandon a fixed exchange rate in the face of strong inflationary pressures emanating from the need for a real exchange rate appreciation.

Even so, wage and price stickiness does add to the problems associated with any exchange rate regime that seeks to prevent the nominal rate fully

---

[19]It is often carelessly asserted that a small open economy which fixes its exchange rate to the currency of a larger trading partner will simply import whatever inflation rate that is ruling there. This conclusion is only true, however, on the assumption that the real exchange rate between the two economies is constant. A more accurate statement would be that the small economy's price level will behave so as to accommodate its time path to that of its partner's price level, given whatever movements might be taking place in the real exchange rate.

[20]There have, of course, been redistributions of wealth over the past year from the unanticipated appreciation of the currency, involving losses on the part of those who were holding substantial US dollar denominated assets, for example holiday homes in the US, or unhedged investments in US stocks.

adjusting to real shocks, and, as is well understood, this matter becomes particularly important when a real exchange rate depreciation is required. Again an illustration from recent Canadian experience is telling: Robson and Laidler (2002) have estimated that, had a fixed exchange rate on the US dollar been in place between early 1998 and 2002, the Canadian price level would have had to fall at a rate of close to 2 per cent per annum in order to bring about the real depreciation that in fact took place. In the best of circumstances, tight monetary policy and a significant temporary contraction of real income and employment would have been required to bring this about, and in the worst, under which markets proved strongly resistant to deflation, temporary real contraction would have been replaced by something closer to stagnation.[21]

Phenomena of the type just postulated here are well documented under just about any kind of fixed or managed exchange rate regime, and it is equally well documented that the political pressures they generate make such regimes fragile and prone to destructive speculative attacks.[22] That is why protagonists on opposite sides of the recent debate about North American monetary integration, for example, Grubel (1998) and Laidler and Poschmann (2000), have sometimes agreed that the middle ground between a common currency and a market determined exchange rate is distinctly inferior to either extreme, and hence to be shunned. But this view has not been universally shared. Courchene and Harris (1999) and Robert Mundell (see Alan Freeman 1999) have urged that Canada adopt a rigidly fixed exchange rate on the US dollar, the former as a way station on the way to fuller monetary integration (along the lines of the European Monetary system in the 1990s) and the latter as an essentially permanent arrangement.

Not everyone will share these authors' view that a fixed exchange rate regime would be feasible provided only that macroeconomic policy in Canada were to be devoted single-mindedly to its maintenance, because the key question here is not so much technical as political. It is far from clear that so single-minded a policy would be sustainable in a country such as Canada which has conspicuously chosen to withhold goal independence from its central bank, and instead has evolved a set of arrangements in which the ultimate responsibility resides with elected politicians. Even so, it is possible to envision institutional changes that would improve such a regime's chances of survival were it to be put

---

[21]For this reason, it is hard to give much credence to claims that Canada's productivity performance would have been better in the late 1990s, had the exchange rate been fixed, or a common North American currency been in place. Indeed, recent work by Edwards and Yeyati (2003) suggest that the shock absorbing properties of flexible exchange rate regimes generally have a systematically beneficial effect on the real performance of the economies that have adopted them.

[22]Osakwe and Schembri (1998), for example, list no fewer than 38 exchange rate crises that occurred between 1990 and 1997 as a consequence of such forces, each one ending in a devaluation or the outright abandonment of a fixed exchange rate. These problems would be exacerbated in the Canadian case by the fact that the Bank of Canada Act explicitly makes the Bank the agent of the federal government in the foreign exchange market. It would have no legal authority to resist political pressures to abandon any exchange rate target.

in place. Some of these could be brought about unilaterally, but others would require the co-operation of the US, and of Mexico too, if the arrangement were to be extended to the whole of the NAFTA.

It has already been noted that money wage and price stickiness make any kind of nominal exchange rate target painful to sustain in an economy where the real exchange rate needs to move from time to time, so it follows immediately that more flexibility in markets in general, and in the labour market in particular, would make this sort of monetary order more viable. As the European example shows, what would be needed here is not just wages and prices that move more easily, but also a reduction in other rigidities associated with the workings of the welfare state; this European example also shows that such changes are extremely hard to bring about, even in countries which have already self-consciously and totally given up their capacity to implement domestic monetary policy and accepted serious limits on their capacity to deploy fiscal tools as well.

The stresses here could, no doubt, be somewhat reduced if the maintenance of a stable or even fixed exchange rate between the Canadian and US dollars (and perhaps between both of these and the Peso) became a joint responsibility of the Federal Reserve system and the Bank of Canada (and, perhaps, of the Bank of Mexico), rather than being the unilateral responsibility of the latter institution(s). If the Fed would support the Canadian dollar and/or the Peso when real shocks were requiring them to depreciate, this would both take some of the pressure of those currencies, and also ensure that some of the required adjustment was brought about by US inflation; and if the Fed. were willing to deflate when their real exchange rates needed to rise, this too would make adjustments easier for Canada and/or Mexico. As we have seen above, much of the machinery needed to enable monetary policy to be formulated on a co-operative basis within North America is already in place, so it would not be technically difficult to bring such a regime into being. As we have also seen above, however, the US has important interests in monetary relations with Europe and Asia, that have no real parallels in the Canadian and Mexican cases, and these might sometimes conflict with an obligation to stabilise exchange rates within North America.[23].

One other change within North America that would lessen the monetary strains associated with the adoption of exchange rate targets should be mentioned; namely, the enhancement of cross border labour mobility, again either between Canada and the US alone, or throughout the NAFTA. One of the more telling points made by advocates of full North American monetary integration in recent debates was that the US monetary system could itself be regarded as a monetary union among disparate regional economies, whose real exchange rates were prone to vary over time without threatening the stability of the union, however, an equally telling response to this was that labour and private capital mobility, not to

---

[23] As John Murray has reminded me, the US has recently been party to discussions about possibly co-ordinated action to deal with current account imbalances, including its own, and to alter the configuration of certain exchange rate regimes, particularly that ruling between the Yuan and the US dollar, though so far, the discussions in question have yielded no practical results. From a US standpoint, these issues are far more important than any that are currently on a purely North American agenda.

mention fiscal transfers, among the regions of the United States provided extra cushions against these effects that would not be available to the same extent, if at all, on a continent-wide basis.

Though there is no sign that co-operation in fiscal matters is on the table, there have recently been discussions of the desirability of regulatory harmonisation between Canada and the US that might, as a side effect, enhance the already a high degree of capital mobility that exists between the two economies. Furthermore, in the wake of the events of September 11th 2001, there have already been speculations about the creation of a North American economic perimeter at which common rules for the movement of goods and people would be enforced, but within which they could move freely.[24]

To discuss the feasibility of regulatory harmonization and labour market integration is well beyond the scope of this paper. Labour market integration in particular would be complicated to arrange, particularly if, in addition to Canada and the US, it were to involve Mexico, whose inclusion in the NAFTA was seen by the US as an alternative, rather than a prelude, to permitting more labour mobility across its southern border. And even if it were decided that such an arrangement could reasonably be confined to the US and Canada, there are more issues implicit in it, having to do with interactions among refugee and immigration policies of both countries and the domestic labour market rights of their citizens and residents, than can be even listed, let alone discussed, here. However, the fact remains that, from the point of view of simple economics, there are strong complementarities between North American labour market integration and the feasibility of active monetary co-operation of any kind within the area, and it will be important to keep these clearly in view as the discussion of these matters progresses.

Summary and Conclusions

A salient fact about recent North American history is that, although a high degree of economic integration has come into being in recent years, this development has had no parallels on the political front. North America differs sharply from Europe in this respect, but not only in this respect. The asymmetries among Canada, Mexico and the United States that stem from the dominant economic and political size of the latter, not just within North America but in the world as a whole, are also without parallels in Europe. The nature of the interests that the US pursues, and of the constraints it faces as it does so, mean that North American concerns will not always take pride of place in its policies. It bears repeating that this does not mean that the US's actions will always, or even usually, run contrary to the interests of Canada and Mexico, but, short of some unexpected events capable of generating a political dynamic in North America similar to that which has been in play for so long in Europe, it does mean that any initiatives aimed at bringing North American economic and political institutions into line with the interests of that area considered in isolation are probably going

---

[24]These proposals have taken a variety of forms, and their discussion is beyond the scope of this paper. See however Danielle Goldfarb (2003) for a survey of them that pays particular attention to looking for common elements among them.

to have to come from these smaller countries. And it also means that among these initiatives, the ones which also happen to promote broader US interests are more likely to be successful.

US interests in the monetary area are quite evidently global in scope, and US policy pronouncements on these matters have made their authorities' awareness of this fact quite clear. Though Assistant Secretary Summers, quoted above, spoke for a previous administration, there is no reason to believe that the policies of the Bush administration on this matter are any different. On the contrary, the silence from Washington in response to President Fox's raising the question of North American monetary integration in 2000, and from Ambassador Cellucci in the face of ongoing Canadian discussions of the same issue, was extremely eloquent. The management of trade in natural resources, including perhaps water, and since September 11th 2001, security, are all areas in which the US has expressed a keen interest in closer North American co-operation, but monetary policy does not seem to be on the list.

A lengthy debate in Canada has nevertheless shown that US political co-operation would be essential to the creation of a fully fledged North American monetary union or indeed to the viability of any kind of arrangement whereby Canada (and presumably Mexico) adopted the US dollar. In this paper, I have shown that similar considerations would usually be at play in any move towards giving the nominal Canadian/US dollar exchange rate an important place among the goals of Canadian monetary policy. Unilateral attempts simply to fine tune the rate's behaviour within a version of the inflation targeting regime currently in place would, at the very least, degrade the transparency of Canadian monetary policy with no obvious benefits to offset this loss. Any scheme to control the nominal exchange rate more actively, so that real pressures emanating from world markets would sometimes be transmitted to domestic money wages and prices with greater force than they currently are, would impose economic and political stresses that would be hard to deal with unilaterally. Co-operation from the Federal Reserve in managing such a regime would ease these pressures, but it is not to be expected. A higher degree of integration among North American labour markets would also help, but to suggest such a possibility is to open up a set of economic and political questions that we have barely begun to analyse.

Even so, it has also been argued above that monetary stability within the separate currency areas of a highly integrated economic space such as North America makes its own contribution to overall economic performance, and it has also been suggested that the more communication there is about policy among the monetary authorities of the separate areas, the greater is this contribution likely to be. Great strides towards monetary stability have been taken in all three NAFTA countries in the last ten years, and the institutions through which communication can and does take place among them are highly developed. There is, however, room for improvement in all three countries. Canada's inflation targeting regime still looks a little tentative - is two per cent really price stability? - and at the time of writing, there are also concerns about the fiscal situation, particularly at a provincial level; Mexico introduced inflation targets later than did Canada, and perhaps still has some way to go in establishing their credibility, with fiscal issues still proving politically difficult there; and in the US, the Fed's mandate is still uncomfortably vague for some tastes, while the long run fiscal outlook, particularly when it is viewed against the background of the current account balance, is positively alarming.

Perhaps the scarce political energy that is available to address monetary questions in all three countries would be usefully deployed in fixing these problems. Successes here would at least ensure that a functional (if untidy) set of North American monetary arrangements continue to serve the continent at least as well in the future as they have in the recent past, and perhaps better. This may be a modest goal, but it is both attractive and viable. In matters of economic policy it is sometimes dangerous to ask for more.

Bibliography

Amano, R. and S. van Norden (1993) "A forecasting equation for the Canada-US dollar exchange rate" in *The Exchange Rate and the Economy*: proceedings of a conference held at the Bank of Canada 22-23 June, Ottawa, Bank of Canada

Amano, R. and S. van Norden (1995) "Terms of trade and real exchange rates: the Canadian evidence" *Journal of International Money and Finance* 14 (April) 83-104

Bailliu, J., A. Dib and L. Schembri (2005) "Multilateral adjustment and the Canadian dollar International Department" Bank of Canada, (mimeo)

Balassa, B. (1964) "The purchasing power parity doctrine - a reappraisal" *Journal of Political Economy* 72, (Dec.) 584-596

Bank of Canada (2003a) Correction (Press Release) Ottawa, Bank of Canada, 29th October

Bank of Canada (2003b) Intervention in the foreign exchange market (Backgrounder), Ottawa, Bank of Canada, 3rd December

Carr, J. L. and J. E. Floyd (2002) "Real and monetary shocks to the Canadian dollar: do Canada and the US form an optimal currency area?" *North American Journal of Economics and Finance* 13, 21-39

Chen, Y-C and K. Rogoff (2002) "Commodity currencies and empirical exchange rate puzzles" *IMF Working Paper WP/02/27* Washington DC., IMF

Clinton, K. (2001) "On commodity sensitive currencies and inflation targeting" *Working Paper* 01-03, Ottawa, Bank of Canada

Cohen, B. (2003) "North American monetary integration: a United States perspective" paper presented at a conference on Britain and Canada and their Large Neighbouring Monetary Unions, University of Victoria 17-18 Oct

Cooper, S. (2001) "Time for US loonie" *National Post,* November 9, 13

Courchene, T. J. and R. Harris (1999) "From fixing to monetary union: options for North American monetary integration", *Commentary 127,* Toronto, C. D. Howe Institute

Devereux, M. and C. Engel, (2004) "Expenditure switching vs. real exchange rate stabilization: competing objectives for exchange rate policy", University of Wisconsin, (mimeo)

Djoudade, R., J. Murray, T. Chan and J. Daw (2001) "The role of chartists and fundamentalists in currency markets: the experience of Australia, Canada and New Zealand", in Bank of Canada, *Revisiting the Case for Flexible Exchange Rates,* Ottawa, Bank of Canada

Flood, R. P. and A. K. Rose (1998) "Understanding exchange rate volatility without the contrivance of macroeconomics", *Discussion Paper 1944,* London, Centre for Economic Policy Research

Freedman, C. (1994) "The use of indicators and of the monetary conditions index in Canada, in T Balino and C. Cottarelli (eds.) *Frameworks for Monetary Stability: Policy Issues and Country Experiences,* Washington, DC. IMF

Freeman A. (1999) "Nobel economist urges tying loonie to US greenback" *The Globe and Mail,* Oct 14, A11

Goldfarb, D. (2003) "Beyond labels: comparing proposals for closer Canada-US economic relations", *Backgrounder No 76,* Toronto, C. D. Howe Institute, October

Grubel, H. (1999) "The case for the Amero: the economics and politics of a North American monetary union", *Critical Issues Bulletin,* Vancouver. the Fraser Institute (September)

Guillemette, Y., D. Laidler, and W. Robson (2004) "The real reason for the Canadian dollar's power trip - and what not to do about it." (e-brief, December 7th) Toronto, C. D. Howe Institute

Howard, D. (2003) "The use of foreign currencies: the United States perspective", in *Regional Currency Areas and The Use of Foreign Currencies, BIS Papers 17,* Basel

Lafrance R.., J. F. Helliwell, R. Issa, and Q. Zhang (2004)" NEMO: an equation for the Canadian dollar", Bank of Canada, (mimeo)

Laidler, D. (1999) *Fabricating the Keynesian Revolution,* Cambridge UK, Cambridge University Press

Laidler D. and W. Robson (2004) *"Two Percent Target: Canadian Monetary Policy Since 1991",* Toronto, C. D. Howe Institute

Laidler, D, and F. Poschmann (2000) "Leaving well enough alone: Canada's monetary order in a changing international environment", *Commentary No. 142,* Toronto, C. D. Howe Institute, May

Mayer, T. (1999) *Monetary Policy and the Great Inflation in the United States* Edward Elgar

McKinnon R. I. (2002) "The world dollar standard and globalization: new rules for the game?" paper presented at a conference on Exchange Rates, Economic Integration and the International Economy, Ryerson University, 17-19 May

Meltzer, A. H. (2003) *A History of the Federal Reserve, Vol. I,* Chicago, University of Chicago Press

Murray, J. and J. Powell (2002) "Dollarization in Canada: the buck stops here" *Technical Report No. 90,* Ottawa, Bank of Canada, August

Murray, J., M. Zelmer and Z. Antia (2000) "International financial crises and flexible exchange rates: some policy lessons from Canada" *Technical Report No. 88,* Ottawa, Bank of Canada, April

Osakwe, P. and L. Schembri (1998) "Currency crises and fixed exchange rates in the 1990s: a review", *Bank of Canada Review* (Autumn)

Robson, W. P. B. and D. Laidler (2002) "No small change: the awkward economics and politics of North American monetary integration" *Commentary No. 167* toronto, the C. D. howe Institute

Rogoff, K. (1966) "The purchasing power parity puzzle" *Journal of Economic Literature* 34 (June) 647-668

Samuelson, P. A. (1964) "Theoretical notes on trade problems" *Review of Economics and Statistics* 46 (May) 145-154

Summers, L. (1999) Statement to the Senate Banking Committee Subcommittee on Economic Policy, Trade and Finance, Washington DC, April 23

193

Thiessen, G. (1999) *The Thiessen Lectures,* Ottawa, Bank of Canada

Timberlake R (1993) *Monetary Policy in the United States* Chicago, University of Chicago

International Competitiveness and Regulatory Framework: A Canadian Perspective

Someshwar Rao
Industry Canada & Prakash Sharma
Industry Canada

Introduction

Although Canadians enjoy one of the highest living standards in the world, there is about 15 percent per-capita income gap between Canada and the U.S., and the gap has widened since 1990. Research done for Industry Canada suggests that close to 85 percent of the Canada-U.S. per-capita income gap is due to the productivity gap between the two countries, and the rest of the income gap is due to the differences in the employment to population ratio in the two countries.[1] Industry Canada research also implies that the productivity gap can be largely explained by the gaps in innovation, capital intensity and skills.[2]

In recent years, the OECD has done a good deal of research in quantifying various product and labour market regulations in the OECD countries. They have also examined the role of differences in regulations in explaining differences in competitiveness across OECD member countries. Their findings suggest that regulatory differences explain a significant part of the inter-country differences in innovation and productivity – key drivers of long-term competitiveness.[3]

The main objective of this chapter is to examine the relationship between regulatory framework and competitiveness, with a focus on Canada. We aim to address the following four policy research questions:

- How does Canada's regulatory framework compare with other G7 countries?
- Is there a regulatory gap between Canada and the U.S., and has it widened or narrowed in the 1990s?
- What are the main sources of the Canada-U.S. regulatory gap? and
- How much of the Canada-U.S. innovation and productivity gap can be explained by the regulatory gap?

---

[1] Someshwar Rao, Jianmin Tang and Weimin Wang, *Measuring the Canada-U.S. Productivity Gap: Industry Dimensions*, International Productivity Monitor, Ottawa: Fall 2005.

[2] Mun S. Ho, Someshwar Rao and Jianmin Tang, *Sources of Output Growth in Canadian and U.S. Industries in the Information Age*, in Dale W. Jorgenson (ed.), *Economic Growth in Canada and the United States in the Information Age*, Industry Canada Research Monograph, Ottawa: 2004.

[3] Stefano Scarpetta and Thierry Tressel, *Productivity and Convergence in a Panel of OECD Industries: Do Regulations and Institutions Matter?*, OECD Economics Department Working Paper (2002) 28, Paris: September 2002. Also, Sanghoon Ahn, *Competition, Innovation and Productivity Growth: A Review of Theory and Evidence*, OECD Economics Department Working Paper (2002) 3, Paris: January 2002.

We tackle the above policy research questions using two approaches: first, we rely on the existing research, particularly the OECD work; and second, using the International Institute for Management Development (IMD) survey data on regulations, we construct time series data on different types of product market regulations in G7 countries for the period 1991-2003. These regulatory variables in turn are used to explain differences in productivity among G7 countries.

Regulatory Framework

Regulation refers to rule-making activity by governments and the courts. Constitutions, parliamentary laws, subordinate legislation, decrees, orders, norms, licenses, plans, codes, and even some forms of administrative guidance can all be considered "regulation". Canada, like other advanced industrialized countries, has over the course of a century and a half constructed an elaborate and complex regulatory system to provide Canadians a wide range of vital services and protections, ranging from accessible buildings to safe food to universal healthcare to a cleaner environment. For markets to function efficiently some regulations, such as framework or market organizing regulations, are necessary. The regulatory framework is a set of the rules within which individual actors operate and includes contract, tort and property law, competition law, bankruptcy law, securities law and intellectual property law.

The use of regulation by governments has both costs and benefits. The OECD estimates that the cost of regulation might be as much as 10% of GDP for some countries.[4] In light of such costs of regulation, many OECD countries are examining ways to improve the cost-effectiveness of their regulations.

Regulatory reform refers to changes that improve regulatory quality, that is, enhance the performance, cost-effectiveness, or legal quality of regulations and related government formalities. Governments in advanced economies are implementing regulatory reforms to make the regulatory environment friendlier to domestic and international competition. The regulatory changes are aimed at boosting productivity growth by providing incentives for incumbent firms to adopt innovative technologies, and encouraging the entry of new and innovative firms in the market place. Governments have also adopted deregulation policy, whereby regulation in a sector is completely or partially eliminated to improve economic performance.[5]

Governments use a variety of regulatory instruments to implement programs and other agendas. The OECD classifies regulations into three categories: economic, social and administrative.[6]

---

[4] Organization for Economic Co-Operation and Development, *The OECD Report on Regulatory Reform Synthesis*, Paris: 1997, p. 14.

[5] Rauf Gonenc, Maria Maher and Giuseppe Nicoletti, *The Implementation and the Effects of Regulatory Reform: Past Experience and Current Issues*, OECD Economics Department Working Paper (2000) 24, Paris: June 2000.

[6] For a more detailed description, please see Annex B.

- **Economic regulation** can include restrictions on entrepreneurship, firm decisions over prices, quantity, service, entry and exit, ownership restrictions, tariffs, quantitative restrictions, inward and outward investment polices, antitrust regulations, and regulations of natural monopolies.
- **Social regulation** can include protection of the environment, health and safety in the workplace, protection of worker rights, rules for industrial relations (e.g., labour market regulations such as hiring and firing restrictions), and protection of buyers from fraudulent or incompetent behaviour by sellers.
- **Administrative regulation** can entail regulations relating to state control of legal framework regulations, taxes, business operations, distribution systems, health care administration, and intellectual property rights.

Different types of regulations

Product market institutions and policies affect firm governance and ownership structures, entrepreneurial incentives, and the ability of firms to enter markets (e.g. by creating fixed costs) or compete effectively with other firms (e.g. by distorting market mechanisms). We describe below various summary indicators of product market regulations. Product market reforms would include privatization, liberalization of potentially competitive markets and pro-competitive regulation of natural monopoly markets.

Labour market regulations in most countries encompass three bodies of law: employment law, industrial and collective relations law, and social security law.

- *Employment laws* govern the individual employment relationship, including the formation of the individual labour contract, the mandatory minimum terms and conditions of such contracts, and the termination of contractual relations.
- *Occupational licensing regulation* deals with entry and standards of practice in such professions as medicine, law, teachers, engineers, dentists, and accountants. Professional societies regulate their own practices by determining standards of entry and by developing a code of ethics. Local and state governments often delegate the regulatory powers of professional licensing to representatives of the professions themselves.
- *Industrial relations laws* aim at collectively protecting workers from employers. They govern the balance of power between labour unions and other forms of organized work, and employers and associations of employers.
- *Social security laws* across most countries address old-age pensions, sickness and healthcare coverage, and unemployment.

Environmental and health and safety regulations impose a variety of direct and indirect costs on regulated firms, consumers, and workers. The environment consists of a large number of attributes (anything affecting the well-being of Canadians) such as clean air and clean water. Environmental policy aims to produce the socially optimal quantities of these attributes, given that market forces alone might not bring about such outcomes in the presence of externalities.

197

Main characteristics of a good regulatory system

The OECD Report of 1997 on Regulatory Reform suggests that "good regulation" should include the following key features:[7]

- Be needed to serve clearly identified policy, and effective in achieving those goals;
- Have a sound legal basis;
- Produce benefits that justify costs, considering the distribution of effects across society;
- Minimize costs and market distortions;
- Promote innovation through market incentives and goal-based approaches;
- Be clear, simple, and practical for users;
- Be consistent with other regulations and policies; and
- Be compatible as far as possible with competition, trade and investment-facilitating principles at domestic and international levels.

Canada's regulatory framework

Canada has a mature and well-functioning system of regulatory governance. It has been consistent in the pursuit of efficient, transparent and accountable regulatory institutions and procedures. Canada's regulatory evolution has been characterized by important regulatory quality principles, such as the role of efficient markets and the need for benefits to exceed costs. A law, dating back to 1950, requires that every regulation be published and tabled in Parliament. In 1977, regulatory agencies were required to perform periodic evaluation of regulatory programs.[8] The Department of Justice drafts legislation and reviews draft regulations for internal consistency. In passing statute law, legislatures may consider distributive and efficiency aspects. Common law reflects past judicial decisions, which some interpret to be concerned with facilitating efficient allocation of resources by firms and households.[9]

In a series of studies in 1978 on the effects of regulation, the Economic Council found "regulation inflation" on account of an increase in federal regulations by almost 350% between 1955 and 1975. In response to such a growth in regulation, the Regulatory Reform Strategy of 1986 saw deregulation in a number of sectors, and regulatory quality became an important policy goal in Canada. A number of institutional, guidance and process reforms were put in place. The trend that started in 1986 was expanded in 1992, when an explicit policy was adopted which set out the overall objective of "maximizing the net

---

[7] OECD, *The OECD Report on Regulatory Reform: Synthesis*, (Paris: 1997).

[8] Serious economic problems in the 1970s that resulted in structural reforms (including tax, labour market and sectoral reforms, free trade agreements with the U.S. and Mexico, and measures to tackle the fiscal deficit) also led to an appraisal of the regulatory system in Canada. Among the OECD countries, starting in the 1950s Canada is viewed as being in the vanguard of having integrated regulatory considerations in its policy making process.

[9] OECD, *OECD Reviews of Regulatory Reform: Canada – Maintaining Leadership Through Innovation*, (Paris: OECD, 2002), esp. pp.32-34.

198

benefit to Canadians". The Regulatory Affairs and Orders in Council Secretariat (RAOICS) of the Privy Council Office (PCO) supports the Treasury Board Secretariat, the Cabinet-level Committee responsible for the oversight, review and overall government co-ordination of federal regulation making in Canada. Both general-purpose and industry-specific regulations exist. General-purpose regulations tend to affect all industries alike, as would be the case for administrative restrictions or antitrust exemptions for public enterprises. Industry-specific regulations are tailored to specific industries or set of industries, such as manufacturing and non-manufacturing industries. Industry level regulations can have economy-wide effects.[10]

Although provinces have exclusive legislative authority in such matters as education, transportation, social services, health and safety, there are also a number of important areas of shared jurisdiction, including agriculture, environment and some aspects of natural resources (federal law prevails in case of conflict). A large body of technical regulation is developed and implemented at the provincial level. It is within provincial powers to adopt laws that might represent barriers to the free movement of products, services, investment and workers, and impair competition in local markets and that inhibit inter-provincial trade and competition. The Agreement on Internal Trade (AIT) of 1994 has a formal and detailed program (including a dispute resolution mechanism) to remove barriers but progress has been limited.

Recent trends in Canada's regulatory framework

Over the last quarter-century, Canadian governments have made several efforts to refine the regulatory regime and have remodeled certain statutes. The major thrust of existing laws and regulations is largely reflective of Canada's domestic orientation rather than forging a competitive position in global markets from a Canadian-base of operations. Regulations in Canada that limit foreign investment constrain the ability of firms in Canada to access foreign-based knowledge and technology, which narrows the scope of innovation achievements in Canada. For example, Canada retains a range of foreign investment ownership restrictions, sclerotic market approval systems for drugs, chemicals and food, continuing barriers to internal trade, and sub-optimal restrictions on financial services.

In a survey of economic and administrative regulations, the OECD distinguished between regulations affecting domestic firms from those affecting foreign firms in an economy.[11] In terms of friendliness of various types of regulations to competition, Canada's regulatory regime ranked in the middle of the 10-country comparison and significantly behind that of the United Kingdom, Australia and the U.S.

---

[10] *Ibid.*, esp. pp. 35-36 and 46-80.
[11] Nicoletti, Scarpetta and Boylaud, *Summary Indicators of Product Market Regulation with an Extension to Employment Protection Legislation*, Economic Department Working Paper No. 226 (Paris: OECD, 2000).

- By international standards, Canada's economic and administrative regulatory climate for incumbent firms compares favourably in terms of its friendliness to competition.
- However, Canada's regulatory regime is relatively more restrictive with respect to foreign businesses considering new investment or trade in Canada. That is, overall product market regulations in Canada are more favourable to Canadian firms than to foreign firms.

To review and reform Canada's regulatory regime, the Government of Canada introduced a smart regulation strategy in 2002. In an increasingly knowledge intensive economy, new approaches to regulation need to enhance the climate for investment and trust in the markets to better achieve the public good. Using a smart regulation strategy the Government of Canada aimed to accelerate reforms in key areas to promote health and sustainability, to contribute to innovation and economic growth, and to reduce the administrative burden on business in both domestic and international environments to obtain desired outcomes.[12]

Starting in the late-1980s and continuing over the past several years, there has been a marked general downward trend in the annual rate of increase of regulations (including new, amended, repealed, and revised). The OECD notes that it appears that Canada has been unusually successful in tackling regulatory inflation.[13]

There is an ongoing debate in Canada pertaining to regulation in sectors such as banking, telecommunications and foreign direct investment. At this time, it is not clear whether the government will consider a total review of these regulations, a review of some specific sectors or industries, or take no action.

Foreign direct investment regulations

Research done at Industry Canada, Statistics Canada, the OECD and elsewhere clearly shows the importance of inward FDI for trade, innovation and productivity in Canada. Therefore, all types of barriers and restrictions, formal and informal, that impact on attracting and retaining FDI need to be assessed. Canada has one of the highest levels of FDI restrictions among OECD countries, especially in the telecommunications, finance and air transport sectors. An OECD study computed an FDI restrictions index by assigning varying importance (weights) of statutory restrictions such as: (a) limits on foreign equity/ownership; (b) screening and approval procedures; and (c) constraints on foreign personnel and operational freedom.[14] The study found that across OECD countries, the most heavily restricted sectors are those that are highly sensitive to national security or national sovereignty considerations: telecommunications, air and maritime transport, finance, public utilities and media. Table 1 shows that Canada was more

---

[12] Government of Canada, *The Canada That We Want*, The Speech From the Throne 2002, Ottawa: 2002.

[13] *OECD Reviews of Regulatory Reform: Canada – Maintaining Leadership Through Innovation*, (2002), *op. cit.*

[14] Stephen S. Golub, *Measures of Restrictions on Inward Foreign Direct Investment for OECD Countries* by, OECD Economics Department Working Paper No. 357, (Paris: OECD), 2003.

restrictive than the U.S. in areas such as telecommunications, finance, business services and manufacturing; while, the U.S. was more restrictive in transport.

In addition, Industry Canada researchers, in a study published by the C. D. Howe Institute in 1996, found that the impact of *informal* barriers to FDI, such as impediments arising from differences in market structure, corporate governance practices, unpublished policies, and non-transparent administrative procedures and actions of government and private, has to be considered because the importance of informal barriers may be gaining importance in making the Canadian investment market place less attractive for foreign investors.[15]

Table 1: Discriminatory Foreign Direct Investment Restrictions, by sector		
Sector	Canada	US
Business Services	.225	.025
Telecommunications	.525	.375
Construction	.225	.025
Distribution	.225	.025
Finance	.506	.125
Hotels and Restaurants	.225	.025
Transportation	.590	.690
Electricity	.725	.475
Manufacturing	.225	.025
Total	**.352**	**.173**
Note: Indices of FDI Restrictions, by competing regions for N.A-bound FDI and major source countries of FDI to Canada, 1998 (0=no restriction, 1=complete restriction)		
Source: *Policies and International Integration: Influences on Trade and Foreign Direct Investment*, Annex 4: *Foreign Direct Investment Restriction Indexes*, (Paris: OECD), March 2003.		

Competition policy

The 1986 Competition Act broadened the objective of competition policy in Canada to include consumer interests and the promotion of sectoral pro-competitive reforms. As of the early 1970s, direct economic regulation of price or output (or both) had an impact on about 29% of the Canadian economy. That share has decreased as a result of subsequent deregulation and reform in transport, energy, telecoms, and financial services. However, the impact of reform on competition policy is diluted by a near-monopoly airline and foreign ownership restrictions to protect Canadian-based companies from international competition.[16]

Intellectual property protection policy

Intellectual property rights (IPRs) are legally enforceable instruments designed to provide protection for investments in innovations. IPRs include patents, copyrights, trademarks, trade secrets (a product or process kept secret

---

[15] Someshwar Rao, and A. Ahmad (1996), *Formal and Informal Investment Barriers in the G7.* in Pierre Sauvé and Daniel Schwanen (eds.), "Investment Rules for the Global Economy: Enhancing Access to Markets", C.D. Howe Institute, Policy Study no. 28. 1996.

[16] *OECD Reviews of Regulatory Reform: Canada – Maintaining Leadership Through Innovation*, (2002), *op. cit.*

from competitors), industrial designs, plant breeder's rights, and integrated circuit topographies. This view encapsulates the argument that entrepreneurs would see increased profitability resulting from expanded IPRs, giving them incentives to come up with innovations. IPRs, such as patents that entail new information disclosure, would also encourage diffusion of new knowledge and would boost social benefits.[17] Moreover, evidence suggests that foreign direct investment in R&D flows to locations where IPRs are securely protected and strongly enforced.[18]

Although Canada's IPRs regime has become somewhat stronger since the late 1980s, tracking the global trend toward stronger IPRs system, Canada's IPRs regime appears not to have followed the trend, as exemplified by the Ginarte-Park index that placed Canada's patent system second last, behind the U.S. and the U.K., and seven other countries.[19]

Telecommunications regulations

Telecommunications infrastructure is a significant driving force of economic growth. Numerous studies have been conducted to quantify the contribution of telecommunications services to economic growth. Despite its rapid growth, Canada's telecommunication services industry fell behind the average of the OECD countries during the 1990s, with telecommunications infrastructure declining from the second place to 23rd place among the 29 OECD countries. In recent research done for Industry Canada, Professor Chen found that two factors mainly contributed to this decline in Canada's relative standing.[20]

- Canada's highly developed fixed-network services, in particular, a well developed payphone system, reduced the need for cellular mobile services and thus slowed down its adoption; and
- Relatively high barriers to ongoing operations and direct investment hindered the growth of cellular mobile services.

If these barriers were reduced to the average restriction level of OECD countries, Canada's telecommunications penetration rate would have been above the OECD average. Furthermore, estimates from Professor Chen's analysis show that Canada's GDP per working-age person would be increased by about 1.7% over a ten-year period if Canada were to remove all barriers to foreign direct investment in telecommunications services.

---

[17] However, as an anonymous referee points out, the impact on profits of the innovator/patent holder is clear, but the net impact on the economy or innovation is not.

[18] Porter and Stern, *The New Challenge to America's Prosperity: Findings from the Innovation Index*, Washington, D.C.: Council on Competitiveness, 1999.

[19] Ginarte and Park, *Determinants of Patent Rights: A Cross National Study*, Research Policy, vol. 26, 1997.

[20] Zhiqi Chen, *Liberalization of Trade and Investment in Telecommunications Services: A Canadian Perspective*, a paper presented at the Industry Canada conference in October 2003, Winnipeg, on "Service Industries and Knowledge-Based Economy", in Richard Lipsey and Alice Nakamura (eds.), an Industry Canada research volume, (forthcoming).

Labour market regulations

The labour market and its reforms have a major impact on an economy's performance. Canada's unemployment rates have been higher than in a number of advanced countries, such as the U.S. Labour market policies have generally not brought about incentives to observed labour mobility, though the amount of human capital embodied in the workforce has increased substantially over the last two decades. After several modifications in the 1990s, the unemployment-insurance system (now Employment Insurance) was restructured in 1996 to restore the insurance principle which had been undermined over time. At the same time, Employment Benefits and Support Measures (EBSMs) restructured employment benefits such as job subsidies and various forms of job search assistance. The management of these programs has been largely decentralized to the provincial level, through Labour Market Development Agreements. The EBSM, though expensive, has been largely successful.[21]

A National Bureau of Economic Research study found that patterns of labour regulations across 88 sample countries generally support the view that regulations across countries are shaped by their legal structures, most of which are adaptations of Europe's common and civil law traditions. Moreover, the study pointed out that the historical origins of a country's labour laws also correlated with other measures of regulations. For example, countries that regulated business entry also regulated labour markets and judicial proceedings. The study concluded that countries have regulatory styles that are pervasive across activities and are shaped by the origin of their laws.[22]

Trends in regulatory burden

One can take the pulse of regulatory activity over time in a number of ways. One is to calculate the rate of growth in government regulatory expenditures (in real terms) over time. Another is to calculate the rate of growth in the number of regulations or in the number of pages of regulations.

The Fraser Institute estimated that between 1975 and 1999, over 117,000 new federal and provincial regulations were enacted, an average of 4,700 every year. Over this period, the federal government alone enacted 25,000 regulations. Between 1975 and 1999, the three levels of governments published over 505,000 pages of regulations (or an average of over 20,000 pages per year), of which the federal government accounted for more than one-fifth.[23]

Accurately measuring the cost of regulation to the entire economy is almost impossible. The Fraser Institute has collected from the public accounts the amounts federal, provincial and local governments spend, or what it calls the public sector "administration costs", to design and implement regulations. It found that in fiscal year 1997/1998, the federal government and provincial, territorial, and local governments in Canada spent $5.2 billion administering their regulatory

---

[21] OECD, OECD Reviews of Regulatory Reform: Canada – Maintaining Leadership Through Innovation, (Paris: OECD, 2002).

[22] Botero, et al., *The Regulation of Labour*, NBER Working Paper 9756, June 2003.

[23] Laura Jones and S. Graf, *Canada's Regulatory Burden: How Many Regulations? At What Cost?*, Vancouver, BC: The Fraser Institute, 2001, p. 9.

activities, down from a price-change adjusted $5.3 billion in 1995/1996. Moreover, it estimated that in fiscal year 1997/1998, the private sector spent $103 billion or $13,700 per family of four to comply with federal and provincial government regulations.[24] Earlier, Milhar had estimated that complying with regulations in 1996 exceeded $83 billion, or just over $11,000 per family of four.[25]

In attempting to obtain crude estimates of additional indirect costs of regulations, the Fraser Institute considered three categories of lobbyists under the *Lobbyists Registration Act.* (a) Consultant lobbyists who lobby on behalf of a client and might include government-relations consultants, lawyers, accountants; (b) In-house lobbyists are corporate employees managing public affairs or government relations; and (c) Non-profit organizations who must register when one or more employees lobby federal politicians. The Fraser Institute reported that between 1998 and 2000:

- The number of consultants lobbyists increased 20 percent from 584 to 702;
- The number of in-house lobbyists fell from 367 to 335; and
- The number of organizations registered increased roughly 15 percent from 322 to 370.

These estimates of the cost of regulation are to be relied on less for the dollar figure but rather to underscore the point that regulation is costly and that it might be growing increasingly costly.

Comparison of Regulations among G7 Countries

In this section, we turn to discuss the OECD work that compares regulations across G7countries and industries. The OECD has compiled summary indicators of *product market regulatory systems* across countries and industries. Product market regulations consist of: (a) inward-oriented policies, and (b) outward-oriented policies. Each indicator is ranked on a scale ranging from 0 to 6, reflecting the least to the most restrictive regime. The data can be divided along three alternative formats:

(a) the economy-wide or industry-specific **scope** of regulations;

(b) the "**thematic**" domains or types of restrictions that indicate channels through which regulations may restrict market mechanisms; and

(c) "**functional**" regulations.

The *thematic domains* consist of three broad categories:

1. **State control over business enterprises** consisting of: (a) public ownership; and (b) involvement in business operation.
2. **Barriers to entrepreneurship** consisting of: (a) administrative burdens on start ups, including burdens at both the economy-wide and sectoral

---

[24] L. Jones and S. Graf, ibid, p. 24.

[25] Fazil Milhar, *The Cost of Regulation in Canada*, Public Policy Sources, Number 12, Vancouver, BC: The Fraser Institute, 1998. Milhar used a multiplier derived by Widenbaum and DeFina (1976), who estimated for the U.S. that for every dollar that the public sector spent to administer regulatory activity, the private sector spent $20 in compliance costs.

levels; (b) regulatory and administrative opacity, including the features of the licenses and permits system and the communication and simplification of rules and procedures; and (c) barriers to competition, including legal limitations on the number of competitors and exemptions to competition law provisions for public enterprises or state-mandated actions.

3. **Barriers to international trade and investment** consisting of: (a) explicit barriers, including average tariffs, discriminatory procedures and restrictions to foreign participations in domestic companies; and (b) other regulatory barriers.

Under the alternative *functional compilation*, data fall in two categories:

- **Administrative regulation** consisting of: (a) administrative burdens of start-ups, including economy-wide and sector-specific burdens; and (b) regulatory and administrative opacity, including the feature of licence and permit system and the communication and simplification of rules and procedures.
- **Economic regulation** consisting of: (a) regulation of economic structure, including the size and scope of public ownership, legal barriers to entry and control of public enterprises by the legislature; (b) regulation of economic behaviour, including command and control regulations, and special voting rights; and (c) regulation of competition, including competition law exemptions and price controls.

In addition to the above product market regulatory indicators, the OECD studies often factor in *employment protection legislation* (EPL) consisting of:

- Regular contracts, including procedural requirements, notice and severance pay, and prevailing standards of and penalties for "unfair" dismissals; and
- Temporary contracts, including "objective" reasons under which a fixed-term contract could be offered, the maximum number of successive renewals, and the maximum cumulated duration of the contract.

In our review of the OECD work below, we will return to the above description of regulatory indicators.

Product Market Regulations

Countries differ much more in the degree of state control than in the extent of barriers to entrepreneurship, partly reflecting differences in the timing and scope of privatization and in the extent to which past regulatory reform has been successful in shifting from command and control to incentive-based regulations. Economic and administrative regulations shape the inward-oriented regulatory environments. Table 2 shows that among G7 countries:

- Overall, Canada's product market regime was inward-liberal and outward-restrictive, whereas the U.S. was characterized by a combination of relatively liberal inward and outward-oriented regulatory policies.
- The United Kingdom was the least restrictive country.
- The United Kingdom, the United States, and Germany had fewer barriers than Canada in the overall product market regulatory regime.

205

- Canada had the most barriers to trade and investment of all G7 countries, making it the least outward-oriented regulatory system in G7.
- The United States had less restrictive regime than Canada with regard to state control and overall economic regulations.
- Canada had less restrictive regime than the U.S. in such domains as entrepreneurship and overall administrative regulations.
- The friendliness of regulatory environments to product market competition still varies substantially across countries, in particular for inward-oriented (economic and administrative) regulations.

Table 2: Synopsis of summary OECD indicators of product market regulation by domain

Overall indicator		*Domains*				
	Product market regulation	State control	Barriers to entrepreneur-ship	Barriers to trade & investment	Economic regulation	Administrative regulation
Canada	**1.5**	1.3	0.8	2.2	1.1	0.9
United States	**1.0**	0.9	1.3	0.9	1.0	1.2
Japan	**1.5**	1.3	2.3	1.0	1.4	2.7
Germany	**1.4**	1.8	2.1	0.5	1.4	2.7
France	**2.1**	2.6	2.7	1.0	2.3	3.1
Italy	**2.3**	3.9	2.7	0.5	3.5	3.0
United Kingdom	**0.5**	0.6	0.5	0.4	0.6	0.5

Source: Nicoletti, Scarpetta & Boylaud, OECD Working Paper 226, (2000), Table A2.7.

State Control Regulations: Provisions that aim at establishing partial or full state control over resources or economic activities could be managed, in principle, by agents (e.g., public ownership and/or control, restrictions on price setting and/or other firm's choices). Table 3 shows that:
- Canada was more restrictive than the U.S. and U.K. in the use of (a) command and controls; (b) price controls; and (c) the size of the public sector.
- The U.S. was more restrictive in regard to the scope of public enterprises.
- Overall, the U.S., U.K. and Canada were less apt to resort to state controls than the other G7 countries.

Table 3: The Composition of OECD State Control Indicator

	Scope of public enterprise sector	Size of public enterprise sector	Special voting rights	Control of public enterprises by legislative bodies	Use of command and control regulation	Price controls
Canada	1.8	1.4	2.0	0.0	1.6	1.0
United States	2.0	0.0	2.0	0.0	1.1	0.0
Japan	1.5	0.0	2.0	0.0	1.4	2.9
Germany	1.8	1.4	2.0	0.0	3.4	1.7
France	3.8	2.6	3.0	0.0	4.8	0.9
Italy	5.3	2.3	6.0	5.3	3.1	2.2
United Kingdom	0.0	0.0	0.0	0.0	2.3	0.6

Source: Nicoletti, Scarpetta & Boylaud, OECD Working Paper 226, (2000), Table A2.2.1

Barriers to entrepreneurship: Table 4 shows that:
- Canada was more restrictive than the U.S. in regard to administrative burdens on: (a) corporations; (b) sole proprietor firms; and (c) specific sectors.
- The U.S. had a less liberal regime than Canada in the use of (a) licenses and permits; (b) communication and simplification of rules and procedures; (c) legal barriers to entry; and (c) antitrust exemptions.
- Overall, the U.K., the U.S., and Canada had a more liberal regulation regime pertaining to entrepreneurship of all the G7 countries.

Table 4: The Composition of OECD Barriers to entrepreneurship Indicator

	Licenses & permits system	Communication & simplification of rules and procedures	Administrative burdens for corporations	Administrative burdens for sole proprietor firms	Sector specific Administrative burdens	Legal barriers to entry	Antitrust exemptions
Canada	0.0	0.3	1.5	1.5	1.0	0.7	0.5
United States	4.0	0.6	0.5	1.3	0.5	1.0	1.3
Japan	6.0	1.5	2.3	2.3	1.5	2.3	0.3
Germany	4.0	1.3	2.5	3.3	2.3	0.5	0.0
France	4.0	0.9	3.3	3.8	3.6	2.0	1.1
Italy	0.0	0.8	5.3	4.3	4.5	3.0	1.3
United Kingdom	0.0	0.0	0.8	1.3	0.4	1.3	0.0

Source: Nicoletti, Scarpetta & Boylaud, OECD Working Paper 226, (2000), Table A2.2.2

In **barriers to trade and investment**, the message that jumps out of table 5 is that Canada had the most restrictive regulatory regime of all the G7 countries. Considering all the other OECD regulation indicators, Canada could be found in the company of less restrictive countries such as the U.K. and the U.S. among the G7 countries.

- Canada broke ranks with its liberal-regulatory cohorts by turning out to be the most restrictive country in regard to all the three indicators of: (a) tariffs; (b) ownership barriers; and (c) discriminatory procedures.

Table 5: The Composition of OECD Barriers to Trade & Investment Indicator				
	Ownership barriers	Discriminatory procedures	Regulatory barriers	Tariffs
Canada	3.6	1.4	0.0	4.0
United States	2.2	0.3	0.0	1.0
Japan	1.9	1.4	0.0	1.0
Germany	0.0	0.5	0.0	2.0
France	1.8	0.5	0.0	2.0
Italy	0.0	0.3	0.0	2.0
United Kingdom	0.0	0.0	0.0	2.0

Source: Nicoletti, Scarpetta & Boylaud, OECD Working Paper 226, (2000), Table A2.2.3.

Employment Protection Legislation (EPL)

Table 6 shows that Canada, United Kingdom, and the United States, are at the one end of the spectrum, with relatively lax EPL systems, while continental European countries and Japan have a much more stringent EPL system. Although the EPL regimes in Canada and the U.S. remained stable in the 1990s, the composite EPL indicators show that:

- The gap between Canada and the U.S. of EPL system continues, with the U.S. being more liberal in employment protection regulations.
- Overall, the U.S., followed by the U.K. and Canada had the least restrictive EPL system, while all the other the G7 economies had more restrictive labour market regimes.

Table 6: Synopsis of OECD summary indicator of employment protection legislation (EPL)

	1990			1998		
	EPL	EPL regular contracts	EPL temporary contracts	**EPL**	EPL regular contracts	EPL temporary contracts
Canada	0.6	0.9	0.3	0.6	0.9	0.3
United States	0.2	0.1	0.3	0.2	0.1	0.3
Japan	2.6	2.5	2.7	2.6	3.0	2.3
Germany	3.6	2.9	4.2	2.8	3.0	2.5
France	2.7	2.4	3.0	3.1	2.5	3.7
Italy	4.2	3.0	5.3	3.3	3.0	3.6
United Kingdom	0.5	0.7	0.3	0.5	0.7	0.3

Source: Nicoletti, Scarpetta & Boylaud, OECD Working Paper 226, (2000), Table A3.11.

In summing up, Canada among the G7: The available "subjective" data from IMD and the "objective" data from the OECD point to a similar overall conclusion concerning Canada's regulation system among the G7, and particularly in comparison to the U.S.

- The overall Canada-U.S. gap regulatory gap exists in both the production and labour market regulation system;
- The U.S. edges out Canada in being more liberal in product market regulations, particularly in regard to barriers to ownership, discriminatory procedures and tariffs; and
- The U.S. has consistently maintained a much more flexible labour market regulatory environment than Canada throughout the 1990s.

Canada-U.S. Regulatory System Comparisons: Recent Trends

The overall comparison of regulatory systems in Canada and the U.S. can be done using data published by international organizations such as the OECD, the World Economic Forum, and the International Institute for Management Development (IMD). In this study, we use annual IMD indicator data over the 1991 to 2003 period complied annually from surveying responses from over 3,000 top business executives of large international and domestic firms in about 50 countries.[26] Following Koch et al, we consider the following indicators of regulations across the G7 economies:

---

[26] The IMD publishes in the *World Competitiveness Yearbook*, its annual survey data on national economic competitiveness, which include some regulation indicators. The discussion of IMD indicator follows closely the discussion in, Kevin Koch, M. Rafiquzzaman, and S. Rao, *The Impact of Regulatory Policies on Innovation: Evidence from G7 Countries*, Industry Canada Working Paper (mimeo.), Ottawa: Industry Canada, 2003.

1. **INVREG** compiled to measure the intensity of **inward foreign direct investment** restrictiveness by asking: "Are foreign investors free to acquire control in a domestic company?"
2. **IPRLAW** set out to measure the effectiveness of **intellectual property rights** by asking: "Is intellectual property adequately protected in your country?"
3. **COMPLAW** aimed to measure the effectiveness of **competition policy** or antitrust laws by asking the question: "Do antitrust laws prevent unfair competition in your country?"
4. **TRANS** aimed to measure the degree of **transparency of government communications** by asking: "Does the government communicate its policy intentions clearly in your country?"
5. **LABREGS** designed to capture the degree of effectiveness of **labour market policies** by asking: "Are labour market regulations (hiring and firing practices, minimum wages) flexible enough in your country?"

The IMD indicator data range from a value of 0, reflecting disagreement with the question, to a maximum value of 10, indicating strong agreement. Notice that the above indicators include both product market and labour market regulations. Koch *et al.* report that despite the "subjective" nature of the IMD data, the above listed indicators are statistically significantly correlated with the "objective" type data collected by the OECD, which we will have an opportunity to analyze below.

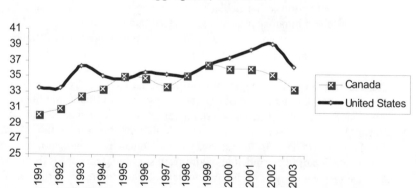

Figure 1: Canada -U.S. Regulatory Gap, IMD Indicators Aggregated, 1991-2003

Figure 1 presents the results of aggregating the IMD indicators for Canada and the U.S. The early 1990s were marked by a regulatory gap between Canada and the U.S., when the U.S. regulatory regime was more liberal than that in Canada. In the mid-1990s, the Canada-U.S. regulatory gap narrowed as the Canadian regulatory regime moved in the more liberal direction while the U.S.

turned less liberal. By the late 1990s, the Canada-U.S. regulation gap reemerged and continued into 2003, as regulations in the two countries turned less liberal. Our reading of the overall picture is that there exists a regulatory gap between Canada and the U.S., with the U.S. system continuing to be more liberal than the Canadian regulatory regime.

Below, we present Canada-U.S. regulatory comparisons based on individual IMD indicators in Figure 2 to Figure 5.

Figure 2: IPRLAW - Effective Intellectual Property Protection

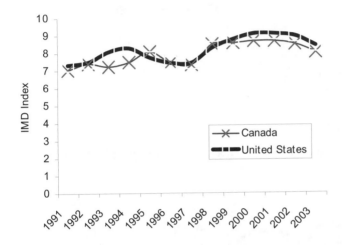

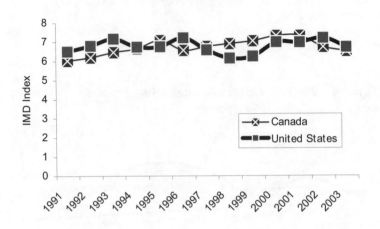

Figure 3: COMPLAW - Effectiveness of Competition Law

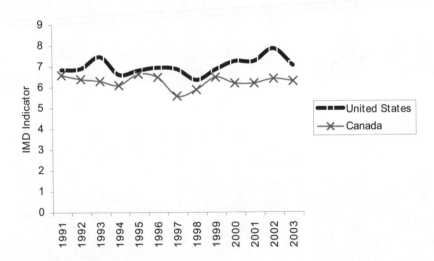

Figure 4: Flexibility of Labour Regulations (hiring/firing)

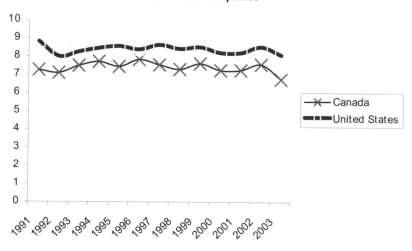

Figure 5: INVREG - Foreign Investors Free to Acquire Control of Domestic companies

To explain the overall Canada-U.S. regulatory gap we observe the following trends, using the IMD data:

- A significant part of the regulatory gap is associated with the less liberal foreign direct investment regime in Canada than the U.S.[27]
- A good part of the regulatory gap is accompanied by the relatively less flexible labour market regulations in Canada than the U.S. Moreover, the gap with respect to Canada-U.S. labour market regulation has widened over the past half a decade.
- Canada, having narrowed the regulatory gap in the mid-1990s, has re-opened the deficit gap with the U.S. in intellectual property rights and in competition policy regulations.

Competitiveness and Regulatory Framework

Competitiveness is the efficiency with which an industry or an economy uses its productive resources, such as natural resources, physical and human capital, in maintaining and expanding real incomes. Competitiveness plays a key role over time in determining how successful a country is in achieving high and rising real wages and incomes. A fundamental objective of regulation is to improve the efficiency of the Canadian economy, while remaining flexible enough to adapt to change and sustain international competitiveness. In this sub-section of the paper, we argue that Canada's international competitiveness is shaped by Canada's productivity performance vis-à-vis its trading partners, and the U.S. in particular. Canada's relative productivity performance, in turn, is driven in part by Canada's regulatory regime. A key hypothesis of this paper is that the impact of regulation

---

[27] The evidence presented in Table 1 above reinforces this observation.

213

on Canada's relative productivity performance will also shape Canada's international competitiveness.

What is international competitiveness?

International competitiveness of a country is determined by how much more efficient it is, compared to competitor economies, in using its resources in meeting the test of international competition. In other words, total factor productivity (TFP) is an ideal measure of the overall health of a country. TFP is measured as the weighted sum of all individual input productivities – natural resources, capital and labour.[28]

In international competitiveness comparisons, labour productivity is commonly used as a good proxy for TFP, given that the two measures are related and over time tend to move closely across countries. The patterns of international trade are governed by comparative advantage that a country enjoys on account of how efficient the country is in using technology to transform its natural resources, human and physical capital relative to its trading partners. A significant improvement in productivity, unmatched by competitors abroad, not only will sustain an industry's comparative advantage but also will enhance its international competitiveness.

Cost competitiveness: Competitiveness is often also expressed in terms of cost competitiveness of one country relative to competitor countries. It is easy to show that Canada-U.S. relative unit labour cost equals the difference between the relative wage rate and relative labour productivity. If labour compensation in Canada and the U.S. is the same, then relative productivity directly determines the relative unit labour cost. Should there be exchange rate swings in the short-term or prolonged deviations from purchasing power parity, unit labour costs would be distorted. In general, sustained improvements in cost competitiveness and living standards can only come from continuous improvements in Canada's productivity performance relative to that of the U.S. and its other trading partners.

Canada's productivity performance

Between 1995 and 2003, real income per capita in Canada grew at 2.5% per year, compared to 2.2% in the U.S. But, in 2003, the real per capita income gap with the U.S. was $5,810. Per capita income in the U.S. on average was about 15% higher than in Canada. Lower productivity explains about 83% of the Canada-U.S. income level gap. The remainder is due to fewer people working and fewer hours worked per person employed. The Canada-U.S. aggregate labour productivity level gap increased from 10% in 1995 to 17% in 2003, as illustrated in Figure 6. Productivity in manufacturing, the key to international competitiveness, and the Canada-U.S. productivity gap widened to 23 percent, in 2001, from 17% in 1995. Research done at Industry Canada suggests that differences in capital intensities in the two countries can explain about 60 percent of the aggregate Canada-U.S. labour productivity gap. In the manufacturing

---

[28] Someshwar Rao and Jiamin Tang, *Competitiveness Challenges Facing Canadian Industries*, Industry Canada Research Paper, Government of Canada, Ottawa: Industry Canada, 2003 (memo.), pp. 5-6.

214

sector, more than 80 percent of the gap can be attributed to the capital intensity gap.[29]

Figure 6
Relative labour Productivity in Canada, 1987- 2003
(U.S.= 1.0)

Note: Labour productivity is defined as real GDP per worker, PPP based.
Source: Figure 1 in Rao, Tang and Wang, May 2004.

Industry Canada research suggests further that the innovation and skills gaps, the larger role of the small medium sized enterprises (SMEs) in the Canadian economy and the smaller size of the high-tech sector explain the remaining Canada-U.S. labour productivity.[30]

Canada's innovation performance

Canada lags behind the U.S. in all indicators of innovation. Canada also ranks 5th to 7th among the G7 countries in all the innovation measures (see figure 7). Canada's business R&D intensity is still only slightly more than 50 percent of the intensity level in the U.S. But, Canada has narrowed some of the R&D-intensity gap in the 1990s. The same is true for other indicators of innovation. As well, since 1990, Canada made progress compared to other G7 countries.

---

[29] Someshwar Rao, Jianmin Tang and Weimin Wang, *Productivity Levels Between Canadian and U.S. Industries*, mimeo., Industry Canada, May 2004.
[30] For example, Rao and Tang (2003), ibid, pp. 16-20; Richard G. Harris, *Determinants of Canadian Productivity Growth: Issues and Prospects*, in Someshwar Rao and Andrew Sharpe, eds., *Productivity Issues in Canada*, Calgary: University of Calgary Press, 2002.

215

Figure 7: Canada's Innovation Performance Relative to G7, 2002

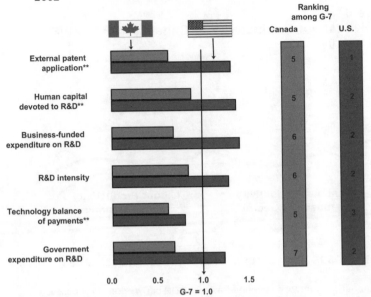

Productivity and regulatory framework

The impact of regulations and institutions on productivity and economic performance depends on market and technology conditions. The link between employment protection legislation (EPL) and productivity is also complex. Over the 1984-98 period there was evidence, across 18 OECD countries, of multifactor productivity (MFP) catch-up in most industries, with a stronger effect in service than in manufacturing.[31] An OECD paper found that:

- Anti-competitive product market regulations had a negative effect on productivity by reducing incentives to adopt better technology thereby catching-up the technological leader;
- Stringent employment protection legislation had a negative effect on productivity growth in countries where wages or internal training did not offset the adjustment costs associated with high firing costs;
- R&D intensity had a positive impact on productivity growth;
- Three countries – the U.S., Canada and Japan – exhibited the highest level of multi-factor productivity in each industry at the beginning and at the end of the sample and were often at the frontier (or close to it) in most industries;

---

[31] Stefano Scarpetta and Thierry Tressel, *Productivity and Convergence in a Panel of OECD Industries: Do Regulations and Institutions Matter?* OECD Economics Department Working Paper No. 342, Paris: OECD, September 2002.

216

- A one standard deviation increase in product market regulations would lead to a decrease by 2.2 percent of the long-run level of MFP (relative to the frontier) in the U.S.; and
- The long-run impact of a one standard deviation increase of EPL was such that it would lead to a decrease of 10.8 percent of the level of MFP. [32]

Another recent OECD study examined the link between product market regulations and productivity performance. Regression results suggested that:[33]

- An anti-competitive regulatory environment and delays in implementing pro-market reforms, including improved market access and state retrenchment, were associated with relatively poor multifactor productivity performance.
- Countries in which public ownership in the business sector was limited and barriers to entry were low have been more successful in improving multifactor productivity than countries in which regulations curb competition and public enterprises were widespread.
- Both privatization and entry liberalization were estimated to have a positive impact on productivity.
- The negative effects stemming from a more timid regulatory reform might have been particularly strong in those industries where European countries had a significant technology gap (e.g., ICT-related industries).

Innovation and regulatory framework

Innovation, the development and implementation of ideas which lead to new or improved products and processes, is widely recognized as a driver of productivity, and hence competitiveness, and economic growth. Public policy across countries often use the regulatory framework to effect economy-wide and specific industry innovation performance.

As noted above, recent research at Industry Canada found that regulatory regimes were important determinants of innovation activity, as measured by R&D intensity, in Canada and G7 economies.[34] The authors found that intellectual property rights (IPRs) and competition policy accounted for about 60 percent of R&D-intensity in Canada from 1991 to 2000. IPRs and competition policy, found to be substitute policies, had a positive impact on innovations. Flexible labour market regulations, in terms of flexibility in hiring and firing as well as the minimum wage restrictions, increased innovation activity. More importantly, the study concludes that differences in regulations (or the regulatory gap between Canada and the U.S.) were responsible for one-third of the R&D intensity gap between the countries.

---

[32] *Ibid*, pp. 17-18.

[33] Nicoletti and Scarpetta, *Regulation, Productivity and Growth: OECD Evidence*, The OECD Working Papers No. 347, January 2003, *op. cit.*, pp. 11-12.

[34] Kevin Koch, M. Rafiquzzaman, and S. Rao, *The Impact of Regulatory Policies on Innovation: Evidence from G7 Countries*, Industry Canada Working Paper (mimeo.), Ottawa: Industry Canada, 2003.

Productivity and a regulatory framework: An empirical analysis

In this section, we pursue regression analysis to examine whether differences in labour productivity across G7 countries could be explained by differences in economic regulations across these countries. Towards this objective, we use the IMD survey data on five types of regulations for the G7 countries over the 1991-2003 period. We discussed the IMD data above in section 5.

Industry Canada's research suggests that the Canada-U.S. labour productivity gap can be explained by the gaps in capital-intensity, innovation, and human capital. In this section, we examine directly the impact of regulations on labour productivity via their impact on capital-intensity, innovation and skills. We estimated the following reduced form equation, using the data on G7 countries:

$$LP_{it} = \alpha_1 KL_{tit} + \alpha_2 IPRLAW_{it} + \alpha_3 IPRLAW_{it} *COMPLAW_{it} + \alpha_4 FDIRES_{it} + \alpha_5 LABREGS + \alpha_6 LP_{it}(-1) + \varepsilon_t \qquad \text{(Eq. 1)}$$

where LP_{it} is labour productivity for country i at time t; KL_{tit} is capital-labour ratio; $IPRLAW_{it}$ is an indicator for intellectual property law; $COMPLAW_{it}$ is an indicator for competition laws; $FDIRES_{it}$ is a foreign direct investment restriction indicator; $LP_{it}(-1)$ is lagged labour productivity; and ε_t is the error term. The equation is estimated using the aggregate time series data over the period 1991 to 2003.

Intellectual property rights protection (IPRLAW) improves resource allocation by enabling inventors to capture more of the profits from their inventive activity. As protection of intellectual property rights increases, the profits from secure proprietary knowledge that a business sources from outside or within the firm would allow a firm to achieve efficiencies and higher productivity.[35] The hypothesis here would be that a strong protection of IPRs will be positively associated with productivity.

The interaction term between competition policy and the intellectual property regime (*IPRLAW *COMPLAW*) is added to capture the complementarity or substitutability between the two policies. Their complementarity implies a positive coefficient. On the other hand, a negative coefficient would suggest substitutability between IPRs and competition policy.

Inward foreign direct investment adds to capital formation, transfers and diffuses technology, skills, innovative capacity, and organizational and managerial practices – all activities leading to productivity enhancements. In addition, research done for Industry Canada and by others suggests that foreign-owned

---

[35] Although the IMD data are based upon perceptions by business decision makers of our regulatory system, they are highly correlated with the objective OECD data set. Due to limited data availability, we neither analyze the particular form (copyrights, patents, trademarks, trade secrets, etc.) of intellectual property protection nor aspects of each form (the framework laws, their enforcement, or their administration). The conclusions that we offer from our analysis should be interpreted with this limitation in mind. Further research is required to determine these specific relationships.

firms on average are more productive than domestically controlled firms.[36] Therefore, it is hypothesized that fewer restrictions on FDI (FDIRES) would positively impact labour productivity.

Labour market regulations (LABREGS), such as hiring/firing and minimum wage rules or strict statutory employment protection legislation increase the cost of production and introduce labour market rigidity which may not allow firms to achieve optimal and most efficient capital to labour combination in producing output and, thus, would limit productivity growth that firms may realize. Therefore, the lower the impact of employment protection legislation, the smaller the distortions and higher the scope for productivity growth. It is hypothesized that there would be a positive link between lower employment protection legislation and productivity.

The capital to labour ratio (KL) measures the capital-intensity with which production is characterized in the economy. Capital deepening is essential to productivity and economic growth. Therefore, it is hypothesized that a higher capital to labour ratio would be positively related with productivity. We do not expect KL variable to be significant in the presence of regulatory variables, because the latter would capture the influence of KL, since KL it self will be influenced by these variables.

The lagged dependant variable (LP-1) is included to take into account the lagged effect of independent variables on labour productivity. The larger the coefficient on the lagged dependent variable, the longer it takes for independent variables to have their full impact on labour productivity, and vice versa.

Regression results

The empirical estimation of the above regression equation is based on a cross-section of the G7 countries over the 1991-2003 period. We followed a standard pooled cross-country time series analysis.

In both the regression equations, the coefficient on the lagged dependent variable is over 0.9 and is statistically highly significant. The large coefficient on the lagged dependant variable suggests a lengthy lag, about ten years, between the independent variables and labour productivity, which is not unreasonable. The regulatory variables we considered might also be picking the influence of other framework conditions that are not considered here.[37]

As expected, the coefficient on capital-intensity is positive in the two regression equations. But, the coefficient is not statistically significant. This is not surprising, because the regulation variables are expected to capture much of the impact of capital-intensity on labour productivity. Differences in regulations are expected to explain differences in capital formation in G7 countries.

The regression coefficients on intellectual property protection and foreign direct investment regulations, as expected, are positive and statistically significant,

---

[36] Someshwar Rao and Jianmin Tang, *Are Canadian-controlled manufacturing firms less productive than their foreign-controlled counterparts?,* Industry Canada Working Paper Number 31, Ottawa: February 2000.

[37] Koch, Rafiquzzman and Rao, *op. cit.,* (2003) also reported similar results, where the R&D intensity served as a proxy for innovation.

implying differences in these two variables explain much of the variation in labour productivity between G7 countries.

The coefficient on competition policy and intellectual property protection interaction term is negative and statistically significant, suggesting substitutability between the two policy variables. This result is consistent with the findings an earlier Industry Canada study.[38]

The coefficient on employment regulations (see the first equation) is negative; this result is much in contrast to the OECD work. Large differences in the interpretation of good labour market regulations across G7 countries perhaps explain the unexpected negative coefficient. But it is not statistically significant. Furthermore, the coefficients of other independent variables are not impacted by the inclusion or exclusion of labour market regulations variable.[39]

In short, differences in regulations and policies with regard to intellectual property protection, competition and FDI explain much of the variation in labour productivity across G7 countries. More importantly, the regression coefficients imply that 55 percent of the Canada-U.S. labour productivity gap can be explained by the regulatory gap between the two countries.

Table 7: Regression Analysis of Regulation and Productivity: Fixed-effect Model

Variable	Parameter estimate (Eq.1)	Parameter estimate (Eq.2)
KL	.019 (0.828)	.0285 (1.277)
IPRLAW	.009*** (3.108)	.0094*** (3.014)
IPRLAW$_{it}$ *COMPLAW$_{it}$	-0.0007** (-2.187)	-0.0007** (-2.244)
LABREGS	-0.002 (-1.385)	
FDIRES	.0075** (2.188)	.0074** (2.185)
LP(-1)	0.903*** (30.364)	.907*** (30.125)
Adj. R-squared	.995	0.99
Observations	91	91

*** , ** = Significant at 1% level and less, and 5% level and less. Fixed country effects not reported here.

---

[38] Koch, Rafiquzzman and Rao, *op. cit.*, (2003).

[39] We ran additional regressions, not reported here, that largely confirmed our hypotheses: (a) without the regulation variables, K/L variable is highly significant; and (b) the regulatory variables explain very well the variation in K/L and the signs of the variables are the same as in the productivity equation.

Conclusions

The principal goal of this study has been to analyse the impact of various types of product market regulations on innovation and productivity performance in OECD countries, with a special focus on G7 countries. Towards this goal we have drawn on available research as well as some new research.

Using IMD survey data, which are highly correlated with the objective OECD data, we developed time series data on several types of economic regulations for G7 countries over the period 1991-2003. These in turn are used as explanatory variables in the innovation and labour productivity regressions.

The following are the key findings of our study:

- Regulation frameworks generally improved in Canada and in other G7 countries;
- There is a regulatory gap between Canada and the U.S. and the gap widened since 1999;
- Differences in intellectual property protection and FDI appear to have largely contributed to the Canada-U.S. regulatory gap;
- Differences in economic regulations, particularly FDI and intellectual property rights, appear to be correlated with R&D-intensity and labour productivity differences among G7 countries; and
- The Canada-U.S. regulatory gap explains about one-third of the innovation gap and over 55 percent of the labour productivity gap between the two countries during the 1991 to 2003 period.

These findings in general are consistent with the conclusions of other research, especially the OECD cross-country evidence. The findings on FDI regulations and productivity are consistent with the conclusions of Rao and Tang (2004) with regard to FDI's positive impact on capital accumulation, R&D, trade flows and productivity.

Our results imply that by closing the regulatory gap with the U.S., Canada could narrow significantly the real income gap with its southern neighbour. Therefore, Canada should undertake a through review of the costs and benefits of its regulations and policies with respect to FDI and intellectual property protection with the objective of closing this gap. Future research should undertake an in-depth industry analysis of specific components of various regulatory variables and the linkages between the Canada-U.S. regulatory gaps, and the innovation and productivity gaps between the two countries.

221

Bibliography

Botero, Juan, S. Djankov, R.L. Porta, F. Lopez-de-Silanes and Andrei Shleifer (2003) *"The Regulation of Labour"*, NBER Working Paper 9756, June.

Chen, Zhiqi, (2003) *"Liberalization of Trade and Investment in Telecommunications Services: A Canadian Perspective"*, a paper presented at the Industry Canada conference on "Service Industries and Knowledge-Based Economy", in Richard Lipsey and Alice Nakamura (eds.), an Industry Canada research volume, (forthcoming).

Ginarte, J.C., and W.G. Park, (1997) *"Determinants of Patent Rights: A Cross National Study"*, Research Policy, vol. 26.

Golub, Stephen S., (2003) *"Measures of Restrictions on Inward Foreign Direct Investment for OECD Countries"* OECD Economic Department Working Paper No. 357, (Paris: OECD).

Harris, Richard G, (2002) *"Determinants of Canadian Productivity Growth: Issues and Prospects"*, in Someshwar Rao and Andrew Sharpe, eds., *Productivity Issues in Canada*, Calgary: University of Calgary Press.

Ho, Mun S., Someshwar Rao and Jinmin Tang (2004) "Sources of Output Growth in Canadian and U.S. Industries in the Information Age" in Dale W. Jorgenson (ed.), Economic Growth in Canada and the United States in the Information Age, Industry Canada Research Monograph, Ottawa.

Jones, Luara and S. Graf, (2001) *"Canada's Regulatory Burden: How Many Regulations? At What Cost?"*, Vancour, BC: The Fraser Institute.

Koch, Kevin, M. Rafiquzzaman, and S. Rao, (2003) *"The Impact of Regulatory Policies on Innovation: Evidence from G7 Countries"*, Industry Canada Working Paper (mimeo.), Ottawa: Industry Canada.

Milhar, Fazil, (1998) *"The Cost of Regulation in Canada"*, Public Policy Sources, Number 12, Vancouver, BC: The Fraser Institute.

Nicoletti, Giuseppe, and Stefano Scarpetta, (2003) *"Regulation, Productivity and Growth: OECD Evidence"*, The OECD Working Papers No. 347, (Paris: January 2003).

Nicoletti, Giuseppe, (2001) *"Regulation in Services: OECD Patterns and Economic Implications"*, Economics Depart Working Paper No. 287, (Paris: OECD), February.

Nicoletti, Giueseppe, Stefano Scarpetta and Olivier Boylaud, (1999) *"Summary Indicators of Product Market Regulation with an Extension to Employment Protection Legislation"*, OECD Economic Department Working Paper No. 226 (Paris: OECD).

Nicoletti, G., S. Golub, D. Hajkova, D. Mirza and K-Y Yool, (2003) *"The Influence of Policies on Trade and Foreign Direct Investment"*, OECD Economic Department Working Paper No. 357, (Paris: OECD).

OECD (1997), *The OECD Report on Regulatory Reform, Volume II Thematic Studies*, Paris.

-------- (1999), *OECD Reviews of Regulatory Reform: Regulatory Reform in the United States – Government Capacity to Assure High Quality Regulation in the United States*, (Paris: OECD).

222

-------- (2002) *OECD Reviews of Regulatory Reform: Canada – Maintaining Leadership Through Innovation*, (Paris: OECD).

-------- (2003), *Foreign Direct Investment Restrictions in OECD Countries,* chapter 7 in *OECD Economic Outlook 73, 2003,* (Paris: OECD).

-------- (2004) *Economic Survey – United States 2004*, (Paris: April).

Porter, Michael and Scott Stern, (1999) *"The New Challenge to America's Prosperity: Findings from the Innovation Index"*, Washington, D.C.: Council on Competitiveness.

Rao, S and A. Ahmad (1996) "Formal and Informal Investment Barriers in the G7. In *Investment Rules for the Global Economy: Enhancing Access to Markets"*, in Pierre Suavé and Daniel Schwanen (eds). C.D. Howe Institute, Policy Study no. 28.

Rao, Someshwar, and Jiamin Tang, (2003) *"Competitiveness Challenges Facing Canadian Industries"*, Industry Canada Research Paper, Government of Canada, Ottawa: Industry Canada (mimeo.).

Rao, Someshwar, Jianmin Tang and Weimin Wang (2005) "Measuring he Canada-U.S. Productivity Gap: Industry Dimensions" International Productivity Monitor, Ottawa, Fall, 2005.

Rao, Someshwar, Jianmin Tang and Weimin Wang, *(2004) "Productivity Levels Between Canadian and U.S. Industries"*, mimeo., Industry Canada, May.

Scarpetta, Stefano and Thierry Tressel, (2002) *"Productivity and Convergence in a Panel of OECD Industries: Do Regulations and Institutions Matter?"* OECD Economics Department Working Paper No. 342, Paris: OECD, September 2002.

Steiner, F., (2000) *"Regulation, Industry Structure and Performance in the Electricity Supply Industry"*, OECD Economics Department Working Papers, No. 238, (Paris: OECD).

U.S. Office of Information and Regulatory Affairs, Office of Management and Budget (OMB), *Report to the President on the Costs and Benefits of Federal Regulations*, Washington, D.C., September 1997.

Annex A: International Patterns: Regulation in Services

Service industries have traditionally been a highly regulated area internationally. Regulation has typically concerned entry, output and/or price choices of firms, restricting actual and potential competition. Since 1980s, many service markets have been extensively liberalized and elsewhere service regulation has often been overhauled. However, initial conditions differed a lot across countries, and the pace and extent of regulatory reform has been variable internationally. An OECD study of potential efficiency gains in several service industries in eight countries reported that:[40]

- Long-run potential output gains ranged from 3 to 6 percent in some European countries and Japan, and about 1 percent in the U.S.

The OECD report summarized empirical studies covering competitive and network industries in different countries and concluded the following:

Retail distribution: Regulations in retail distribution are legal or administrative entry barriers. Studies point to potentially large gains from liberalization of entry and prices in retail trade:[41]

- Distribution systems become more efficient (as large outlet restrictions are removed);
- Employment and the volume of sales increase; and
- Margin decline putting downward pressure on consumer prices.

Road freight: Road freight restrictions include discriminations against foreign haulers, limitations on own-account transport and price controls. The effect of reform on a cross-country basis point to:[42]

- Industry employment and output rise;
- Productive efficiency and the quality of services are enhanced, partly due to network rationalization and an increased rate of innovation; and
- Fares fall by a significant amount.

Mobile telephony: There has been ample evidence of the benefits of competition in the mobile telephony industry. The empirical findings show:[43]

- Productivity increases (defined as cellular subscribers per industry employee) increases as liberalization approaches; but
- Average prices (defined as mobile revenue per cellular subscriber) decline only as competition in the market unfolds; and
- Neither ownership nor prospective privatization per se has positive effects on the performance variables.

Air passenger transportation: Cross-country examinations of the relationship between regulatory frameworks, market structures and performance

---

[40] OECD, The OECD Report on Regulatory Reform, Volume II Thematic Studies, Paris: 1997.

[41] Giuseppe Nicoletti, *Regulation in Services: OECD Patterns and Economic Implications*, Economics Depart Working Paper No. 287, (Paris: OECD), February 2001.

[42] *Ibid.*, p.14.

[43] *Ibid.*, p. 15.

224

in air transportation have been few given the complexity of analysis involved. Nonetheless, the following results stand out:[44]

- At the national, restrictive regulatory and, especially, market environments are associated with lower overall efficiency of the domestic industry;
- Efficiency (as measured by the highest load factor) improves significantly in competitive markets, but entry deregulation by itself may have adverse consequences, as incumbents adopt pre-emptive strategies against potential new entrants;
- Business and economy fares tend to decline significantly when the route-specific regulatory environment is relaxed; and
- Business and economy fares tend to rise with the tightness of infrastructure access conditions at route ends, the capacity share of airline alliances and the role of government-controlled carriers on the route.

Railway transportation: Because of economies of scale leading to natural monopoly, railway is a highly regulated industry. Reforms have concerned mainly the reorganization of the industry, with attempts at separating various functions and opening up of the rail freight business. The available evidence suggests that:[45]

- The U.S. reform had led to a significant reduction in rail passenger transportation and a relatively strong growth in freight services, with fare declining by 30 to 50 percent in certain markets and efficiency and quality of service being enhanced; and
- The Mexican reform has led to a moderate decline in freight fares and an improvement in the quality of service, but the effects on efficiency are unclear.

Electricity supply: Some countries are beginning to consider changing the regulatory environment of the electricity supply industry by reforming functions that do not possess natural monopoly component, while other countries are contemplating opening up to competition the generation segment of the industry. An OECD study looked in a sample of 19 countries over the 1986-1996 period at the impact on electricity prices and industry efficiency of privatization, liberalization, vertical separation, third party access to the grid, creation of an electricity pool and the degree of consumer choice of supplier and offered the following conclusions:[46]

- Electricity prices (measured as the ratio of industrial to residential end-user tariffs) tend to fall when generation and transmission are unbundled, third party access to the grid is expanded and an electricity market is created;

---

[44] *Ibid.,* p. 16.

[45] *Ibid.,* p. 18.

[46] F. Steiner, *"Regulation, Industry Structure and Performance in the Electricity Supply Industry"*, OECD Economics Department Working Papers, No. 238, (Paris: OECD), 2000.

- Productive efficiency of generation plants (measured by both the rate of capacity utilization and reserve margins) tends to increase when ownership in private and generation and transmission are unbundled;
- Private ownership, or the prospects of privatization, tend to increase industrial end-user prices; and
- In countries, such as the United Kingdom, New Zealand and Norway, which have reformed extensively their regulatory framework had the positive impact of liberalization.

Telecommunications industry: Liberalization of entry into long-distance (trunk and international) telecommunications is already progressed well in most advanced industrialized countries. However, the debate is still open on the best kind of interconnection pricing rule and the degree of network unbundling to be ensured by the incumbent. The available empirical cross-country analysis of economic benefits of entry liberalization and competition in long-distance fixed telephony suggest that:

- Anticipated entry liberalization (measured as the time remaining to announced liberalization) has a significant impact on the performance of trunk and international services, leading to increases in productivity, improvements in quality and lower prices;
- Competitive pressures following liberalization (measured by the share of new entrants) further increase productivity and lower prices of both trunk and international services; and
- The effects of ownership and privatization per se are unclear.

In general, to take full advantage of the reform process, policies in network service industries would have to consider regulatory settings that impinge on incentives to invest and innovate:

- Structural interventions in these industries, such as vertical separation of infrastructure and services, need to strike a balance between the incentives to encourage competition and the incentives to encourage investment and innovation by the owner of the non-competitive component;
- The design of network access provisions needs to seek to prevent inefficient bypass while maintaining (or creating) sufficient and correct investment incentives for network operators; and
- Institutional design and regulatory policies need to avoid cross-sector inconsistencies to avoid distortions in the allocation of capital.

Annex B: The OECD Regulatory Indicators

To make cross-country comparisons of regulatory regimes, the OECD has compiled summary indicators, which are further classified in three broad regulatory domains and ranked each on a scale ranging from 0 to6, which reflects the least to most restrictive nature of the regulatory regime:

- **State control** over business enterprises consisting of:
    1. The overall size of the public enterprise sector;
    2. The scope of the public enterprise sector;
    3. The existence and extent of special rights over business enterprises;
    4. Legislative control over public enterprises;
    5. The existence of price controls in competitive industries; and
    6. The use of command and control regulations, both economy-wide and at the industry level.
- **Barriers to entrepreneurship** consisting of:
    1. The features of the licensing and permit system;
    2. The communication and simplification of rules and procedures;
    3. Economy-wide administrative burdens on startups of corporate firms and sole-proprietor firms;
    4. Industry-specific administrative burdens on startups of retail distribution and road freight companies;
    5. The scope of legal barriers to entry; and
    6. Exemptions from competition law for public enterprises or state-mandated behaviour.
- **Barriers to trade and investment** consisting of:
    1. Barriers to share-ownership for non-resident operators (economy-wide and in the telecommunications and air travel industries);
    2. Discriminatory procedures in international trade and competition policies;
    3. Regulatory barriers to trade; and
    4. Average tariffs.

Moreover, the state control and barriers to entrepreneurship are classified in the following two alternative broad regulatory areas:

- **Administrative regulation** consisting of (a) administrative burdens of startups, including economy-wide and sector-specific burdens; and (b) regulatory and administrative opacity, including the feature of license and permit system and the communication and simplification of rules and procedures.
- **Economic regulation** consisting of (a) regulation of economic structure, including the size and scope of public ownership, legal barriers to entry and control of public enterprises by the legislature; (b) regulation of economic behaviour, including command and control regulations, and special voting rights; and (c) regulation of competition, including competition law exemptions and price controls.
- **Product market regulation** consisting of (a) inward-oriented policies; and (b) outward-oriented policies.

- **Employment protection legislation** consisting of (a) regular contracts, including procedural requirements, notice and severance pay, and prevailing standards of and penalties for "unfair" dismissals; and (b) temporary contracts, including "objective" reasons under which a fixed-term contract could be offered, the maximum number of successive renewals, and the maximum cumulated duration of the contract.

The Potential Gains of Deeper Canada-US Regulatory Cooperation: A Cash Flow Analysis of Faster Drug Approvals

Doug Blair, André Downs & Fidèle Ndayisenga
Policy Research Initiative

Introduction

There is considerable evidence and widespread conviction that NAFTA has generated substantial economic benefits for Canada.[1] Recently, in the context of the 10th anniversary of NAFTA, concerns have been expressed that the full potential benefits of NAFTA are not being realized due, in part, to the different regulatory approaches of Canada and the United States. For a small economy whose trade largely depends on a single giant neighbouring market, it is important for Canada to carefully weigh the benefits and costs for its industry, governments, and citizens of maintaining exiting regulatory differences with the United States.

Research to date suggests that there are clear economic benefits to regulatory convergence between Canada and the United States. For example, Ndayisenga and Downs (2004) found that investment in Canada could have been substantially higher if our regulatory reforms had kept pace with the U.S. from 1976 to 1998. They also estimated that if the level of regulatory reforms in Canada had kept pace with U.S. levels over this time period, Canada's per capita income would have been, on average, 1.9% higher.

Much can be gained, therefore, by exploring ways and means in which regulatory differences can be bridged or their impact ameliorated. More regulatory co-operation with the United States would be one means to capture these economic benefits while simultaneously safeguarding and improving the integrity of the regulatory system.

The External Advisory Committee on Smart Regulations (EACSR) recognized this, and recommended "primary and immediate focus" on North American regulatory cooperation. Further, the Security and Prosperity Partnership of North America (SPP) agreement signed by leaders in March 2005 committed Canada, the U.S. and Mexico to work together to enhance North American regulatory cooperation to promote competitiveness, productivity and growth, while maintaining high standards for health and safety. The International Policy statement issued in April 2005 re-confirmed the Government of Canada's commitment to pursue regulatory compatibility within North America under this new partnership agreement.

---

[1] See Downs, 2004 and Canada, 2005. p.3.

229

One of the key policy questions now facing the Canadian government is where to focus efforts to deepen regulatory cooperation with the United States. This chapter begins to address this issue by examining the potential gains from faster new drug approvals: an area that has long been at the heart of the discussion of deeper regulatory cooperation.

First, the chapter discusses the reasons why drug approvals are the focus of the analysis; the cash flow model is then used to derive estimates of potential economic gains. Results from the cash-flow model are presented at the product level, and sector wide effects are derived from these estimates based on studies concerning the effects of new drug introduction on total drug expenditures. Macroeconomic effects are estimated using Statistics Canada input/output multipliers. Finally, potential societal benefits and limitations to the analysis are discussed.

Focusing on Regulatory Approvals

The EACSR (2004) observed a "lack of harmonization between Canadian and American regulations, approval processes, long wait times in Canada, and a 'tyranny of small differences' between Canada and the U.S." (External Advisory Committee on Smart Regulation 2003). Differences in regulatory requirements to get products approved or registered for the Canadian market impose additional costs on industries and consumers. Examples described in Blair (2004a) include the costs of additional testing for the Canadian market for pesticides products (specific Canadian field trials for residue, efficacy, and crop tolerance data) and for new chemicals. The EASCR (2004) cited differences in fortification of food and beverage products and trans-fat labelling, among others.

Differences in product standards between Canada and the United States can create impediments to domestic production (by shortening production runs to serve different markets or by diminishing the ability to promote products, secure investment, or service niche markets in Canada), and can impede the ability to export Canadian production to the United States, for example, differences in food product regulation (health claims, nutrition labelling, fortification) and differences in automobile standards (seat belt standards, daytime running lights).

Impediments to timely market access have been a particular concern across a number of economic sectors. For industry, regulatory decision times directly affect time to market that, in turn, affects the ability to earn a return on investment in product development. While these issues have been highlighted for many years, there is surprisingly little in the way of quantitative estimates of the actual economic implications of longer regulatory approval times and higher regulatory costs in Canada.

New drug approvals in particular have been the subject of much discussion, dating back to the 1992 Review of the Canadian Drug Approval System, also known as the Gagnon Report. The Gagnon Report argued in favour of improved timeliness and efficiency of new drug approvals while transforming the regulatory system as a whole. Since that time there has been an ongoing debate between establishing a timely and efficient regulatory system and the protection of Canadians.

In 2002, the Speech from the Throne introduced the Smart Regulation Strategy. A key commitment in the strategy was to "speed up the regulatory process for drug approvals to ensure that Canadians have faster access to the safe drugs they need, creating a better climate for research in pharmaceuticals." (Government of Canada, 2002).

The External Advisory Committee on Smart Regulation looked into specific regulatory issues surrounding the Canadian drug review process. The Committee determined that the drug approvals process in Canada is the slowest among industrialized countries, that it was lacking in transparency, that there are significant backlogs in the system, and that a slower process does not necessarily indicate a more rigorous regulatory regime, but rather a regulator with limited resources and capacity.

The Committee suggested that Canada focus its energies in areas where the potential for risk is greater, or where Canada can contribute value-added to the regulatory process. It recommended developing a Canadian framework for international regulatory cooperation as a means to developing a more strategic regulatory approach, "when an independent Canadian process does not add to the quality of outcomes." (External Advisory Committee on Smart Regulation, 2004).

What would be the economic consequences of enhanced regulatory cooperation with the US? For the purposes of the analysis presented here, we attempt to estimate the potential economic gains that could accrue if regulatory cooperation with the U.S. (either bilateral or unilateral) led to a reduction in decision times for new drugs. It should be noted that there may be other means to reduce regulatory decision times for new drugs, such as adding resources to the drug review process in Canada.

A Cash Flow Model

To assess these issues, we use a cash flow approach to compute measures of the profitability of commercial ventures including R&D projects, and to assess the impacts of regulatory costs on firm decision-making. Cash flow models have the advantage of capturing not just the hard costs, such as those of research and development, production and marketing, and regulation, but also the potential opportunity costs, as well as the risks and uncertainty of investments. A cash flow analysis better captures the dynamic nature of investment decisions and a full range of the financial considerations of businesses.

Heller (1995) developed quantitative estimates of the impact of regulatory delays using discounted cash flow scenarios for commercializing biotechnology products in Canada and the United States. Heller found that the profitability of drug firms is most seriously affected by protracted delays in regulatory approval. Heller estimated that if regulatory approval delays were reduced by 2 years, it would improve the rate of return on investments for drug firms by at least 5.5 percentage points.[2]

---

[2] Background Economic Study of the Canadian Biotechnology Industry. James G. Heller Consulting Inc., June 1995.

231

More recently, DiMasi (2002) studied a sample of 68 randomly selected investigational drugs from 10 pharmaceutical firms to determine the effects of shorter development and regulatory review times on capitalized costs for the drug industry. DiMasi found that a 50% reduction in regulatory review times would reduce capitalized costs by 7.6%.

Schwartz (2003) also developed a model to estimate the financial impacts of product approval delays at the firm level. While Schwartz bases his work on the pharmaceutical industry, he notes that the model can be used to evaluate the effects of regulatory delays on net present value for any product approval process.

Grabowski et al (2002) developed a rate of return model to examine the worldwide returns on R&D for drugs introduced into the U.S. market. The study assesses the impact of changes in various model parameters (margins, tax rates, sales profiles, cost of capital and regulatory review times) on after-tax cash flows, R&D costs, net present value and internal rates of return.

Cash flow modeling has also been used in regulatory impact analysis in the United States. The U.S. EPA Office of Pollution Prevention and Toxics developed a cash flow model to assess the impacts of regulations on biotechnology products in 1997 (United States Environmental Protection Agency, 1997).

Using the academic literature as a guide, a basic cash flow model of regulatory cost was developed and then applied to the issue of new drug approvals. The analysis involved developing "typical" product profiles for new human drugs based on estimated product development costs, expected regulatory costs and approval times, market sales over the product life-cycle, and the average number of new drug products introduced to the Canadian market each year.

The cash-flow model was applied to simulate the effects of various policy scenarios (reduced regulatory decision times and reduced regulatory costs – scenarios that might be achieved through greater regulatory cooperation with the U.S.) on sales, net income and rates of return for new products. Preliminary estimates at the product level were then used to derive sector-level estimates.

The model is of a general nature and can be applied to assess a range of policy options and how they affect private sector investment decisions.

A Basic Cash Flow Model

A basic model for examining firm decisions in light of regulatory costs considers changes in revenue and costs, as well as changes in one-time and annual regulatory compliance costs. The basic model can be expressed as follows:

$$PV = -CO - \int CA_t \, e^{-rt} \, dt + \int \pi_t q_t \, e^{-rt} \, dt$$

Where;
q_t = quantity sold in period t
π_t = is profit per unit in period t
CA_t = annual regulatory compliance costs in period t
CO = one-time regulatory costs
r = the discount rate.

232

A firm will find it profitable to enter the market if the present value of net revenues (i.e., profits) from the sale of a good or service exceeds the present value of the regulatory costs i.e. $PV > 0$.

In developing a model relevant to examining Canadian policy variables, we refined and added a number of important considerations that allow the model to focus on specific regulatory parameters, namely Canadian regulatory costs and regulatory decision times. We also refined a number of model parameters to reflect Canadian business realities.

The model with refined regulatory cost parameters is as follows:

$$PV = \int_{t0}^{T} [CF_t] \, e^{-rt} \, dt,$$
$$\text{where } CF_t = Rev_t - RD_t - M_t - Rac_t - Rcc_t - TX_t$$

Where:
CF_t = Cash flow at time t
Rev_t = Revenues at time t
RD_t = Research and development expenditures at time t
M_t = Production and marketing cost at time t
Rac_t = Regulatory approval costs at time t; and
Rcc_t = Ongoing regulatory compliance at time t.
TX_t = taxes at time t

Regulatory Decision Times

A regulatory "delay" can be defined as the difference between the expected time of decision (i.e., based on performance standards set by the regulator, or based on decision times observed in other jurisdictions) and the actual time of regulatory decision.[3] Figure 1 shows a stylized depiction of the life-cycle cash flows for a patented drug product where sales peak around the time of patent expiry, followed by a sharp sales decline due to generic competition. The product life-cycle covers the period $T-t_0$ where t_0 is the date at which product discovery and development begins and T is the date at which sales are no longer viable to maintain the product on the market.

---

[3] For a detailed discussion of factors that influence decision times, see Public Policy Forum (2003).

Figure 1: Stylized Cash Flow Scenario for a Regulated Product

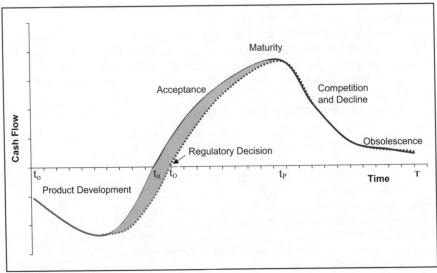

The shaded area represents the change in cash flow resulting from faster regulatory decisions.

The net present value of the cash flow in Figure 1 is given by:

$$PV = \int_{t0}^{tR} [CF_t]e^{-rt} \, dt + \int_{tR}^{TD} [CF_t] \, e^{-rt} \, dt + \int_{TD}^{TP} [CF_t] e^{-rt} \, dt + \int_{TP}^{T} [CF_t]e^{-rt} \, dt$$

$\int_{t0}^{tR} [CF_t]e^{-rt} \, dt$ is the value cash flow from inception to expected time of regulatory approval;

$\int_{tR}^{TD} [CF_t] e^{-rt} \, dt$ is the present value cash flow lost or gained due to actual regulatory approval time;

$\int_{TD}^{TP} [CF_t] e^{-rt} \, dt$ is the present value cash flow during period of exclusivity (from entry restrictions, such as patent protection); and,

$\int_{TP}^{T} [CF_t] e^{-rt} \, dt$ = Present value cash flow after patent expiration.

As modeled, the direct cost of regulatory decision time has two distinct components. First, there are foregone sales because of the very existence of "delay". Second, in the presence of delays, sales occur at a later period than it would be the case in the absence of delay imposing a cost that can be attributed

234

solely to the time value of money. Our estimates of the impact of regulatory decision times include these two costs, but do not distinguish between them.

Limitations to the Analysis

The cash flow analysis summarized in this paper provides estimates of potential economic gains of faster approvals for new drug products in Canada. These estimates are based on synthetic scenarios of R&D and market size derived from the academic literature, not observed Canadian-specific data. We do not assess whether faster regulatory decisions in Canada would affect the quality of those decisions. Safety, quality and efficacy are held constant in the analysis, under the assumption that those new drugs that would be approved in Canada are simply approved sooner.

The cash flow model is a closed, static model: it assumes no other policy or economic changes (e.g., tax incentives, exchange rate fluctuations, etc.) and does not include dynamic effects such as potential increases in investment and higher rates of product introduction due to improved financial returns in Canada. Based on anecdotal evidence from industry, the hypothesis was put forward that faster decisions and lower regulatory costs would make more products financially viable in the Canadian market and increase the number of new products introduced in Canada each year. There are two potential effects:

- Our cash flow analysis suggests that potential rates of return could increase significantly if new drugs were approved more quickly. This could make more products financially viable in the Canadian market and increase the number of new drugs introduced in Canada each year.
- If faster decisions were achieved through granting of conditional approvals based on US approvals, then in theory we could expect as many new drug introductions in Canada as in the US (or about 200 more new drug approvals in Canada each year - a 75% increase over the current number of new drug approvals).[4]

However, these effects have not been estimated empirically.

Societal benefits are discussed, but not estimated empirically. A number of academic studies are cited which suggest that faster drug approvals could lead to decreased spending on other health care (e.g., hospital spending) coupled with long-term benefits to the health of Canadians (as measured by decreased morbidity, mortality, and improved quality of life).

Finally, we do not attempt to quantify the potential gains from more effective regulatory approaches. One of the recognized benefits of regulatory cooperation is to potentially improve the capacity of regulators to meet their health, safety and environmental objectives. The analysis contained in this paper focuses on potential cost savings to the regulated industries, but not on the potential gains to government regulatory programs. For a discussion of the potential effectiveness gains for regulatory programs, see Griller (2004) and Rawson, West and Appel (2000).

---

[4] This is based on a 5-year average of the number of NDS and NAS approvals in Canada compared to NDA and NME approvals in the US over the period from 1999 to 2003.

Parameters and Assumptions Used in the Model

Below we describe the parameters we used in our cash flow model and draw comparisons to the parameters used in other studies.

R&D Expenditures:

Heller (1996) assumed R&D investment for a drug product of $100 million, and evenly distributed expenditures over a 10-year period. Schwartz used a similar approach, with the caveat that the distribution oversimplifies the relationship with the different phases of R&D. Grabowski et al (2002) used more recent estimates of $480 million in after-tax R&D expenditures from Di Masi for the average new drug. To develop scenarios typical to the Canadian market, we used estimates of worldwide R&D expenditures for product development, convert edto Canadian dollars, and scale based on the ratio of Canadian to worldwide market size. This assumes that the Canadian market is expected to recover its share of worldwide R&D expenditures for product development.[5] For new human drugs, we applied this approach to the $480 million Di Masi estimate. According to data from the Patented Medicine Prices Review Board (PMPRD), the Canadian pharmaceutical market represents 2.6% of the world market. The figure we then derive is a capitalized, after tax R&D contribution for a typical new medicine introduced in Canada of $16.9 million ($480 million x Can-US exchange rate x 2.6%).

Capital Costs and Depreciation:

Heller included capital costs of $50 million for manufacturing process development and quality control, written off using a straight-line depreciation in the first five years of income. We employed the same approach as Grabowski, allowing for plant and equipment capital expenditures equal to 40% of tenth-year sales, half applied in the 2 years prior to marketing, and the remaining distributed over the first 10 years of the product's market life.

Production/distribution Costs (COGS):

Heller assumed cost of goods sold (COGS) to be 40% of sales with 2% cost efficiency gains every 2 years. In Grabowski, COGS are 42% in the first year of product sales, and grow by 0.3% annually to 48% by year 20. The average of the 20-year period is 45%. We applied a contribution rate for production and distribution costs of 45% of gross sales in each year of the product life cycle.

Working Capital:

Heller applied working capital in the first year of sales. Like Grabowski, we estimated working capital to be two months of sales for accounts receivables and five months of sales for inventories. These costs are recovered from revenues in the final year of the product life cycle.

---

[5] For a discussion of global product development R&D costs and returns from individual markets, see Jarvis (1998).

236

Marketing Expenses:

Heller applied marketing expenses valued at 10% of sales in each year of product life cycle. Grabowski found that marketing expenses are front-end loaded, valued at 100% of first year sales, 50% in year two, and 25 % in year three. He also allowed for pre-marketing launch expenditures beginning two years prior to product launch, valued at 5% and 10% of first year sales. We followed the Grabowski approach.

Taxes:

We used an effective corporate tax rate (federal + provincial) of 31.8%, as per C.D. Howe, June 2003. For R&D tax credits, we applied a rate of 20% to total R&D expenditures to reduce taxes in first year of sales.

Product Life Cycle and Market Size:

Heller assumed a market life to patent expiry of ten years, with peak sales of $265 million achieved in year two and remaining at that level until year twenty. Grabowski found that the top 10% sellers showed a rapid increase in sales from year zero to year ten, which then plateaus until year fourteen, at which point sales fall off drastically due to generic competition. They observed that the sales profiles for the next decile of products, as well as the mean and median sellers are much less pronounced, both in terms of growth and decline after patent expiry. For the purpose of developing typical Canadian scenarios, we adjusted the worldwide life-cycle patterns from the Grabowski analysis to better reflect the Canadian market. Grabowski's worldwide market profiles are skewed towards the reality of the dominant EU and US markets, where patent term restoration exists. We develop our Canadian market scenarios assuming that peak sales would occur in years nine through twelve, and decline thereafter. Figure 2 provides a comparison of the Grabowski life cycle patterns with our version, applicable to the Canadian situation.

In the absence of time-series sales data for new medicines in Canada, we base our product sales estimates on data from the PMPRB. The PMPRB reports total sales of patented drug products in Canada of $8.8 billion, which implies an average of about $22 million per patented drug.[6] Using this as our basis, we develop product life-cycle scenarios for a top 10% seller and an average seller in the Canadian pharmaceutical market, as shown below in Figure 3. Market scenarios were segmented into top selling and average selling products to give a more accurate depiction of the markets for new drugs in Canada. This approach yields estimates of peak sales for a top 10% seller in Canada of about $200 million. For average sellers in Canada, our approach suggests peak annual sales of about $40 million.

---

[6] Based on data from the Patented Medicine Prices Review Board we estimate that the number of 1,027 patented medicines in Canada in 2002 represents about 400 active substances (which includes various strengths, package sizes and presentations of the active substance) -- from various Annual Reports of the Patented Medicine Prices Review Board (<http://www.pmprb.gc.ca/>).

Figure 2: Market Life-Cycles for Top Selling Drugs, Worldwide and in Canada[7]

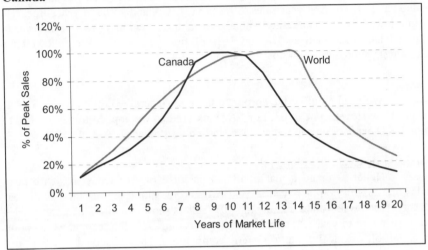

Figure 3: Top and Average Seller Product Life-cycle Scenarios

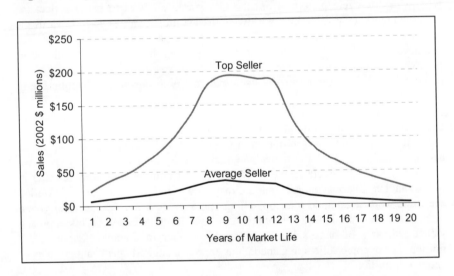

[7] The world life-cycle pattern is based on data from Grabowski (2002). The Canadian product life-cycle pattern is an estimation, based on the Grabowski analysis, but modified to better reflect the Canadian market situation for new drug products.

238

Regulatory Approval Costs:

We assume Canadian-specific approval costs to be $2.5 million, and submission evaluation fees of $250,000. Approval costs are distributed over the five years prior to submission for review; fees are assumed to occur in the year of submission.

Ongoing Regulatory Compliance Costs:

We set these costs at 0.1% of sales for each year of sales. Ongoing regulatory fees were set at $1,000, applied to each year of sales for the product life cycle.

Analytical Results

Below we provide a summary of the potential impacts of six and twlve-month faster decisions for new human drugs, and 50% reduction in Canadian specific regulatory approval costs.

Top Seller Scenario*

Policy Scenarios	Rate of Return		Net Income			Sales		
	%	% Change	PV ($M)	% Change	PV ($M)	% Change	PV Sales Impact ($M)
Baseline Scenario	20.0%		$163.0		$897.3		
6 Month Faster Decision	20.7%	3.7%	$177.8	9.1%	$986.5	9.9%	$89.3
12 Month Faster Decision	21.4%	7.2%	$192.7	18.2%	$1,075.8	19.9%	$178.5
50% Reduced Canadian Specific Approval Costs	20.4%	2.3%	$165.0	1.2%	$897.3		
12 Month Faster Decision and 50% Cost Reduction	21.9%	9.5%	$194.7	19.5%	$1,075.8	19.9%	$178.5

* Assumes peak sales at $200 million, 5% discount rate.

239

Average Seller Scenario*

Policy Scenarios	Rate of Return		Net Income		Sales		
	%	% Change	PV ($M)	% Change	PV ($M)	% Change	PV Sales Impact ($M)
Baseline Scenario	13.4%		$44.3		$289.9		
6 Month Faster Decision	13.7%	1.5%	$45.7	3.0%	$305.7	5.4%	$15.8
12 Month Faster Decision	13.9%	3.0%	$47.0	6.0%	$321.4	10.9%	$31.5
50% Reduced Canadian Specific Approval Costs	13.9%	3.5%	$45.6	2.9%	$289.9		
12 Month Faster Decision and 50% Cost Reduction	14.3%	6.6%	$48.3	8.9%	$321.4	10.9%	$31.5

* Assumes peak sales at $40 million, 5% discount rate.

Our model suggests a present value sales impact of $90 million or $180 million for a top selling drug, for a six-month and twelve-month faster decision respectively. This represents, on average, 9.1% to 16.6% of the present value sales over a twenty-year product life cycle. For average sellers, our model suggests a present value sales impact of $15.8 million to $31.6 million, or 5.2% to 9.8% of sales over a 20-year product life cycle.

In terms of net income, annual gains were estimated to be 8%. Rates of return on new products were estimated to increase by an average of 4.8%, ranging from 4.4% to 5.3%.

Sector-Wide Effects

Data from the PMPRB show that an average of 23 new active substances are introduced to the Canadian market each year.[8] To estimate sector-wide effects of faster drug decisions, we assume that the top sellers (top 10%) would be substantially improved products - about two per year. We assume the remaining twenty-one medicines would be average sellers.

---

[8] 5-year average from 1997 to 2002. PMPRB Annual reports (<http://www.pmprb.gc.ca>).

Policy Scenarios	Rate of Return		Net Income		Sales		
	%	% Change	PV ($M)	% Change	PV ($M)	% Change	PV Sales Impact ($M)
Baseline Scenario	14.7%		$1,457		$8,611		
6 Month Faster Decision	15.0%	2.2%	$1,520	4.3%	$9,155	6.3%	$544
12 Month Faster Decision	15.3%	4.1%	$1,583	8.6%	$9,699	12.6%	$1,088
50% Reduced Canadian Specific Approval Costs	15.2%	3.0%	$1,491	2.3%	$8,611		
12 Month Faster Decision and 50% Cost Reduction	15.8%	7.2%	$1,618	11.0%	$9,699	12.6%	$1,088
Average	15.3%	4.2%	$1,553	6.6%	$9,291	10.5%	$907

Potential annual gains in the present value of sales for new drug products averaged over $900 million, or an average 10.5% increase. By this we mean that, based on various scenarios of reduced regulatory decision times and costs for industry, the present value of their sales over the life-span of a basket of new drug products normally introduced in one year would be about 10% higher on average than the current present value.

In terms of net income, annual gains were estimated to be 6.6% in the present value of net income from the basket of new drugs normally introduced in one year. Average rates of return on new products were estimated to increase by 4.2%.

Indirect and Induced Effects

As noted above, our estimates of the impact of faster approvals on the present value of sales to firms do not equate to increased sales in the marketplace. To assess the induced effects on the economy, we need to understand how faster approvals could affect firm output as measured by growth in market sales.

There has been considerable study of the numerous factors that affect the overall growth in drug sales, including changes in utilization of drugs; changes in prescribing habits of physicians; a tendency to prescribe and use newer and more expensive drugs; a trend towards using drug therapy instead of other treatments; changes in total population; changes in demographics and health status of the population; and the emergence of new diseases to be treated and old diseases which can now be treated more effectively (Patented Medicines Prices Review Board, 1999).

While some of these influences might have been captured in our market profile scenarios for individual products that were based on Grabowski's worldwide product profiles, the simple addition of the product level results from our model might not reflect the practical effect of those factors listed above on sales of new drugs in the Canadian market.

To better assess the potential economic effects in Canada, we examined the trend in total Canadian prescription sales from 1988 to 2002 and the extent to which rates of real growth in prescription drug sales can be attributed to the introduction of new drug products.

The most recent studies from the US indicate that utilization and cost effects of new drugs account for between 37% and 68.5% of overall growth in spending on prescription drugs. Estimates of future impact of new drugs range from 30 to 40% (Merlis, 2000). Canadian studies indicate that new drugs can account for between 30% and 101% of the growth in provincial expenditures on prescription drugs (PMPRB, 1999).

Based on these cost driver studies, we assume that 40% of the increase in future prescription drug expenditures can be attributed to new drug introductions.[9] We then applied this rate to the present value of annual increases in prescription drugs, to calculate the impact of faster new drug approvals in Canada (six and twelve months, as above).

Our analysis indicates that, on average, a six-month faster decision time for new drugs would increase total prescription sales by 1.4% annually. A twelve-month faster decision time would increase sales by 2.7% annually. This implies increased annual sales of new drugs of between $200 million and $400 million, based on the total sales of prescription drugs in 2002 of $14.6 billion. (Canadian Institute for Health Information, 2003).

Below, we use the estimated annual increase in sales ($200 million and $400 million) to assess R&D, growth and employment effects on the economy.

R&D, Growth and Employment Effects

Data from the PMPRB indicates that, on average, 10% of sales are invested in R&D in Canada by the human pharmaceutical industry. Applying this investment rate, we calculate that additional investment in R&D in Canada of between $20 million and $40 million could occur annually if new drugs were approved six or twelve months faster, respectively. This represents an increase in R&D investment of about 2% to 4% for this industry sector.[10]

To estimate the economic growth and employment effects of an increase in output, indirect effects on intermediate industries and suppliers are captured using multipliers from Statistics Canada's national input-output model (Statistics Canada, 1998). We introduced the estimated sector impacts from faster new drug approvals to the I/O model as a one-time shock to manufacturing output.

The I/O multipliers provide estimates of the value of increased business activity in one sector on all other sectors of the economy. They do not take into account the induced business effects from spending or saving by households or the

---

[9] The sales weighted average across the 6 provincial drug reimbursement plans studied by the PMPRB is 49%, as is the simple average of the 3 US study results.

[10] Based on annual R&D expenditures of $1,051 million, Statistics Canada (2004b).

government sector of the increased income.[11] This approach also implies that the potential growth in the pharmaceutical market from faster new drug approvals is a one-time occurrence: it does not enable us to track the cumulative annual effect of increased sales over time. Results should be viewed as long-term effects of a one-time shock to the pharmaceutical market.

Output and Employment Effects (upstream only)

	Industry Sector Values[12]	6 months faster (+$200M/yr)	12 months faster (+$400M/yr)
Increase in Total Output	$14.6 billion	$344 million (2.4%)	$688 million (4.7%)
Direct effect on GDP	$5 billion	$66 million (1.3%)	$133 million (2.6%)
Total direct and indirect effect on GDP		$134 million	$268 million
Direct effect on employment	27,400	1,119 (4.1%)	2,237 (8.2%)
Total direct and indirect effects on employment		2,338	4,676

Potential Societal Benefits

Faster regulatory approvals of new drugs could increase drug expenditures for provincial health plans, private insurers and consumers. But would the potential benefits of these increased expenditures justify the costs?

There have been many studies of the long-term impacts of increased expenditures in health care on mortality, morbidity and quality-adjusted years of life. We cite findings from a number of more recent studies below.

Health Canada's report, Economic Burden of Illness in Canada, assesses the direct and indirect costs of illness in 1998, as determined by the opportunity costs to society of illness or injury (Health Canada, 2002). The report estimates that in 1998 the total cost of illness in Canada was $159.4 billion. This includes direct health care costs of $83.9 billion and indirect costs of $75.5 billion. Hospital care expenditures represent the largest direct cost at $27.6 billion. Major components of the indirect costs include the value of production lost due to long- and short-term disability, which is estimated to be $42 billion. This provides a measure of the potential savings that could be gained if illness and injury were prevented, but it does not address savings due to increased longevity and improvements in quality of life, and it does not assess the potential effect of new drugs on reducing health care costs.

The National Bureau of Economic Research (NBER) has published a number of papers on the benefits and costs of newer drugs. In a series of these

---

[11] Multipliers from the Canadian Open Output Determination Model, based on the Preliminary 1992 Input-Output Tables for total manufacturing.

[12] Sector information are from Statistics Canada (2004a).

243

studies, Lichtenberg (2002) conducted an econometric investigation of the contribution of pharmaceutical innovation to mortality reduction and growth in lifetime per capita income. Results showed a highly significant positive relationship across diseases between life expectancy and rates of introduction of new drugs.

Overall, estimates from the literature suggest that faster drug approvals in Canada could:

- Lead to savings in other areas of health care. For example, Lichtenberg (2002) found that that new drugs lead to a reduction in non-drug expenditures at a rate 7.2 times as much as they increase drug expenditures;
- Generate long-term health benefits. For example, MedTap (2003) provides estimates from a number of recent studies of the value of expenditures in health care in the US. These analyses suggest that each additional dollar spent on health care in the past twenty years has produced health gains worth $2.40 to $3.00;
- Generate societal returns on research and development. For example, a major study of returns to investment in health care found that overall, annual societal rates of return lie between one and five times R&D expenditures (Australian Society for Medical Research, 2003).

Conclusion

In 2003, the Government of Canada launched a new approach to the management of pharmaceuticals in Canada called the Therapeutics Access Strategy (TAS). The main objectives of the TAS are to improve the timeliness of reviews, as measured against international benchmarks, to exercise greater vigilance post-approval, through better surveillance, and finally, to improve access to therapies and contribute to the long-term sustainability of the health system. Improved regulatory cooperation is a key feature of the TAS.

In November 2003, a Memorandum of Understanding (MOU) was signed between Health Canada and the U.S. Food and Drug Administration (FDA) regarding the sharing and exchange of information about therapeutic products. The purpose of this MOU is "to enhance and strengthen the exchange of information and existing public health protection cooperative activities related to the regulation of the specific therapeutic products" (Health Canada and the United States Food and Drug Administration 2003). Since signing the MOU, Health Canada and the FDA have held discussions to identify potential areas for joint projects, and to develop a framework for collaboration activities in product quality, bioequivalence, and compliance.

Based on the results shown here for new drug approvals, our assessment is that if these commitments to greater regulatory cooperation lead to concrete improvements in the speed of regulatory decisions, the economic benefits to Canadians could be substantial.

Societal benefits could also accrue. The academic literature suggests that faster approval of new drugs that represent breakthroughs or substantial improvements in patient therapy could reduce spending on other health care and increase long-term health benefits to Canadians. The literature also suggests regulatory cooperation could improve regulatory protections by allowing regulators to benefit from the expertise of other jurisdictions, and to focus their limited resources on areas of highest risk to Canadians.

Bibliography

Access Economics. (2003) "Exceptional Returns: The Value Of Investing In Health R&D In Australia" Prepared For The Australian Society For Medical Research, Canberra.

Auditor General. (2004) "Chapter 2: Health Canada – Regulation of Medical Devices." Report of the Auditor General of Canada to the House of Commons. Office of the Auditor General of Canada, March 2004.

Blair, Doug. (2004a) "Measuring the Potential Gains of Regulatory Co-operation: A Cash Flow Model Approach." September. Draft available on request from the PRI.

———. (2004b) "Expanding Regulatory Co-operation with the United States." Horizons 7, no. 1 (June): 73-76.

Canada (2002) "Speech from the Throne 2002: The Canada We Want" <www.sft-ddt.gc.ca/hnav/hnav07_e.htm>.

———. (2003) "Budget 2003: Building the Canada We Want" <http://www.fin.gc.ca/budget03/booklets/bkheae.htm>.

———. (2004) "Joint statement by Canada and the United States on common security, common prosperity: A new partnership in North America" <http://www.pm.gc.ca/eng/news.asp?id=341>.

Canada, (2005) "Canada's International Policy Statement. A Role of Pride and Influence in the World – COMMERCE" <http://itcan-cican.gc.ca/ips/pdf/IPS-commerce-en.pdf>

Canadian Institute for Health Information. (2003) "Drug Expenditure in Canada, 1985 to 2002".

CBS News. (2004) "Prescriptions And Profit" 60 Minutes, August 22.

Chen, Duanjie and Jack M. Mintz. (2003) "Taxing Investments: On the Right Track, But at a Snail's Pace" C.D. Howe Backgrounder 72.

DiMasi, J.A. (2002) "The value of improving the productivity of the drug development process: faster times and better decisions" PharmacoEconomics. Vol. 20, Supp 3.

Downs, André. (2004) "North American Integration Challenges and Potential Policy Responses" Horizons, Volume 7, Number 1.

External Advisory Committee on Smart Regulation. (2003) "Regulating in the 21st Century: Global Changes and Implications for Regulation."

———. (2004) "Smart Regulation for Canada- A Regulatory Strategy for Canada" Report to the Government of Canada.

Grabowski, Henry, John Vernon and Joseph A. DiMasi. (2002) "Returns on Research and Development for 1990s New Drug Introductions" PharmacoEconomics. Vol. 20, Supp 3.

Griller, David. (2004) "Can Regulatory Collaboration Improve Safety in Health Care?" Horizons, Volume 7, Number 1.

Health Canada. (2003a) Annual Drug Submission Performance Report - Part I. Therapeutic Products Directorate.

Health Canada and the United States Food and Drug Administration. (2003) Memorandum of Understanding Regarding Sharing And Exchange Of

Information About Therapeutic Products.
<www.fda.gov/oia/agreements/HCFDAMOU111803.html>

Heller, James G. (1995) Background Economic Study of the Canadian Biotechnology Industry.

IMS Health Canada. (2003) "Retail Prescriptions Grow at Record Level in 2003 - Cholesterol-lowering medications fastest growing drug class" Canadian NewsWire, March 25.

Jarvis, B. (1998) "A Question of Balance" Public Policy Forum.

Kaitin, Kenneth I. (2002) "Regulatory Reform At A Crossroads". Drug Information Journal, Volume 36, pp. 245-246.

Lichtenberg, Frank. (2002) "Benefits and Costs of Newer Drugs: An Update." NBER Working Paper No. 8996. Cambridge, MA: National Bureau of Economic Research.

Medtap International. (2003) "The Value of Investment in Health Care: Better Care, Better Lives" Bethesda, MD: Medtap.

Merlis, M. (2000) Explaining the Growth in Prescription Drug Spending: A Review of Recent Studies" <http://aspe.hhs.gov/health/reports/Drug-papers/merlis/Merlis-Final.htm>.

Ndayisenga, Fidèle. (2004) "Economic Impacts of Regulatory Convergence Between Canada and the United States." Horizons 7, no. 1 (June): 9-16.

Ndayisenga, Fidèle and André Downs. (2004) "Economic Impacts of Regulations: Effects of Regulatory Convergence between Canada and the United States." Paper presented at the Canadian Economics Association Annual Meeting, June 3-6, 2004, Toronto, Canada.

Patented Medicines Price Review Board. (1999) "Price and Expenditure Trend Analysis Of Prescription Drugs In Six Provincial Plans 1990-1997" Federal/Provincial/ Territorial Task Force On Pharmaceutical Prices.

———. (2000) "Cost Driver Analysis of Provincial Drug Plans" Federal/ Provincial/ Territorial Working Group On Drug Prices.

Pettigrew, The Honourable Pierre. (2004) Keynote speech at BIOTECanada's Annual Convention. Montreal, Quebec.

Perchorowicz , John T. (1995) "Appraising Inventions: The Key to Technology Management" <http://www.autm.net/pubs/journal/95/AI95.html>.

Public Policy Forum. (2003) "Improving Canada's Regulatory Process for Therapeutic Products"

Rawson, N., R. West and W.C. Appel. (2000) "Could conditional release of new drugs provide the information required to study drug effectiveness?" Canadian Journal of Clinical Pharmacology. Winter;7(4):185-90.

Rawson, Nigel S. (2002) "Human resources for the approval of new drugs in Canada, Australia, Sweden, the United Kingdom and the United States." Canadian Journal of Clinical Pharmacology, Summer; 9(2): 73-8.

Schwartz, Eduardo S. (2003) "Patents and R&D as Real Options." NBER Working Paper No. 10114. Cambridge, MA: National Bureau of Economic Research.

Standing Committee on Finance. (2000) "Challenge for Change: A Study of Cost Recovery" Report of the Standing Committee on Finance. June.

Statistics Canada. National Input-Output Model 1992.

———. (2004a) Canadian Industry Statistics. http://strategis.ic.gc.ca/canadian_industry_statistics/cis.nsf/idE/cis3254defE.html

———. (2004b) Total Intramural Expenditures in Selected Industries, 1999-2003.

United States Environmental Protection Agency. (1997) "Regulatory Impact Analysis of Regulations On Microbial Products Of Biotechnology. Volume I: Technical Report" Economics, Exposure and Technology Division, Office of Pollution Prevention and Toxics. January 21, 1997

United States Food and Drug Administration. (2003) "Approval Times for Priority and Standard NDAs, Calendar Years 1993-2003" Center for Drug Evaluation and Research, <http://www.fda.gov/cder/rdmt/NDAapps93-03.htm>.

Stay the Course or Find a New Path?
Canada's Reliance on the U.S.
as an Export Market

Eugene Beaulieu   &   Herb Emery
The University of Calgary[1]   The University of Calgary

Introduction

Canada is currently at a cross-road in terms of the direction to take with respect to international trade policy. After over fifteen years of increased market integration through the Canada-U.S. Free Trade Agreement (CUSTA) and the North American Free Trade Agreement (NAFTA) the Canadian economy is more closely integrated with the United States than at any time in history. At the same time that the North American economy has become more integrated, tremendous changes have occurred outside North America as economic growth and international trade has expanded considerably in the developing world. Concern over trade dependence with the United States, and the sense that Canadian firms are missing out on profitable markets outside of North America, has led to calls for government policy to encourage Canadian firms to look beyond North America. The important policy questions are thus: whether or not Canada would benefit from deeper integration with the United States; whether Canada should extend market integration on a regional basis; or pursue integration with other regions of the world. Some have argued for a multi-facet approach whereby Canada simultaneously pursues all of these objectives.

In part, the increased dependence on the U.S. is the result of policy directions taken in the 1980s – a time when Canada was at another cross-road in international trade policy. The policy debate at the time was whether Canada should continue to engage in incremental trade policy and negotiate sector-by-sector with the United States or should Canada pursue an ambitious trade policy agenda to increase and lock-in economic ties with the United States? Some argued, at that time, that Canada was already too closely tied to the American economy (receiving approximately 70 percent of Canadian exports) and argued that the extent of the dependence was not healthy for economic and political reasons. Others argued that Canada had no choice – it had to secure market access in the U.S. given the rise in U.S. protectionism. Still others argued that guaranteeing and securing access to the American market and increasing competition by lowering import barriers would lead to more competitive Canadian firms. These firms, it was argued, would thus be more successful in the world market.

---

[1] Part of this research was conducted while Eugene Beaulieu was a visiting professor at Carleton University and was the Norman Robertson Fellow at International Trade Canada. Dr. Beaulieu acknowledges financial support from SSHRC.

Canadian policy makers and political leaders decided to follow the Macdonald Commission recommendations (1985) to take a bold new direction in Canadian trade policy and negotiate and sign a comprehensive trade and investment agreement with the United States – which eventually led to the CUSTA. The agreement was in response to the decidedly unilateral direction American international trade policy had taken and was an effort to maintain market share with its largest trading partner, and to forge a deeper economic integration with the largest and most dominant economy in the world. Canadian voters agreed with this new direction in trade policy and re-elected the Mulroney government in the great "free trade" election of 1988.[2]

It is inevitable that Canadian trade flows to the United States will be large given the proximity, size and wealth of the U.S. market. As an economy, Canada has been reliant on exports of raw and processed natural resources and since the 1840s, increasingly dependent upon the United States as a trading partner. The combination of these two features of the economy has resulted in volatile incomes and employment in Canada. Prices received for natural resources such as oil, wheat and potash, are determined in the global marketplace and are volatile. Reliance on the United States as a trading partner also exposes Canada to the risk of income changes being tied to U.S. economic conditions and trade policies. Recent events such as the "mad cow" crisis, the softwood lumber dispute, a rapidly appreciating Canadian dollar, and Canada's lack of direct support for U.S. actions in Iraq have all highlighted the risks of having trade specialized so heavily with one trading partner, particularly one with greater economic and bargaining power in trade arrangements. While the benefits of this specialization in production and trade flows has been higher Canadian incomes and employment, the benefits have been acquired by Canada taking on greater income risk and potentially by accelerating the rate of resource depletion such that whatever increases in income that occurred, they might not be sustainable.

In this chapter, we examine the evolution and the extent of Canadian and American economic integration. We analyse and show that Canada's economy has become more dependent on the United States in terms of international trade. We then examine and discuss the costs and benefits of being part of such an integrated North American economy. The two main concerns raised about the deep dependence are: 1) an economic (portfolio type) argument that the status quo delivers volatility; and 2) a political argument that policy dependence (or loss of sovereignty) is the result of economic dependence. Moreover, we argue that although the Canadian economy is extremely dependent on the U.S. economy, the main feature of the relationship is that there is a trade-off between the gains from specialization derived from deep integration and the volatility that the lack of market diversification affords. We argue that income smoothing policies and institutions are the proper instrument for addressing these issues of volatility in

---

[2] See Beaulieu (2002) for an analysis of the political-economy of the CUSTA and preferences of Canadian voters.

250

economic markets. Whereas income-smoothing policies are the proper instrument for market volatility, diplomacy is the proper instrument in the political sphere.

We provide evidence that the CUSTA and NAFTA were very successful at increasing the integration of the North American economy and argue that market forces should determine whether we have ever deeper integration with the United States. It is important to point out that Canada's move to regional trade agreements and a more integrated regional economy in the 1980s and 1990s was part of a decision by Canadians that diversification via protection was too costly. Ergo the choice to sacrifice income level to reduce volatility may not be a palatable choice for voters.

From close ties to deeper integration

Figure 1 shows the evolution of Canada's export trade with the United States since 1840. During the period of Reciprocity from 1854 to 1866, the share of merchandise exports destined for the U.S. reached as high as 70%. Britain resumed its dominant position as Canada's trade partner after the abrogation of Reciprocity. From 1886 to 1947, exports to the United States were usually 35% to 40% of total exports, and exports accounted for 25% to 40% of Canada's Gross National Product (GNP). From 1886 to 1913, exports to Britain accounted for over half of Canadian exports, but fell abruptly during World War I to 25% to 30% of total Canadian exports. Canada's reliance on the United States as an export destination has been increasing as a series of steps after World War II. In 1947, 39% of exports went to the U.S., and 27.5% to the UK. In 1950, the UK share had fallen to 15%, and the share of exports to the U.S. increased to 65% (Rooth 2000).

Even as early as the late 1950s, the extent of Canadian dependence on trade with the United States was considered an exceptional and unprecedented economic relationship between two sovereign nations. Moreover, the exceptionally close economic ties between Canada and the United States had already become a concern for Canadian politicians, policymakers and academics. At a speech at Carleton University in 1958, the great Canadian-born trade economist Jacob Viner remarked that "These are all exceptionally high ratios for economic relations of one country to another. They cannot be matched, taken together, I feel certain, for any other two countries in the free world." (Viner, 1958 p. 37).[3]

Although Canadian exports to the United States had already reached 60% of total Canadian exports, the trend continued upward. From 1950 to 1967, the share of exports to the U.S. remained at around 60%, but increased to 70% for the period 1969 to 1983. Since 1983, the share of exports to the U.S. has increased to reach a peak of 86% in 2000.

---

[3] Note that Jacob Viner's seminal work established the economic model of customs unions that became the foundation for economic thinking on regional trade agreements.

Figure 1

Percentage of Total Exports to the US, 1850-2002

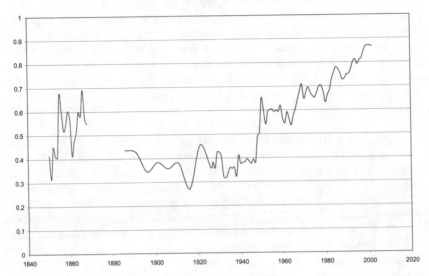

Source: F. H. Leacy (1982); CANSIM; Marr and Paterson (1980)

Figure 2

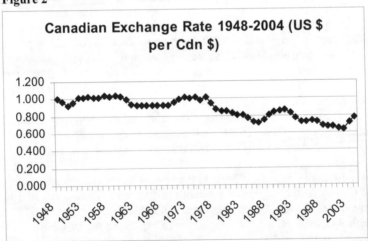

Canadian Exchange Rate 1948-2004 (US $ per Cdn $)

Exports to the U.S. continued to grow in absolute and relative importance in the 1960s, but the composition of exports shifted from reliance on pulp and paper and minerals to manufactured goods. The expansion of Canada's manufacturing exports after 1960 was stimulated by the devaluation of the Canadian dollar from $1.04 in 1959 to $0.925 (US dollars per Canadian dollar),

252

and by policy developments like the Autopact of 1965 (Norrie, Owram and Emery 2002). Figure 2 presents the Canadian exchange rate vis-à-vis the U.S. dollar from 1948 to 2004.

Figure 3 shows that the real value of exports to destinations other than the U.S. grew until 1980, but by much less than exports to the U.S. It is the expansion in total exports, particularly to the U.S., that dominates the expansion of Canadian trade after 1960. One of the notable features of the real value of exports is that export values reached a plateau in the 1980s, the value of exports to the U.S. levelled off while exports to the rest of the world showed some decline.

With the expansion of trade with the United States, Canada's reliance on external trade as measured by the ratio of exports to GNP/GDP increased. Figure 4 shows the ratio of exports to output in Canada from 1870 to 2000. Other than during World War I and World War II, when exports were exceptionally high, until 1960 exports were normally between 15 and 20% of GNP. Since 1960, the ratio of the value of exports to GDP has increased such that today the ratio is over 35 percent. As Canada experienced a severe recession in the early 1980s coincident with the stagnation in growth of its exports, the Macdonald Commission investigated what was needed to re-invigorate the Canadian economy. The Commission concluded that a movement towards freer trade with the United States would be a positive development, and in 1989, the Mulroney Conservative government implemented the CUSTA and in 1994, the NAFTA. Following the implementation of these policies, exports to the U.S. grew rapidly, and while exports to the rest of the world showed no growth, the share of total exports destined for the U.S. grew to a high of 86%.

Figure 3

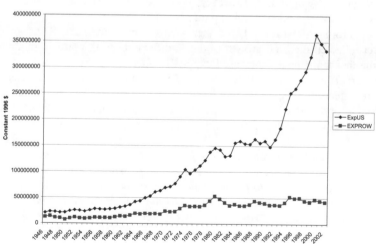

Value of Exports to US and Rest of the World (ROW), 1946-2002, in Constant 1996 $

Source: Leacy (1982); CANSIM

253

Figure 4

Exports to GNP and GDP, 1870-2001

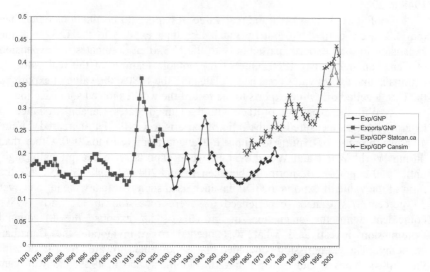

Source: Urquhart (1993); Leacy (1982); CANSIM

The importance of exports for the Canadian economy measured by the ratio of exports to GDP is higher now than at any other time in Canadian history with perhaps the exceptions of WWI and WWII and the Reciprocity era of 1854 to 1866.[4] In the 1950s and 1960s, there was an expectation that increasing reliance on the U.S. was likely a short run situation and once other markets emerged, the export reliance would fall. However, when economic stagnation struck in the 1980s, Canada responded by relying more on the lucrative U.S. market.

From 1870 to 1980, the increased reliance on the U.S. as an export market reflected the high growth of demand for industrial inputs in that country, and the fact that Canada increased exports by increasing the number of products for export. The increased reliance on the U.S. as an export destination after World War II reflects the expansion of the level of exports in response to rising U.S. demand as opposed to diverting exports away from alternative markets to the U.S. According to Viner (1958, 37) the high degree of trade dependence

> ...cannot be accounted for solely by the relative size of the two countries, or even by relative size plus proximity. An additional factor operative to tie the Canadian into the American economy is the complementary character of the two economies; Canada has surpluses of raw materials of which the United States has

---

[4] The ratio of exports to GDP has fallen-off somewhat in recent years, but remains at historically high levels.

254

deficiencies; standard American capital goods are well adapted to Canadian production techniques; the consumption standards and tastes of the two countries are almost identical, so that Canadian consumers' goods find a ready market in the United States.[5]

The U.S. industrial demands for commodities in which Canada was abundant caused the expansion in exports and the Canadian capital boom of the 1950s. David Slater (1955, 4) found:

The changes in content and geographical destination are closely related. The decline of the United Kingdom as a market is closely related to the enormous decline in exports of animal products, lumber and timber, and the more recent decline in agricultural and vegetable products. The relative rise of the United States as a market is related to the enormous expansion of wood products, particularly pulp and paper, and non-ferrous metals. To a considerable degree, for Canada to sell to different areas she must sell (and produce) different things; to sell different things she must sell to different areas.

The 1957 Final Report of the Royal Commission on Canada's Economic Prospects (the Gordon Commission) included forecasts of Canada's export to GDP ratio and percentage of exports to the U.S. for 1980. With a forecast based on a basic premise that there would be no severe economic depressions, world conflicts or radical changes in policies (among others), the report forecast that total exports to GNP would fall from 21.7% to 18.4% while the share of total exports to the U.S. would rise from 62% to 69.5%. Amongst merchandise exports, the only sub-groups expected to increase their share of total exports between 1955 and 1980 were Chemicals, Aluminum and products, and Petroleum and Products. All other sub-groups including agricultural and food products, pulp and paper, lumber, and copper and nickel were predicted to have falling shares of total exports (Kuznets 1959, Table 3). In many respects, these forecasts were remarkably accurate as in 1980 the export to GNP ratio was around 20% and the share of exports to the U.S. was around 70%. This would suggest that the Autopact, the abandonment of the Bretton-Woods fixed exchange rate systems and large shocks like the OPEC oil crises that took place between 1957 and 1980 had little effect on the ratio of exports to GDP over the long run. All told, this

---

[5] Note that last sentence segment in the original passage from Viner reads: "*; the consumption standards and tastes of the two countries are almost identical, so that American consumers' goods find a ready market in the United States.*" This appears to be a typographical error – so we changed "American consumers' goods" to "Canadian consumers' goods."

suggests remarkable stability and predictability of the Canada-US trade relationship prior to the CUSTA.

As late as 1980, increased specialization in the destination for exports was accompanied by greater diversification of products for export. Since 1980, the volume of Canadian international trade has continued to increase rapidly and has become even more specialized in its destination market partner, i.e. increasingly specialized in trade with the U.S. However, Acharya, Sharma and Rao (2003) find that most of the increase in trade has been intra-industry, rather than inter-industry trade. The rapid increase in intra-industry trade suggests that trade flows have become more diversified in the variety of goods traded – but the authors also find that Canada's comparative advantage remains in commodity intensive sectors. Acharya et al (2003) examine the changes in export intensities and import penetrations for 84 industries between 1985 and 1997. They find that the number of industries with increased trade (larger export intensities and import penetration) increased during this period. In 1985, 30 of the 84 industries (or 36 percent) had export intensities of more than 30 percent and by 1997, 50 industries (or 60 percent) had export intensities of more than 30 percent. Similar increases occurred in import penetration rates.

Note that although there was a large increase in trade over a broad cross section of industries, the relative pattern of export intensity and import penetration was very stable from 1985 to 1997. Since 1997, however, the value of exports has increased due to increases in intra-industry trade in autos and in energy exports where high prices have resulted in a highly specialized export composition. Figure 5 shows the top industries by exports to the United States in 1993 and 2002 with all industries related to automobiles, trucks, engines and parts aggregated into one category. The figure shows the large increases in total Canadian exports since 1993, and especially since 1997, from increases in the exports of automobiles and light trucks and from exports of oil and gas. At the same time, the figure also shows that increased values of exports are across a large number of industries. In fact, although the magnitude is less than for autos, trucks and parts, real exports grew for all of the top 25 exporting industries except the computer and peripheral equipment industry and the semiconductor and other electronic component industry. The "All Others" residual category represents an enormous increase in the real value of exports for a large number of industries representing a large number of products.

There is strong evidence in the literature that CUSTA and NAFTA had a significant impact on trade flows. A recent working paper by Romalis (2002) makes the point that it is difficult to measure the impact of CUSTA or NAFTA. Part of the problem is the level of aggregation. Romalis uses very detailed trade data and finds large impacts of the CUSTA and NAFTA tariff changes on North American trade flows. The problem with using more aggregate data is that much of the cross-commodity variation in tariffs occurs within quite detailed industry sectors. There is additional evidence based on Helliwell (1998) that the border effect between Canada and the United States has declined since NAFTA. Again, evidence that the trade agreements had some impact on the degree of integration.

Figure 5

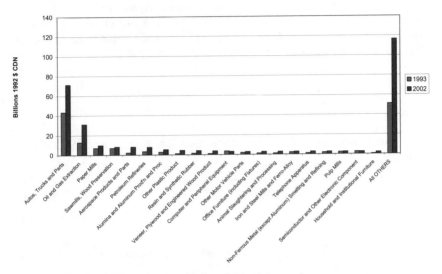

Figure 5: Exports to US for Top 25 Industries (5 Digit NAICS Code) 1993 and 2002 in Constant 1992 Billions of $CDN

Source: Strategis Web Page (Industry Canada): *http://strategis.ic.gc.ca/*

Deeper bilateral integration in a regional world

Figure 6 shows that the ratio of Canada's exports to GDP has been high compared to the average ratio for high income countries since 1965. However, it also shows that Canada's ratio of exports to GDP grew faster than the average ratio for high income countries after 1990. In 1965, the ratio of exports to GDP was approximately 19 percent in Canada and 12 percent on average among high income countries (representing a 53 percent differential). The increase in the ratio from 1965 to 1990 was similar for Canada and for the average of high income countries (the differential did not change much). However, after 1990 the ratio increased faster in Canada than it did for the averages across the other countries. By 2001, the ratio was 44 percent in Canada and 23 percent on average among high income countries – a differential of over 87 percent.

Note, however, that comparing Canada to country averages obscures the fact that a large number of countries have much higher export to GDP ratios than Canada. In fact, out of the 166 countries for which data are available, Canada's ratio of exports to GDP ranked 64th in 2001. Figure 7 presents a scatter plot of the ratio of exports to GDP against country size (measured by GDP) for the high income countries.[6] Canada is not at all an outlier in terms of the ratio of exports to

---

[6] High income countries are defined as those with GDP measured in US dollars greater than $12,000 in 2001. Note that the three largest world economies (Germany, Japan and the

GDP given the size of the country. Canada has a higher ratio than the largest countries in the world – but as the regression line shows – the ratio is inversely related to country size. The outlier countries include Luxemburg and Hong Kong with export to GDP ratios greater than 100 percent. Ireland (IRL), Belgium (BEL) and the Netherlands (NLD) also have higher ratios of exports to GDP than their size suggests. On the other hand, Australia (AUS) and Greece (GRC) have lower than average export to GDP ratios given their economic size.

Figure 6

Export Share of GDP for Canada and Country Groups: 1965-2001

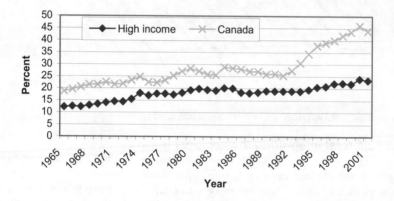

It is also important to recognize that Canada was not the only country to recently experience an increase in trade dependence. In fact, the rapid growth of world exports in the post-war period caused export revenues to be an increasingly important portion of domestic income for numerous countries. As Moore and Rugman (2001) point out, world trade flows have become increasingly regional, and less global in nature. Figure 8 provides an illustration of how trade flows became more regional between 1980 and 2000. As seen in the figure, intra-NAFTA trade went from 34% of North American trade in 1980 to 56% in 2000. Europe and Asia experienced similar growth in the share of regional trade.

United States) are excluded from the figure for scale and space considerations. The diagram is very similar including the slope of the regression line.

Although world trade flows have become more regional, Canadian trade flows became even more concentrated.

Figure 7

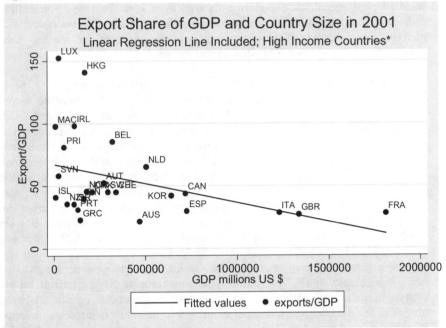

Export Share of GDP and Country Size in 2001
Linear Regression Line Included; High Income Countries*

* Japan, Germany and the US are excluded due to scale and space constraints. These are the three largest countries and the picture is similar (but difficult to read) when they are included. High income countries are defined here as those with GDP per capita greater than US$12,000.
Source: World Development Indicators

Figure 8: Intra-regional vs inter-regional trade

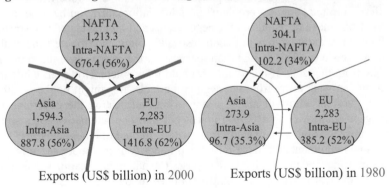

The problems with economic dependence on the U.S.

As noted above, at the present time, Canada is more dependent on exports to a single market than at any point in its history. The obvious policy question that arises is whether or not this is a problem. Part of the static welfare gains in standard neoclassical trade models is derived from specialization in production and trade flows. These gains can be offset by the increased risk associated with increased specialization. This section examines the concerns that are expressed over the lack of diversity in Canadian export markets.

Irreversible investments and strategic trade considerations

There is a potentially critical strategic problem with negotiating deeper economic ties with a much larger trading partner. The problem is similar to what is known as a "hold-up" problem in the industrial organization literature. The basic idea is that in a world with irreversible investments, anticipated trade negotiations between a large country and a small country might make the small country worse off. Investors anticipating liberalized trade will invest in export opportunities making the small country dependent on trade with the large country and destroying the small country's bargaining position. A version of this argument was popularized during the CUSTA debates by the retired Judge Marjorie Bowker (1988) and was also expressed by economist Brian Copeland (1989). The idea was then formalized in economic theory by John McLaren (1997). Judge Bowker was part of a grass-roots movement opposed to CUSTA and pointed out that the abrogation clause in CUSTA (either side can abrogate the agreement on six months notice) could place Canada in a serious predicament regardless of who abrogates the deal because Canadian industry will have restructured and invested in export related activities. The key point is that Canada will gain from CUSTA by re-adjusting its economy toward the U.S. export market. When these investments are irreversible, however, Canada becomes extremely vulnerable to threats of abrogation. As Copeland (1989) points out, this weakens Canada's bargaining position on any trade issue.

McLaren (1997) makes the point, however, that this trade negotiations case differs from the "hold-up problem" in industrial organization because in the latter case firms make decisions on the negotiations and on the related investment. In the trade case, the government negotiates trade policy and private firms make investment decisions. This is important because in the former case the firm can walk away from the table, if it anticipates a hold-up problem. However, while the government can walk away from the negotiating table, this might not be credible to private investors who will invest in any event and destroy the government's bargaining position. McLaren (1997) points out that one alternative for a small country in this situation is to diversify trade with a number of other countries.

Some commentators have raised additional concerns more recently that Canada's trade dependence on the U.S. exposes Canada to uncertainties due to the increasingly evident move by the U.S. to politicize trade relations by connecting

260

trade policy to other political objectives.[7] In May, 2003 the then U.S. Trade Representative Robert Zoellick announced that co-operation in foreign policy and security issues are a pre-condition for any country wanting to negotiate a free trade agreement with the U.S., for example, confirming these concerns.

The "Portfolio" concern with dependence on a small number of markets and excess reliance on natural resources

Canada's early economic development up to 1840 was fostered by British mercantile policies (Navigation Acts, Corn Laws and Timber Tariffs) that provided Canadian products with preferential treatment and access into the British market. Canada lost this privileged access to the British market after 1840 with the repeal of the timber tariffs and the Corn Laws a few years later in 1846 and the Navigation Acts in 1849. The loss of this preferential access coincided with an economic slump in the British North American (BNA) colonies and the consequences of the loss of an important market became clear. In the short run, the BNA colonies responded by seeking a new market for their resources and eventually entered into the Reciprocity Treaty of 1854 with the United States. Over the period of the Treaty, 1854-1866, reported Canadian exports grew by over 300% but the effect of the Treaty was a small one-time gain in the level of exports to the U.S (Norrie, Owram and Emery 2002). With the abrogation of the Treaty in 1866, Canada continued to orient itself increasingly towards trade with the United States, even negotiating an ill-fated Reciprocity Agreement with the U.S. in 1911 (see Beaulieu and Emery 2002).

The Depression of the 1930s was a hard lesson for a small economy like Canada's dependent on the exports of a few commodities to a small number of markets. In 1929, merchandise exports represented 22% of Canadian GNP. In contrast, merchandise exports were only 5% of GNP in the U.S. The importance of exports for income was more acute in some sectors like forestry, farming and mining where 80% of produce was exported. Canada's wheat exports alone were 40% of world wheat exports. Canada also had a lack of diversification in export goods as 80% of Canada's exports were made up of three primary products: grains, animal products and forest products. Wheat and flour alone comprised 36% of total exports. Canada was also reliant on two export markets, the U.S. and the UK (In 1929, over 1/3 of exports went to U.S. while another 1/3 were destined for the UK) and through the gold standard, the monetary policies of the three countries were bound together. With the glut of wheat and other primary products on world markets by the late-1920s, commodity prices were low and Canadian exporters were not doing well. The U.S. and U.K. moves to protectionism, the 1930 Smoot-Hawley Tariff in the U.S. in particular, resulted in draconian reductions in Canadian exports. By 1932, exports to the U.S. were half of their 1929 level and to the U.K., 2/3 of their 1929 level. While it is clear that the high reliance on exports of a few commodities left the Canadian economy particularly vulnerable in the 1930s, it is not clear if there were arrangements that Canada

---

[7] See Winham and Ostry (2003).

261

could have pursued to avoid the devastating effects of the Depression. Most, if not all, economies were moving in protectionist directions in the 1930s and had experienced precipitous drops in incomes. There were no alternative export markets to which Canada could have turned.

After World War II, the growing share of Canadian exports to the U.S. was cause for some concern in Canada, but it was not clear what alternatives existed. Gibson (1956, 423) argued that:

> *Many Canadians feel a little uneasy because we now send such a large proportion of our exports to the United States. Though a feeling of concern is understandable, the fact is that we have had no practicable alternative to increasing our exports to the United States. In the post-war period the big increase in demand has come from the United States and it must be admitted that the increase has been very welcome in Canada. No remotely comparable opportunity for expanding our export markets has been available in the sterling area or elsewhere, particularly in the early post-war period when we were worried about obtaining adequate markets.*

Similarly, Simon Kuznets (1959, 378) wrote:

> *There is a conflict between apprehension over the recently increased "dominance" of the United States in the foreign trade of Canada, its foreign capital, and some of its important industries, and recognition that these ties with its larger neighbor to the south are an important and increasing source of economic strength, a basis for past growth and a promise for the future which it would be irrational to forego... Yet there is apprehension... lest the increased dependence upon United States markets, for imports and particularly for exports, make Canada more sensitive to the vagaries of United States economic policy...*

Gibson (1956, 424) argued that the reliance on the U.S. as an export market was likely to diminish once the economies of Europe stabilized and hence, not reason for concern:

> *The kind of goods produced by our basic industries and particularly our minerals and wood products are in growing demand throughout the world. The economic recovery of Europe has much increased the continent's requirements for industrial raw materials. The growth of nationalism all over the world, with its emphasis on industrialization, has added further to demand. The most powerful impulse is, of course, the recent surge in growth in the world's population, perhaps the most*

262

rapid in recorded history. We are thus not so completely dependent on the United States for the disposal of our basic exports as the trade figures appear to suggest.

Gibson's expectation that the reliance on the U.S. market for Canada's exports would diminish could not have been more incorrect. As noted above, Canada's reliance on the U.S. has grown and concerns over the reliance on trade with United States continue to be voiced. "This concentration of trade creates vulnerability, much the same as a company that makes most of its sales to a single buyer" (Winham and Ostry (2003)). At a recent "Borderlines" conference, one "dooms-dayer" opined that Canadians "have pinned our prosperity to trade with a single convenient customer on a cheap Canadian dollar. Any of us with brains enough to run a lemonade stand knows the risk of a single customer."[8] Although the logic of the argument is questionable and the analogy is completely fallacious (are Canadian businesses with access to a market of over 290 million people really selling to a single customer?), it does raise important concerns that the Canadian economy may be "too dependent" on the American market. Recent events such as the softwood lumber dispute, the "mad cow" disease scare which closed the border to Canadian beef exports, and tensions between the two countries over Canada's choice not to support the U.S. in Iraq, have shown the risk of relying on preferential access to one, albeit large and wealthy, economy.

According to Winham and Ostry (2003) Canada is facing a new crisis due to the vulnerability created by its trade-dependence on the United States. The authors point out that there are two basic alternative strategies Canada can follow: 1) move Canada to deeper economic and political ties with the United States; and 2) diversify trade in a "second policy direction." Even the Governor of the Bank of Canada has argued that Canadians need to look beyond the North American continent. In a recent speech, David Dodge (Nov 2003) argues:

> *During the 1980s and 1990s, free-trade agreements with the United States and Mexico focused Canada's attention on the opportunities south of the border. Individual Canadians and businesses have been making the tough adjustments that are necessary to face increased competition and to take advantage of new opportunities. While keeping that continental focus, it is now important that we broaden our sights and focus on opportunities that are opening up in the rest of the world.*

Winham and Ostry also come down with an argument for the latter policy direction. They argue that the free trade agreement was the proper response to the

---

[8] This quote is attributed to Desmond Morton from McGill Univeristy in "Ideas that Matter," Vol. 2 #4, p. 36 published by Zephyr Press, Toronto. This issue is devoted to ideas expressed at a series of conferences "*BorderLines: Canada in North America*" sponsored by the Institute for Research on Public Policy (IRPP).

263

uncertainty over trade policy in the late-1970s and early 1980s as the United States pursued a "unilateral" approach to international policy during that period, however, today, a policy of closer ties with the United States would be a mistake. Their argument of vulnerability comes down to the standard analogy that treats Canada as one agent selling one product to one large buyer which leaves one vulnerable and exposed. However, as pointed out above, Canada is not one seller peddling one good to one large buyer. Canadian export dependence on the U.S. is comprised of thousands producers peddling thousands of different goods to millions of American firms and consumers. According to Statistics Canada's data based on the Exporter Registry, 41,267 establishments exported goods in 2001 – up from 30,589 enterprises exporting in 1993.[9] The "lack of diversification" argument looks pretty weak in this context.

The impact of trade dependence on export performance

A central question regarding the impact of Canadian trade dependence on the United States is whether Canadian export performance has suffered. A starting point from which to address this empirical question is to examine whether Canada managed to export more as a percentage of world trade over time. The next step is to decompose the change in world export shares into structural changes and residual – or unexplained changes. A common approach used in the literature to evaluate why the exports of one country grew faster (or more slowly) than world exports is the Constant Market Share (CMS) analysis. The CMS analysis applies a "structural decomposition analysis" methodology to exports. The CMS analysis decomposes export growth into one of four factors: a) the general growth of world exports (i.e. growth in global demand for exports), b) the composition of the country's exports; c) the destination of the country's exports; and d) a residual term which includes all other factors not captured by a), b), and c). The residual term has become interpreted as a "competitiveness index".

Taszynski (1951) was the first to apply this structural decomposition methodology to exports. Leamer and Stern (1970) provide a detailed discussion of CMS analysis and propose a new version of the method. The methodology has been used extensively in applied international applications including work on the United States by Bowen and Pelzman (1984) and more recently by Azam and Azam (1994). The mathematical foundation of the approach (based on Leamer and Stern (1970)) is presented in the appendix.

Swisterski (2002) employs the CMS approach to decompose sources of export revenues in the OECD from 1972 to 1992. Some results from his analysis for Canada are summarized in Table 1. For the 1972-76 period, if Canadian exports had grown at the rate of world exports, they would have been 1.65 times greater than the actual level. Canada was unable to maintain its market share during this period primarily due to negative competitiveness (-48.5%) and destination (-15.0%) effects and to a much lesser extent by commodity (-1.5%) effects.

---

[9] See Statistics Canada Catalogue no. 65-506-XIE "A profile of Canadian exporters".

Table 1: Constant Market Share Analysis for Canada

	1972-76	1976-80	1980-84	1984-88	1988-92	1980-88	1980-92
a) World Trade	165.0	132.9	-18.5	179.2	170.4	57.4	85.0
b) Commodity	-1.5	-7.6	-5.5	14.9	-37.1	3.6	-11.3
c) Destination	-15.0	3.5	61.9	-39.6	-53.9	32.3	12.3
d) Competitiveness	-48.5	-28.8	62.1	-54.6	20.6	6.7	13.9
Total %	*100*	100	100	100	100	100	100

During the 1976-80 period, Canadian export growth was again below the world average, and again the commodity and the competitiveness effects were negative (-7.6% and –28.8% respectively). The competitiveness effect increased by 20 percentage points, from –49% in the previous period to –29%. However, there was a positive destination effect on Canadian exports during the period of 3.5%. As seen in Table 1, the destination effect was very large and positive from 1980-84 and again from 1988-92 – although it was negative from 1984-88.

If Canadian exports had grown at the global rate of export growth from 1984 to 1988, they would have been 1.79 times larger than was actually the case. The destination and the competitiveness effects were both negative at –39.6% and –54.6% respectively, but the commodity effect was positive (at 14.9%). The positive commodity effect coincided with a structural change among Canada's principal exports. Whereas machinery was still Canada's leading export, manufactured goods became the second largest export group, pushing crude material exports into third place.

During the 1988-92 period, however, Canada experienced a positive competitiveness effect of 20.6%. Notwithstanding the positive competitiveness effect, Canadian export growth was below the world average rate, with negative commodity and destination effects, at –37.1% and -53.9% respectively. The negative destination effect was to a great extent due to the 1991 recession in the United States.

Between 1972 and 1992, Canadian exports grew at well below the world average rate, with negative commodity (-25.5%) and competitiveness (-18.4%) effects, and only a marginally positive destination effect (0.9%). One of the key factors contributing to the decline in Canada's market share of world exports over this 20 year period was the falling demand for (and thus relative value of) the Food and the Crude Materials commodity groups; both of which comprise a large share of Canadian exports.

Table 2 from Swisterski (2002) presents the CMS results for all OECD countries between 1972 and 1992. The columns show the percentage contribution of individual CMS effects to the overall change in exports. As Table 2 indicates in the first column, growth in world trade accounted for most of the growth in trade for all OECD countries. Export growth can be accounted for by overall growth in world trade in New Zealand, Sweden, Canada, Australia and the Netherlands. Since this table is one of relative contributions of the four factors of trade growth, the overall impact of commodity, destination and competitiveness in these countries will be negative. Canada's commodity composition and competitiveness effects are negative, but note that the destination effect is almost neutral. New Zealand, Australia, Iceland and Canada had high and negative commodity effects whereas Switzerland, Japan, Germany, the U.S. and Italy had large positive commodity composition effects. Although the destination effect was neutral in Canada, it was positive and large in Australia, Japan, New Zealand and the U.S. Ireland had one of the highest competitiveness effects.

The results of the CMS analysis conducted by Swisterski (2002) provide some evidence that Canadian export performance from 1972 to 1992 was not adversely affected by the degree of trade dependence on the American economy. Canadian exports grew more slowly than the world growth in exports over the period but this had more to do with the commodity composition of Canadian exports and the competitiveness residual. Note that Richardson (1971) is critical of the CMS approach pointing out that the signs and values of the various effects may change depending on how the base period is constructed. That is, the values and signs of the effects may change if the final year, instead of the initial year of the period under study is used as the base year. Fagerberg and Sollie (1987) address the Richardson (1971) criticisms and perform a revised CMS study of 20 OECD countries from 1961-83. Fagerberg and Sollie (1987) find similar results for Canada over that period – that is – they also find a positive "destination" effect for Canadian exports.

Has increased dependence on the United States as a Trading partner increased the volatility of exports and income for Canada?

Another approach to examining whether trade dependence on the United States has adversely affected Canadian export performance is to analyse the long term trend and variability of Canadian exports. This provides an alternative approach to the CMS analysis. Ideally it would be useful to conduct a counter-factual experiment whereby the variance of exports for the actual "portfolio" of Canadian exports is compared to a hypothetical export portfolio with less dependence on trade with the United States. This approach would require the estimation of an export trade model which is beyond the scope of this study. However, we compare the variation of Canadian exports to the variation of exports of a similar country that is not as dependent on trade with one large trading partner. One way to compare the income risk associated with specializing on a single export market is to compare the volatility of income and exports of Australia and Canada since World War II. Whereas Canada was oriented towards the U.S., Australia went towards Asia and only recently to the U.S.

266

Table 2: Constant Market Share for OECD countries: 1972-92

	World Trade	Commodity Effect	Destination Effect	Competitiveness Effect
Australia	130.7	-53.7	32.3	-9.3
Austria	77.7	3.8	-9.2	27.8
Belgium & Luxemburg	121.0	7.1	3.3	-31.4
Canada	143.0	-25.5	0.9	-18.4
Denmark	97.3	-3.4	-4.2	10.3
Finland	113.2	-15.4	-13.3	15.5
France	101.2	6.5	-4.9	-2.8
Germany	99.0	19.6	-5.8	-12.8
Greece	79.1	-11.1	-6.3	38.2
Iceland	115.1	-36.5	-8.5	30.0
Ireland	48.2	-3.3	3.1	51.9
Italy	94.2	15.6	-5.1	-4.8
Japan	71.0	24.1	23.1	-18.1
Netherlands	126.4	15.6	0.8	-42.8
New Zealand	183.7	-78.9	10.5	-15.3
Norway	84.9	-4.6	-2.5	22.2
Portugal	60.8	0.2	-6.1	45.2
Spain	46.5	0.0	-2.9	56.5
Sweden	156.5	0.1	-4.7	-51.9
Switzerland	93.5	25.9	3.4	-22.8
Turkey	49.9	-15.7	-0.5	66.2
U.K.	109.2	13.9	-0.9	-22.2
U.S.A.	100.1	16.9	21.7	-38.6

Table 3: Comparing the Growth and Variation of Canadian and Australian Exports, GDP and GDP per capita from 1949 to 2003

		1949-64		1965-73		1974-88		1989-03		1949-03	
		Growth	Variation	Growth	Variation	Growth	Variation	Growth	Variation	Growth	Variation
Exports	Australia	8.6%	0.25	10.7%	0.31	14.2%	0.51	6.9%	0.31	10.1%	1.25
	Canada	6.8%	0.26	12.9%	0.30	12.1%	0.43	7.5%	0.37	9.5%	1.23
GDP	Australia	11.1%	0.41	10.7%	0.27	13.1%	0.47	5.9%	0.24	10.2%	1.13
	Canada	7.7%	0.30	10.5%	0.25	11.0%	0.39	4.7%	0.21	8.3%	1.00
GDP per capita	Australia	8.6%	0.31	8.5%	0.22	11.6%	0.42	4.6%	0.19	8.3%	1.01
	Canada	5.2%	0.19	8.6%	0.20	9.7%	0.35	3.6%	0.16	6.6%	0.89

Growth is the average annual growth of the variable over the period. **Variation** is the standard deviation divided by the average of that variable for the period.

Table 3 presents the average annual growth rates and variation of exports, GDP and GDP per capita for Canada and Australia from 1949 to 2003 (last column). There are several important aspects of this comparison that are worth mentioning. First, over the entire period from 1949 to 2003, the variation of exports was almost the same in Canada and Australia but the GDP and GDP per capita had higher variation in Australia. Second, on average over the entire period Australian exports, GDP and GDP per capita grew faster than they did for Canada but that was also associated with greater variation in the measures. Although we do not look at causal relationships and are looking at only two countries, in this case there does not appear to be much of a trade-off between variability and growth. Third, the growth rates of the variables in the two countries follow a similar pattern over time: high and low growth episodes correspond with each other in both countries and across all three variables. The highest average annual growth rates of all three variables for both countries was 1974-88 while the lowest growth occurred in the 1989-03 period. Relative to the experience of Australia, an economy much less dependent on the United States as a trading partner, it appears that Canada does not have any greater volatility in her trade patterns and incomes. Recognizing that income per capita in Canada is higher than it is for Australia leads us to conclude that deeper integration with the United States has benefited Canada.

Both the CMS analysis and the comparison of variation and growth of exports and income between Canada and Australia provide evidence that Canadian export dependence on the American economy did not adversely affect Canadian export performance. Australia and Canada sell their exports in a world market that is interconnected. Based on the evidence above, it would be highly dubious to argue that Canada would have benefited a great deal from pursuing policies designed to diversify export markets.

There does not appear to be a large potential for Canadian exporters to diversify their markets. In particular, for natural resource exports, there are not multiple independent markets across which any country can diversify its sales. Natural resource demand has always been global and when one export destination deteriorates in its demand position, so do most of the others. The Great Depression showed that there were no alternative markets for exporters to exploit; the collapse of potash demand in the 1970s illustrated the same problem for that commodity and we saw it again with respect to oil in the 1980s. Wheat has also had this problem for over a century. Another question to ponder is whether there exists an alternative market to the U.S. for Canadian produced auto-parts? All of this indicates that there is limited potential for diversifying the market risk across destinations.

Trade policy and trade diversification

What role is there for policy to diversify the portfolio of destination markets? As discussed earlier, the 1957 Final Report of the Royal Commission on Canada's Economic Prospects forecasts of Canada's export to GDP ratio and percentage of exports to the U.S. for 1980 were remarkably accurate as in 1980 the export to GNP ratio was around 20% and the share of exports to the U.S. was around 70%. This would suggest that the Autopact, the abandonment of the Bretton-Woods fixed exchange rate system and large shocks like the OPEC oil crises that took place between 1957 and 1980 had little effect over the long run. What scope would the Canadian government have to influence the structure of Canadian trade flows?

The alternative approach to trade diversion policies, or trade promotion to markets that currently do not import a great deal from Canada, is to continue

268

having Canada export to the markets that pay the highest prices for our produce. This will mean that we remain highly dependent on the U.S. market and subject to considerable income risk and income volatility. What a government may be able to do is develop institutions to smooth incomes.

Can, or even should, the federal government encourage Canadian exporters to divert some of its trade away from the high price market in the name of greater income stability? The answer to this question is not obvious. First, in a global marketplace, are there many segregated markets, which is a necessary condition for this sort of diversification, or is there really one large integrated/global market? If all markets are subject to the same business cycles as the U.S., then there may be little scope for true diversification. The relevant policy issue might not be trade specialization versus diversification per se, but one of how Canada should address its income volatility. Incomes from trade can be expected to be high and low depending on demand for Canada's exports, but total income over time will presumably be maximized by Canada specializing in its comparative advantage and exporting to the highest price buyer. Thus, the issue is really one of smoothing income over time. This can be done by Canada not fully pursuing its comparative advantage, or by not putting all its exports into a small number of markets, but it can also be achieved through other "income-smoothing" institutions that can be designed and run by government.

Consider that federal equalization payments in Canada were part of a strategy encouraging regional specialization in production within a diversified national economy. These payments smooth the incomes of the resource producing provinces. Unemployment/Employment insurance, personal savings etc... are ways in which individual workers smooth incomes over the business cycle. The Canada Pension Plan reserve fund, Registered Retirement Savings Plan, etc... are ways in which governments seek to have pension incomes and payouts smoothed over time. On a more aggregate level, oil economies like Norway, Alaska and Alberta have established savings/stabilization/endowment funds to smooth government revenues and in some cases personal incomes over the oil price cycles. The Canadian Wheat Board was established, following the Great Depression, to stabilize prices for farmers over the wheat price cycle. All of these arrangements are alternatives to the trade diversification strategy that smooth incomes over time while encouraging exporters to maximize incomes by selling to the high price markets. Thus it would appear that the federal government may want to consider institutions for smoothing income as a practical alternative to a strategy of diversifying export markets.

Conclusions

The analysis above provides a framework for examining the desirability of pursuing policies aimed at diversifying Canadian export markets. The study confirms that the concentration of Canadian exports on U.S. markets are at an all time high. It also argues that this lack of diversity in export markets exposes Canadian exports to any barriers that arise at the U.S. border or in the U.S. market place. However, the study argues that there are no compelling reasons to adopt policies designed to diversify exports. First, at a time when over 70 percent of

269

Canadian exports went to the U.S. market, Canadian voters endorsed a free trade agreement that fundamentally changed the direction of Canadian trade policy. The new trade policy direction contributed to even higher shares of Canadian exports going to the U.S. market. Furthermore, policies designed to diversify exports to other markets are at a minimum ineffective and might sacrifice income growth.

Bibliography

Acharya, Ram, Prakash Sharma and Someshwar Rao (2003) "Canada-US Trade and Foreign Direct Investment Patterns," in Richard G. Harris edited North American Linkages: Opportunities and Challenges for Canada. (The Industry Canada Research Series, University of Calgary Press).

Azam, Golam and Farida Azam (1994) "Sources of Changes in US Manufactured Exports During the Eighties," Journal of Economics and Finance 18(1) 31-42.

Baland, J. M. and P. Francios (2000) "Rent-seeking and Resource Booms," *Journal of Development Economics.* 61, p. 527-42.

Beaulieu, Eugene (2002) "Factor or Industry Cleavages in Trade Policy: An Empirical Analysis of the Stolper-Samuelson Theorem," *Economics & Politics.* Vol. 14 No. 2, pp. 99-132, July.

Beaulieu, Eugene and J. C. Herbert Emery. (2001) "Pork Packers, Reciprocity and Laurier's Defeat in the 1911 General Election," *Journal of Economic History.* Volume 61; December 2001; Number 4. 1082-1100.

Bowen, Harry P., and Joseph Pelzman. (1984) "US Export Competitiveness: 1962-77" Applied Economics 16 461-473.

Courchene, Thomas J. and Colin R. Telmer (1998) From Heartland to North American Region State: The Social, Fiscal and Federal Evolution of Ontario. Toronto: University of Toronto Press.

Fagerberg, Jan and Gunnar Sollie (1987) "The Method of Constant Market Shares Analysis Reconsidered," Applied Economics 19 1571-83, 1987.

Gibson, (1956) "The Changing Influence of the United States on the Canadian Economy," *Canadian Journal of Economics and Political Science*, 22 (4), 421-36.

Helliwell, John F. (1998), *How Much Do National Borders Matter?*, Washington, D.C.: Brookings Institution Press.

Kuznets, Simon (1959) "Canada's Economic Prospects: A Review Article," *American Economic Review* 49 (3), 359-85.

Larsen, Erling Røed (2003) "Are Rich Countries Immune to the Resource Curse? Evidence from Norway's Management of Its Oil Riches," Discussion Papers No. 362, October 2003. Statistics Norway, Research Department

Leacy, F. H. (1982) "Historical Statistics of Canada, 2nd edition." (Ottawa: Statistics Canada).

Leamer, Edward, and Robert M. Stern. (1970) Quantitative International Economics Chapter 7, Allyn and Bacon, Boston.

Marr, William L., and Donald G. Patterson (1986) Canada: An economic History. Toronto: Gage.

Moore, Karl and Alan Rugman (2001) "The Myths of Globalization" Ivey Business Journal 66:1 (September 2001): 64-68.

Norrie, Kenneth, Douglas Owram and J. C. Herbert Emery (2002) A History of the Canadian Economy. (Toronto, Harcourt Brace & Company, Canada).

Ostry, Sylvia and Gilbert R. Winham (2003) "The second trade crisis," *Globe and Mail.* Tuesday June 17, 2003.

Rodriguez, Francisco and Dani Rodrik (1999) "Trade Policy and Economic Growth: A Skeptic's Guide to Cross-National Evidence" *NBER Working Paper* No. w7081. Issued in April 1999.

Romalis, John, (2002) "NAFTA's and CUSFTA's Impact on North American Trade," University of Chicago GSB mimeo, July.

Rooth, Tim (2000) "Australia, Canada, and the International Economy in the Era of Postwar Reconstruction, 1945–50", *Australian Economic History Review* 40(2), 127-152

Sachs, J. D. and A. M. Warner (2001) "The Curse of Natural Resources," *European Economic Review*,45, s 827-838.

Sachs, J. D. and A. M. Warner (1999) "The Big Push, Natural Resource Booms and Growth," *Journal of Development Economics*, 59, pp. 43-76.

Sala-i-Martin, Xavier X. (1997) "I Just Ran Two Million Regressions." *American Economic Review* 87(2): 178-83.

Slater, David W. (1955) "Changes in the Structure of Canada's International Trade," The Canadian Journal of Economics and Political Science, Vol. 21, No. 1. (Feb., 1955), pp. 1-19.

Stevens, P. (2003) "Resource Impact: Curse or Blessing? A Literature Survey," *Journal of Energy Literature*, 9 (1), pp. 3-42.

Swisterski, Pawel (2002) "A Constant Market Share Analysis of OECD Export Performance, 1972-1992," University of Calgary, Department of Economics, MA Thesis.

Torvik, R. (2001) "Learning by Doing and the Dutch Disease," *European Economic Review*, 45, pp. 285-306.

Tyszynski, H., (1951) "World Trade in Manufactured Commodities, 1899-1950", The Manchester School, XIX, 272-304, September.

Urquhart, M.C. (1993) *Gross National Product, Canada 1870-1926: The Derivation of the Estimates.* (Kingston and Montreal: McGill-Queens Press).

Winham, Gilbert R. and Sylvia Ostry (2003) "The Second Trade Crisis," *The Globe and Mail.* Tuesday, June 17, 2003.

Viner, Jacob (1958) <u>Canada and Its Giant Neighbour</u>. Alan B. Plaunt Memorial Lectures, Carleton University, Ottawa. 30 January and 1 February 1958. (Copyright 1958, Carleton University).

APPENDIX: Constant Market Share Analysis (CMS)

In its most general form, the CMS model measures a country's total export growth relative to total global export growth:

1) $\quad V^2 - V^1 = rV^1 + (V^2 - V^1 - rV^1)$

Where: V^2 = Value of the country's total exports in period 2

$\quad\quad V^1$ = Value of the country's total exports in period 1

$\quad\quad r \quad$ = percent increase in total world exports between periods 1 and 2.

The last term in equation 1, "$(V^2-V^1-rV^1)$" captures the difference between the growth of exports due to the world's growth of exports (rV^1), and actual growth of a country's exports (V^2-V^1). This residual term is identified as the "competitiveness effect."

A more detailed CMS model can be expressed as follows:

2) $\quad V^2_{ij} - V^1_{ij} = r_{ij}V^1_{ij} + (V^2_{ij} - V^1_{ij} - r_{ij}V^1_{ij})$

Where V^2_{ij} = Value of the country's exports of commodity "i" to region "j" in period 2

$\quad\quad r_{ij} \quad$ = percent increase in world exports of commodity "i" to region "j" between periods 1 and 2

Aggregating equation 2) over all exports and destinations yields:

3) $\quad V^2.. - V^1.. = \Sigma_i\Sigma_j r_{ij}V^1_{ij} + \Sigma_i\Sigma_j(V^2_{ij} - V^1_{ij} - r_{ij}V^1_{ij})$

Where $V^1.., V^2..$ = Total value of the country's exports in periods 1 and 2 respectively.

In turn, equation 3) can be re-written:

4) $\quad V^2.. - V^1.. = rV^1.. + \Sigma_i(r_i - r)V^1_i. + \Sigma_i\Sigma_j(r_{ij} - r_i)V^1_{ij} + \Sigma_i\Sigma_j(V^2_{ij} - V^1_{ij} - r_{ij}V^1_{ij})$

$\quad\quad\quad\quad$ (a) $\quad\quad\quad$ (b) $\quad\quad\quad\quad$ (c) $\quad\quad\quad$ (d)

Where r_i = percent increase in world exports of commodity "i" between periods 1 and 2

$\quad\quad V^1_i.$ = Value of the country's exports of commodity "i" in period 1

As Leamer and Stern (1970) point out, the difference between equation 1) and 4) is the "level" of analysis. Equation 1 explains the change in a country's value of exports only in terms of change in world demand (i.e. general growth of world exports), and the competitiveness residual. Equation 4 decomposes the growth in the country's exports in terms of: (a) the growth of the world exports; (b) the composition of the country's exports; (c) export destination; and (d) the competitiveness residual.

The "competitiveness residual" shows the difference between a country's actual export growth rate and the export growth rate it would have achieved had it maintained its market share of exports of each commodity group to each region. The competitiveness residual reveals how a country is able to compete with other exporters, controlling for the structural effects (commodity and destination factors).

NAFTA Rules of Origin

Robert (Bob) Kunimoto
Policy Research Initiative
&
Gary Sawchuk
Policy Research Initiative

Introduction[1]

Over the last several years, increased public attention has focused on the potential for deeper North American integration. Discussions prior to 2001 had already demonstrated growing support for further facilitating the cross-border movement of goods and people given that Canada – U.S. trade had reached the point where traditional approaches to border administration and border management had become increasingly problematic. Moreover, the post September 11th environment has elicited growing Canadian interest towards rethinking the Canada-U.S economic relationship and NAFTA in the larger context of an overall security perimeter that would protect and ensure our economic security, our border security and U.S. homeland security.

Much of the attention deals with the feasibility and desirability of a Canada-U.S. customs union, a perimeter approach and various NAFTA plus proposals. Proponents of a Canada-U.S customs union often stress the administrative and compliance cost savings and efficiency gains that would be associated with the elimination of rules of origin, regulatory differences and other barriers to trade and the difficulties arising from the application of trade remedies. NAFTA rules of origin (ROO), government procurement restrictions, anti-dumping procedures, intrusive countervailing duty investigations, burdensome regulatory requirements, and other restrictive trade measures, discourage cross-border investment decisions, reduce Canada-U.S. trade flows, and reduce the potential benefits accruing to Canada and the United States as members of a preferential trade agreement.

The purpose of this study is to examine and assess the key issues and evidence associated with the growing concern related to the restrictive nature of NAFTA ROO. In particular this paper attempts to shed empirical light on the degree to which NAFTA ROO impose significant compliance costs on traders, restricts the use of NAFTA, and reduces the potential benefits from NAFTA.[2]

---

[1] The authors wish to thank André Downs and Jean-Pierre Voyer of the Policy Research Initiative (PRI) for their helpful comments and direction, David Dodds (Statistics Canada) and his staff for assistance with the Canadian data, the United States International Trade Commission for the US data, Antoni Estevadeordal (IADB) for the restrictiveness index data, and to the participants of the PRI/SSHRC Policy Research Roundtable "Moving Toward a Customs Union" for their insights and suggestions.

[2] This paper is part of a larger research project on *Moving Toward a Customs Union* involving research partners from the Canadian Border Services Agency, Industry Canada, Foreign Affairs and International Trade Canada, Statistics Canada, the Department of Finance Canada and the Policy Research Initiative.

Are NAFTA ROO Necessary?

Under NAFTA, as under other free trade agreements, each member country retains their respective external tariffs and other import restrictions against non-members while lowering or eliminating tariffs on goods "originating" from other member countries. All trade under NAFTA is supported by an extensive system of ROO.

ROO are the criteria used to define where a product "originates". There are two classes of ROO: non-preferential and preferential. Non-preferential ROO are used to distinguish foreign from domestic products in establishing anti-dumping and countervailing duties, safeguard measures, origin marking requirements and/or discriminatory quantitative restrictions or quotas.[3] Preferential ROO define the conditions under which the importing country will regard a product as originating in an exporting country that receives preferential treatment under a free trade agreement (FTA). They are used to prevent imports from non-member countries from taking advantage of the concessions that have been made by member countries of the free trade agreement.

In the absence of preferential ROO, imports to the free trade region would come through the country with the lowest external tariff and, in theory, serve the entire free trade region. This would force a convergence of external tariffs and possibly a competitive decline of external tariffs. In essence, ROO are thus a means to operate the FTA and operate independent external trade policy.

Preferential ROO provide the method for customs officials to determine which goods are entitled to preferential tariff treatment. Preferential ROO are a necessary and integral part of any free trade agreement.

What Are NAFTA ROO?

Under NAFTA, a good is considered to be an **originating good** and is entitled to preferential tariff treatment; if it meets one of the five requirements set out in the NAFTA ROO:[4]

1. the good is **wholly obtained or produced** in a NAFTA country (including those goods that are entirely grown, fished, or mined in a member country - it does **not** include goods purchased in a NAFTA country that were imported from a non-NAFTA country);
2. the good is made up entirely of **components and materials** that qualify in their own right as goods that originate in a NAFTA country;
3. the good meets the requirements of a **specific rule of origin** for that product, as listed in NAFTA Annex 401.[5] With respect to Canadian

---

[3] The WTO agreement on ROO aims at harmonizing non-preferential rules of origin so that all WTO members apply the same criteria, ensuring that these rules do not themselves create unnecessary obstacles to trade. The agreement sets out a work programme for the harmonization of these rules to be undertaken by the WTO in conjunction with the World Customs Organization (WCO).

[4] Canada Customs and Revenue Agency (1995), Information for Importers, Exporters or Producers. CCRA document C-144.

[5] For this requirement each of the non-originating materials used in the production of the good undergoes an applicable change in tariff classification set out in Annex 401 as a result

276

imports, this normally applies when goods are produced from material imported from countries other than the United States or Mexico;

4. the good qualifies under NAFTA **Article 401(d)**,[6] which only applies to a few cases; or

5. the good is automatic data processing equipment or parts qualifying under the provisions of Annex 308.1.

Of these five requirements, the most commonly used is the ***specific rule of origin***, which applies to a good that includes any non-originating materials in its production. These specific ROO are based on the substantial transformation criteria. There are at least three methods that are used in the NAFTA agreement to determine whether there has been sufficient transformation to warrant preferential tariff treatment of the good:

- a change in tariff classification (CTC) requiring the product to change its tariff classification at the item, sub-heading, heading or chapter level under the Harmonized Commodity Description and Coding System[7] (Harmonized System or HS) in the originating country[8];

- a domestic or regional value content (RVC) rule requiring a minimum percentage of local value added in the originating country (or setting the maximum percentage of value originating in non-member countries); or

- a technical requirement prescribing that the product must undergo specific manufacturing processing operations in the originating country.

The first step to understanding the NAFTA Annex 401 specific rules of origin is to understand the Harmonized System. The HS uses a 6-digit number to identify basic commodities or sub-headings. The HS is organized around 96 chapters arranged in 21 sections. The first two digits indicates the chapter, the first four digits indicate the heading level while six digits identifies the sub-heading level. Within the HS structure, there are over 1200 headings and over 5000 subheadings.

---

of production occurring entirely in the territory of one or more of the Parties, or the good otherwise satisfies the applicable requirements of that Annex where no change in tariff classification is required, and the good satisfies all other applicable requirements of this chapter.

[6]Article 401 (d) applies when the good is produced entirely in one or more of the NAFTA countries but one or more of the non-originating materials provided for as parts under the Harmonized System that are used in the production of the good does not undergo a change in tariff classification for either of two particular reasons, and provided the good meets the regional value content criteria as outlined in Article 402.

[7] The Harmonized Commodity Description and Coding System (HS) was developed and is maintained by the World Customs Organization, an independent intergovernmental organization with over 150 member countries based in Brussels, Belgium. Over 170 countries, representing about 98% of world trade, use the HS as a basis for trade negotiations, collecting international trade statistics, quota controls, rules of origin, and statistical and economic research and analysis.

[8] We will use the notation CC to denote a change at the chapter level, CH to indicate a change in heading; CS to represent a change in sub-heading and CI to designate a change in tariff classification at the item level.

Each country is allowed to add additional digits to make their tariff classifications more specific. In Canada, an additional two digits are used for exports and an additional four digits for imports while the United States uses a 10-digit system for imports and exports.

Most of the specific ROO require a certain HS classification change from the non-originating materials to the finished good. The CTC must result from processing in one or more of the NAFTA countries. For example, orange marmalade is classified under heading 20.07 while fresh oranges are 08.05. The specific NAFTA rule of origin for orange marmalade requires a chapter change. If fresh oranges from Brazil are transformed into orange marmalade in the United States, the orange marmalade is an originating good since a change from chapter 08 to chapter 20 has occurred.

Often the CTC has an additional requirement that must be met for a good to qualify for NAFTA status. Usually this additional requirement tests the good's regional value content or adds a technical requirement. RVC rules are used extensively for automotive goods and chemicals, but are quite limited in other product areas.[9] If a rule requires a CTC and a RVC test, the good must meet both of these requirements to qualify as an originating good.

Moreover, in some preferential trade agreements, a choice of origin test is offered for some tariff items. In NAFTA and other agreements based on NAFTA, one test is commonly based on a CTC rule alone, while a second test, for the same tariff items, may involve a CTC rule at a lower level together with a technical test and/or RVC requirement. About 34 per cent of all tariff line items at the 6-digit level in NAFTA specify a RVC requirement as part of the first or second test.

According to the WTO (2002) survey of ROO, the average threshold on domestic content or RVC varies from 40-60% using any method of calculation. The NAFTA RVC threshold is 60% if calculated by the transaction value method or 50% if calculated by the net cost method.[10]

NAFTA introduced a highly disaggregated system of ROO with specific rules at the product level (generally using a HS 6 level of disaggregation). Those specific rules were adopted to close loopholes that might allow third country-producers to benefit from NAFTA status by performing assembly, processing or minimal production operations in the territory of one of the parties (Carrére and de Melo (2004)).

---

[9] RVC may be calculated using one of two methods: transaction value or net cost. Usually, the exporter or producer can choose between either method. However, there are a number of situations where the exporter or producer cannot use the transaction value method. The producer can also revert to the net cost method if using the transaction value method is unfavourable

[10] The net cost method calculates RVC as a percentage of the net cost to produce the good while the transaction value method calculates the value of the non-originating materials as a percentage of the GATT transaction value of the good. Because the transaction value method permits the producer to count all of its costs and profit as originating, the required percentage of RVC under this method is higher than under the net cost method.

NAFTA Certificate of Origin and Verification

The three NAFTA members adopted a uniform certificate of origin to certify that goods imported into NAFTA territories qualify for the preferential tariff treatment accorded by NAFTA. NAFTA relies on the process of self-certification where the certificate of origin must be completed and signed by the producer or exporter of the goods. When the exporter is not the producer, the exporter can complete the certificate on the basis of knowledge that the good originates, reasonable reliance on the producer's written representation that the good originates, or a completed and signed certificate of origin for the good voluntarily provided to the exporter by the producer.

Only importers who possess a valid certificate of origin can claim preferential tariff treatment. A certificate of origin can cover a single importation of goods or multiple importations of identical goods. Certificates that cover multiple shipments are called blanket certificates, and can apply to goods imported within any 12-month period specified on the certificate.

The certificate of origin is only one of the several documents required by importers of goods seeking preferential tariff treatment under NAFTA. Importers must maintain records pertaining to the importation for at least five years, or any longer period that may be specified by their country. Exporters or producers that provide a certificate of origin must maintain records pertaining to the exportation for five years.

Under NAFTA, the importing country's customs administration can conduct verifications with the exporter or producer to confirm whether goods qualify as originating as certified by the certificate of origin. Verifications are principally conducted by written questionnaires and verification visits. Additional verification can be done by telephone, facsimile, and information from the supplier as well as on-site audits. Since imports claiming NAFTA status can be subject to post-entry audits while imports from NAFTA members using the most favoured nation (MFN) tariff are not subject to this process, there is a tendency for importers to take more care in meeting NAFTA requirements.[11] Therefore, we would expect to observe higher NAFTA compliance rates. However, discussions with importers/exporters revealed that some might use MFN status rather than NAFTA in order to avoid the possibility of post-entry verification, and in particular verification visits. Therefore, the higher costs associated with the use of NAFTA and the greater the possibility of post-entry audit, the lower NAFTA utilization rates.

Are NAFTA ROO Costly?

ROO impose administrative and compliance costs on parties involved in international transactions. Administrative costs refer to the costs incurred by governments in implementing, administering, and monitoring the system of ROO while compliance costs refer to the financial costs incurred by importers, exporters or producers to meet the ROO requirements to qualify for preferential treatment.

Compliance costs can be thought of as the cost of "paperwork" or "red tape" associated with filling out forms in order to satisfy Customs requirements

---

[11] Officials from Canadian Border Services pointed this out to the authors.

and the cost to business associated with determining, meeting and proving origin (Australia Productivity Commission, 2004a). This could also include the office systems and computer programs for meeting and proving origin and the cost of maintaining records. These compliance costs are distinct from the economic costs associated with ROO such as the costs associated with changing production methods or input mixes and changing input sourcing to meet origin requirements. The economic effects of NAFTA ROO are examined in section 6.

Earlier estimates of the compliance and administrative costs associated with ROO were often based on pre-computer technology procedures and may overestimate current NAFTA transaction costs. Koskinen (1983) estimated the compliance costs for Finnish exporters under the European Community (EC) – EFTA FTA at 1.4 to 5.7 % of the value of export transactions. Herin (1986) estimated the compliance cost to meet the ROO within EFTA at 3 to 5 % of the price of the good. Those estimates are based on a paper intensive system. Holmes and Shepard (1983) found the average export transaction from EFTA to the EC required 35 documents and 360 copies.

In the NAFTA case, the empirical evidence on the administrative and compliance costs is very limited. Krueger (1997) reported, "Canadian producers have on occasion chosen to pay the relevant duties rather than incur the cost of proving origin". Recent discussions with Canadian exporters and importers revealed that for small shipments and exporters with limited knowledge of NAFTA and small-sized firms are likely to pay MFN duties rather than incur the additional expense of meeting the NAFTA requirements. In addition, firms who could not get sufficient numbers of certificates of origin from their suppliers chose MFN and paid duty rather than claiming NAFTA status.

Two recent studies, Cadot et. al. (2002) and Carrère and de Melo (2004), employ an indirect approach similar to Herin (1986) to estimate the compliance cost of NAFTA rule. Both of these studies utilize a revealed preference approach and both studies provide only an approximation of the compliance cost of NAFTA ROO for imports into the United States from Mexico.

The authors assume that the compliance cost to import the ith good, c_i, is:

$$c_i = \delta_i + \sigma_i \qquad (1)$$

where δ_i is the NAFTA compliance component and σ_i is the non-ROO costs.[12]

If NAFTA utilization rates U_i are 100% for the ith good, then the NAFTA tariff preference is revealed larger than the compliance costs and the preference margin can be used as an upper bound for the compliance costs. For items with U_i = 0%, the preference margin is revealed smaller that the cost of the compliance costs and provides a lower-bound estimate.

Where NAFTA utilization rates are $0 < U_i < 100\%$, Cadot et. al. (2002) and Carrère and de Melo (2004) assumed the firms were revealed indifferent

---

[12] Cadot et. al. (2002) and Carrère and de Melo (2004) use the terminology administrative and distortionary cost as components of trade compliance cost. We follow the Australian Productivity Commission (2004a, b) use of terminology.

between shipping under NAFTA or MFN. This would imply that the expected cost of using NAFTA and the MFN are the same. Therefore, given revealed indifference between the MFN rate and cost of using NAFTA, the authors use the MFN rate or the difference between the MFN and NAFTA rate as a proxy for the costs associated with the use of NAFTA.[13] This provides an estimate of the average NAFTA compliance costs.

The authors assumed that NAFTA compliance component is negligible when U_i is close to 100% and NAFTA ROO is not restrictive, $r_i \leq 2$. The tariff preference when U_i is close to 100% and $r_i \leq 2$ would provide an estimate of the non-ROO administrative costs, σ_i.

Employing this revealed preference approach, Cadot et. al. (2002) calculated the cost of compliance and other NAFTA related administrative procedures for imports in 2000 from Mexico into the United States at 5.06% of the value of Mexican exports. When non-ROO administrative costs, estimated at 3.12%, are subtracted from the preceding estimates, the authors find that the compliance costs of NAFTA ROO to the private sector for exports from Mexico into the United States at 1.94% of value of Mexican exports.

Carrère and de Melo (2004), using 2001 data on Mexican exports to the United States, arrives at an average compliance cost estimate of 1.72% of the value of exports based on a total estimated cost of 6.16%.[14]

Following Cadot et. al. (2002) and Carrère and de Melo (2004) we employ this non-parametric indirect approach based on revealed preferences to approximate the upper bounds on the compliance cost of NAFTA ROO using HS 6 digit data on imports into the United States from Canada for 2003.

Where NAFTA utilization rates are $0 < U_i < 100\%$, we find the trade compliance costs to be 5.37% of the price for Canadian goods imported into the United States. Examining cases where $95\% \leq U_i < 100\%\%$ and $r \leq 2$ we find the non-ROO costs associated with importation to be approximately 4.32%.[15] Subtracting the non-ROO costs from the trade compliance costs provides an estimate of 1.05% for the NAFTA ROO compliance costs. This is significantly lower than estimates from the Mexican data and might be due to the wider use of information and communication technologies, the greater maturity of Canadian and American firms, and the Canada – U.S. FTA experience by firms engaged in trade on the northern border compared to their Mexican counterparts.

It should be noted that these estimates need to be viewed with caution since they provide only an upper-bound proxy for the compliance cost of ROO. The question remains how much this upper bound might deviate from the true cost of NAFTA ROO or a statistically unbiased estimate.

---

[13] This applies to individual importers where the NAFTA tariff rate is zero. For 2002 data, almost 100% of NAFTA rates were duty free.

[14] Carrère and de Melo (2004) follow Cadot et. al. (2002) using the term "administrative costs" to the firm to refer to compliance costs.

[15] There are 68 observations meeting the requirement that $95\% \leq u < 100$ and $r \leq 2$. We eliminate one observation since this outlier has an abnormally high effective tariff rate and is not representative of the trade cost within this group. With all 68 observations the compliance costs are estimated at .83% of the price of U.S. imports from Canada.

Table 1: Non-Parametric NAFTA Compliance Cost Estimates

Study	Imports to U.S from	NAFTA ROO compliance cost
Cadot et. al.(2002)	Mexico	1.94
Carrère and de Melo (2004)	Mexico	1.72
This study	Canada	1.05

Are NAFTA ROO Too Restrictive?

As an integral component of a free trade agreement, ROO are intended to ensure that the benefits from an FTA accrue to its members. However, a particular ROO system can be liberal, promoting the flow of intra-bloc trade, or restrictive,[16] acting as a non-tariff barrier to trade within the preferential trade region.

Estevadeordal (2000) developed a categorical index on the restrictiveness of a given type of ROO ranging from 1 (least restrictive) to 7 (most restrictive). The index is based on two assumptions:

1. a required CTC at the level of chapter is more restrictive than a CTC at the level of heading, and a CTC at the level of heading is more restrictive than a CTC at the level of sub-heading, and so on; and
2. regional value content and technical requirement criteria attached to a given change in tariff classification add to the level of restrictiveness of the specific ROO.

Estevadeordal (2000) constructed the categorical variable, r, assigning to each HS 8-digit category an ordered numerical value according to the observation rules in Table 1.[17]

Table 2: ROO Restrictiveness Index Criteria

r = 1	If a change at the item level is required
r = 2	If a change at the subheading level is required
r = 3	If a change at the subheading level plus an additional requirement is specified
r = 4	If a change at the heading level is required
r = 5	If a change at the heading level plus an additional requirement is specified
r = 6	If a change at the chapter level is required
r = 7	If a change at the chapter level plus an additional requirement is specified

---

[16] ROO can be restrictive in terms of the difficulty to meet the ROO criteria or restrictive in their effects on trade or utilization of the preferential trade agreement.

[17] This table is a simplification of the table found in Estevadeordal and Suominen (2004b).

The index can be aggregated to the chapter, section or agreement level. Examining NAFTA exports from Canada to the United States, approximately 45% of all tariff lines (HS 8 digit) required a change in classification at the chapter level or more. Correspondingly, the majority of all tariff lines (51%) were represented by an index of 5 or higher while 11.4% of all tariff lines have an index of 3 or less (see Figure 1).[18] Almost 75% of all NAFTA tariff lines applied to Canadian exports to the United States required a change in tariff classification at the heading level (r=4) or at the chapter level (r=6).

Figure 1: NAFTA ROO Restrictiveness Index and Tariff Lines for Canadian Exports to the U.S. (2003)

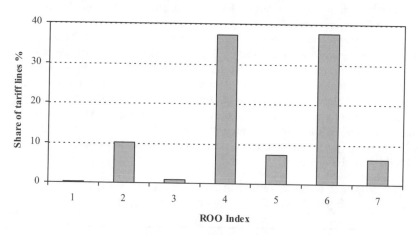

Source: USITC data for 2003 and Estevadeordal (2000) index.

Estevadeordal (2000) found that compared to other FTAs, NAFTA ROO are very restrictive with an average restrictiveness index of 5.1 compared to the pan-European ROO rated at 4.5, the EFTA-Mexico[19] ROO rated at 4.2 and the non-preferential ROO average at 3.9. NAFTA ROO are stringent due to the predominant use of the change in chapter criterion.

The Australian Productivity Commission (2004a, b) extended the ROO restrictiveness index to include 11 restrictiveness categories and normalized the index to a scale from 0 to 1 (see Figure 2). Since this methodology features a weighted sum over the 11 categories, it is particularly well suited for inter-preferential trade agreement (PTA) comparisons of ROO restrictiveness.

Compared to the ROO restrictiveness level associated with other preferential trade agreements (PTA), NAFTA ROO are the most restrictive in the sample of 18 PTAs. In addition, a comparison of the restrictiveness of NAFTA

---

[18] We have updated the Estevadeordal index at the 6-digit level to incorporate the changes made to NAFTA ROO up until January 2003.

[19] European Free Trade Association (EFTA) is comprised of Iceland, Liechtenstein, Norway and Switzerland.

283

ROO to the four other U.S. FTAs (U.S.- Israel, U.S.-Singapore, U.S.-Jordan and U.S.-Chile) indicates that NAFTA ROO are the most restrictive.

Why are NAFTA ROO so restrictive? ROO can be used as a means of industrial policy; it is this factor that often leads to differences in restrictiveness between sectors and specific ROO for selected products. In this regard, ROO raises a larger question about the possible role of industrial policy, with the trade-off being between less strict ROO and hence more intra-NAFTA trade versus stricter ROO that potentially protects domestic sectors. Restrictive ROO can be viewed as a new form of hidden protectionism acting as a substitute for inter-FTA tariff barriers that were eliminated and as tool of industrial policy.[20] This appears to be the core of the problem with respect to restrictive ROO where some free trade agreements have in effect negotiated industrial policy into their free trade agreements by using more restrictive ROO in specific sectors and for specific products as substitutes for tariffs.

In many agreements, special treatment or more restrictive ROO are found in sensitive sectors such as textiles and clothing, the automotive sector, agriculture and some electronics industries. A sectoral examination of NAFTA ROO by Estevadeordal and Miller (2002) documents "missed preferences"—i.e., utilization rates below 100 percent—between the United States and Canada, which they attribute to the tightening of the ROO under NAFTA in 1994. Estevadeordal and Miller demonstrated that agriculture, textiles and apparel, transportation equipment and automobiles sectors implemented stricter ROO with NAFTA compared to the FTA.

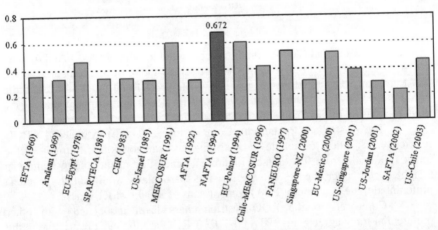

Figure 2: Restrictiveness Index for Preferential ROO
0 (least restrictive) to 1 (most restrictive)

Source: Australian Productivity Commission (2004a, b)

For the automobile sector, NAFTA introduced stricter ROO compared to earlier trade agreements. While under the Auto Pact and the former Canada-U.S. FTA, duty-free trade between participants was contingent on a 50% Canadian or

---

[20] See Estevadeordal, Antoni and Kati Suominen (2004a).

284

U.S. content; the threshold increased to 56% on January 1, 1998 and to 62.5% on January 1, 2002 for passenger cars, light trucks, small buses (transport of 15 or fewer persons), their engines and transmissions. The corresponding level for heavy-duty vehicles, large buses and all other parts is 60% since January 1, 2002. Companies operating in Canada are required to meet these increased regional value content levels plus in most cases in the automobile sector a change in tariff classification at the heading level in order to export to Mexico and the United States at the NAFTA rates.

For textiles and apparel, the origin criterion requires that most of the production occurs in North America. The production of most textile and apparel goods is a four-step process:

- Fibres, hair, wool and other raw materials are gathered or harvested.
- Fibres are spun to make a yarn.
- The yarn is woven into a fabric.
- The fabric is cut and sewn (or assembled) into a garment.

The basic origin rules for textile and apparel are "yarn forward" and "fiber forward". This means that the yarn or fiber, whichever applies, used to form the fabric must originate in a NAFTA country. Put differently, apparel products imported into the United States must satisfy a "triple transformation" rule requiring domestic content of each one of three transformations stages: fiber to yarn, yarn to fabric, and fabric to garment.[21]

According to the WTO (2002), the NAFTA ROO might have increased trade diversion in favour of NAFTA partners, notably in the clothing sector (the yarn forward rule) and the motor vehicle component sector. They may have also penalized Canadian clothing manufacturers using inputs from MFN sources and contributed to the lack of international competitiveness of the North American textiles and clothing industries.

An alternative way of examining the coverage of the ROO index is to examine the relationship between the index and the share of imports as shown in Figure 3. In 2003, 67.7% of U.S. imports from Canada under NAFTA were covered by a restrictiveness index of 5 or more. In addition, 25% of U.S. imports from Canada under NAFTA required a change at the chapter level (r= 6) or higher. This compares with only 57.9% of Canadian NAFTA imports from the United States being covered by an index of 5 or more, while about 19% of NAFTA imports into Canada from the U.S. required a change of tariff classification at the chapter level (r=6 or 7) or higher.

This suggests that even though Canada and the United States face the same set of NAFTA ROO, the composition of trade results in imports into the United States from Canada experiencing more stringent NAFTA ROO than imports into Canada from the United States.

---

[21] Cadot et. al. (2002) "Assessing the Effects of NAFTA Rules of Origin"

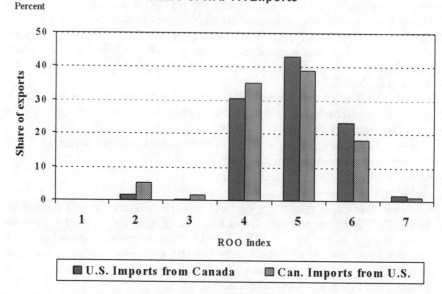

Figure 3: NAFTA's ROO Restrictiveness Index and Share of NAFTA Exports

Percent

Share of exports (y-axis), ROO Index (x-axis)

■ U.S. Imports from Canada   ▨ Can. Imports from U.S.

Source: Compilations based on Statistics Canada and USITC 2003 data

Restrictive and costly NAFTA ROO creates an incentive to use the MFN tariff rates rather than NAFTA in order to avoid the ROO compliance costs associated with the latter. As such, restrictive ROO result in reducing the NAFTA utilization rates and reducing the benefits resulting from the free trade agreement.

When importers of NAFTA goods into the United States have the choice of paying a higher MFN tariff or using the lower NAFTA rate (positive tariff preferences) but incur the costs of the NAFTA ROO, the importers will have a preference to choose the least-cost method of importation. Without any additional transaction costs, when NAFTA and MFN rates are the same (i.e. no positive tariff preference), importers will choose to use the MFN rate since it does not involve the NAFTA ROO related costs and avoids the possibility of origin verification.[22] Hence, all else remaining equal, as MFN rates fall due to multilateral trade liberalization, we should observe fewer importers using NAFTA and more using MFN on bilateral trade between Canada and the United States.

It is interesting to note that there appears to be a common misconception among the public that most intra-North American trade occurs using NAFTA. In 2002, 54% of total U.S. imports from Canada entered under the NAFTA regime and 45% entered at MFN rates.[23] Similarly, approximately 50% of imports to Canada from the United States entered under NAFTA while 62% of imports into

---

[22] By choosing MFN, however, the importer must incur the Merchandise Processing Fee.
[23] WTO (2004) indicates the remaining 1% fell under a variety of programs such as civil aviation and pharmaceuticals

286

the United States from Mexico used the NAFTA regime and 37% at MFN rates for 2002. The intra-North America trade outside of the NAFTA regime may reflect exporters taking advantage of the prevailing zero or low MFN rates since the NAFTA margin of preference is not sufficiently attractive to offset the cost of complying with ROO requirements.

Are There Sectional Differences in NAFTA Utilization?

Examining NAFTA utilization rates by sector for Canadian exports into the United States reveals large inter-sectional differences (see Table 3). Canada has high utilization rates for fats and oils (98%), textiles and apparels (95%), plastics (94%) and transportation equipment (85%). However, Canadian exporters have extremely low NAFTA utilization rates for jewellery (14%), wood products (17%), pulp and paper (19%), arms and ammunitions (22%) and chemicals (26%).

These sectional differences may be a reflection of the restrictiveness associated with the specific ROO, the inter-sectional differences in the MFN tariff rates versus the NAFTA rate, the difference in the ability to qualify for NAFTA status and/or the degree of trade friction found within the sector. Carrère and de Melo (2004), using an econometric approach, find for Mexican exports into the United States that the NAFTA utilization rates are positively influenced by the tariff preference margins. Moreover, Carrère and de Melo find that additional technical requirements, regional value content and the change in tariff classification at the chapter level are an impediment to NAFTA utilization.

In a later section of this paper, we report the findings of our econometric work, which takes advantage of section, chapter and sub-heading trade data. Our results based on U.S. imports from Canada data confirm the Carrère and de Melo (2004) findings, which focused on U.S. imports from Mexico.

Are There Differences in Canadian and U.S. NAFTA Utilization?

Do Canada and the United States differ in their pattern of use of NAFTA? Importers into the United States should have a greater tendency to use NAFTA compared to importers into Canada due to a fee that is charged on imports into the United States using MFN/NTR[24] that is not charged when using NAFTA. The merchandise processing fee (MPF) is a fee collected by the U.S. Bureau of Customs and Border Protection on most goods imported into the United States that do not qualify for any special programs such as NAFTA. This non-refundable fee charged by U.S. Customs for administrative expenses for processing an imported shipment requiring formal entry is accessed at 0.21% of the value subject to a $25.00 minimum and a $485.00 maximum. However, shipments valued at less than $2,000.00 are assessed a $2.00 fee. There is no comparable fee for imports into Canada.

---

[24] The United States adopted the term Normal Trade Relations (NTR) status replacing Most Favoured-Nation (MFN) status in 1998. We use the term MFN/NTR.

287

Table 3: NAFTA Utilization Rates and Restrictiveness Index Imports from Canada into the U.S.

	NAFTA Utilization Rate[1]	Estevadeordal Restrictiveness Index[2]
1. Live Animals, Animal Products	33	6.0
2. Vegetable Products	72	6.0
3. Fats and Oils	98	5.9
4. Prepared Food, Beverages, Tobacco	64	5.7
5. Mineral Products	45	5.6
6. Chemicals	26	3.1
7. Plastics	93	4.8
8. Leather Goods	57	5.6
9. Wood Products	19	4.1
10. Pulp and Paper	26	5.4
11. Textiles and Apparel	94	6.0
12. Footwear, Headgear, etc	72	4.8
13. Article of Stone, Plastic, Glass, etc	58	5.1
14. Jewellery	14	5.3
15. Base Metals	62	4.8
16. Machinery, Electrical Equipment	41	3.8
17. Vehicles,Transport Equipment, etc	85	4.2
18. Optical, Photographic, etc	40	4.3
19. Arms & Ammunition	22	5.4
20 Miscellaneous	15	5.8
Average	**52**	**5.1**

[1] Authors' calculations based on 2003 USITC data.
[2] Estevadeordal (2000) and updates on the restrictiveness index.

Discussions with large Canadian exporters of goods into the United States indicate that the MPF is one factor taken into consideration when deciding between using NAFTA preferences and MFN rates. It is viewed as a major irritant to Canadian shippers but makes using NAFTA status marginally more appealing.

A preliminary comparison between Canadian and U.S. NAFTA utilization rates for bilateral trade (see Table 4) reveals that, based on the sections average, imports from the United States into Canada use NAFTA preferences about 48% of the time compared to 52% for imports from Canada into the United States. More striking are the large inter-country differences for NAFTA utilization rates between Canada and the United States at the section level. Out of the twenty sections compared, six sections reflect an inter-country difference in NAFTA utilization rates of less than 10 percentage points, six sections with an inter-country difference between 10 and 20 points and eight sections with an inter-country difference in NAFTA utilization rates of greater than 20.

To date, these large inter-country differences within sections have not been explained. We speculate that inter-country differences in MFN rates, trade patterns within sections, and trade policy differences may be partly responsible for these differences.

Using overall NAFTA utilization[25] rates reveals that 57% of all imports into the United States from Canada used NAFTA status while only 44% of all imports into Canada from the United States used NAFTA. Given the relative size of the Canadian market, Canadian producers and manufacturers tend to be more export orientated with a particular focus on the United States. More importantly, a small number of large firms account for a major share of Canada's exports to the United States. According to Sulzenko (2003), in 2001 the top five exporters accounted for almost half, and the largest 2,000 firms accounted for over 80 percent of Canada's exports to the United States. With the paramount importance of the United States as Canada's principal export market and the concentration of firms who export to the U.S. market, Canadian producers and exporters tend to be more focused on meeting NAFTA ROO requirements in production and manufacturing and, as a matter of course, provide the necessary certificates of origin to U.S. importers. This is reflected in the higher NAFTA utilization rates.

Has the Pattern of NAFTA and MFN Imports Changed?

The growth in U.S. imports from Canada under both the NAFTA[26] and MFN programs during the period 1990-2003 is illustrated in Figure 4. This period was witness to considerable trade liberalization, including the implementation of the Canada-U.S. FTA, NAFTA, and the general downward drift of MFN tariffs as a result of multilateral initiatives. However, there are two distinct sub-periods over this 14-year span. The period from 1990 to 1999 witnessed spectacular growth in U.S. imports from Canada under NAFTA; rising over 300% from $29 billion to $127 billion (constant 2000 U.S. dollars). NAFTA imports from Canada to the United States levelled off and remained relatively stable at $180 billion (constant 2000 U.S. dollars) over the period 2000 to 2003. MFN imports also increased but at a somewhat slower pace until 1997 at which time they grew more quickly than NAFTA imports until 2000. By 2000, however, MFN imports into the United States from Canada levelled off. Since the mid-1990s most U.S. imports from Canada has taken place under NAFTA. But by 2003, the difference between NAFTA and MFN imports amounted to only some US$ 14 billion on total imports of some US$ 226 billion.

---

[25] The NAFTA utilization rate base on the average of section rates, the most common rate reported, provides a biased estimate of the actual NAFTA utilization rate when compared to the overall NAFTA utilization rate based on HS 6 data. The former is calculated as the average of the 20 or 21 sections utilization rates while the overall NAFTA utilization, for example for imports into Canada from the United States, is calculated as the total value of imports using NAFTA status from the United States divided by total value of imports into Canada from the United States. The overall utilization rate can be viewed as a trade weighted measure of utilization.

[26] In this section, we will use 'NAFTA' when referring to either the NAFTA or its predecessor, the Canada-U.S. FTA.

Table 4: NAFTA Utilization Rates by Sectors for Canada – United States Trade, 2003

	U.S. Imports from Canada[1]	Canadian Imports from U.S.[2]	Inter-Country Difference
1. Live Animals, Animal Products	33	50	-16
2. Vegetable Products	72	21	51
3. Fats and Oils	98	93	5
4. Prepared Food, Beverages, Tobacco	64	81	-16
5. Mineral Products	45	24	21
6. Chemicals	26	53	-27
7. Plastics	93	82	11
8. Leather Goods	57	37	21
9. Wood Products	19	30	-11
10. Pulp and Paper	26	28	-2
11. Textiles and Apparel	94	84	10
12. Footwear, Headgear, etc	72	71	0
13. Article of Stone, Plastic, Glass, etc	58	43	15
14. Jewellery	14	17	-3
15. Base Metals	62	49	14
16. Machinery, Electrical Equipment	41	23	18
17. Vehicles, Transport Equipment, etc	85	55	30
18. Optical, Photographic, etc	40	16	25
19. Arms & Ammunition	22	52	-29
20 Miscellaneous	15	55	-40
Average utilization rate based on sections	52	48	6
Overall utilization rate:[3] aggregate	57	44	13

[1] Authors' calculations based on 2003 USITC data
[2] Authors' calculations based on 2003 Statistics Canada data
[3] Overall utilization rate does not include section 21

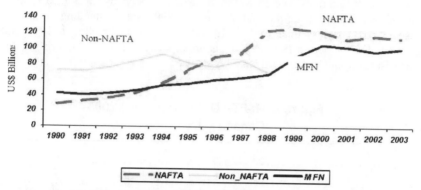

Figure 4: U.S. Imports from Canada By NAFTA and MFN

Source: Authors' calculations based on USITC data in 2000 US constant dollars.

Disaggregating NAFTA imports into dutiable and duty-free imports, we observe that the spectacular rise in NAFTA imports till 1997 was due to the growth in the duty-free component (see Figure 5). Although the NAFTA duty-free component was initially the smaller of the two components, the duty-free component has risen quickly so that by 1997 NAFTA imports were almost exclusively duty-free. This pattern of NAFTA duty-free imports is a reflection of the phase-in of FTA and NAFTA tariff reductions between Canada and the United States.

Figure 5: U.S. NAFTA Imports from Canada (Dutiable and Duty Free)

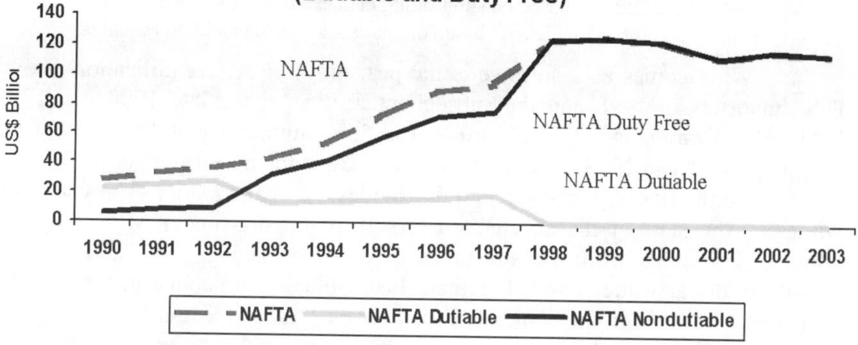

Source: Authors' calculations based on USITC data in 2000 US constant dollars

291

An alternative way to examine the growth in the use of NAFTA is to focus on utilization rates. The growth in the use of NAFTA by Canadian exporters to the United States during the first half of the 1990s was outstanding; utilization rates moved from less than 25% in 1989 to approximately 68% in 1998 (see Figure 6). For the period 1998 to 2003, approximately 54% of all imports into the United States from Canada used NAFTA status.

Figure 6: NAFTA Utilization[1] 1989-2003
Canada - U.S.Trade

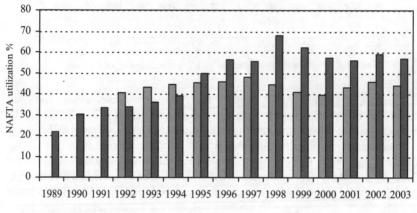

$\boxed{\text{▨ Canadian Imports from U.S.} \quad \text{■ U.S. Imports from Canada}}$

[1] NAFTA utilization based on subheading data excluding section 21.
Source: Authors' calculations based on Statistics Canada and USITC data

What comes as a surprise is the peak in the NAFTA utilization rate by U.S. importers in 1998 and the subsequent decline in the late 1990s. In 1997, NAFTA utilization by U.S. importers was 56%, jumping to 68% in 1998 but declining to 62% in 1999 - averaging around 57% in the post-1998 period.

Comparing Figures 4, 5 and 6 provides a revealing story. The year 1997 witnessed the start of the accelerated growth in imports under MFN duty-free while U.S. imports from Canada under NAFTA peaked in 1997 and declined slightly in dollar value. Taken together, this resulted in a decline in the NAFTA utilization rate. Given the choice between NAFTA duty free and MFN duty free, importers will choose the latter since it costs less to import despite the additional cost of the Merchandise Processing Fee.

The pattern of NAFTA utilization for Canadian imports from the United States reveals a slightly different pattern.[27] The growth in the use of NAFTA was considerably less pronounced for imports into Canada from the United States moving from a 40% utilization rate in 1992 and peaking at a 48% utilization rate

---

[27] We use 1992 to 2003 data only for Canadian imports from the United States provided by Statistics Canada.

in 1997. Post-1997 shows a declining utilization rate to the 44% range in 2001 to 2003. From 1992 to 2003, NAFTA utilization rates for imports into Canada from the United States remained in the 40 to 50% range.

Comparing NAFTA utilization on Canada–U.S. bilateral trade shows that U.S. imports from Canada had a significantly higher NAFTA utilization rate than Canadian imports from the United States. During the period 1997 to 2003, 56% of U.S. imports from Canada used NAFTA status while only 44% of Canadian imports from the United States used NAFTA. NAFTA utilization rates peaked in 1997 on Canada-U.S. bilateral trade and have subsequently declined since then. Overall, Canadian importers of U.S. goods use NAFTA about ten percentage points less than U.S. importers of Canada goods.

Do MFN Rates Influence NAFTA Utilization?

The level of NAFTA utilization has changed over the 1989-2003 time period as tariff rates under both NAFTA and the MFN have fallen. The average overall NAFTA utilization rate rose steadily between 1989 and 1997, declined thereafter until 2000, and has been relatively stable since then. This was illustrated earlier in Figure 6.

In order to gain additional insight into the behaviour of NAFTA imports, we segment the NAFTA import data into situations where tariffs are positive or zero. In particular, we calculate NAFTA utilization rates through time for five cases:

- Overall NAFTA utilization (U)
- MFN tariffs rates are positive (U when MFN>0)
- MFN tariffs rates are zero (U when MFN=0)
- NAFTA tariff rates are positive (U when NAFTA>0)
- NAFTA tariffs rates are zero (U when NAFTA=0)

These NAFTA utilization rates are shown in Figure 7. Several striking features become apparent. First, NAFTA utilization is very high at around 80% when the MFN tariff is positive. Firms attempting to minimize costs will weight

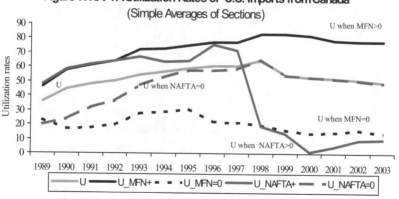

Figure 7: NAFTA Utilization Rates of U.S. Imports from Canada
(Simple Averages of Sections)

Source: Based on USITC data.

293

the cost of NAFTA ROO against the cost of the MFN tariff. The higher the MFN tariff, the more likely firms will use NAFTA. Second, NAFTA utilization rates have been relatively stable but low when the MFN tariff was zero. In this case, NAFTA utilization has been around 15% since the mid 1990s. When both the MFN tariff and NAFTA tariff rate are zero, it costs less to use MFN than NAFTA. Hence firms will import MFN duty free rather than NAFTA duty free since the former does not involve the additional costs associated with NAFTA ROO. Third, FTA utilization for those commodities that had not yet become NAFTA duty free plummeted around 1998. NAFTA utilization fell where NAFTA duty was positive since the number of dutiable NAFTA goods fell rapidly as a result of the final phase in NAFTA duty-free status for Canada–U.S. bilateral trade. Finally, the overall NAFTA utilization rate increased through 1990s peaking during the late 1990s. Since then, NAFTA utilization has fallen to the 50% range where about half of all goods imported into the United States from Canada use NAFTA.

A Disaggregate Look At NAFTA Utilization

We examine the frequency of subheadings and its relationship to NAFTA utilization rates over the 1989-2003 period for U.S. imports from Canada. Our results are illustrated in Figure 8a.

Comparing the two extremes through time, we observe that zero or low NAFTA utilization has increased since 1998 while high or 100% NAFTA utilization has fallen since 1998. Moreover, there has been a "hollowing" out of the middle of NAFTA's utilization range over time (commodities in each of the 10-20 to 80-90 utilization levels). This represents the distribution across subheadings of the declining in the use of NAFTA particularly from 1998 to 2002.

The data for Canadian imports from the United States reveal a different story as shown on Figure 8b. NAFTA utilization rates for Canadian imports is clustered at the upper end while the remainder is distributed relatively uniformly

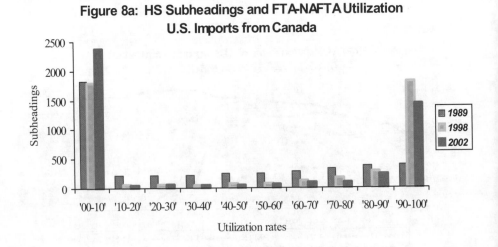

Figure 8a: HS Subheadings and FTA-NAFTA Utilization
U.S. Imports from Canada

Source: Based on USITC data.

294

across the spectrum of utilization. Historically we observe utilization rates declining for those sectors with utilization rates greater than 50% while utilization rates are growing for sectors with less than 50% NAFTA utilization.

We must note that the utilization rates vary among sections and through time. For U.S. imports from Canada, as illustrated in Table 5a, NAFTA utilization rates in some HS sections such as Fats and Oils remained high and stable throughout the time period while others sections such as Vegetables reflected continual growth. The most dramatic growth in NAFTA utilization has been in Transport Equipment, from 4.4% in 1989 to 91.7 in 1998 and 85.0% in 2003. NAFTA utilization for Footwear was high until 1998 but has fallen back to its pre-FTA level. NAFTA utilization in several other HS sections fell right after 1998 with the most dramatic decrease occurring in Arms and Ammunition from a 90% NAFTA utilization rate to 22 % between 1998 and 2003. The 33% NAFTA utilization rate recorded for Live Animals in 2003 marked the first time in ten years that its NAFTA utilization rate fell below 40% and might reflect the mad cow fall-out.

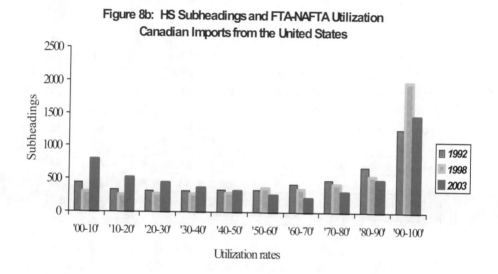

Figure 8b: HS Subheadings and FTA-NAFTA Utilization
Canadian Imports from the United States

Source: Authors' calculations based on Statistics Canada data.

In fact, in 9 out of the 21 sections for U.S. imports from Canada, NAFTA utilization rates fell more than 10 percentage points between 1998 to 2003 pulling down the overall 2003 utilization average. NAFTA utilization rates peaked in 1998 for 13 of the 21 sections causing the average NAFTA utilization rate also to peak. The question remains; what caused this peak in NAFTA utilization rate and what caused the subsequent decline?

295

Table 5a: NAFTA Utilization By Section, 1989-2003
U.S. Imports from Canada

		1989	1992	1995	1998	2003
1	Live Animals, Animal Products	35	54	49	49	33
2	Vegetable Products	49	65	68	71	72
3	Fats and Oils	86	97	96	97	98
4	Prepared Food, Beverages, Tobacco	58	74	70	71	64
5	Mineral Products	47	57	54	47	45
6	Chemicals	30	44	45	43	26
7	Plastics	70	84	87	93	93
8	Leather Goods	47	42	48	52	57
9	Wood Products	4	5	17	26	19
10	Pulp and Paper	6	12	17	23	26
11	Textiles and Apparel	66	89	90	96	94
12	Footwear, Headgear, etc	76	95	97	98	72
13	Article of Stone, Plastic, Glass, etc	44	57	69	81	58
14	Jewellery	1	21	40	37	14
15	Base Metals	42	59	57	69	62
16	Machinery, Electrical Equipment	23	42	53	63	41
17	Vehicles,Transport Equipment, etc	4	11	49	92	85
18	Optical, Photographic, etc	22	43	57	72	40
19	Arms & Ammunition	6	48	89	90	22
20	Miscellaneous	44	66	86	93	15
	Average of Sections[1]	**38**	**53**	**62**	**68**	**52**
	Overall Utilization	**28**	**34**	**50**	**68**	**57**

[1] Average of sections and overall utilization are calculated excluding section 21.
Source: Authors' calculations with USITC data for various years

The historical usage of NAFTA across HS sections for imports from the United States into Canada shows a different pattern as illustrated in Figure 5b. In 18 out of 20 sections for imports into Canada from the United States, NAFTA utilization rates fell from 1998 to 2003 with 12 sections falling more than 10 percentage points. Transport equipment (section 17) posted the only increase in NAFTA utilization moving from 20% to 55% while Plastics (section 7) remained the same at 82%. The overall utilization rate for imports into Canada, calculated as the value of imports using NAFTA divided by the value of imports from the United States, has remained relatively constant over the last ten years while the utilization rate calculated as the average of sections shows a rising trend, peaking in 1998 and subsequently declining.

296

Table 5b: NAFTA Utilization By Section, 1992-2002
Canadian Imports from United States

		1992	1995	1998	2002	2003
1	Live Animals, Animal Products	67	66	65	49	50
2	Vegetable Products	68	70	64	26	21
3	Fats and Oils	85	92	95	93	93
4	Prepared Food, Beverages, Tobacco	80	84	86	83	81
5	Mineral Products	20	33	34	19	24
6	Chemicals	65	67	65	56	53
7	Plastics	70	81	82	82	82
8	Leather Goods	63	58	58	46	37
9	Wood Products	31	33	37	30	30
10	Pulp and Paper	54	60	61	43	28
11	Textiles and Apparel	81	87	89	87	84
12	Footwear, Headgear, etc	70	78	81	74	76
13	Article of Stone, Plastic, Glass, etc	60	61	56	43	43
14	Jewellery	20	20	41	19	17
15	Base Metals	64	69	67	56	49
16	Machinery, Electrical Equipment	39	44	37	25	23
17	Vehicles,Transport Equipment, etc	18	15	20	53	55
18	Optical, Photographic, etc	28	28	26	20	16
19	Arms & Ammunition	22	44	62	59	52
20	Miscellaneous	71	68	67	58	56
	Average of Sections^1	**54**	**58**	**60**	**51**	**48**
	Overall Utilization	**41**	**45**	**44**	**46**	**44**

^{1} Average of sections and overall utilization are calculated excluding section 21.
Source: Authors' calculations based on Statistics Canada data for various years

What Are the Economic Effects of NAFTA ROO?

There are several drawbacks to the use of restrictive ROO as outlined in the research literature. The three most often cited adverse effects created by restrictive ROO are that they restrict trade, misdirect investment, and distort sourcing and production decisions.[28]

First, with restrictive ROO and high transaction costs, there can be significant resource costs associated with the application of ROO. As noted earlier in this chapter, the private sector incurs compliance costs (broker fees, additional accounting costs, audit costs, etc.) to meet the origin requirements while the public sector incurs administrative costs (customs costs, audit costs, etc.). The costs associated with ROO would have the effect of raising consumer

---

[28] See Australian Productivity Commission (2004b), Krishna (2004), Krueger (1993, 1997, 1999) and Estevadeordal and Suominen (2004a) for example.

297

prices, lowering producer returns and decreasing the volume of exports that otherwise would have occurred thereby directly reducing the net benefits accruing to NAFTA members. The more restrictive and costly the ROO, the greater the reduction in net benefits from a free trade agreement. In this case, restrictive ROO serve as a traditional barrier to trade, *i.e.*, to protect domestic producers of final goods when the rules of origin are so administratively or technically difficult to comply that they serve as a non-tariff barrier to trade (LaNasa (1995)).

Second, restrictive ROO may distort the location of production and investment decisions. Estevadeordal and Suominen (2004) identify two types of investment diversion that could occur as a result of restrictive ROO. First, there is the case where final goods producers from outside the FTA "jump" the ROO by locating plants within a FTA region in order to satisfy the ROO even if the FTA region was not the optimal location for investment. Second, ROO can result in investment diversion within the FTA area since outside producers could have an incentive to locate in the largest FTA market or the FTA member region with the lowest external tariffs such as the United States in the context of NAFTA.

NAFTA ROO can create a bias toward investment in the United States since multinational firms seeking larger markets have the incentive to minimize the uncertainty and resource costs associated with ROO. The costs associated with ROO, border costs, additional transportation charges for goods targeted for the U.S. market and investors' desires to secure access to the U.S. market add a bias towards investing in the United States compared to Canada or Mexico. This may be a contributing factor explaining why Canada witnessed a decline in the share of North American bound FDI.

Third, restrictive ROO can create incentives for producers to use member country inputs to satisfy ROO requirements rather than third country inputs even though third country inputs may be available at lower cost. The incentive is to increase the amount of intermediate and final good manufacturing, processing and assembly done within NAFTA, when regional value content requirements are binding, at the expense of facilities in other countries that would otherwise have a comparative advantage. This distortion of the sourcing and purchasing decision causes policy-induced allocation inefficiency where firms and industries are producing goods at a higher cost even though less costly inputs are available (trade diversion). Krishna (2004) indicates that that this provides hidden protection to suppliers within an FTA.

Estevadeordal and Suominen (2004), employing a 156-country gravity model, carried out the most extensive investigation to date regarding estimating the trade effects of ROO. The authors find that regimes with restrictive ROO and with high degrees of sectoral selectivity discourage aggregate trade flows. In addition, they find that at the sectoral level (in vehicles), restrictive ROO in final goods encourage trade in intermediate goods, and could thus engender trade diversion in inputs.

What do the quantitative studies reveal about the economic costs of NAFTA ROO? Appiah (1999) incorporated the NAFTA ROO into a multi-sector general equilibrium model, modeling NAFTA ROO as an RVC requirement he found, in his intermediate case, the welfare costs of the NAFTA ROO to be 1.5 to

2.3% of GDP.[29] The author finds that the more restrictive the ROO, the more the cost in terms of forgone GDP. With non-restrictive ROO, the cost of ROO to the Canadian economy is 0.3 to 0.61% of GDP while restrictive ROO could cost the Canadian economy 2.8% of GDP. In addition, Appiah (1999) found that welfare costs of the NAFTA ROO to the U.S. economy are approximately 0.47% to 1.22% of U.S. GDP in the intermediate case.

Cadot et. al. (2002) employed data on Mexican exports to the United States, exports to the rest of the world, NAFTA preferences, Estevadeordal's restrictiveness index, and dummy variables to estimate a model explaining the effects of NAFTA ROO on Mexican exports to the United States. The authors found that relaxing the NAFTA ROO would increase Mexican exports to the United States between 17.8% and 35%.[30] In addition, relaxing the change in tariff classification at the chapter level would increase Mexican exports by 35.3%. This suggests that NAFTA ROO significantly reduce exports from member countries.

Ghosh and Rao (2004), assessing the likely effects from a Canada–U.S. customs union in a dynamic multi-sector, multi-country general equilibrium model, find that eliminating the NAFTA ROO alone between Canada and the United States would increase Canada's GDP by 1.04%, U.S. GDP by 0.13% and would increase Canadian exports to the United States by 19% and American exports to Canada by 22.7%.[31] In addition, the simulations indicate that the elimination of NAFTA ROO between the two countries would increase investment into Canada by 1.3% and the United States by 0.23%.

Examining NAFTA ROO and Bilateral Trade

In this section, we explore the relationship between NAFTA utilization rates, Estevadeordal's ROO restrictiveness index, and tariff preferences. To simplify, we can conceptually view the producer/exporter facing a two-stage problem.

In the first stage, the producer/exporter must make a sourcing and/or production decision. We can think of this sourcing and production decision when ROO are binding within the framework of the producer's/exporter's profit maximization problem with the additional ROO binding constraint. The formulation of the constraint(s) is different depending on whether ROO are characterized by CTC, CTC plus RVC, or CTC plus technical requirements. It is the producer/exporter that provides the certificates of origin to the purchaser/importer of the good.

---

[29] Appiah (1999) models the NAFTA ROO as changes in the tariff classification and as regional value content requirements. The change in tariff classification is approximated by the percentage increase in value added per unit of foreign inputs to achieve the tariff classification change. His intermediate case simulates a change in tariff classification (tariff shift) equal to 30% in value added per unit cost of foreign input. Two other simulations are a tariff shift of 20% and 40% in value added per unit cost of foreign input.

[30] Cadot et. al. (2002) found that relaxing ROO to r = 3 would increase Mexican exports to the United States by 17.8% but setting it to r = 2 would increase exports by 35%.

[31] Ghosh and Rao (2004) provide upper-bound estimates and denote the maximum values that may occur. These are preliminary results and are subject to subsequent modification.

In the second stage, the choice of using NAFTA with its compliance costs versus MFN can be thought of in the context of a cost minimization problem of the importer. If the good for importation satisfies the ROO binding constraint within stage one, the importer can choose between NAFTA and MFN status. However, not satisfying the binding ROO constraint in stage one implies that the importer is only entitled to MFN status. It is the importer that must provide the necessary documentation to customs for clearance of the imported shipment.

We separate the choice of input mix in the production decision and the sourcing problem by producers/exporters from the importers' decision to use NAFTA or MFN. For our analysis, we focus on the use of NAFTA or MFN as a means to import into a member country and abstract from the sourcing and production decision.

The importer will seek the mode of importation, NAFTA versus MFN, which minimizes the cost of importation. It is assumed the logistical costs (transportation charges, insurance, brokers' fees, etc.) are the same under NAFTA and MFN. As mentioned before, the key cost factors that influence the choice of using NAFTA versus MFN are tariff preferences and the requirements associated with ROO.

It is expected that NAFTA utilization is positively related to tariff preferences since the greater the difference between MFN and NAFTA tariffs, the greater the cost savings from not paying MFN duty net of NAFTA ROO costs if one uses NAFTA. It is also expected that NAFTA utilization is negatively related to the degree of restrictiveness of ROO so that the more restrictive ROO, the less the use of NAFTA. The predominant use of the CTC at the chapter level makes it more difficult to satisfy compliance with ROO requirements compared to CTC at lower levels within the HS code and hence should result in lower utilization rates.

To capture the effects of ROO restrictiveness on utilization rates, we first employ the Estevadeordal restrictiveness index. The Estevadeordal index performs well in regressions with cross-country aggregate data (Estevadeordal and Suominen 2003). With single country trade data, the index performs well with disaggregated data (Anson et. al. 2003).

In addition, given the large percent of ROO requiring a chapter change, we also employ a chapter change dummy as an alternative to the restrictiveness index. Our regression strategy is to use the restrictiveness index and to compare these results to our regressions where dummies capture the CTC at the chapter level as specified in Annex 401 of NAFTA. Following Cadot et. al. (2002) and Carrère and de Melo (2004), we also include a sector specific dummy variable to capture the heterogeneity within certain sectors.

Our regression equation is:

$$\ln U = \beta_0 + \beta_1 \ln\tau + \beta_2 \ln r + \delta D \qquad (2)$$

where:

τ is the tariff preference rate calculated as
$(t^{MFN} - t^{NAFTA})/(1 + t^{NAFTA})$ where t is the tariff rate

300

r is the Estevadeordal restrictiveness index of the ith good
D is a sector dummy

It is expected that $\beta_1 > 0$ and $\beta_2 < 0$.

Our first set of regressions, reported in Table 6, use section level data. The results show that tariff preferences are positively related to NAFTA utilization – the greater the tariff preferences (the higher the MFN rate) the greater the use of NAFTA. In all cases, tariff preferences are statistically significant. With every 1 percentage reduction in tariff preferences, there would be approximately ½ percentage reduction in the NAFTA utilization rate as importers find it relatively less costly to use the MFN and relatively less attractive to use NAFTA.

	Table 6: NAFTA Utilization Regressions					
	1	2	3	4	5	6
Independent variables	Dependent Variable NAFTA Utilization Rates					
Constant	3.177* (2.336)	2.951** (15.76)	3.192* (2.126)	3.203** (17.26)	2.959** (3.245)	3.175** (19.59)
Tariff preference	0.538** (3.837)	0.578** (4.074)	0.354* (2.126)	0.391 (2.081)	0.411** (3.544)	0.405** (3.492)
Restrictiveness index	-0.159 (-0.185)		0.016 (0.026)		0.156 (0.274)	
Section dummy	0.702* (2.336)	0.861* (2.495)	0.572* (2.177)	0.604* (2.212)	0.553* (2.327)	0.570* (2.484)
CC dummy		-0.363 (-1.024)		-0.105 (-0.382)		.099 (.533)
Country dummy					-0.078 (-0.420)	-0.076 (-0.409)
adj R^2	.57	.60	.48	.48	.44	.45
Data	U.S. HS sections	U.S. HS sections	Canada HS sections	Canada HS Sections	Pooled	Pooled
t-ratio in parenthesis * and ** denotes significance at the 5% and 1% level, respectively						

The Estevadeordal restrictiveness index is not statistically significant. This finding is not surprising given the data sets that we are using for these regressions. As a result, we replace the restrictiveness index with a restrictiveness dummy following Carrère and de Melo (2004). For our second regression equation, we replace the Estevadeordal index with a restrictiveness dummy (CC dummy) which takes on the value of 1 when $r \geq 6$ and 0 otherwise. The results indicate that the restrictiveness dummy has the correct sign, suggesting that CTC

301

at the chapter level reduces NAFTA utilization. However, the coefficient is not statistically significant. The section dummy captures the effects of selected sections on NAFTA utilization and is positive and statistically significant.

Running the regressions with pooled Canada–U.S. bilateral trade data reveals no change in the value of the estimated parameters compared to the single country analysis (see column 5 and 6). Again the restrictiveness index and the change in chapter dummy are not statistically significant. It is interesting to note that the country dummy is not statistically significant, suggesting similar behaviour in both countries. This would suggest that composition differences may explain the sectoral differences in utilization between the two countries.

We take an initial look at 2002 data for U.S. imports from Canada at the chapter level. Although there are 99 chapters designated, chapter 77 is reserved for future use while 98 and 99 are reserved for special use. Consequently, the chapter data allows for 96 observations. Inspecting the chapter data, we observe the dependent variable, NAFTA utilization rates U_i, with values $0 \leq U_i < 1$.[32] With a dependent variable that is zero for a significant fraction of the observations, conventional regressions fail to account for the qualitative difference between limit (zero) observations and nonlimit (continuous) observations.[33] If we only use the observations where $U_i > 0$ to estimate the regression equation by ordinary least squares, then the mean stochastic error would not equal zero violating the first assumption of the classical linear model.[34] Therefore, we estimate the coefficients using the Tobit regression model applied to HS chapter import data set.

This disaggregated data allows us to expand the range of dummy variables in an attempt to capture the effects of NAFTA ROO on utilization rates. Our strategy will be to run our first regression with the Estevadeordal restrictiveness index and then a second regression with the change in chapter dummy variable, reflecting the value of 1 when $r \geq 6$ and CC dummy = 0 otherwise. Our third regression includes three restrictiveness dummies: CC dummy for chapter changes, CHplus dummy for heading changes including a regional value content requirement, and a technical requirement and CH dummy for changes in headings. The results are reported in Table 7.

Tariff preferences and the sector dummy are statistically significant and hence NAFTA utilization rates are positively related to tariff preference in all three regressions. We find that the restrictiveness index has the right sign but again is not statistically significant. Similarly, none of change in tariff classification dummies are significant in regressions 8 and 9.

---

[32] There is no HS chapter with a NAFTA utilization rate of 1.

[33] Greene (1990) provides an in-depth explanation of several limited dependent variable models.

302

Table 7: NAFTA Utilization Regressions

	7	8	9
Independent variables	Dependent Variable NAFTA Utilization Rates		
Constant	2.10** (2.785)	2.727** (7.302)	2.237** (4.240)
tariff preference	0.308** (3.837)	0.307** (3.751)	0.308** (3.743)
restrictiveness index	-0.123 (-0.1855)		
sector dummy	1.419** (4.678)	1.443** (4.775)	1.390** (4.538)
CC dummy		0.085 (0.389)	0.584 (1.322)
CHplus dummy			0.505 (1.181)
CH dummy			.571 (1.344)

Data: USITC chapter import data for 2002, Estevadeordal index aggregated to the HS2 chapter level, 96 observations
Coefficients estimated with the Tobit model.
t-ratio in parenthesis

** denotes significance at the 1% level.

The empirical results regarding the restrictiveness index and the CTC dummies are to be expected given the level of aggregation in the data. The influence of the restrictiveness index on utilization rates should show up with the single country trade data at the import transaction level, the item level and the subheading level. Anson et. al. (2003) and Cadot et. al. (2002) statistically find the inverse relationship between NAFTA utilization rates and the restrictiveness index employing sub-heading data on U.S. imports from Mexico.

Similarly the effects the CTC dummies on utilization are more likely to be captured in the econometric results the greater the degree of disaggregation. Carrère and de Melo (2004), using HS 6 data for U.S imports from Mexico, found the CTC dummies to be highly significant. This micro data also allowed the authors to explore how the stages of production (intermediate and final goods) influence utilization rates and the cost of compliance.

Does ROO Reduce U.S. NAFTA Imports From Canada

In this section, we will rely on the 2003 HS 6 data for imports into the United States from Canada in our regressions.[35] This data poses some challenges given the large number of subheadings where NAFTA utilization rates are zero or

---

[35] We will not use the data for Canadian imports from the United States since the Canadian data contains noise in the tariff revenue component that may bias the econometric results.

100%. There are 1492 subheading observations where the NAFTA utilization rate is zero and 743 subheading observations where the NAFTA utilization rate is 100%.

The restrictiveness index was updated to incorporate the various changes in the NAFTA ROO that have occurred since 1998.

We chose to estimate our model using a two-limit Tobit model. This approach allows one to use the entire sample including observations where the dependent variable, the NAFTA utilization rate, might take on values of zero, one or any value in between.

Our regression equation is:

$$U = \beta_0 + \beta_1\tau + \beta_2 r + \beta_3 F + \delta_1 D_1 + \delta_2 D_2 + \delta_3 D_3 + \ldots + \delta_n D_n$$

where:

τ is the tariff preference rate calculated as $(t^{MFN} - t^{NAFTA})/(1 + t^{NAFTA})$ where t is the tariff rate
r is the Estevadeordal restrictiveness index,
D_i are section dummy variables representing 19 sections.[36]

Again it is expected that the greater the tariff preference, the greater the use of NAFTA ($\beta_1 > 0$) and the more restrictive ROO the less the use of NAFTA ($\beta_2 < 0$). The section dummies should pick up the extent to which NAFTA is used more or less than average after correcting for the influence of the restrictiveness index, tariff preferences and freight and insurance charges.

The results are shown in Table 8. The coefficients associated with tariff preferences and the restrictiveness index are statistically significant and have the expected signs. Nine dummies are significant at the 1% level of confidence while an additional two section dummies are significant at the 5% level.

Section 2 (Vegetable Products), section 3 (Fats and Oils), section 4 (Food, Beverage and Tobacco), section 7 (Plastics), section 11 (Textile and Textile Articles) and section 15 (Base Metals) all reflect greater NAFTA utilization after correcting for the influence of the restrictiveness index, tariff preferences, and freight and insurance charges.[37] On the other hand, section 5 (Mineral Products), section 9 (Wood and Articles of Wood) and section 16 (Machinery and Mechanical Appliances) have a statistically smaller utilization rates after correcting for the restrictiveness index, tariff preferences and freight and insurance charges compared to the average section.

---

[36] See appendix 1 for a listing of chapters and sections. Section 21 has been eliminated from the data set since there are no index numbers assigned to this section.
[37] Each of these sections have a dummy coefficient that is statistically significant at the 1% level.

Table 8: Determinants of NAFTA Utilization

Independent Variables			Independent Variables (continued)	
Intercept	0.6720** (6.78)		D9	-0.3973** (-3.35)
Restrictiveness index	-0.0784** (-6.48)		D10	0.0651 (0.68)
Tariff preference	0.0194** (7.69)		D11	0.6537** (8.40)
D1	-0.0555 (-0.60)		D12	0.1162 (0.90)
D2	0.4759** (5.27)		D13	0.2008* (2.05)
D3	0.6723** (4.64)		D14	-0.0695 (-0.50)
D4	0.4467** (4.84)		D15	0.4263** (5.41)
D5	-0.7943** (-6.68)		D16	-0.2718** (-3.41)
D6	0.0861 (1.02)		D17	-0.0911 (-0.89)
D7	0.3331** (3.77)		D18	-0.0526 (-0.58)
D8	0.2531* (2.16)		D19	-0.2860 (-1.39)
			Observations	4489
			Log likelihood	-4385

USITC trade data for 2003
Coefficients estimated with Two-Limit Tobit
T-ratios in brackets
** and * denotes 1% and 5% level of significance

To assist in our understanding of these parameter estimates, we undertake the following conceptual experiments of hypothetically decreasing:

i.   the average restrictiveness index from 5 to 4, and
ii. the average tariff preference by 1 percentage point

separately and examine the impact on NAFTA utilization.[38] Reducing the average NAFTA ROO restrictiveness index from 5 to 4 would result in a 13% increase in the use of NAFTA. This would be equivalent to relaxing NAFTA ROO to the

---

[38] We calculate the relevant elasticity evaluated at the mean of the data and simulate the effects of each scenario based in these elasticities.

point where the average NAFTA ROO would be a change in tariff classification at the heading level and would be equivalent to the ROO restrictiveness level of the Canada-Israel FTA. Similarly, redrafting NAFTA ROO so that average restrictiveness index fell to 3 would result in a 26% increase in NAFTA exports from Canada to the United States.

Reducing tariff preferences by 1 percentage point would decrease NAFTA utilization by 3.4%. As MFN rates fall, this makes the use of MFN more attractive. Our results indicate that reducing the restrictiveness of NAFTA ROO would bring about considerably larger increases in NAFTA imports compared to reducing MFN tariffs.

These results are consistent with the general conclusions of Ghosh and Rao (2004) who found that the gain from the reduction in NAFTA ROO was significantly larger than the gain from tariff harmonization. The econometric results confirm our earlier expectations that the restrictiveness of NAFTA ROO have dampened the use of NAFTA while the remaining MFN rates have encouraged the use of NAFTA.

Concluding Remarks

For Canada and the United States, improved access to each other's market has been beneficial. The security concerns in the wake of September 11th have made Canadians acutely aware of the strategic importance of the border and introduced new issues that must be resolved to facilitate the movement of goods and individuals between Canada and the United States.

The available empirical evidence suggests that NAFTA ROO, although intended to distinguish between NAFTA originating goods and non-originating goods, can result in significant, unexpected economic costs that alter the expected net benefits from trade. Importers are using NAFTA less than expected given that NAFTA utilization is around 50% of Canada-U.S. bilateral trade. NAFTA utilization for U.S. imports from Canada peaked in 1998 and has declined since then. About half of the Canada-U.S. trade is imported under NAFTA while almost all tariff lines under NAFTA are duty free. When MFN rates are zero, importers use NAFTA only to a very limited extent, likely as a result of costs of using NAFTA; when MFN rates are positive, importers rely more heavily on NAFTA.

Other studies based on data related to U.S. imports from Mexico indicated that NAFTA ROO are costly. Our analysis suggests that NAFTA compliance costs for U.S. imports from Canada are about 1% of the exports. In addition, Anson et. al. (2003), Cadot et. al. (2002) and Carrère and de Melo (2004) demonstrate that NAFTA ROO have significant negative effects on NAFTA utilization rates for U.S. imports from Mexico. For U.S. imports from Canada, we also find that NAFTA ROO significantly reduce NAFTA utilization rates.

The maturity of the bilateral trade relationship between Canada and the United States as reflected in the success of the Auto Pact, the FTA and the NAFTA, coupled with liberalized tariff environments witnessed by the historical reductions of Canadian MFN and U.S. NTR tariff rates over the last 15 years, may be eroding the usefulness of NAFTA as demonstrated by the declining NAFTA utilization rates on both sides of the northern border. If we want to capture additional gains from trade, reduce inefficient and costly sourcing and production, and reduce compliance and administration costs associated with NAFTA rules of origin, then action is required to change the current NAFTA ROO environment.

There are several approaches that could be employed to address the adverse effects of ROO. The elimination of ROO for all intra-bloc trade between Canada and the United States could occur by moving toward a Canada-United States customs union. Alternatively, ROO could be eliminated for intra-bloc trade on a sectoral basis where the difference in level of MFN between the two countries is small or zero. Some have suggested that this as a potential option where the inter-country differences in tariffs are less than 1 percentage point. Our earlier work on a potential customs union suggested that the relative small differences in the external tariff between Canada and the United States for non-agriculture would make a sectoral approach towards the removal of NAFTA ROO attractive. Sensitive sectors such as automotives, agriculture and textiles might require special consideration. Reducing MFN rates could also eliminate some of the adverse effects of the NAFTA ROO. As we have seen as MFN rates decline, importers move from using NAFTA towards using MFN tariff rates.

At a minimum, NAFTA rules of origin should be liberalized in order to make it easier, less costly, and less burdensome for firms to establish origin, to comply with ROO and to use NAFTA. Although there are numerous options and variations to be considered in liberalizing NAFTA ROO, we explore three possible options below.

The first option to liberalize NAFTA ROO is to reduce the current regional value content threshold, currently at 60% if calculated by the transaction value method or 50% if calculated by the net cost method. Lowering the RVC threshold would allow greater choice in sourcing inputs, reduce ROO-induced inefficiency in production, and reduce some of the barriers to trade caused by NAFTA ROO. Moreover, reducing the RVC threshold would be relatively simple to implement and would involve minimal transaction costs. Currently, 35% of the tariff items have a RVC component.

Currently under the Canada–Chile FTA, the RVC is 25% (net cost method) and 35% (transaction value method) and for the Mexico – Israel FTA the RVC is 35% (net cost method) and 45% (transaction value method). The United States bilateral agreements with Israel and Jordan diverge markedly from the NAFTA model, operating with only RVC rules. The RVC threshold is 35% in both agreements. The application of a single test across all activities and the relatively low RVC requirement would be reflected in a lower restrictiveness index.

A second option to reduce the restrictiveness of NAFTA ROO would be to diminish the discriminatory nature of NAFTA CTC rules by downward harmonization. Estevadeordal (2000), Estevadeordal and Suominen (2004a, b) and the Australia Productivity Commission (2004a,b) identified the CTC ROO at the chapter level as a major cause of the restrictiveness of NAFTA ROO. The incidence of CTC ROO at the chapter level in the first test is significantly lower in the United States–Singapore FTA at 33% and the United States–Chile FTA at

37% compared to NAFTA at 54%.[39] Downward harmonization of the NAFTA CTC rules would require the modification of those CTC rules currently at the chapter (and perhaps heading) level downwards to CTC at the headings (or sub-heading) level. Again this option would reduce the policy-induced inefficiencies created by the current NAFTA ROO.

A third option would be to re-examine the exceptions to the CTC rules with the objective to eliminate these exceptions. About 50% of NAFTA ROO in the first test are CTC alone while 38% contain exceptions. Exceptions in CTC rules serve to restrict the application of the particular ROO.

A fourth option would be to simplify the second rule or test for the same tariff item. As outlined earlier, there is a wide range of tariff items where there is a choice of rules given. In NAFTA, the first test is commonly based on a CTC rule alone, while a second test, for the same tariff item, may involve a CTC rule at a lower level, together with a technical test and/or RVC requirement. For any tariff item where a choice of rules is given, simplification could involve CTC for rule one and a RVC only for rule two.

These options could be implemented independently or combined as a NAFTA ROO reform package.

It should be noted that although RVC threshold reduction, downward harmonization of CTC and the simplification of the second rule would all generate efficiency gains to the economy and benefits to producers and traders. However, these options would not address, to any large extent, the compliance and administration costs associated with NAFTA ROO. A review of NAFTA ROO transaction requirements for customs purposes and business and customs operational procedures to meet NAFTA ROO is required to identify any potential sources of administrative and compliance gains.

In conclusion, our present analysis suggests that NAFTA rules of origin are restrictive, create policy-induced inefficiencies in sourcing and production, impose compliance costs on firms engaged in intra-NAFTA trade, and inhibit NAFTA trade. The elimination or reduction of these costs associated with the NAFTA rules of origin would provide positive economic benefits to Canada by lowering costs to producers and prices to consumers, by increasing intra-NAFTA trade, and by reducing NAFTA ROO-induced inefficiencies.

---

[39] See Estevadeordal and Suiminon (2004b) or the Australia Productivity Commission (2004b)

Bibliography

Adams, Richard, Philippa Dee, Jyothi Gali and Greg McGuire (2003). "The Trade and Investment Effects of Preferential Trading Arrangements - Old and New Evidence". Australian Government Productivity Commission Staff Working Paper. Canberra: Productivity Commission.

Agama, Laurie-Ann and Christine A. McDaniel (2003). "The NAFTA Preference and U.S.-Mexico Trade: Aggregate-Level Analysis" World Economy 26pp. 935-955.

Anson, José, Olivier Cadot, Jaime de Melo, Antoni Estevadeordal, Akiko Suwa-Eisenmann and Bolormaa Tumurchudur (2003). "Rules of Origin in North-South Preferential Trading Arrangements with an Application to NAFTA" Centre for Economic Policy Research discussion paper 4166. London: Centre for Economic Policy Research.

Appiah, Alex Jameson (1999). *Applied General Equilibrium Model of North American Integration with Rules of Origin*. PhD. Dissertation. Burnaby: Simon Fraser University.

Australia. Productivity Commission (2004a). *Rules of Origin under the Australia - New Zealand Closer Economic Relations Trade Agreement*. Canberra: Productivity Commission

——— (2004b). *Restrictiveness Index for Preferential Rules of Origin Supplement to Research Report, Rules of Origin under the Australia - New Zealand Closer Economic Relations Trade Agreement*. Canberra: Productivity Commission.

Bartholomew, Ann (2002). "Trade Creation and Trade Diversion: The Welfare Impact of MERCOSUR on Argentina and Brazil." *University of Oxford Centre for Brazilian Studies Working Paper* CBS-25-2002.

Brown, Drusilla K. and Alan V. Deardorff (2003). "Impacts on NAFTA Members of Multilateral and Regional Trading Arrangements and Tariff Harmonization". In Richard Harris, ed. *North American Linkages: Opportunities and Challenge for Canada*. Calgary: University of Calgary Press.

Cadot, Olivier, Antoni Estevadeordal and Akiko Suwa-Eisenmann (2003). "Rules of Origin as Export Subsidies". Mimeo

——— (2004). "An Assessment of Rules of Origin: The Case of NAFTA." In Cadot, Olivier, Antoni Estevadeordal, Akiko Suwa-Eisenmann, and Thierry Verdier, eds. The Origin of Goods: A Conceptual and Empirical Assessment of Rules of Origin in PTAs." Washington: Inter-American Development Bank and Centre for Economic Policy Research. Canberra.

Cadot, Olivier, Jaime de Melo, Antoni Estevadeordal, Akiko Suwa-Eisenmann and Bolormaa Tumurchudur (2002). "Assessing the Effect of NAFTA's Rules of Origin." Mimeo.

Canada. Auditor General of Canada (2001). "Canada Customs and Revenue Agency - Managing Risk of Non-Compliance from Commercial Shipments Entering into Canada" Report of the Auditor General of Canada Chapter 8. Ottawa:

Canada. Canada Border Services Agency (2000). Compliance Improvement Plan 2000 – 2001. CBSA document at http://www.cbsa-asfc.gc.ca/general/blue_print/compliance/plan-e.html

Canada. Customs and Revenue Agency (1995). *Information for Importers, Exporters or Producers.* CCRA document C-144 at http://www.ccra-adrc.gc.ca/E/pub/cp/c-144/c-144-143-e.pdf

Canada. Standing Committee on Foreign Affairs and International Trade (2002). "Partners in North America: Advancing Canada's Relations with the United States and Mexico" (Report of the Standing Committee on Foreign Affairs and International Trade).

Carrère, Céline and Jaime de Melo (2003) "A Free Trade Area of the Americas: Any Gains for the South" Presentation at the Third Workshop of the Regional Integration Network, Uruguay December 15-18, 2003.

——— (2004) "Are Different Rules of Origin Equally Costly? Estimates from NAFTA" Centre for Economic Policy Research, , Discussion Paper No. 4437.

Chambers, Edward J. and Peter H. Smith (2002). NAFTA in the New Millenium. Edmonton: University of Alberta Press.

Clausing, Kimberley (2001). "Trade creation and trade diversion in the Canada - United States Free Trade Agreement. Canadian Journal of Economics 34, 3.

Dobson, Wendy (2002). "Shaping the Future of the North American Economic Space: A Framework for Action". *C.D. Howe Institute Commentary 162.* Toronto: C.D. Howe.

Estevadeordal, Antoni (2000). "Negotiating Preferential Market Access: The Case of the North American Free Trade Agreement." *Journal of World Trade 34,* 1.

Estevadeordal, Antoni and Kati Suominen (2004a). "Rules of Origin in FTAs in Europe and in the Americas: Issues and Implications for the EU-Mercosur Inter-Regional Association Agreement. INTAL-ITD Working Paper 15. Buenos Aires: Inter-American Development Bank.

——— (2004b). "Rules of Origin: A World Map and Trade Effects." In Cadot, Olivier, Antoni Estevadeordal, Akiko Suwa-Eisenmann, and Thierry Verdier, eds. The Origin of Goods: A Conceptual and Empirical Assessment of Rules of Origin in PTAs." Washington: Inter-American Development Bank and Centre for Economic Policy Research

——— (2003). "Rules of Origin in the World Trading System" mimeo

Ghosh, Madanmohan and Someshwar Rao (2004 forthcoming). "Economic Impacts of a Possible Canada-U.S. Customs Union: A Dynamic CGE Model Analysis". Ottawa: Industry Canada.

Goldfarb, Danielle (2003a). "The Road to a Canada- U.S. Customs Union: Step-by-Step or in a Single Bound?" *C.D. Howe Institute Commentary* 184.

——— (2003b) "Beyond Labels: Comparing Proposals for Closer Canada-U.S. Economic Relations" *C.D. Howe Institute Backgrounder* 76.

Gould, David (1998). "Has NAFTA Changed North American Trade?" Economic Review. Dallas: Federal Reserve Bank of Dallas

310

Greene, William H. (1990). *Econometric Analysis*. New York: MacMillan Publishing Co.

Hakim, Peter and Robert E. Litan, eds. (2002). *The Future of North America: Beyond Free Trade*. Washington: The Brookings Institution.

Harris, Richard, ed. (2003). North American Linkages: Opportunities and Challenges for Canada. Calgary University Press.

——— (2001). *North American Economic Integration: Issues and Research Agenda*. Ottawa: Industry Canada, Research Publications.

Hart, Michael and William Diamond (2001). *Common Borders, Shared Destinies: Canada, the United States and Deepening Integration*. Ottawa: Centre for Trade Policy and Law.

Herin, Jan (1986) *Rules of Origin and Differences Between Tariff Levels in EFTA and the EC* Occasional Paper No. 13, European Free Trade Association (EFTA) Secretariat, Geneva

Holmes, P. and G. Sheppard (1983). Protectionism in the Economic Community. International Economics Study Group, 8th annual conference.

Inter-American Development Bank (2002). *Beyond Borders: The New Regionalism in Latin America*. Washington: Inter-American Development Bank

Koskinen, Matti (1983). "Excess Documentation Costs as a Non-Tariff Measure: An Empirical Analysis of the Effects of Documentation Costs." Working Paper. Swedish School of Economics and Business Administration.

Krishna, Kala (2004). "Understanding Rules of Origin." NBER Working Paper No. W11150 Cambridge, MA: National Bureau of Economic Research.

Krueger, Anne O. (1993). "Free Trade Agreements as Protectionist Devices: Rules of Origin." NBER Working Paper No. W4352. Cambridge, MA: National Bureau of Economic Research

——— (1997). "Free Trade Agreements versus Customs Unions." Journal of Development Economics 54, pp 169-187.

——— (1999). "Trade Creation and Trade Diversion Under NAFTA." NBER Working Paper No. W7429. Cambridge, MA: National Bureau of Economic Research.

Kunimoto, Robert and Gary Sawchuk (2004). *Moving Towards a Customs Union: Perspectives and Evidence*. Ottawa: Policy Research Initiative.

LaNasa, Joseph (1995). "An Evaluation of the Uses and Importance of Rules of Origin, and the Effectiveness of the Uruguay Round's Agreement on Rules of Origin in Harmonizing and Regulating Them" Harvard Jean Monet Working Paper No. 1/96. http://www.jeanmonnetprogram.org/papers/96/9601ind.html

Mirus, Rolf. 2001. "After September 11: A Canada-US Customs Union". *Policy Options November 2001* p. 53-57

Mirus, Rolf and Nataliya Rylska (2002). Economic Integration: Free Trade Areas Vs. Customs Unions. Western Centre for Economic Research.

OECD (Organization for Economic Co-operation and Development) (2002). *The Relationship between Regional Trade Agreements and Multilateral Trading System: The Role of Rules of Origin* Working Party of the Trade Committee.

——— (2003), Regionalism and the Multilateral Trading System, Policy Brief, August.

311

Pastor, Robert (2001). *Toward a North American Community: Lessons from the Old World for the New.* Washington: Institute for International Economics

Policy Research Initiative (2003a), "The North American Linkages Project" Horizons Volume 6, Number 2 pp. 24 –28.

——— (2003b). *The North American Linkages Project: Focusing the Research Agenda.* Discussion paper.

Sawchuk, Gary and Daniel Trefler (2002). "A Time to Sow, A Time to Reap: The FTA and Its Impact on Productivity and Employment," In Productivity in Canada, eds. Someshwar Rao and Andrew Sharpe, Calgary University Press, pp. 537-569.

Schwanen, Daniel (2003). Free Trade and Canada -- Fifteen Years Later. Montreal: Institute for Research on Public Policy.

Sulzenko, Andrei (2003). "Economics of North American Integration: A Canadian Perspective" Horizons 6, Number 2 pp. 35-40

Trefler, Daniel, (2004). The Long and Short of the Canada-U.S. Free Trade Agreement, American Economic Review, 94:870-895.

United States. Customs Service (2002). *FY2001 Trade Compliance Report.* Washington, DC: U.S. Customs Service.

——— (2003). *Performance and Annual Report Fiscal Year 2002* Washington, DC: U.S. Customs Service.

United States. International Trade Commission (1995). *The Economic Effects of Significant US Import Restraints: First Biannual Update.* Washington: International Trade Commission.

——— (1999a). *Economic Effects of Significant US Import Restraints: Second Update.* Washington, DC: International Trade Commission.

——— (1999b). *Probably Economic Effects of the Reduction or Elimination of US Tariffs.* Washington: International Trade Commission

——— (2002). *The Economic Effects of Significant U.S. Import Restraints: Third Update.* Washington, DC: International Trade Commission.

World Trade Organization (2002). *Rules of Origin Regimes in Regional Trade Agreements: Background Survey by the Secretariat*, Committee on Regional Trade Agreements, WT/REG/W/45, WTO, Geneva.

——— (2003a). *Trade Policy Review - Canada.* Trade Policy Review Body.

——— (2003b). *World Trade Report 2003.* Geneva: WTO.

——— (2003c). *International Trade Statistics 2003.* Geneva: WTO.

——— (2003d). *Regional Trade Agreements; Scope of RTAs*, WTO, Geneva, http://www.wto.org/english/tratop_e/region_e/scope_rta_e.htm (accessed 4 December 2003).

——— (2004). *Trade Policy Review – United States.* Trade Policy Review Body.

Toward "Deeper" Canada-U.S. Integration: A Computable General Equilibrium Investigation

Evangelia Papadaki
DFAIT

Yu Lan
DFAIT

&

Marcel Mérette
University of Ottawa

Jorge Hernández
DFAIT

Introduction

A number of respected analysts and economic commentators in Canada have been calling for deeper Canadian economic integration with the U.S. Wendy Dobson, Director of the Institute for International Business at the Rotman School of Management, has argued that deeper bilateral integration with the U.S. would remedy some of the economic weaknesses that became apparent in Canada during the 1990s, as evidenced by lagging standards of living in Canada in comparison to the U.S. and a decline in Canada's share of North American foreign direct investment (FDI) inflows[1]. Dobson argues that the post-September 11 context provides a window of opportunity to propose a "big idea" with respect to economic integration that would at once create new economic opportunities for Canada while addressing the U.S.'s overwhelming interest in improved homeland security.

Michael Hart and William Dymond argue that current cross-border arrangements for the management of common trade, security and immigration issues are inadequate to the demands being placed upon them[2]. They contend that integration will continue to deepen between Canada and the U.S. in virtually every area where the two countries connect; the question for government, in their view, is whether to actively further that integration. They propose that Canada take advantage of the increased importance that the U.S. now attaches to border issues to negotiate comprehensive formal agreements for a more open and secure North America—whether Mexico joins such an effort or not.

The Governor of the Bank of Canada, David Dodge, while making it clear that he was not speaking as an advocate for greater North American integration—which he emphasized is very much a political decision for Canadians—argued from the economist's perspective as follows: "For me, free world trade is still the ideal. We in Canada cannot, and should not, lose sight of that goal by focusing only on free trade in North America. But, if we cannot tear down barriers multilaterally, we should at least continue to tear them down between provinces in Canada, between Canada and the U.S., between Canada and Mexico and, indeed, throughout the Americas.[3]" He argued that the key issue for Canada was to reduce border risk (which in his words amounted to "guaranteeing Canadian producers and service providers access to U.S. markets without hassle

[1] See Wendy Dobson (2002).
[2] See Michael Hart, and William Dymond (2001).
[3] See David Dodge, Governor of the Bank of Canada (2003).

313

and expense at the border, and without the risk of suddenly being shut out of those markets by some discretionary U.S. action."). Mr. Dodge also suggested that broadening and deepening NAFTA would be "extremely valuable"—while at the same time recognizing that this would not be straight forward as the easier steps towards integration had already been taken. Concrete steps towards this would involve harmonization of regulatory standards and practices, particularly with respect to capital and labour markets. And, in a context in which there already existed "a true single market for goods and services, labour, and capital", consideration could be given to moving to a common currency insofar as the then-prevailing industrial structures of Canada and the U.S. would make that an efficient arrangement (i.e., that reduction of transactions costs would outweigh potentially higher adjustment costs).

Most proponents of deepening economic integration favour the European progressive approach[4]. With respect to trade and the market for goods and services, the progressive approach would involve the following steps, as outlined by Governor Dodge[5]:

- A common external tariff and common border practices for imports from, and exports to, overseas markets (which we will term a "basic" customs union);
- Harmonization of trade and commercial policies and regulation ("intermediate" customs union);
- An end to the application of trade remedies within North America ("full" customs union); and
- A uniform policy with respect to federal and state/provincial subsidies.

An "intermediate" customs union would, in the opinion of some observers, be the most that could be realistically attained in the foreseeable future[6]. The next stage of economic integration would be along the lines of the "single market" that Europe forged in 1992; this would basically involve free movement of, and harmonization of regulatory regimes for, not only goods and services, but also labour and capital.

Finally a full-blown economic union, as in the latest stage of the European experiment, would involve harmonization of competition, structural, fiscal and monetary policies and possibly a common currency.

The complexity of negotiating and implementing these arrangements increase from one step to the next. Harmonizing external tariffs is much easier than harmonizing regulatory regimes in areas as diverse as cultural, legal, financial and communication services at the various levels of government. Removal of the use of trade remedies within a customs union could be quite problematic: some observers[7] argue that the U.S. would in fact insist on maintaining its right to use trade remedies such as countervailing and antidumping

---

[4] See, for example, the discussion in the Report of the Standing Committee on Foreign Affairs and International Trade (2002).
[5] See David Dodge, ibid.

[6] See Report of the Standing Committee on Foreign Affairs and International Trade, ibid.
[7] See for example the comments of Professor Hill quoted in: Report of the Standing Committee on Foreign Affairs and International Trade, ibid.

duties. The creation of a common market would necessitate the creation of various new bilateral or NAFTA-based political and legal institutions. An economic union would be considered both impractical and undesirable as long as the structures of the North American economies remain divergent[8].

Without prejudging the outcome of the debate over deeper integration, which as Governor Dodge stressed is a political decision, it is nevertheless useful to ground the discussion of the economic costs and benefits of further economic integration on as rigorous a basis as possible. In this chapter, we use a Computable General Equilibrium (CGE) model to shed quantitative light on two hypothetical scenarios of closer economic integration with the U.S:[9]

1. Harmonisation of external tariffs towards the rest of the world, coupled with the elimination of remaining tariff protection in bilateral trade between the two countries; that is, the "basic customs union".

2. Elimination of "unobserved trade costs" resulting from, *inter alia*, administrative border measures and costs that arise from national differences in technical standards and regulations.

CUSFTA and NAFTA in a Nutshell

The Canada-United Sates Free Trade Agreement (CUSFTA) came into effect on January 1, 1989. It marked an important step in the development of bilateral trade relations between the two countries[10]. The stated objectives of the Agreement were to "eliminate barriers to trade in goods and services between the...Parties", to "facilitate conditions of fair competition within the free-trade area", to "liberalize significantly conditions for investment" and to "lay the foundation for further bilateral and multilateral cooperation to expand and enhance the benefits of this Agreement"[11].

As of January 1, 1998, virtually all tariffs on Canada–U.S. trade in goods originating in the two countries were eliminated. Exceptions involved tariffs that remained in place for certain products in Canada's supply–managed agricultural sectors (e.g., dairy and poultry), as well as for sugar, dairy, peanuts and cotton in the U.S.

CUSFTA was incorporated into the North American Free Trade Agreement (NAFTA) in January 1994, which extended the free trade

---

[8] See David Dodge, ibid.

[9] As demonstrated by previous studies of the impact of NAFTA, it is the changing relationship with the U.S. that has and will have the largest impact in the Canadian economy (see T.J.,Kehoe. 2002). For this reason, not withstanding the added complexity of negotiating a trilateral agreement, only the Canada-U.S. case is considered at this stage of our research. However, in the future, by expanding our data set to include Mexico, we will be able to extend our analysis to a potential trilateral trade agreement.

[10] Prior to the CUSFTA, the General Agreement on Tariff and Trade (GATT) and several bilateral sectoral agreements primarily governed Canada-U.S. trade relations. Duty free trade in farm machinery was approved in 1944. The Defence Production Sharing Agreement of 1958 provided for cooperation weapons development and manufacture. The most important sectoral agreement, prior to the CUSFTA, was the Automotive Products Trade Agreement of 1965.

[11] For a full text of the agreement see:
http://wehner.tamu.edu/mgmt.www/NAFTA/index.htm

315

arrangements to Mexico. Almost all tariffs on goods originating in Canada, the U.S. and Mexico will be eliminated by January 1, 2008. NAFTA, however, goes beyond the CUSFTA to include substantially expanded coverage of government procurement (to services and construction), intellectual property and investor rights (introducing binding investor-state arbitration), as well as a higher local content requirement to meet the rules of origin test for NAFTA products. NAFTA also created some two-dozen working groups, committees and subcommittees to advance the objectives of the Agreement to reduce "barriers to trade" beyond the phasing out of duties to the reduction of non-tariff barriers to trade in goods and services by harmonizing procedures, recognizing standards as equivalent, and encouraging the exchange of information[12].

Since 1989, the year in which the CUSFTA came into force, Canada-U.S. trade has risen by a factor of 2.7, from C$235 billion to C$644 billion in 2003. In 2003, the U.S. accounted for 80 percent of Canada's exports of goods and services and 68 percent of its imports. How much of this expansion of bilateral trade is due to the CUSFTA/NAFTA is disputed. Some analysts argue that the long and sustained decline in the value of the Canadian dollar from the mid 1970s through 2002 contributed importantly to the increase in Canada's export intensity with the U.S.—although this would not explain the associated rise in the share of Canada's market accounted for by imports from the U.S. or the lack of an increase in foreign direct investment inflows from the U.S. (inward foreign direct investment from the U.S. decreased from 72 percent in 1986 to 67 percent in 2001, while outward foreign direct investment in the U.S. in 2001 was at the same level as in 1986[13]). The unprecedented economic boom in the U.S. during the 1990s, especially in technology-intensive sectors such as telecommunications and Internet related businesses, is also held to explain the sectorial distribution of Canadian exports that developed post-FTA, and in particular the significant increase in export intensity in such sectors as industrial goods and materials, sectors that had very low tariff rates prior to the CUSFTA.

Certain developments post-CUSFTA have not evolved as predicted by economic theory. In particular, given the spectacular increase in trade, productivity and real wage growth in Canada would have been expected to converge towards U.S. levels whereas in fact they lagged, resulting in an unexpected relative decline in Canada's standard of living compared to the U.S. From 1977 to 1994, the Canada-U.S. gap in output per hour in manufacturing averaged 14 percent. Since 1994, however, the gap has widened[14].

Canada's adjustment to free trade also appears to have been more difficult and costly than advocates of free trade had expected or economic theory would have predicted. Indeed, Canada's growth performance in the 1990s was worse than in any other decade of the last century except the 1930s. Living standards as expressed by average per capita income fell steadily in the first seven years of the decade and only regained 1989 levels by 1999. By comparison, per

---

[12] For further detail on theses committees and a summary description of how various issues related to the cross-border trade in goods are being managed through the NAFTA see: http://www.dfait-maeci.gc.ca/nafta-alena/2800216b-en.asp?#1

[13] See Globerman (2003).

[14] Source: Statistics Canada

capita income in the U.S. grew 14 percent during this period[15]. Thus Canadian GDP per capita in 2001 was 84.7 percent of the U.S. level, down from 90.7 percent at its peak in 1975[16]. The unemployment in Canada in the 1990s averaged 9.6 percent, higher than in any other decade since the 1930s; the gap with the U.S. rate, at 5.8 percentage points, was double that of the 1980s[17].

The impacts of the CUSFTA and NAFTA have been analyzed using ex-ante general equilibrium models. The estimated impacts have been influenced heavily by the assumptions incorporated in the models. Early models based on the assumption of constant returns to scale showed very modest gains for Canada; later models that incorporated economies of scale showed significantly larger gains for Canada in terms of welfare and every major economic indicator[18]. New generation models that varied the type of pricing rule employed by the firms, that included capital mobility, and dealt with types of protection other than nominal tariff rates, showed positive welfare gains ranging from a modest 0.7 percent of GDP to a quite spectacular 3 percent of GDP. Table 1 compares the estimates for major economic indicators such as welfare, trade volumes, terms of trade, based on variants of CGE models employed to capture the impact of CUSFTA and NAFTA.

Ex-post, the evidence is persuasive that the CUSFTA/NAFTA increased trade. Trefler (2001) found that over the 1988-1996 period, half of the decline in manufacturing employment and output in sectors subject to the largest tariff cuts[19] was due to the CUSFTA. Furthermore, he found that the CUSFTA tariff concessions raised labour productivity in these sectors by an average compound rate of between 1.7 and 3.3 percent per year. Trefler also found that the CUSFTA tariff cuts explain most of the change in imports in the post-FTA period for the most impacted industries but not for those least impacted. However, it would also appear that the magnitude and scope of the benefits flowing from expanded trade did not meet expectations.

---

[15] See Sharpe (2000).

[16] Centre for the Study of Living Standards (2002).

[17] See Sharpe, ibid.

[18] The major reason for the larger welfare effects in imperfectly competitive models with increasing returns to scale versus perfectly competitive models with constant returns to scale, stem form the fact that tariff reductions in the CUSFTA lead to a terms of trade deterioration for Canada (as average tariffs were higher at the begining of the implementation period in Canada than the U.S.) which in the latter case dominate the welfare effects, leading to welfare losses or small welfare improvements. To the contrary, in models with increasing returns to scale, firms facing foreign competition and having access to larger markets will reduce their price-average costs mark-ups and move down their average costs producing larger output at even lower prices. These additional consumer and efficiency gains overcompensate for the welfare losses resulting from the terms of trade effect.

[19] These sectors are what Trefler calls the "most impacted" and correspond to industries for which tariff cuts exceeded 8 percent on the 1988-1996 period. To the opposite, the "least impacted" industries are those industries for which tariff cuts were between 4 percent and 8 percent.

Against that background, we now turn to a consideration of remaining gains from trade in Canada's economic relationship with the U.S.

TABLE 1
Impact of CUSFTA and NAFTA, Summary of CGE Results

	CUSFTA Simulation Results			NAFTA Simulation Results		
	Cox & Harris [1]	Wigle [1]	Hamilton & Whalley [2]	Cox & Harris [1]	Cox [1]	BDS [1]
Real GDP	4.57			4.93	5.11	
Gross Output	7.80			8.74	9.05	
Labour Productivity	9.96			11.21	10.82	
Total Factor Product.	4.27			4.48	4.47	
Trade Volume	14.77			14.81	19.28	
Trade Volume (Canada-USA)	25.70			25.32	22.95	
Imports						4.20
Exports						4.30
Terms of Trade	-0.92	-2.60	0.70	0.03	0.01	-0.70
Welfare	3.09	-0.1 bil. CND$*		3.14	3.18	0.70

[1] Imperfect competition

[2] Perfect competition

*Percentage change if not specified

Source: Brown,Deardorff and Stern (BDS) (1992/1995), Cox & Harris (1992), David Cox (1995), Hamilton & Whalley (1985)
and Randall Wigle (1988)

Methodology: Description of the CGE model

The CGE model utilized in this paper is standard in its general approach. Its framework has been inspired by a generation of models following the seminal work of Mercenier (1995). The model is static, featuring perfect competition, constant returns to scale, and national product differentiation.

A unique feature of the model is that it disaggregates Canada into three regions[20]. Canada's recent experience has demonstrated that free trade agreements can have differential effects at the national and provincial level. Econometric studies have shown that the Canada-U.S. free trade agreement has diverted East-West inter-provincial trade to North-South state-province trade[21]. A CGE model with regional specification thus enables us to assess the impact of hypothetical policy changes not only on inter-provincial flows, but also on the industrial structure, revenue and welfare of the Canada's diverse regions.

The model consists of a multi-region, multi-sector applied general equilibrium model with perfectly competitive markets and constant returns to scale. The regions of the model currently consist of three Canadian regions, the U.S. and the Rest of the World.

---

[20] Though a three Canadian region model is presented here, a six Canadian region model has been also developed.

[21] John F. Helliwell, Frank C. Lee, and Hans Messinger (1999).

In the model, we first define different commodity sets. Sectors of activity are identified by s and t, with S representing the set of all industries so that $s, t =1,...S$. Regions are identified by indices i and j, with W representing the set of all regions so that $i, j=1,..,W$. In a multicountry, multisector framework, it is necessary to keep track of trade flows by their geographical and sectoral origin and destination. Thus, a subscript $isjt$ indicates a flow that originated in sector s of country i with industry t of country j as recipient. Since it will be necessary more than once to aggregate variables with respect to a particular subscript, to avoid unnecessary proliferation of symbols, occasionally we substitute a dot for the subscript on which aggregation has been performed; for instance, $c_{.si}$ is an aggregate of c_{jsi} with respect to the first subscript.

Household

Final consumption decisions in each region are made by a representative household (consumer), which considers products of industries from different regions as imperfect substitutes [Armington (1969)]. The household's preferences are given by a log-linear transformation of a Cobb-Douglas utility function

$$U_i = \sum_{s \in S} \rho_{si} \log c_{.si} \quad \text{where} \quad \sum_{s \in S} \rho_{si} = 1 \tag{1}$$

whereas its preference between local and external origin of a given good s are given by a CES function

$$c_{.si} = \left(\sum_{j \in W} \delta_{jsi} c_{jsi}^{(\sigma_{si}-1)/\sigma_{si}} \right)^{\frac{\sigma_{si}}{(\sigma_{si}-1)}} \tag{2}$$

where c_{jsi} is the consumption in region i of goods s produced in region j, $c_{.si}$ is the composite of domestic and imported goods, δ_{jsi} are consumption share parameters in region i of goods s produced in region j, σ_{si} are the Armington elasticities of substitution for consumption in region i for good s.

In fact, consumption decisions are made at two levels. At the first level, the household chooses the optimal amount of a composite good $c_{.si}$ given constant expenditure shares ρ_{si}. At the second level it chooses the optimal composition of the composite goods in terms of geographic origin (Armington specification). Final demands c_{jsi} are given by maximization of (1) subject to (2) and to the consumer's budget constraint, that is to say, the sum of wage earnings, capital rental and the proceeds of tariff revenues, distributed as a lump sum transfer from the government.

319

$$Y_i = \sum_{s \in S} \omega_i L_{is} + \sum_{s \in S} r_i K_{is} + \sum_{j \in W} \sum_{s \in S} \tau_{jsi} p_{jsi} c_{jsi} + \sum_{j \in W} \sum_{t \in S} \sum_{s \in S} \tau_{jti} p_{jti} x_{jtis}$$

where p_{jsi} denotes the price in region i of goods s produced in region j; L_{is}, K_{is} are labour and capital supply in region i of sectors s, respectively; ω_i, r_i are wages and rental rates of capital of region i, respectively and τ_{jti} are tariff rates that region i impose on good t of region j. In this formulation it is assumed that both capital and labour are mobile between sectors but not between regions.

Firms

Each region is characterized by perfectly competitive industrial sectors. Demand for capital, labour and intermediate inputs by producers result from minimization of variable unit costs v_{is}

$$v_{is} Q_{is} = \sum_{j \in W} \sum_{t \in S} \left(1 + \tau_{jti}\right) p_{jti} x_{jtis} + \omega_i L_{is} + r_i K_{is} \tag{4}$$

subject to a Cobb Douglas production function

$$\log Q_{is} = \alpha_{L_{is}} \log L_{is} + \alpha_{K_{is}} \log K_{is} + \sum_{t \in S} \alpha_{tis} \log x_{.tis} \tag{5}$$

where α are share parameters and where

$$x_{.tis} = \left(\sum_{j \in W} \beta_{jtis} x_{jtis}^{(\sigma_{si}-1)/\sigma_{si}} \right)^{\frac{\sigma_{si}}{\sigma_{si}-1}} \tag{6}$$

are composite intermediate inputs in terms of geographical origin, x_{jtis} is the amount of intermediate goods purchased by sector s of region i from sector t of region j, and p_{jti} is the price of goods t sold by region j to region i, and σ_{si} is the elasticity of substitution of sector s in region i (as households, firms consider intermediate inputs from different regions as imperfect substitutes).

To guarantee homogeneity of degree one of the unit costs in prices, we set

$$\alpha_{L_{is}} + \alpha_{K_{is}} + \sum_{t \in S} \alpha_{tis} = 1 \tag{7}$$

320

where α and β are share parameters and $\beta_{jtis} = 0, \forall j \neq i$ if t is non-tradable. Profit maximization, in this perfect competitive setting, implies prices equal marginal cost.

$$p_{is} = v_{is}$$

Equilibrium conditions

There are two types of production conditions in the model. First, in each region demand for primary factors must equal their supply. Second, supply for goods and services equals its demand in each market (i,s). The Rest of the World (ROW) rental rate of capital is the numeraire.

Dataset and calibration procedure

The base year is 1999. The current model consists of five regions, three Canadian regions, the U.S., and the rest of the world (ROW) aggregated as one region. The three Canadian regions are:

(i) **Canada East** comprising Atlantic Canada and Québec.
(ii) **Ontario**
(iii) **Canada West** comprising the Prairies, North West Territories, Nunavut, Alberta, British Columbia and Yukon.

The fifty-five commodities, level S^{22}, from the trade flow data were mapped into 24 sectors. Table 2 sets out the elasticities of substitution adopted in this study, and describes how they were constructed.

Data requirements for our model consist of nominal bilateral (international and inter-regional) trade flows; input-output tables, national accounts data (consumption demand by sector, labor and capital earnings[23]). Moreover, consistency among the sources must be ensured. This is a challenging and time-consuming task. Therefore, many CGE models have used existing databases such as the Global Trade Assistance and Production (GTAP) data package. Despite the convenience, GTAP data has some major disadvantages: the latest update of the database at the time of model building for this study was 1997[24]; furthermore, the GTAP database does not provide us with Canadian provincial data. For this reason, we opted to develop our own database, collecting data from a variety of national and international sources.

---

[22] Level S accounts for the *small* level industrial category according to NAICS, North-American Industrial Classification System

[23] Labour and capital remunerations, value added, in Canada and The United States, were extracted from the Input-Output tables and double checked with the respective Nationals Income Accounts. For ROW, we used the "Sources of Factor Income" from GTAP database as a proxy for labor and capital earnings.

[24] A new database based on the year 2001 was released in 2005.

321

TABLE 2
Elasticity of Substitution between Domestic Goods and Services and Imports

	Canada	USA	ROW*
Agriculture and Forestry	5.3	5.3	3.5
Food, Beverages and Tobacco	5.4	5.4	3.6
Textiles	6.2	6.2	3.3
Clothing	4.5	4.5	3.0
Wood Products	6.4	6.4	4.2
Furniture and Fixtures	6.8	6.8	4.5
Paper Products	4.1	4.1	2.7
Printing and Publishing	5.6	5.6	2.7
Chemicals, Fertilizers and Pharmaceuticals	4.8	4.8	3.3
Petroleum Products and Mineral Fuels	4.4	4.4	2.9
Leather, Rubber and Plastic Products	5.0	5.0	3.3
Non-metal Mineral Products	8.3	8.3	4.2
Metal Products	5.1	5.1	4.2
Non-electrical Machinery	8.6	8.6	4.2
Electrical Machinery	6.3	6.3	4.2
Transport Equipment	7.5	7.5	5.0
Miscellaneous Manufacturers	6.3	6.3	4.2
Mining and Quarrying other than Petrol.	6.3	6.3	4.2
Communication Services and Other Utilities	5.3	5.3	3.6
Construction	4.3	4.3	2.9
Wholesale Trade	4.3	4.3	2.9
Transportation and Storage	4.3	4.3	2.9
Financial Services	4.3	4.3	2.9
Personal, Business and Other Services	4.3	4.3	2.9

* Values in italics: the elasticities of substitution were calculated using the average of the elasticity of substitution between domestic and composite imported goods, and between the different sources of imports from the GTAP 5 for the ROW. As per convention, we multiplied the ROW estimates by 1.5 to derive the Canadian and U.S. elasticities. Values in bold: were retrieved from Erkel-Rousse H. and Daniel Mirza, (2002) for Canada. We assumed the same elasticities as for the U.S. The ROW estimates were obtained by dividing the Canadian estimates by 1.5.

The Canadian inter-provincial and international trade flows data were obtained from the National Accounts Division of Statistics Canada and Industry Canada Trade Data[25]. The trade flows of the U.S. and the Rest of the World were retrieved exclusively from Industry Canada Trade Data.

The three Canadian economic regions were assumed to share the same production technology as Canada as a whole; therefore the Canadian input-output table was used to derive the production technology coefficients; i.e., the share of intermediate inputs, labour and capital in final production. Due to confidentiality issues, provincial input-output tables have many cells with non-available data ("suppressed") that renders their use not always convenient[26]. The Canadian Input-Output tables were retrieved from CANSIM II database (tables 381009 and 3810010) for 1999. The Bureau of Economic Analysis provided the U.S. Input-Output tables. We have approximated a technological profile for the Rest of the World economies as one region, retrieving information on the "intermediate goods purchases" of firms in the Rest of the World economies, as provided in the GTAP database.

Information on tariffs originates from GTAP version 5, which provides us with weighted average tariffs for trade flows with the U.S. and the Rest of the World (and tariff equivalents of some non-tariff barriers) for the year 1997.

As data is collected from various sources, a major challenge consists of ensuring consistency of the dataset, or otherwise balancing the social accounting matrix for every region. This implies that: a) supply equals demand for all goods and services; b) budget constraints for firms and consumers are satisfied; c) domestic external trade balances equal to zero; and, d) firms in all sectors make no excess profits.

Once consistency of the dataset is established, the next step is the calibration of the model; determination of the share parameters in the supply side ($\alpha_{L_{is}}, \alpha_{K_{is}}, \alpha_{tis}$) and demand side of the model ($\rho_{si}, \delta_{jsi}, \beta_{jtis}$), such that the various supply and demand equations given the benchmark year dataset are satisfied. This approach is quite standard (see for instance, Srinivasan and Whalley 1986) for the case of the experiment of external tariff harmonization-customs union.

However, the calibration procedure for the experiment of abolishment of unobserved trade costs (UTCs) diverges from the norm. Unobserved trade costs are calibrated using a variation of a procedure that has been adopted by various researchers to estimate the impacts of EU enlargement[29]. The basic methodology uses gravity results for Canada-USA trade to estimate the potential trade flows in the absence of any UTCs. Appendix 1 describes in more detail the gravity equations and the approach adopted in this paper. Preference (demand side) parameters are calibrated such that the demand equations are consistent with the

---

[25] Industry Canada Trade Data. Canadian Trade By Industry- NAICS codes: http:/strategis.ic.gc.ca

[26] Though not available at the time of the construction of our database, Wilfrid Laurier University, has since produced a micro -consistent input-output data for Canada's provinces: CREAP 1998 Version 2 data (Snoddon and Wigle, 2004)

[29] See A.M. Lejour. et al (2001) and Dihel, N. P. Walkenhorst (2002).

323

new dataset. Using the new set of preference parameters, and the original benchmark data, tariff equivalents of the unobserved trade costs that are consistent with the demand and supply equations are calibrated.

Scenario 1: A "Basic Customs Unions"

In scenario 1, we model a "Basic Customs Union" - A common external tariff and abolition of all remaining tariff protection in Canada-U.S. trade.

Common external tariff harmonization implies reconciliation of Canadian and U.S. MFN rates, of general preferential rates extended to developing countries, and of preferential tariffs facing countries with which either Canada, or the U.S., or both has/have a bilateral FTA or other preferential arrangement[32]. With few exceptions[33], there are significant similarities between Canadian and USA lists of actual and expected preferential trade agreements; accordingly, the latter task would not be exceptionally difficult.

In economic terms, the impact of regional trade agreements (RTAs) is measured in terms of their welfare-enhancing effects. Generally speaking, a positive global welfare result obtains if the trade creation effects of an RTA are greater than its trade diversion effects. If trade diversion is greater, welfare losses can exceed the welfare gains for the members of the RTA. In the latter case, lower-cost production in the Rest of the World might well be displaced by higher-cost producers within the RTA who gain an expanded market within the RTA zone under the protection of MFN tariffs applied to third parties. Empirical evidence suggests that the trade created by CUSFTA/NAFTA exceeded the amount of trade diverted; that being said, the amount of trade diverted by CUSFTA/NAFTA was not insignificant—studies suggest that as much as 35 percent of the increased Canadian and Mexican exports to the USA following CUSFTA/NAFTA was due to trade diversion[34].

Insofar as moving to a common external tariff decreases average tariff rates, a "basic" customs union would be expected to reduce the trade diversion effects generated by the CUSFTA and NAFTA.
Indeed, this is likely the case for two reasons:

1) Most Canadian and USA MFN rates are "bound" under GATT/WTO agreements; accordingly, any increase in rates requires negotiated compensation to other trading partners. Harmonizing tariff rates within a customs union by lowering the higher rate is thus much less complicated than by raising the lower rate. While the tariff rates of one or the other

---

[32] They would also have to reconcile rates on Mexican agricultural exports because the agricultural provisions of NAFTA were not negotiated trilaterally. In principle, a customs union would also involve eliminating tariffs between Canada and the U.S. on agriculture, which did not occur under NAFTA.

[33] For example, the U.S. has a current bilateral agreement with Jordan, is pursuing FTAs with Morocco and the South African customs union, and has initiated discussions with Bahrain. In the case of Chile, though both Canada and the U.S. have bilateral agreements, the Canada-Chile agreement applies to fewer categories. For a list of similarities and differences, see Goldfarb (2003), Table 2, page 14.

[34] See John Romalis. (January 2004), Kimberly A. Clausing (2001).

partner to a customs union could potentially rise for certain goods, on average they would be expected to fall.

2) Negotiating asymmetries between Canada and the USA imply that it is more likely for Canada to harmonise its levels to the USA levels than vice versa. Given that in general Canadian rates are higher than USA rates, a customs union is likely to produce lower tariff rates.

It is therefore expected that Canada-USA harmonization of external tariffs would have a welfare enhancing effect, both for the partners and also for the rest of the world.

Furthermore, it is argued that the gains provided from the application of a common external tariff (CET) could be minimal compared to the potential gains from elimination of Rules of Origin NAFTA provisions. Rules of origin impose significant administrative costs on exporters, create production inefficiencies by inducing producers to buy from higher cost NAFTA sources than from "tariff ridden" cheaper world sources, and may also affect firms location decisions in favour of the largest market, the U.S. in the NAFTA case[35]. Estimating the cost of rules of origin and modelling its various transmission mechanisms, however is an extensive endeavour, beyond the scope of this paper.

Design of the experiment

We use our CGE model to simulate the impact of a hypothetical policy change that consists of: a) adoption of a common external tariff (CET) between the USA and Canada against all third countries, and b) and the elimination of remaining tariffs in Canada-USA trade. The combination of these two policies would resemble a basic customs union[36] between the two countries. Taking into consideration the GATT provisions and negotiating asymmetries discussed above, we have adopted two alternative assumptions for a CET, which we will henceforth refer to as: *scenario a* when CET is set equal to the USA external tariff; and *scenario b* when CET is set equal to the minimum of Canada-USA MFN tariff rates.

Table 3 sets out the bilateral export and import tariffs between Canada and the U.S. (columns 2 and 3), the tariffs applied to the Rest of the World by Canada and the U.S. (columns 3 and 4), and vice-versa (columns 5 and 6). There are only two sectors that would be affected by elimination of remaining tariff protection in bilateral trade: the primary sectors and the food sector. Furthermore, the food sector is considerably more protected in Canada than in the U.S. In terms of tariffs applied to imports from the Rest of the World, the sectors mostly protected in both countries are the primary sectors, food, textiles and clothing.

With the notable exception of the primary sector, and to a much lesser degree the non-metal mineral products and non-electrical machinery sectors, tariff protection in Canada remains greater than it in the U.S.

---

[35] See Appiah (1999).

[36] As mentioned earlier, a customs union would also eliminate the ROO provisions. In a forthcoming paper, we have used a conventional methodology for capturing "upper bound" estimates of gains from elimination of NAFTA's ROO.

Bilateral trade effects

The results of the simulations are reported in terms of the impact of the hypothetical policy change. In *scenario 1a,* Canadian tariffs imposed on imports from the Rest of the World decrease in all sectors but those of agriculture, non-metal mineral and non-electrical machinery whose tariff protection to the contrary increases. These changes lead to an overall larger inflow of Canadian importations from the Rest of the World (see Table 4). Thus, Ontario's imports from this region increase by 4.08 percent and Canada's East by 5.55 percent. Though there will be some diversion of imports from the U.S. to imports from the Rest of the World following the CET, the later will be overcompensated by an increase in trade between Canada and the U.S. following the bilateral tariff elimination in the agricultural and food sectors, leading to an overall increase of imports from the U.S. Thus, Ontario's imports from the U.S. increase by 1.47 percent while those from Canada's West increase by 5.01 percent[37]. As expected, some of the increase in international trade is trade diverted from Canadian regions: trade between Canadian regions decreases across Canada.

A CET does not affect tariff levels imposed on U.S. imports from the Rest of the World. However, the Canada-U.S. bilateral tariff elimination leads to an increase of U.S. demand for Canadian goods, ranging from 2.61 to 3.66 percent. This will happen at the expense of imports from the Rest of the World, which decrease by 0.22 percent.

Results in *scenario 1b* are similar to those of *scenario 1a,* as in most cases the U.S. external tariff is indeed the minimum of the current Canadian and U.S. external tariffs. The only substantial policy differences among the two scenarios are relevant to the agricultural sector. Under a CET in this scenario, tariff protection of this sector towards the Rest the World remains unchanged in Canada and decreases in the U.S. In the aggregate, this leads to slightly larger increases in imports from the Rest of the World for most Canadian regions, and only a slight decrease in U.S. imports from that region.

---

[37] We break down scenario 1 into its components: a) a CET and b) CAN-US zero bilateral tariff . These tables are not presented in this paper, but are available from the authors upon request.

326

TABLE 3
Import Weighted Average Tariff Rates, 1997, in percent.

	Canada on USA	USA on Canada	Canada on ROW	USA on ROW	ROW on Canada	ROW on USA
Agriculture and Forestry	3.4	3.6	2.9	11.9	51.4	31.3
Food, Beverages and Tobacco	25.4	8.8	33.7	11.7	35.4	35.4
Textiles	0	0	15.0	9.7	10.3	9.7
Clothing	0	0	20.9	11.9	12.7	14.8
Wood Products	0	0	4.9	1.7	2.5	4.4
Furniture and Fixtures	0	0	3.3	2.1	5.6	4.8
Paper Products	0	0	1.9	1.0	2.6	4.1
Printing and Publishing	0	0	3.3	2.1	5.6	1.6
Chemicals, Fertilizers and Pharmaceuticals	0	0	7.0	6.1	5.1	5.1
Petroleum Products and Mineral Fuels	0	0	6.1	2.2	5.4	4.0
Leather, Rubber and Plastic Products	0	0	7.0	6.1	5.1	5.1
Non-metal Mineral Products	0	0	5.2	5.4	6.3	6.0
Metal Products	0	0	3.5	2.7	2.6	4.6
Non-electrical Machinery	0	0	5.2	5.4	6.3	6.0
Electrical Machinery	0	0	1.1	1.1	5.5	3.6
Transport Equipment	0	0	3.6	1.9	8.0	4.2
Miscellaneous Manufacturers	0	0	3.3	2.1	5.6	4.8
Mining and Quarrying other than Petrol.	0	0	0	0.3	0.8	1.0
Communication Services and Other Utilities	0	0	0	0	0.4	0.4
Construction	0	0	0	0	0.2	0.1
Wholesale Trade	0	0	0	0	0.4	0.3
Transportation and Storage	0	0	0	0	0.1	0.1
Financial Services	0	0	0	0	0.2	0.2
Personal, Business and Other Services	0	0	0	0	0.2	0.2

Source: GTAP 5, 1997.

TABLE 4
Impact of a Canada-USA Customs Union on Bilateral Trade Flows
(Percentage change over the base case)
Scenario a: CET is set to USA MFN rates.

Exporters	Importers				
	Canada East	Ontario	Canada West	USA	ROW
Canada East	-0.82	-2.65	-2.24	3.66	1.07
Ontario	-1.56	-1.18	-1.62	2.61	0.88
Canada West	-2.03	-1.85	-0.74	3.53	0.79
USA	1.91	1.47	5.01	-0.04	0.11
ROW	5.55	4.08	5.23	-0.22	0.00

Scenario b: CET is set to the minimum of Canada-USA MFN rates.

Canada East	-0.84	-2.62	-2.24	3.67	1.67
Ontario	-1.56	-1.20	-1.66	2.64	1.45
Canada West	-2.01	-1.85	-0.79	3.52	1.45
USA	1.91	1.49	4.98	-0.07	0.59
ROW	5.57	4.06	5.67	-0.02	-0.07

Sectoral trade effects

In terms of imports, the most obvious difference between the two CET scenarios is their relative impact on the sector of agriculture. Under *scenario 1a,* protection of this sector towards the Rest of the World actually increases. While this increase is compensated by the elimination of Canada-U.S. tariffs, the overall impact is a slight decrease in the international agricultural imports of all three Canadian regions, in the range of 0.24 to 1.89 percent (Table 5). In *scenario 1b,* tariff protection towards imports from the Rest of the World in the agricultural sector does not change in Canada, but it decreases by 75 percent in the U.S. As a result, across Canadian regions international imports of agricultural goods will rise, by a modest 9.27 percent in the case of Canada West, whereas agricultural imports in the U.S. will increase by a more impressive 37.49 percent (Table 6).

In both scenarios, the sector most impacted in Canada is food, whose tariff protection is reduced by 100 percent with respect to imports from the U.S., and by 65 percent with respect to imports from the Rest of the World. Subsequently, international imports of food rise by a spectacular 147.20 percent in the case of Canada West (*scenario 1b*)[38]. The second most impacted sector in Canada as a whole is clothing whose tariff protection from imports from Rest of the World declines by 43 percent. Thus, in *scenario 1b,* our model estimates that

---

[38] The increase of international trade is of course compensated by a decrease in inter-Canadian regional trade, leading to smaller increases in total trade. Thus, in the case of Canada West, total imports of food (including imports from other Canadian regions) increase by 37.03 percent (tables of total sectoral trade impacts are available upon request).

imports of clothing increase by 18.35 percent in Canada East, and by 19.46 percent in Canada West[39].

TABLE 5

Impact on Trade Flows for Selected Sectors[a]

(Percentage change over the base case)

Scenario a: CET is set to USA MFN rates.

		Agriculture and Forestry	Food, Beverages and Tobacco	Textiles	Clothing
Canada East	EXP.	18.61	46.71	1.64	1.72
	IMP.	-1.10	133.30	9.08	18.83
Ontario	EXP.	19.89	57.36	1.25	1.11
	IMP.	-1.89	114.50	2.95	11.90
Canada West	EXP.	11.96	46.10	0.81	0.92
	IMP.	-0.24	147.40	6.18	20.01
USA	EXP.	3.45	19.27	-0.59	-0.48
	IMP.	3.96	10.04	-0.01	-0.07
ROW	EXP.	-3.56	6.11	1.48	0.96
	IMP.	0.44	0.43	0.20	0.16

[a] Interprovincial trade is not taken into account

TABLE 6

Impact on Trade Flows for Selected Sectors[a]

(Percentage change over the base case)

Scenario b: CET is set to the minimum of Canada-USA MFN rates.

		Agriculture and Forestry	Food, Beverages and Tobacco	Textiles	Clothing
Canada East	EXP.	13.58	46.96	1.95	1.89
	IMP.	8.05	131.50	8.67	18.35
Ontario	EXP.	13.01	57.37	1.70	1.47
	IMP.	5.41	114.20	2.76	11.59
Canada West	EXP.	10.06	45.97	1.32	1.21
	IMP.	9.27	147.20	5.84	19.46
USA	EXP.	4.01	20.52	-0.22	-0.11
	IMP.	37.49	8.54	-0.55	-0.58
ROW	EXP.	39.01	4.24	0.79	0.42
	IMP.	1.60	1.69	0.62	0.55

[a] Interprovincial trade is not taken into account

Following the elimination of remaining Canada-U.S. tariffs, international exports of food increase by 57.37 percent in Ontario and by 45.97 percent in

---

[39] When inter-Canadian region imports are taken into account, the respective increases are 12.29 percent in Canada East and 4.52 percent in Canada West.

329

Canada West, while agricultural exports rise by 13.58 percent in Canada East (*scenario 1b*). In the U.S. exports of food and agricultural goods increase by 20.52 percent and 4.01 percent respectively.

Sectoral output effects

As the sectors most impacted by the proposed policies are those of agriculture, food, textile and clothing, we focus on these sectors for the following discussion of sectoral effects. Thus in *scenario 1a,* agricultural output increases across regions from 4.15 percent in Ontario to 1.91 percent in Canada East (Table 7a). This is the result of reduced competition from imports from the Rest of the World and an increased demand for agricultural exports in the USA. In the sectors of food, textiles and clothing, output decreases as local producers face increased competition from imported goods. The biggest decline is experienced in Ontario's food production, by 7.30 percent.

The only substantive difference in *scenario1b* is again relevant to the agricultural sector: agricultural output increases by less in *scenario b*, as local producers do not benefit from the tariff protection from the Rest of the World afforded to them in *scenario 1a* (Table 7b).

TABLE 7a

Impact of a Canada-USA Customs Union on Sectoral Output

(Percentage change over the base case)

Scenario a: CET is set to USA MFN rates.

	Canada East	Ontario	Canada West	USA	ROW
Agriculture and Forestry	1.91	4.15	2.43	0.04	-0.61
Food, Beverages and Tobacco	-4.13	-7.30	-4.81	0.52	0.68
Textiles	-2.76	-1.80	-1.49	-0.13	0.17
Clothing	-6.39	-5.76	-5.88	-0.04	0.24

TABLE 7b

Impact of a Canada-USA Customs Union on Sectoral Output

(Percentage change over the base case)

Scenario b: CET is set to the minumim of Canada-USA MFN rates.

	Canada East	Ontario	Canada West	USA	ROW
Agriculture and Forestry	0.22	0.73	1.31	-2.31	8.82
Food, Beverages and Tobacco	-3.89	-7.16	-4.89	0.81	0.37
Textiles	-2.53	-1.47	-1.21	0.06	0.08
Clothing	-6.21	-5.42	-5.62	0.16	0.10

Aggregate economy effects

Overall, the impact of the proposed policies on the economy of Canadian regions (Table 8) are of a very small magnitude, as Canadian trade with the Rest of the World consist only a small percentage of total Canadian trade, and Canada-USA bilateral liberalization affects only two sectors, agriculture and food.

In *scenario 1a*, international imports increase in all three Canadian regions: from 2.06 percent in Ontario to 5.08 percent in Canada West. The smaller increase in total import flows (in parenthesis, in Table 8) ranging from 1.30 to 2.16 percent demonstrates the shift form West-East trade to North-South trade. As in the aggregate tariff protection towards international imports declines, there is deterioration in the terms of trade in all Canadian regions, particularly so with respect to its international trade partners. However, real revenue increases in all Canadian regions, leading to an increase in real consumer spending (welfare). The largest gains are witnessed in Canada West, with increases in real revenue and real spending of 0.12 to 0.09 percent respectively, or the equivalent of C$ 879.48 million and C$ 508.65 million.

The slight aggregate decline in output in Canada East is mostly due to a decline in domestic demand in three sectors in particular: food, textiles and clothing. These sectors contribute more to value added in Canada East than in Canada West and Ontario.

The U.S. economy, in the aggregate, is hardly impacted at all in this scenario as its external tariff towards the rest of the world is not affected and the impact of U.S.-Canada bilateral tariff has a negligible impact in the U.S. economy as a whole. However, because of the later, the impact on its terms of trade is positive rather than negative as in the Canadian case.

TABLE 8
Impact of a Canada-USA Customs Union on Aggregate Economic Variables
(Percentage change over the base case)
Scenario a: CET is set to USA MFN rates.

	Exports[a]	Imports[a]	Terms of Trade[a]	Output	Real Revenue	Welfare
Canada East	3.27 (1.53)	3.76 (1.48)	-0.27 (-0.17)	-0.01	0.10	0.08
Ontario	2.48 (1.42)	2.06 (1.30)	-0.21 (-0.18)	0.01	0.07	0.05
Canada West	2.94 (1.86)	5.08 (2.16)	-0.19 (-0.09)	0.01	0.12	0.09
USA	0.44	0.33	0.01	0.00	0.00	0.00
ROW	0.07	0.14	0.04	0.01	0.01	0.01
Scenario b: CET is set to the minimum of Canada-USA MFN rates.						
Canada East	3.37 (1.60)	3.78 (1.49)	-0.37 (-0.23)	0.00	0.08	0.06
Ontario	2.56 (1.47)	2.07 (1.31)	-0.26 (-0.22)	0.02	0.05	0.03
Canada West	3.07 (1.97)	5.21 (2.22)	-0.27 (-0.14)	0.01	0.10	0.07
USA	0.84	0.50	-0.12	0.01	-0.01	-0.01
ROW	0.26	0.62	0.20	-0.01	0.05	0.06

[a] For Canadian regions, numbers in bracket take into account interprovincial trade.

The overall impact on the Rest of the World is also positive, slightly larger than the USA, but considerably smaller than in Canada as whole.

In *scenario1b,* aggregate tariff reduction on goods imported to Canada is larger, leading to a further deterioration in the terms of trade of all Canadian regions. As a result, the gains in real revenue and real consumer spending are smaller than in *scenario 1a.*

As the external tariff towards U.S. imports from the Rest of the World declines, USA terms of trade deteriorate in this scenario, leading to a slight decrease in its real revenue and real consumer spending. The reduction in tariffs imposed on exports of the Rest of the World region to the U.S. lead to a further improvement in the terms of trade of the ROW region and a further improvement in its real revenue and real consumer spending.

Scenario 2: The Elimination of Unobserved Trade Costs

Given the long history of Canada-U.S. trade, the huge bilateral trade volume boosted by a free trade agreement and significantly reduced transportation and communication costs, economists expected that the Canada-USA border would no longer be an important determinant of geographic trade patterns. Accordingly, John McCallum's (1995) finding that, after controlling for distance, trading partner sizes and a small number of other factors, trade between two individual Canadian provinces was on average 22 times larger that trade between Canadian provinces and USA states, became one of the most puzzling empirical findings in the recent international trade literature. Subsequent research challenged both the measurement and theoretical underpinnings of the McCallum estimates. Though more recent estimates have reduced the "border" effect to more than half the size estimated by McCallum, they nevertheless have confirmed the existence of a sizable "border" effect in Canada-USA merchandise trade.

While the existence of a "border effect" in Canada-USA trade has now become generally accepted, its interpretation is still a matter of debate. Two popular interpretations have competing policy implications: (a) the border effect could be due to differing national preferences: i.e., consumers prefer to buy from domestic producers; or (b) the border effect could be due to unobserved trade costs (UTCs), such as costs due to customs controls and administrative formalities, costs that arise out of national differences in technical standards and regulation, transactions costs related to currency exchange and hedging of currency risks, and costs associated with developing trade relations in different cultural and legal environments.

The first interpretation would imply that further integration between Canada and the USA would not provide any further economic advantages to either of the two countries. The second implies, however, that co-coordination of regulatory, monetary and transportation policies to lower or remove these implicit costs of trade could facilitate cross-border exchange.

Efforts to empirically test the alternative hypotheses in the Canada-USA context and more generally have been hampered by two factors. [40] First, the lack

---

[40] See Head and Ries (1999) for a demonstration of the linkages and attempt to separate the two factors on the border effect.

of reliable data on "unobserved" trade costs has led to a reliance on proxies that only poorly reflect the real size of these costs. Secondly, estimation complexities have been encountered in establishing a causal link (covariance issues arising between the estimated border coefficients and measures of border related costs).

Even though empirical research has not yet succeeded in providing a definitive answer on the source of the border effect[41], it is generally accepted that even apparently small trade impediments can potentially have large effects on bilateral trade[42] if traded goods are close substitutes, which recent research evidence seems to confirm to be the case. As the CUSFTA has significantly reduced the border effect in Canada-USA bilateral trade[43], the "border" gravity literature suggests that reduction or elimination of UTCs by means of a common market, monetary union, or even smaller scope agreements such as closer regulatory co-operation would lead to significant increases in bilateral trade. Gravity models, however, cannot predict the impact of policy change on other aspects of the economy such as gross domestic product, industry structure, prices, etc. This is one area where a computable general equilibrium model can provide useful insights on the impact of trade policy on economic factors besides bilateral trade flows.

Design of the experiment

We use our CGE model to simulate the impact of a hypothetical policy change that completely abolishes the unobserved trade costs in Canada-USA trade. Given that unobserved trade costs arise from a broad range of sources, only the most ambitious economic union scenarios, including a common currency, would likely come close to eliminating them.

Our model calibrates the UTCs as ad-valorem tariff equivalents following the methodology described under 'dataset and calibration proceedure'. Given that we are implicitly assuming that the border effect captured by the gravity models is fully due to unobserved trade costs, these calibrated values can only be considered as upper bound approximations. The resulting UTCs are reported in Table 9. We observe that in most sectors, UTCs are larger trade impediments to U.S. exports in Canada than vice versa.

In the wholesale trade sector for instance, UTCs are the equivalent of a 45 percent tariff facing U.S. exports to Canada. As expected, UTCs in the services sectors (communications, finance/business and personal services) are also particularly high, especially so in Canada. The same observation applies to the

---

[41] Two alternative explanations: a) Canada and the U.S. are very similar countries, thus unlikely to trade (the comparative advantage hypothesis) and b) the border induces changes in the composition of trade are either not tested directly or their estimations are also prone to the criticism mentioned above.

[42] See Obstfeld and Rogoff (2000).

[43] Helliwell (1998) examines the impact of the CUSFTA on border effects for Canada's trade flows. His estimates cover the period 1988-1993. He finds that the average border effect was constant from 1988-1990 and then fell substantially from 1990-1993. The border effect was the same as in 1973 and about 60 percent of the estimated 1990 value.

petroleum industry. UTCs according to our estimations are higher in the U.S. only in the electrical and leather sectors.

TABLE 9

Calibrated Unobserved Trade Costs, in percent.

	USA	Canada
Agriculture and Forestry	10.05	22.57
Food, Beverages and Tobacco	8.61	19.43
Textiles	5.65	10.35
Clothing	3.98	5.96
Wood Products	6.89	18.88
Furniture and Fixtures	3.83	8.74
Paper Products	13.22	26.33
Printing and Publishing	10.13	27.21
Chemicals, Fertilizers and Pharmaceuticals	8.68	17.95
Petroleum Products and Mineral Fuels	7.83	37.80
Leather, Rubber and Plastic Products	12.06	10.31
Non-metal Mineral Products	4.50	9.99
Metal Products	10.44	15.36
Non-electrical Machinery	3.18	3.28
Electrical Machinery	7.45	4.66
Transport Equipment	2.97	5.11
Miscellaneous Manufacturers	4.45	11.37
Mining and Quarrying other than Petrol.	6.64	17.95
Communication Services and Other Utilities	12.68	36.47
Construction	7.34	9.54
Wholesale Trade	16.70	45.43
Transportation and Storage	15.22	27.77
Financial Services	12.56	42.50
Personal, Business and Other Services	15.05	38.79

Bilateral trade effects

As UTCs are of significant magnitude, their elimination leads to a large increase of Canadian exports to the USA (Table 10). Ontario increases its exports to the USA by 48.62 percent while Canada East and Canada West increase their exports by 62.15 and 72.84 percent, respectively.

Canadian imports from the U.S. are even more impacted as UTCs in Canada are larger. Canada East and Canada West experience the largest increases in imports, following the elimination of UTCs, as high as 162.80 percent in the case of Canada West. Ontario's imports from the USA increase by less, at 53.55 percent.

TABLE 10

Impact of Elimination of all UTCs between Canada-USA on Bilateral Trade Flows
(Percentage change over the base case)

Exporters	Importers				
	Canada East	Ontario	Canada West	USA	ROW
Canada East	-14.00	-16.30	-19.90	62.15	-1.94
Ontario	-16.60	-18.10	-23.50	48.62	-4.66
Canada West	-9.59	-13.20	-15.20	72.84	0.19
USA	152.30	53.55	162.80	-1.16	-0.88
ROW	-6.82	-7.33	-13.80	0.15	0.07

The lowering of costs of doing business with the USA results in some degree of trade diversion. For example, Canada West's imports from the Rest of the World decrease by 13.80 percent in this simulation. By the same token, aggregate imports from the Rest of the World decrease in Canada East and Ontario. As expected, the rise in Canada-USA trade is also accompanied by a significant decline in intra-regional trade within Canada.

Sectoral trade effects

Sectoral trade effects are very impressive, in particular with regards to imports (Tables 11a and 11b). Thus, international imports in Canada West will increase by 200 percent or more in the sectors of agriculture, petroleum, communications and financial services. Increases in international exports, though of smaller magnitude, exceed 80 percent in the food sector and range between 95.33 to 110.50 percent in wholesale trade.

In the U.S., increases in trade volumes are of smaller magnitude. The largest increases in terms of imports are in the sectors of mining and wholesale trade, by 29.48 and 33.88 percent, respectively. U.S. exports of financial services increase by 83.86 percent, while agricultural exports increase by 41.05 percent.

Aggregate economy effects

As expected, the economic impact of the elimination of UTCs in the economy as a whole are of an impressive magnitude (Table 12). Given the large volume of Canadian exports to the USA, the elimination of UTCs leads to a slight improvement in the terms of trade of two out of three Canadian regions. Real revenue increases in all Canadian regions by 6.01 percent to 7.29 percent. Consequently, real consumer spending rises by as high as 7.15 percent in the case of Ontario. The U.S. will also experience positive gains in terms of increases in real output, real revenue and real consumer spending, but the size of these gains are comparatively very small. As expected, the Rest of the World will be negatively impacted from "freer" trade between Canada and the USA.

TABLE 11a

Impact of Elimination of all UTCs between Canada-USA on Sectoral Trade Flows[a]
(Percentage change over the base case)

	Canada East		Ontario		Canada West	
	EXP.	IMP.	EXP.	IMP.	EXP.	IMP.
Agriculture and Forestry	61.58	161.30	45.11	69.20	54.28	203.00
Food, Beverages and Tobacco	80.97	83.43	85.71	75.83	86.44	144.70
Textiles	22.71	23.67	5.37	19.05	-0.46	30.43
Clothing	13.96	6.22	8.37	9.84	16.86	9.34
Wood Products	48.65	128.00	32.71	69.24	51.49	132.80
Furniture and Fixtures	44.12	71.99	32.75	26.14	53.08	52.00
Paper Products	53.39	122.30	52.47	50.84	35.97	104.60
Printing and Publishing	86.79	176.20	67.77	118.40	79.60	228.50
Chemicals, Fertilizers and Pharmaceuticals	29.72	32.39	31.13	17.17	31.64	72.30
Petroleum Products and Mineral Fuels	27.83	68.14	23.12	186.00	44.39	263.30
Leather, Rubber and Plastic Products	60.23	28.06	51.49	16.48	57.82	34.13
Non-metal Mineral Products	38.80	72.09	27.82	35.96	45.75	95.76
Metal Products	64.86	47.90	54.55	37.38	44.25	57.26
Non-electrical Machinery	1.44	8.94	-4.27	5.92	11.06	12.35
Electrical Machinery	47.96	10.02	36.51	5.44	43.06	11.26
Transport Equipment	25.69	13.28	33.11	12.17	23.96	8.14
Miscellaneous Manufacturers	24.75	24.04	17.56	12.52	25.48	20.85
Mining and Quarrying other than Petrol.	24.01	9.31	34.65	57.49	54.16	193.90
Communication Services and Other Utilities	75.18	134.20	59.73	63.67	79.75	227.30
Construction	56.43	51.56	54.53	36.13	65.88	88.77
Wholesale Trade	95.98	144.60	95.33	70.71	110.50	138.40
Transportation and Storage	64.69	157.30	52.82	100.60	75.60	186.00
Financial Services	62.19	189.40	65.22	137.10	65.19	250.50
Personal, Business and Other Services	76.74	161.10	73.53	95.45	84.92	198.90

[a] Interprovincial trade is not taken into account

336

TABLE 11b

Impact of Elimination of all UTCs between Canada-USA on Sectoral Trade Flows[a]
(Percentage change over the base case)

	USA		ROW	
	EXP.	IMP.	EXP.	IMP.
Agriculture and Forestry	41.05	15.75	-1.13	-0.51
Food, Beverages and Tobacco	21.46	18.05	-1.60	-0.67
Textiles	4.19	2.98	0.79	-1.20
Clothing	1.38	1.20	0.71	-0.89
Wood Products	29.53	18.49	-1.53	-1.18
Furniture and Fixtures	13.71	8.88	-0.44	-1.69
Paper Products	19.21	19.18	-2.22	-0.66
Printing and Publishing	35.42	16.01	0.34	-0.84
Chemicals, Fertilizers and Pharmaceuticals	6.45	5.83	-0.46	-0.91
Petroleum Products and Mineral Fuels	29.86	2.26	0.12	-0.71
Leather, Rubber and Plastic Products	4.47	10.71	-0.55	-0.85
Non-metal Mineral Products	15.39	5.45	0.92	-1.39
Metal Products	16.17	13.41	-1.76	-1.06
Non-electrical Machinery	0.03	1.20	1.21	-1.07
Electrical Machinery	1.67	7.72	0.24	-1.18
Transport Equipment	5.31	7.82	-1.52	-1.30
Miscellaneous Manufacturers	0.61	1.79	0.86	-1.14
Mining and Quarrying other than Petrol.	19.51	29.48	-0.57	-1.76
Communication Services and Other Utilities	33.06	15.66	-0.61	-0.81
Construction	14.77	10.80	-0.96	-0.49
Wholesale Trade	13.03	33.88	-0.89	-0.55
Transportation and Storage	8.57	5.55	0.02	-0.54
Financial Services	83.86	14.96	-0.93	-0.62
Personal, Business and Other Services	26.82	19.44	-1.18	-0.76

[a] Interprovincial trade is not taken into account

TABLE 12

Impact of Elimination of all UTCs between Canada-USA on Aggregate Economic Variables
(Percentage change over the base case)

	Exports[a]	Imports[a]	Terms of Trade[a]	Output	Real Revenue	Welfare
Canada East	52.55 (31.55)	71.07 (34.49)	0.23 (0.09)	1.63	6.01	5.94
Ontario	44.65 (27.91)	39.73 (30.16)	0.79 (0.84)	2.82	7.29	7.15
Canada West	57.25 (41.83)	105.10(50.66)	-0.45 (-0.66)	1.31	6.62	6.62
USA	13.39	9.80	0.14	0.14	0.18	0.19
ROW	-0.34	-0.92	-0.29	-0.01	-0.09	-0.13

[a] For Canadian regions, numbers in bracket take into account interprovincial trade.

TABLE 13

Sensitivity Analysis for Scenario 1

(Percentage change over the base case)

CET is set to the minimum of Canada-USA MFN rates.

With Original Elasticity Substitution Parameters

	Exports[a]	Imports[a]	Terms of Trade[a]	Output	Real Revenue	Welfare
Canada East	3.37 (1.60)	3.78 (1.49)	-0.37 (-0.23)	0.00	0.08	0.06
Ontario	2.56 (1.47)	2.07 (1.31)	-0.26 (-0.22)	0.02	0.05	0.03
Canada West	3.07 (1.97)	5.21 (2.22)	-0.27 (-0.14)	0.01	0.10	0.07
USA	0.84	0.50	-0.12	0.01	-0.01	-0.01
ROW	0.26	0.62	0.20	-0.01	0.05	0.06

Elasticity Substitution Parameters Decrease by 25%

	Exports[a]	Imports[a]	Terms of Trade[a]	Output	Real Revenue	Welfare
Canada East	2.45 (1.19)	2.63 (1.05)	-0.36 (-0.22)	0.00	0.03	0.01
Ontario	1.87 (1.10)	1.46 (0.92)	-0.26 (-0.22)	0.02	0.01	-0.01
Canada West	2.24 (1.44)	3.63 (1.57)	-0.27 (-0.14)	0.01	0.07	0.03
USA	0.62	0.35	-0.12	0.01	-0.02	-0.01
ROW	0.17	0.48	0.20	0.00	0.05	0.05

Elasticity Substitution Parameters Increase by 25%

	Exports[a]	Imports[a]	Terms of Trade[a]	Output	Real Revenue	Welfare
Canada East	4.37 (2.06)	5.06 (1.99)	-0.38 (-0.23)	-0.01	0.12	0.10
Ontario	3.28 (1.86)	2.71 (1.71)	-0.26 (-0.22)	0.01	0.09	0.07
Canada West	3.98 (2.55)	6.96 (2.93)	-0.27 (-0.15)	0.00	0.14	0.11
USA	1.09	0.67	-0.12	0.02	-0.01	-0.01
ROW	0.36	0.78	0.20	-0.01	0.05	0.06

[a] For Canadian regions, numbers in bracket take into account interprovincial trade.

Sensitivity Analysis

The magnitudes of the elasticities of substitution are critical determinants of the direction and size of the impact of any hypothetical trade policy change. The higher the degree of substitution between goods produced locally and imported goods, the larger the impact of a reduction in the external tariff or tariff equivalent protection on trade flows and consequently on domestic production, prices and economic welfare. Furthermore, the value of the elasticity of substitution directly affects the size of the unobserved trade costs: the smaller the elasticity, the larger the UTCs calibrated and vice versa. To check for the robustness of our model, we have run sensitivity results for the different experiments that we have undertaken. We have first reduced the values of the elasticities of substitution by 25 percent and then increased them by 25 percent. Sensitivity analysis for *scenario 1b* of CET (Table 13) demonstrates that trade flows fluctuate by approximately 25 to 35 percent from the base case scenario in

338

each case. Changes in real income and welfare also vary in the expected direction, offering a minimum and a maximum bound to the base case scenario. Finally, Table 14 illustrates the impact of a variation of the elasticity of substitution relative to the value of the unobserved trade costs.

TABLE 14				
Sensitivity Analysis of Calibrated Unobserved Trade Costs (UTCs)				
	Elasticity Substitution Parameters Decrease by 25%		Elasticity Substitution Parameters Increase by 25%	
	Calibrated UTCs, in percent.			
	USA	Canada	USA	Canada
Agriculture and Forestry	9.85	35.44	7.93	17.52
Food, Beverages and Tobacco	7.70	31.72	6.81	15.19
Textiles	4.71	18.03	4.46	8.11
Clothing	1.69	14.69	3.16	4.74
Wood Products	6.47	29.62	5.46	14.78
Furniture and Fixtures	2.54	14.72	3.04	6.88
Paper Products	13.35	41.77	10.47	20.57
Printing and Publishing	10.33	42.74	8.00	21.08
Chemicals, Fertilizers and Pharmaceuticals	7.97	29.28	6.88	14.06
Petroleum Products and Mineral Fuels	6.70	60.76	6.21	29.10
Leather, Rubber and Plastic Products	12.51	17.92	9.45	8.07
Non-metal Mineral Products	3.92	16.01	3.57	7.87
Metal Products	10.62	25.06	8.22	12.02
Non-electrical Machinery	2.31	6.39	2.52	2.59
Electrical Machinery	7.23	8.70	5.88	3.67
Transport Equipment	1.66	9.19	2.36	4.02
Miscellaneous Manufacturers	3.26	18.38	3.52	8.92
Mining and Quarrying other than Petrol.	6.06	27.60	5.24	14.00
Communication Services and Other Utilities	13.48	24.55	10.05	28.19
Construction	10.11	13.36	5.75	7.42
Wholesale Trade	18.39	73.01	13.07	34.42
Transportation and Storage	16.66	44.85	11.93	21.34
Financial Services	12.65	66.82	9.83	32.50
Personal, Business and Other Services	16.09	61.20	11.79	29.72

Concluding Remarks

In this chapter, we have attempted to contribute to the debate over closer economic integration with the U.S. We have developed a computable general equilibrium model and dataset to implement the hypothetical scenarios of: a) Canada and the U.S. adopting a common external tariff towards imports from third countries; and, b) the elimination of remaining bilateral trade protection between Canada and the U.S. In order to assess the differential impact of these scenarios on Canadian regions, our model features three such regions: Canada West, Ontario, and Canada East. Our findings suggest that due to previous free trade agreements between Canada and the U.S., the impact of these policy scenarios, with respect to the economy as a whole, was generally positive, as expected, yet of almost negligible size. However, certain sectors, food in particular, but also agriculture and clothing, will experience notable impacts, mostly in terms of a significant increase in trade activity. Our results also capture the differential impact of these policies on Canadian regions and the trade-off between international and inter-Canadian trade. However, our model does not capture the gains that would result from the elimination of the NAFTA provisions of rules of origin.

In combination with econometric "gravity" results, we have used our CGE model to calibrate "unobserved" trade costs between Canada and the U.S., and subsequently assessed the impact of elimination of these costs following the adoption of ambitious economic integration/union policies. The impact of such a hypothetical policy scenario is substantive for all Canadian regions in terms of increased trade flows, and positive gains in real revenue, output, and real consumer spending. One may want to interpret these substantive results as an upper bound to "deep" integration between Canada and the U.S. as the border effect detected by gravity models is assumed to be fully due to unobserved trade costs.

Bibliography

Acharya, R.C., Sharma, P. and S. Rao (2001). "Canada's Trade and Foreign Direct Investment Patterns with the United States", Micro-Economic Policy Analysis. Paper presented for Industry Canada conference *North American Linkages: Opportunities and Challenges for Canada.*

Anderson, J. and E. Wincoop (2001a). "Gravity with Gravitas: A Solution to the Border Puzzle", NBER Working Paper 8079 (January)

Anderson, M. A., and S.Smith (1999). "Canadian Provinces in World Trade: Engagement and Detachment", *Canadian Journal of Economics* 32, (February), pp22-38

Appiah, J. A. (1999) "Applied General Equilibrium Analysis of North American Integration with Rules of Origin", doctoral dissertation, Simon Fraser University

Armington P. (1969). "A Theory of Demand for Products Distinguished by Place of Production", *International Monetary Fund Staff Papers*, 16, pp159-176

Brown, D.K., A.V. Deardorff, and R.M. Stern (1989). "U.S.-Canada Bilateral Tariff Elimination: The Role of Product Differentiation and Market Structure" in R.C. Feenstra, editor, *Trade Policies for International Competitiveness*, Chicago: University of Chicago Press, pp217-245

Brown, D.K., A.V. Deardorff, and R.M. Stern (1992). "A North American Free Trade Agreement: Analytical Issues and a Computational Assessment", *The World Economy*, 15, pp11-30

Brown, D.K., A.V. Deardorff, and R.M. Stern (1995). "Estimates of a North American Free Trade Agreement", in P.J.Kehoe and T.J.Kehoe, editors, *Modeling North American Economic Integration*, Boston: Kluwer Academic Publishers, pp59-74

Brown, D.K., and R.M.Stern (1987). "A Modeling Persperctive", in R.M.Stern, P.H. Trezise and J.Whalley editors, *Perspectives on a U.S.-Canadian Free Trade Agreement*, pp155-182

Brown, F. and J. Whalley (1980). "General Equilibrium Evaluation of Tariff Cutting Proposals in the Tokyo Round and Comparisons with More Extensive Liberalisation of World Trade", *Economic Journal*, 90, (December), pp838-866

Centre for the Study of Living Standards (2002). "Raising Canadian Standards: A framework for Discussion", TD forum on Canada's Living Standards.

Clausing, K. A. (2001). "Trade Creation and Trade Diversion in the Canada-Unites States Free Trade Agreement", *Canadian Journal of Economics*, 34, (3), pp677-696

Coulombe, S. (2002). "Border Effects and North American Economic Integration: Where Are We Up To?", first draft, prepared for the workshop, Social and Labour Market Aspects of North American Linkages (August)

Cox, D.J. (1994). "Some Applied General Equilibrium Estimates of the Impact of a North American Free Trade Agreement on Canada", in J.F. Francois and C.R. Shiells, editors, *Modeling Trade Policy: Applied General Equilibrium Assessments of North American Free Trade*, New York: Cambridge University Press, pp100-123

Cox, D.J. (1995). "An Applied General Equilibrium Analysis of NAFTA's Impact on Canada", in P.J.Kehoe and T.J.Kehoe, editors, *Modeling North American Economic Integration*, Boston: Kluwer Academic Publishers, pp75-89

Cox, D.J. and R.G. Harris (1985). "Trade Liberalization and Industrial Organization: Some Estimates for Canada," *Journal of Political Economy*, 93, pp115-145

Cox, D.J. and R.G. Harris (1992b). "North American Free Trade and its Implications for Canada: Results from a CGE Model of North American Trade," *The World Economy*, 15, pp31-44

Deardorff, A.V., and R.M. Stern (1981). "Aggregated Model of World Production and Trade: An Estimate of the Impact of the Tokyo Round", *Journal of Political Modeling*, 3 , pp127-152

Dihel, N. and P. Walkenhorst (2002). "European Union trade and non-tariff measures" OECD, 5th Conference on Global Economic Analysis.

Dixit, A.K. and J.E. Stiglitz (1977). "Monopolistic Competition and Optimum Product Diversity", *American Economic Review*, 67(3), pp297-308

Dobson, W (2002). "Shaping the Future of North American Economic Space", *Commentary: The Border Papers*. C.D. Howe Institute.

Dodge, D. (2003) Economic Integration in North America", Speech to the Couchiching Institute on Public Affairs, Geneva Park, Ontario, (August)

Dungan, P. and S. Murphy (1999). "The Changing Industry and Skill Mix of Canada's International Trade", *Perspectives on North American Free Trade*. Paper No. 4. Industry Canada

Dymond, B. and M. Hart (2003). "Canada and the Global Challenge: Finding a Place to Stand", *Commentary: The Border Papers*. C.D. Howe Institute

Erkel-Rousse H. and D. Mirza (2002). "Import Prices Elasticities: Reconsidering the Evidence", *Canadian Journal of Economics*, 35 (2), pp282-306

Ethier, W.J. (1982). "National and International Returns to Scale in the Modern Theory of International Trade", *American Economic Review*, 72, pp389-405

Fox, A.K. (1999). "Evaluating the Success of a CGE Model of the Canada-U.S. Free Trade Agreement", University of Michigan

Globerman, S. and P. Storer (2003). "Canada-U.S. Economic Integration Following CUSFTA and NAFTA, Western Washington University.

Goldfarb, D. (2003). "The Road to a Canada-U.S. Customs Union: *Step-by-Step or in a Single Bound?" Commentary: The Border Papers*. C.D. Howe Institute.

GTAP (2001). Global Trade, Assistance, and Production: The GTAP 5 Data Package, Centre for Global Trade Analysis, Purdue University

Hamilton, R. W. and J. Whalley (1985). "Geographically Discriminatory Trade Arrangements", *The Review of Economics & Statistics*, 67 (3), pp446-55

Harris, R.G. (1984). "Applied General Equilibrium Analysis of Small Open Economies with Scale Economies and Imperfect Competition", *The American Economic Review*, 74(5), pp1016-1032

Harris, R.G. (2003). "Canada's Economic Interest and the CUSFTA-NAFTA Agreements: A Review of Evidence" *Perspectives on North American Free Trade*. Industry Canada

Hart, M. and W. Dymond (2001). "Canada, the United States and Deepening Economic Integration: Issues and Research Agenda", University of Ottawa, Center for Trade Policy and Law

Hazledine, T. (1990). "Why do the Free Trade Gain Numbers Differ So Much? The Role of Industrial Organisation in General Equilibrium", *Canadian Journal of Economics*, 4 (4), pp791-806

Head, K. and J.Ries (1999). "Can Small Country Manufacturing Survive Trade Liberalization? Evidence from the Canada-U.S. Free Trade Agreement", *Perspectives on North American Free Trade*. Industry Canada

Head, K. and T.Mayer (1998). "Non-Europe: the Magnitude and Causes of Market Fragmentation in the EU", mimeo (October)

Helliwell, J. F. (1996). "Do National Borders Matter for Quebec's Trade?" *Canadian Journal of Economics* 29 (3), pp.507-522

Helliwell, J. F. (1997). "National Borders, Trade and Migration", NBER Working Paper 6027 (March)

Helliwell, J. F. (1998). "How Much Do National Borders Matter", Washington, DC: Brookings Institution Press.

Helliwell, J. F. (2002). "Border Effects: Assessing Their Implications for Canadian Policy in a North-American Context". (September)

Helliwell, J. F., F C. Lee, and Messinger, H (1999). "Effects of the Canada-United States Free Trade Agreement on Inter-provincial Trade", *Perspectives on North American Free Trade*. Industry Canada

Helliwell, J.F., and L.C. Frank (1999). "Effects of the Canada-United States Free Trade Agreement on Inter-provincial Trade", *Perspectives on North American Free Trade*. Industry Canada

Hillberry, R. (1998). "Regional Trade and the 'Medecine Line': The National Border Effect in US Commodity Flow Data", *Journal of Borderlands Studies* (Fall), pp1-17

Hillberry, R. (1999). "Explaining the 'Border Effect': What Can We Learn from Disaggregated Commodity Flow Data?" Indiana University Graduate Student Economics Working Paper Series, No.9802 (April)

Hillberry, R. (2000). "Interpreting 'Home Bias' in U.S.-Canada Trade", *International Economic Review*, (June/July)

Hillberry, R. (2002). "Aggregation Bias, Compositional Change, and The Border Effect", *Canadian Journal of Economics* (August), pp517-530

Hillberry, R. and D. Hummels (2002). "Explaining Home Bias in Consumption: the Role of Intermediate Input Trade", NBER Working Paper 9020 (June)

Huw Edwards, T. (2002). "Modeling the Accession of the Central and Eastern European Countries to the EU Single Market" Centre for the Study of Globalisation and Regionalisation, Warwick UK.

Kehoe, T.J. (2002). "An Evaluation of the Performance of Applied General Equilibrium Models of the Impact of NAFTA", Research Department Staff Report, Federal Reserve Bank of Minneapolis (April)

Krueger, A. (1999). "Trade Creation and Trade Diversion under NAFTA", NBER Working Paper 7429 (December)

Lavoie, Claude, Mérette, M. and M. Souissi. (2001). "A Multi-sector Multi-country Dynamic General Equilibrium Model with Imperfect Competition", Department of Finance. Working Paper No. 2001-10.

Lejour, A.M and R.A. de Mooij, and R. Nahuis (2001). "EU enlargement: Economic implications for countries and industries", CPB Netherlands Bureau for Economic Policy Analysis.

McCallum J. T. (1995). "National Borders Matter: Canada-U.S. Regional Trade Patterns", *American Economic Review* 85 (June), pp615-623

Mehanna, R. and H. Shamrub (2002). "Who is Benefiting the Most from NAFTA? An Intervention Time Series Analysis", *Journal of Economic Development*, 27(2)

Mercenier, J. (1995). "Can "1992" Reduce Unemployment in Europe? On Welfare and Employment Effects of Europe's Move to A Single Market", *Journal of Policy Modeling*, 17, pp1-37

Mirus, R. and N. Rylska. "Economic Integration: Free Trade Areas vs. Customs Unions", Western Centre for Economic Research (August)

Nguyen, T.T. and R.M. Wigle (1992). "Trade Liberalisation with Imperfect Competition The Large and Small of It", *European Economic Review*, 36, pp17-35

Obstfeld, M. and K. Rogoff (2000). "The Six Major Puzzles in International Macroeconomics: is there a Common Cause?", NBER Working Paper 7777 (July)

Papadaki, E. (1998). "Welfare Effects of the Completion of the Single European Market on Greece" in *Global Trading Arrangements in Transition,* in C. Paraskevopoulos, editor, Massachusetts, Edward Elgar Publishing

Reed, G. (1996). "The Use of CGE Modelling in the Analysis of Trade Policy Reform", Centre for Research in Economic Development and International Trade, University of Nottingham, Nottingham, UK (January)

Report of the Standing Committee on Foreign Affairs and International Trade. 2002. "Partners in North America: Advancing Canada's Relations with the United States and Mexico"

Romalis, J. (2001). "NAFTA's and CUSFTA's Impact on International Trade", University of Chicago and NBER (December)

Sharpe, A. (2000). "A Comparison of Canadian and U.S. Labour Market Performance in the 1990s," in *Vanishing Borders Canada Among Nations 2000,* in M. Molot and F. Hampson, editors, Toronto: Oxford University Press

Snodon, T. and R. Wigle (2004). "CREAP Data V2.0: Documentation and Methods" Wilfrid Laurier University

Trefler, D. (2001). "The Long and Short of the Canadian –US Free Trade Agreement", *Perspectives on North American Trade*, Industry Canada

Wigle, R.M. (1988). "General Equilibrium Evaluation of Canada-U.S. Trade Liberalisation in a Global Context", *Canadian Journal of Economics*, 20(3), (August), pp539-564

Wigle, R.M. and J. R. Markusen (1989). "Nash Equilibrium Tariffs for the United States and Canada: the Roles of Country Size, Scale Economics, and Capital Mobility", *Journal of Political Economy* 97(2), (April), pp368-386

Appendix 1: The Gravity Model

Economic Gravity models are based on an analogy to the law of gravity in physics: "after controlling for size, trade between two regions is decreasing in their bilateral trade relative to the average barrier of the two regions to trade with all their partners. Intuitively, the more resistant to trade with all others a region is, the more it is pushed to trade with a given bilateral partner".

In his pioneering article, McCallum (1998) estimated the following gravity equation in a Canada-USA context:

$$\ln x_{ij} = \alpha_1 + \alpha_2 \ln y_i + \alpha_3 \ln y_j + \alpha_4 \ln d_{ij} + \alpha_5 \delta_{ij} + \varepsilon_{ij} \qquad \text{(i)}$$

where x_{ij} stands for exports from region i to region j, y_i and y_j are gross domestic product per capita of the importing and exporting regions, d_{ij} is distance between the capitals of regions and δ_{ij} is a dummy equal to 1 for inter-provincial trade and zero for state province trade. The exponential of the dummy variable coefficient, α_5, is the "border effect", or the effect of the border on the ratio of inter-provincial trade to state province trade after controlling for distance and size. Based on 1988 data, McCallum estimated that inter-provincial trade is 22 times larger than state-province trade.

Anderson and Wincoop (2001) have criticized McCallum's work and subsequent studies based on "theoretical" gravity models on the grounds that they failed to capture the key implication of the theoretical gravity equation that "trade between regions is determined by relative trade barriers" and therefore have overestimated the border effect. Anderson and Wincoop (2001) estimated a non-linear regression that is consistent with the theoretical underpinnings of the gravity model as developed by Anderson (1979). In effect they develop a term they call multilateral resistance variable that effectively measures the average barrier implied in the gravity theory. Based on the assumption that the exporter passes on to the importer the trade costs they incur (nominal information costs, design costs, transport costs, legal and regulatory costs) Anderson and Wincoop take into account two price index terms (in a two country model) that take the following form[30]

$$p_j = \left[\sum_i \left(\frac{\beta_i t_{ij} p_i}{p_j} \right)^{1-\sigma} \right]^{\frac{1}{1-\sigma}}, \forall i, j \qquad \text{(ii)}$$

where σ is the elasticity of substitution between imported and domestic goods, t_{ij} are the trade costs that the authors proceed in assuming they are symmetrical

---

[30] This is derived from a CES preferences and goods that are differentiated by region of origin. The authors also assumed that each region is specialized in producing one good following Deardorff (1988).

345

and β_i is a positive distribution parameter implied by the CES utility function assumption. Using 1993 data, they estimate the following theoretical gravity equation in the context of Canada-USA trade (two country model):

$$\ln z_{ij} = \ln\left(\frac{x_{ij}}{y_i y_j}\right) = k + (1-\sigma)\rho \ln d_{ij} + [(1-\sigma)\ln b](1-\delta_{ij}) - \ln p_i^{1-\sigma} - \ln p_j^{1-\sigma} + \varepsilon_{ij}$$

(iii)

where $(b-1)$ represents the ad-valorem tariff-equivalent of the USA-Canada border barrier, and δ_{ij} is the same variable as in equation (i) above.

To take into account the fact that the U.S. and Canada also trade with other countries, A&W also estimate a multi-country model that includes a total of 22 industrialized countries. A&W estimate a border effect of 10.2 and 10.7 for the two-country and multi-country mode respectively. They also re-estimated the McCallum gravity equation border effect for the same year, which as expected yielded a considerably larger estimate of 16.4. After estimating the tariff equivalents of the border barriers for bilateral trade, A&W also consider the implications for bilateral flows. Their estimated ratios of trade flows with border barriers to that under borderless trade (BB/NB) for the multi-country model is reproduced below

Ratio BB/NB					
USA-USA	CAN-CAN	USA-CAN	USA-ROW	CAN-ROW	ROW-ROW
1.25	5.96	0.56	0.40	0.46	0.71

Source: Anderson & Wincoop, 2001

In this paper we have used these ratios to produce "predicted" trade flows on the base of actual trade flow dataset 1999. In a world without unobserved trade costs (UTCs), trade between Canada and the U.S. would be 1.78 (1/0.56) times larger than actual trade flows where UTCs are present.

Editors

John M. Curtis

John M. Curtis is the Chief Economist at Foreign Affairs and International Trade Canada. He is responsible for providing overall international trade and economic policy advice and for managing economic analysis and research within the Department. He played a major role in the development of the Asia Pacific Economic Cooperation (APEC) forum, serving as the founding Chair of the Economic Committee for its first four years (1994-1998). At the same time, he was involved in the work of the OECD Trade Committee and in the Government of Canada's private sector consultative process on trade. Prior to that, he participated in the Canada-USA Free Trade negotiations, was federal government's first coordinator of regulatory reform at the Treasury Board, held various policy advisory and management positions in the Department of Consumer and Corporate Affairs, and served in the economic policy secretariat of the Privy Council Office and on the staff of the International Monetary Fund in Washington, D.C. Having completed his B.A. degree at the University of British Columbia and his Doctorate in Economics at Harvard, Dr. Curtis has continued to lecture on an occasional basis at several universities in Canada and the USA.

Aaron Sydor

Aaron Sydor is A/Director of the Current and Structural Analysis Division within the Office of the Chief Economist at Foreign Affairs and International Trade Canada. The division is responsible for briefing senior management on current economic issues and for producing a number of the Department's regular publications such as the annual report on the "State of Trade" and the "Monthly Trade Report". The division also conducts analysis on special issues of importance to the department which currently includes emerging markets and global value chains. Prior to joining the Department, Mr. Sydor worked in the Micro-Economic Policy Analysis Branch at Industry Canada. He holds a MA in Economics from Carleton University as well as a BA in Economics from Brock University.

Contributing Authors

Ram Acharya
Ram Acharya is an economist with the Micro-Economic Policy Analysis Branch at Industry Canada, where he has conducted research on trade, foreign direct investment, the impact of trade and technology on relative factor earnings, product market competition and productivity, social returns to domestic R&D and spillovers from foreign R&D. Mr. Acharya received his PhD. in economics from University of Ottawa.

Eugene Beaulieu
Eugene Beaulieu is an Associate Professor in the Department of Economics at the University of Calgary and holds a Ph.D. in economics from Columbia University. Dr. Beaulieu's principal area of research is empirical international economics, with an emphasis on political economy, causes and consequences of international trade policy, and economic development. During the 2004/05 academic year, Dr. Beaulieu spent a sabbatical as the Norman Robertson Fellow at International Trade Canada and as a Visiting Scholar at the Department of Economics at Carleton University.

Doug Blair
Doug Blair is a Project Director at the Policy Research Initiative (PRI), responsible for International Regulatory Cooperation under the North American Linkages project. Mr. Blair is currently on executive interchange to the PRI from his position as President of RIAS Inc., a consulting firm specializing in federal regulatory policy and process, regulatory impact assessment and cost-benefit analysis. Mr. Blair has over 20 years experience in the regulatory field, as an economist and as a former regulator within the federal government. He obtained his BA (Honours) in Economics from Queen's University.

Shenjie Chen
Shenjie Chen is a senior policy researcher analyst at Foreign Affairs and International Trade Canada. He received his Ph.D. in Economics from Dalhousie University. His primary area of interest is empirical research relating to international trade theory and policy and has published research papers in several journals and books.

André Downs
André Downs is a Senior Project Director at the Policy Research Initiative (PRI), responsible for three research projects under the North American Linkages umbrella. Dr. Downs has extensive research experience acquired in the academic, private, and public sectors, having taught at a major Canadian business school and worked in two financial institutions, and spent the last 13 years with the Government of Canada, notably in the Department of Finance, the Privy Council Office and the Competition Bureau. Before joining the PRI in December 2001, he held the position of Deputy Commissioner of Competition responsible for the

Competition Policy Branch. Dr. Downs holds a PhD in economics (International Trade) from the London School of Economics.

Herb Emery

J.C. Herbert Emery is an Associate Professor in Economics at the University of Calgary specializing in economic history and labour economics. He received his Ph.D. in economics from the University of British Columbia and holds a B.A. in economics from Queen's University.

Wulong Gu

Wulong Gu is chief of research with the Micro Economic Analysis Division at Statistics Canada. Prior to joining Statistics Canada, he was a policy analyst in the Micro-Economic Policy Analysis Branch at Industry Canada and assistant professor in the Department of Economics at the University of Saskatchewan. His research has been published in *American Economic Review*, *Oxford Review of Economic Policy*, and *Canadian Journal of Economics*. His main research is in the areas of innovation and productivity. He received his Ph.D. in economics from McMaster University.

Richard G. Harris

Richard G. Harris is the Telus Professor of Economics at Simon Fraser University, and Senior Fellow of the C.D. Howe Institute. He is a Fellow of the Royal Society of Canada, a former President of the Canadian Economics Association, and former Fellow of the Canadian Institute for Advanced Studies. He received his Ph.D from the University of British Columbia. His major area of specialization is international economics and in particular the economics of integration. During the 1980's, he worked extensively on economic modeling of the potential impact of the Canada-U.S. Free Trade Agreement and subsequently on NAFTA. He is currently involved in research on North America monetary integration, the New Economy, and labour mobility in North America.

Jorge L. Hernandez

Jorge L. Hernandez is a policy research analyst with the Office of the Chief Economist at Foreign Affairs and International Trade Canada. He holds an M.A. in Economics from the University of Ottawa and a B.A. in Economics from the Central University of Venezuela. Prior to joining the Government of Canada, he was an economic advisor for Nestle Venezuela, S.A. His fields of his interest include mathematical economics, applied general equilibrium modeling and game theory.

John James Kirton

John Kirton is an Associate Professor of Political Science, a Fellow of Trinity College, a Research Associate of the Centre for International Studies, Principal Investigator of the EnviReform Project, and Director of the G8 Research Group in the Munk Centre at the University of Toronto. He has co-authored numerous works assessing the environmental impacts of NAFTA and its institutions. He is co-editor of *Linking Trade, Environment and Social Cohesion: NAFTA*

349

Experiences, Global Challenges (Ashgate, 2002) and *Sustainability, Civil Society and International Governance: Local, Regional and Global Perspectives* (Ashgate, 2005). Kirton is Principal Investigator of the University of Toronto-based project on "Strengthening Canada's Environmental Community through International Regime Reform" (EnviReform), and editor of Ashgate Publishing's book series on *Global Environmental Governance*. He has served as team leader of the Commission on Environmental Cooperation's project on NAFTA's environmental effects (1995–99), founding Chair of the North American Environmental Standards Working Group, a member of the Foreign Policy Committee of the Canadian Prime Minister's National Round Table on the Environment and the Economy (1989–95), and a member of the Government of Canada's International Trade Advisory Committee (1995–97).

Robert (Bob) Kunimoto
Bob Kunimoto is currently a senior policy research officer at the Policy Research Initiative (PRI) responsible for the "Moving Toward a Customs Union" project under the North American Linkages umbrella. Prior to joining the PRI, he worked in the Taxation and Business Framework Directorate at Micro-Economic Policy Analysis, Industry Canada and taught economics at Queen's University, the University of Alberta, the University of Saskatchewan, and Mount Royal. He is a founding member of the Micro-Economic Policy Analysis Branch and the Policy Research Initiative and has undertaken extensive policy research on issues related to international trade, growth, the knowledge-based economy, productivity and technology. Mr. Kunimoto has a M.A. (University of Alberta) and is a Ph.D. candidate at Queen's University with specialization in public finance, natural resources and urban/regional development.

David Laidler
David Laidler is Professor Emeritus at the University of Western Ontario, where he was Professor of Economics from 1975 until 2004, and is Fellow in Residence at the C.D. Howe Institute. He was educated at the London School of Economics (B.Sc. (Econ.) 1959), the University of Syracuse (M.A. 1960), and the University of Chicago (Ph.D. 1964). Professor Laidler's fields of interest are monetary economics and its history. He has written numerous academic articles and books in these areas. From 1998 to 1999, he was Visiting Economist and Special Adviser at the Bank of Canada.

Yu Lan
Yu Lan has a M.B.A. and a M.A. in Economics, both from the University of Ottawa. Currently, she is working as an economist on contract to the Office of the Chief Economist at Foreign Affairs and International Trade Canada.

Marcel Mérette
Marcel Mérette is an associate professor in the Department of Economics and Vice-Dean Research in the Faculty of Social Sciences at the University of Ottawa. He has a Ph.D. from the University of Montreal and was a post-doctorate fellow at Yale University. He is a specialist in computable general equilibrium

350

models and has applied this analytical tool on topics such as international trade and population ageing.

Fidèle Ndayisenga
Fidèle Ndayisenga is a Senior Policy Research Officer at the Policy Research Initiative (PRI). He has worked on projects such as estimating the benefits of regulatory cooperation, estimating government regulatory expenditures and on issues pertaining to regulatory research and data. Dr. Ndayisenga has extensive policy research experience acquired in the academic and public sectors. Prior to joining the PRI, he worked for Agriculture Canada, the Rural Secretariat and Citizenship and Immigration. He holds a Ph.D. in applied Economics from the University of Minnesota.

Evangelia Papadaki
Evangelia (Elina) Papadaki is a senior trade analyst and A/Deputy Director with the Office of the Chief Economist, Foreign Affairs and International Trade Canada. She has also worked as an economist and policy analyst at Industry Canada. She holds a Ph.D. in Economics from the University of Montréal.

Someshwar Rao
Someshwar Rao is the Director of the Strategic Investment Analysis Directorate in the Micro-Economic Policy Analysis Branch at Industry Canada. Prior to joining Industry Canada, he worked as a senior economist at the Economic Council of Canada. He obtained his Ph.D. in economics from Queen's University and has published extensively on both micro- and macro-economic issues.

Gary Sawchuk
Gary Sawchuk is a member of the Policy Research Initiative (PRI), where he participates in projects and undertakes research related to North American integration. He holds a Ph.D. in economics from the University of Manitoba and an MPA degree from Harvard University. Prior to joining the Policy Research Initiative, he worked at Industry Canada.

Prakash Sharma
Prakash Sharma is a Senior Research Coordinator with the Micro-Economic Policy Analysis Branch at Industry Canada. Previously, he was with the Department of Foreign Affairs and International Trade where he was a Senior Research Coordinator and Deputy Director of the Trade and Economic Analysis Division. He has also taught at the University of Ottawa and holds a Ph.D. in economics from Carleton University.

Lori Whewell Rennison
Lori Rennison is chief of the U.S. Economic Analysis and Forecasting group at Finance Canada. Prior to her current position, she was assistant chief and senior economist in the Demand and Labour group at Finance Canada and economist in the Micro-Economic Policy Analysis Branch at Industry Canada, working on issues relating to the labour market and productivity.

351